super
recipe collection

TRIDENT PRESS
INTERNATIONAL

Published by:
TRIDENT PRESS INTERNATIONAL
801 12th Avenue South
Suite 400
Naples, FL 34102 U.S.A.
©Trident Press International
Tel: (239) 649 7077
Fax: (239) 649 5832
Email: tridentpress@worldnet.att.net
Website: www.trident-international.com

acknowledgements

Super Recipe Collection

Packaged by: R&R Publications Marketing Pty Ltd
Brunswick, Victoria, Australia
Creative Director: Paul Sims
Production Manager: Anthony Carroll
Food Photography: Warren Webb,
William Meppem, Andrew Elton,
Quentin Bacon, Gary Smith, Per Ericson,
Paul Grater, Ray Joice, John Stewart,
Ashley Mackevicius, Harm Mol,
Yanto Noerianto,
Andy Payne.
Food Stylists: Stephane Souvlis, Janet Lodge,
Di Kirby, Wendy Berecry, Belinda Clayton,
Rosemary De Santis, Carolyn Fienberg,
Jacqui Hing, Michelle Gorry,
Christine Sheppard, Donna Hay.
Recipe Development: Ellen Argyriou,
Sheryle Eastwood, Kim Freeman,
Lucy Kelly, Donna Hay, Anneka Mitchell,
Penelope Peel, Jody Vassallo,
Belinda Warn, Loukie Werle.

Includes Index
ISBN 1 58279328 X
EAN 9 781582 793283

First Edition Printed October 2002

Printed in Canada by Transcontinental Printing

contents

Welcome to **Super Recipe Collection**

We have planned every part of this wonderful collection of recipes like a poet would arrange an anthology – with a great deal of creative thought and attention to detail.

Our expertise in recipe compilations, together with our professional review of marketplace trends, means that you hold in your hands what will prove to be a comprehensive reference guide for every meal occasion. Keep this cookbook handy because we know it will prove to be a delightful addition to your kitchen.

Whether you are a seasoned chef or an amateur cook, you will find these recipes are fashioned for minimum fuss. Our ultimate aim is to help you make cooking an enjoyable experience, rather than a tedious chore. The thought of cooking an evening meal or hosting a dinner party will not be a daunting one with our imaginative suggestions and step-by-step instructions. Take advantage of our vast experience.

Our unique blend of flavours will surprise you. We take common ingredients and mix and match them to produce magnificent results. Our section on meat recipes, for example, will banish the boring steak-and-vegetables meal from your dinner table forever. Take steak or ground meat and combine it with vegetables and spices in an inspiring and creative way to uncover a whole new world for your taste buds to explore. It's certainly a breath of fresh air for the jaded cook.

You will be delighted to discover we have recipes that focus on quick cooking for those who are strapped for time. We understand that there are other priorities in your life that demand your attention and while you may enjoy cooking, you might like to spend more time doing other things like playing with your children or watching a luminescent sunset.

Recipes for fast and simple meals for your family are a highlight of this wonderful cookbook. The temptation for those with a busy schedule is to resort to takeaway meals or microwave dinners that are often high in fat and low in nutrition. We help you prepare a balanced meal that will give you and your family the best of both worlds: terrific taste in less time.

No stone is left unturned with this recipe collection. Whether you are faced with an impromptu get-together or a scheduled dinner party, we have included recipes for finger foods and barbeques that are nothing short of brilliant. Imagine firing up the grill with a new sense of exhilaration as you marinate meats and sprinkle steaks with a fantastic mix of flavours. Or try preparing finger foods with colourful new combinations that are fit for a caterer. It's easy and it's exciting with this clever cookbook.

In addition, our selection of cake and cookie recipes will show you how to round-off a perfect meal or a late-night supper with an array of appetizing treats. Your mouth will water as we sweeten your tooth with our delectable delights. Let us help you host in style.

We encourage you to familiarise yourself with this book and take advantage of every recipe. Flipping through the pages with their appealing illustrations is sure to capture your imagination. You'll remember that simple family meal whenever you're pressed for time or you'll recall that luscious dessert next time you entertain guests. Your loved ones will thank you for preparing phenomenal food.

Don't be surprised if you get more compliments from your family or more visits from your cherished friends in the future. After all, there's nothing like home cooking and we've got the secrets of the best.

Good luck with your new ventures and bon appetite!

fingerfoods
and antipasto

introduction

introduction

introduction

How often have you thought about giving a party and been put off by the idea of preparing and cooking the food involved? Serving drinks is one thing, catering for a crowd is another.

This book has all the answers. Within these pages you will find a complete selection of delectable fingerfoods designed to entertain your guests, no matter what the occasion – formal or informal, outdoors or indoors, no matter what the season.

All recipes are simple to make, use attractive ingredients, easily found on your supermarket shelves and are designed to allow you maximum time to spend with your guests. Most can be prepared beforehand, with little or no last-minute preparation.

The key here is simplicity. Every single recipe in this book is designed to be eaten with fingers only, no forks or knives need be supplied. The only other things that you as the party-giver have to provide are the occasion, good cheer and plenty of napkins.

Some easy hints-using cheese

All foods have a greater appeal if they are attractively presented, and cheese is no exception. Invest in a cheeseboard, or provide a handsome platter and arrange your selection of cheeses in the centre and surround them with a variety of cracker biscuits, celery, radishes or a lovely wreath of fresh fruit. Cheese and fruit are regarded as the perfect after dinner combination by many European gourmets – and for health and sheer good eating we might follow their example.

salmon cucumber bites

cocktail party

These delicious finger-food recipes

are perfect for your next drinks party. They are easy to
make and serve, and taste great!!

salmon
cucumber bites

Photograph page 11

ingredients

250g/8oz cream cheese, softened
60g/2oz smoked salmon, chopped
2 tablespoons cream (heavy)
2 teaspoons lemon juice
1-2 drops Tabasco sauce
2 cucumbers, cut into
5mm/¼in thick slices
1 lemon, cut into tiny wedges
¼ red pepper, diced

Method:
1 *Place cream cheese, salmon, cream, lemon juice and Tabasco sauce in a food processor and process until smooth. Spoon mixture into a piping bag fitted with a large star nozzle and pipe rosettes onto cucumber slices. Arrange cucumber slices on a serving platter and garnish each with a lemon wedge and a piece of red pepper.*
Makes about 36

devils
on horseback

ingredients

30 blanched almonds
30 soft prunes, pitted
250g/8oz thin rashers bacon,
rind removed

Method:
1 *Place an almond in the cavity of each prune. Cut bacon into pieces just long enough to wrap around prunes and to overlap slightly. Wrap bacon around prunes and secure with wooden toothpicks or cocktail sticks. Place on a baking tray and bake for 12 minutes or until bacon is crisp. Serve hot.*
Makes 30

Oven temperature 220°C, 425°F, Gas 7

spiced
almonds and pecans

Method:

1 *Heat oil in a frying pan over a medium heat, add almonds, pecans and sugar and cook, stirring, until nuts are golden. Transfer to a heatproof bowl.*

2 *Combine cumin, salt and chilli powder, sprinkle over hot nuts and toss to coat. Cool for 5 minutes, then serve.*

Makes 2¹/₂cups/350g/11oz

ingredients

¹/₄ **cup/60mL/2fl oz peanut (groundnut) oil**
220g/7oz **whole blanched almonds**
125g/4oz **whole pecans**
¹/₄ **cup/60g/2oz sugar**
2 **teaspoons ground cumin**
1 **teaspoon salt**
1 **teaspoon chilli powder**

mini
pizzas

Method:

1 To make dough, place yeast, sugar and water in a bowl and mix to dissolve. Set aside in a warm, draught-free place for 5 minutes or until mixture is foamy.

2 Place flour and salt in a food processor and pulse once or twice to sift. With machine running, slowly pour in yeast mixture and oil and process to make a rough dough. Turn dough onto a lightly floured surface and knead for 5 minutes or until soft and shiny. Add more flour if necessary.

3 Place dough in a lightly oiled bowl and roll around bowl to cover surface with oil. Cover bowl with plastic food wrap and place in a warm, draught-free place for 1-1½ hours or until doubled in size. Knock down and knead lightly.

4 Divide dough into 4cm/1½ in balls, press out to make 7cm/2¾in circles and place on greased baking trays. Spread each dough circle with tomato paste (passata), then sprinkle with oregano and top with slices of tomato, peperoni or cabanossi and olives. Sprinkle with cheese and bake for 10 minutes or until pizzas are crisp and brown.

Makes about 80

ingredients

Pizza dough
1 teaspoon active dry yeast
pinch sugar
⅔ cup/170mL/5½fl oz warm water
2 cups/250g/8oz flour
½ teaspoon salt
½ cup/60mL/2fl oz olive oil

Classic pizza topping
¾ cup/185g/6oz concentrated tomato paste (passata)
dried oregano leaves
315g/10oz cherry tomatoes, sliced
125g/4oz peperoni or cabanossi, thinly sliced
10-12 pitted black olives, thinly sliced
2 cups/250g/8oz grated mozzarella cheese

Oven temperature 190°C, 375°F, Gas 5

Oven temperature 220°C, 425°F, Gas 7

lobster
filo triangles

Method:

1 To make filling, remove meat from lobster, chop finely and set aside. Melt 45g/1¹/₂oz butter in a saucepan over a medium heat, add spring onions and garlic and cook, stirring, until onions are tender. Stir in flour and cook for 1 minute.

2 Remove pan from heat and whisk in wine and cream, a little at a time, until well blended. Season to taste with cayenne and black pepper, return to heat and cook, stirring constantly, until sauce boils and thickens. Reduce heat to low and simmer for 3 minutes. Remove from heat, stir in lobster meat and cool completely.

3 Cut pastry sheets lengthwise into 5cm/2in wide strips. Working with one strip of pastry at a time, brush pastry with melted butter. Place a teaspoonful of the filling on one end of strip, fold corner of pastry diagonally over filling, then continue folding up the strip to make a neat triangle.

4 Place triangles on a baking tray, brush with butter and bake for 10-15 minutes or until golden.

Makes 24

ingredients

8 sheets filo pastry
125g/4oz butter, melted and cooled

Lobster cream filling
1 cooked lobster
45g/1¹/₂oz butter
6 spring onions, chopped
2 cloves garlic, crushed
1¹/₂ tablespoons flour
¹/₄ cup/60mL/2fl oz white wine
¹/₄ cup/60mL/2fl oz cream (heavy)
pinch cayenne pepper
freshly ground black pepper

chocolate
macadamia clusters

Method:

1 *Melt chocolate in a bowl over a saucepan of simmering water.*
2 *Chop macadamia nuts into chunks.*
3 *Add nut and shredded coconut to chocolate, stir to coat.*
4 *Place heaped teaspoonfuls mixture onto foil-lined tray, allow to set.*

Makes about 24

ingredients

300g/10oz dark chocolate, chopped
200g/7oz roasted macadamia nuts
¹/₂ cup/45g/1¹/₂oz shredded coconut

continental
salad sticks

Method:

1 *Slice cucumbers, cut capsicum into squares. Combine vegetables in a bowl.*

2 *Combine dressing ingredients in a screwtop jar, shake well, add to vegetables, stand at least an hour.*

3 *Thread vegetables onto toothpicks or short skewers.*

Makes 24

ingredients

4 lebanese cucumbers
1 green capsicum (pepper)
250g/8oz cherry tomatoes
24 pitted black olives

Dressing
$^1/_3$ cup/85ml/3fl oz olive oil
2 tablespoons lemon juice
1 tablespoon chopped fresh basil

oysters
with caviar

ingredients

24 oysters on half shell
$^1/_4$ cup/45g/1$^1/_2$oz caviar
lemon juice
thin lemon slices

Method:

1 Loosen oysters in shell and arrange on large platter. Spoon $^1/_4$ teaspoon caviar onto each oyster. Squeeze some lemon juice over each oyster.

2 Cut lemon slices into quarters and present platter with each oyster garnished with a thin piece of lemon. Serve immediately

Makes 24

ground
beef filo filling

ingredients

White sauce
1 tablespoon butter
1$^1/_2$ tablespoons plain flour
1 cup flour

1 onion, finely chopped
2 tablespoons butter
500g/1lb ground topside beef
$^3/_4$ cup dry white wine
2 tomatoes, peeled, seeded, chopped
1 cup water
salt
pepper
3 hardboiled eggs, chopped
90g/3oz grated Romano cheese

Method:

1 To make white sauce melt butter in a small saucepan, stir in flour; cook 2 minutes, stirring constantly. Off the heat add milk all at once; return to heat and cook, stirring, until mixture thickens. Simmer 5 minutes. Set aside.

2 Cook onion in butter until golden, add ground beef and cook until meat is brown and juices have evaporated. Add wine, tomatoes, salt and freshly ground black pepper and water. Bring to a boil, reduce heat, cover and simmer until juices have evaporated, about 30 minutes. Cool.

3 Stir ground beef mixture into white sauce. Add cheese and eggs. Use mixture to fill buttered filo sheets.

Makes about 48

egg
and onion spirals

Method:

1 To make filling, place eggs in a bowl and mash. Add spring onions, mayonnaise, sour cream and mustard and mix well to combine.

2 Make pinwheels.

Makes 25

ingredients

1 loaf unsliced wholemeal bread
125g/4oz butter, softened

Egg and spring onion filling
8 hard-boiled eggs
4 spring onions, finely chopped
2 tablespoons mayonnaise
2 tablespoons sour cream
2 teaspoons dry mustard

fruit
kebabs

Method:
1 *To make sauce, place mint, honey, sour cream and cream in a bowl and mix to combine. Cover and refrigerate until ready to serve.*
2 *Peel rock melon (cantaloupe), remove seeds and cut into bite-size pieces. Cut kiwifruit in half. Thread two pieces of fruit onto each cocktail stick. Serve with the sauce.*

Makes 16

ingredients

1 small rock melon (cantaloupe)
4 kiwifruit, peeled and quartered
250g/8oz strawberries, hulled
16 wooden cocktail sticks

Honey cream sauce
2 tablespoons chopped fresh mint
2 tablespoons honey
1 cup/250g/8oz sour cream
1 cup/250mL/8fl oz cream (heavy)

sun-dried
tomato dip

Method:

1 *Place sun-dried tomatoes, pine nuts, basil, Parmesan cheese and cream cheese in a food processor or blender and process until smooth. Serve dip with bagel chips or bread and vegetables.*

Serving suggestion: *Place dip in a bowl on a serving platter or tray and surround with bagel chips or bread and/or raw vegetables.*

Serves 4

ingredients

**250g/8oz sun-dried tomatoes
60g/2oz pine nuts
3 tablespoons chopped fresh basil
3 tablespoons grated Parmesan cheese
250g/8oz cream cheese, softened
bagel chips or French bread, sliced
selection of raw vegetables such as
cherry tomatoes, celery sticks, carrot
sticks, broccoli florets, cauliflower
florets and green beans**

Oven temperature 140°C/280°F/Gas 2

coffee
meringues

ingredients

³/₄ **cup/185g raw sugar**
3 tablespoons water
1 egg white
1 teaspoon white vinegar
2 teaspoons cornflour
2 teaspoons coffee essence

Method:

1 *Place sugar and water in a small saucepan, over a medium heat, stirring until sugar dissolves. Bring to the boil and boil for 1-2 minutes. Brush any sugar grains from sides of pan with a wet pastry brush.*

2 *Beat egg white until stiff peaks form. Continue beating while pouring in hot syrup in a thin stream, a little at a time. Beat until meringue is thick. Fold in vinegar, cornflour and coffee essence.*

3 *Place mixture in a large piping bag fitted with a fluted tube. Pipe 4 cm stars onto greased and lined oven trays. Bake at 140°C/280°F for 1 hour or until firm and dry. Cool in oven with door ajar.*

Note: *Who would believe that these delicious morsels are free of fat and cholesterol? They are perfect to serve with coffee or as an afternoon tea treat.*

Makes 30

spicy
curry dip

Method:

1 *Heat oil in a non-stick frypan and cook onion with curry and chilli powders for 4-5 minutes or until onion softens.*

2 *Whisk into yoghurt and season to taste with pepper. Chill until ready to serve.*

Note: *Yogurt is the ideal base for many dips. When a recipe calls for sour cream replace it with yogurt to allow those watching their cholesterol to indulge as well. Serve this dip with vegetables such as blanched asparagus spears, raw carrot and celery sticks and cherry tomatoes.*

Makes 1 cup/250mL

ingredients

2 teaspoons polyunsaturated oil
1 small onion, chopped
1 teaspoon curry powder
pinch chilli powder
1 cup/250mL low fat yogurt
freshly ground black pepper

artichoke
hearts stuffed with two cheeses

Method:

1 *Slice bottoms off artichoke hearts so they will stand upright.*
2 *In a small bowl, combine ricotta, Parmesan, capsicum parsley and pepper; mix well.*
3 *Spoon mixture into the centre of each heart and grill for 1 minute or until the cheese begins to turn golden.*
   Serves 4

ingredients

500g/1lb jar artichoke hearts, drained
3 tablespoons ricotta cheese
2 tablespoons grated Parmesan cheese
1 tablespoon finely chopped red capsicum (pepper)
1 teaspoon finely chopped parsley
1/4 teaspoon black cracked pepper

creamy
oyster dip

Method:

1 *Rinse oysters and place in a small bowl, cover and refrigerate.*
2 *In a small saucepan, over medium heat, combine cream, milk, sour cream, tomato sauce and potato flour. Slowly bring to the boil, stirring constantly until mixture thickens.*
3 *Remove from heat and stir in oysters. Serve with hot toast or biscuits.*

Serves 4

ingredients

24 oysters, removed from shells
¹/₂ cup cream
¹/₄ cup milk
¹/₂ cup sour cream
2 tablespoons tomato sauce
¹/₄ teaspoon potato flour

cherry
tomatoes with parmesan and rosemary

Photograph page 27

Method:
1 *Sprinkle the inside of tomatoes with black pepper.*
2 *In a small bowl, combine cheese, cream, nutmeg and rosemary, mix well.*
3 *Spoon mixture into the tomatoes and grill for 1 minute. Serve immediately.*
Serves 4

ingredients

**8 oz cherry tomatoes, halved and seeded
black pepper
1/4 cup grated Parmesan cheese
1 tablespoon cream
pinch nutmeg
1 tablespoon fresh rosemary, finely chopped**

grilled
eggplant (aubergine) with mozzarella cheese

Photograph page 27

Method:
1 *Lightly brush eggplant slices with combined oil, garlic and pepper. Grill until lightly browned, approximately 3 minutes each side.*
2 *Top each slice with mozzarella cheese and decorate with pimento strips.*
3 *Return to the grill and cook until cheese has melted. Serve immediately and garnish with fresh basil if desired.*
Makes 8

ingredients

**1 medium eggplant (aubergine), cut into 1cm/1/2in slices
3 tablespoons olive oil
1 garlic clove, crushed
1/4 teaspoon pepper
8 thin slices mozzarella
2 pimentos, sliced into strips**

chilli
onion rings

cocktail party

Method:

1 Blend or process buttermilk and chillies for 30 seconds. Pour mixture into a medium bowl, add onion rings and toss, coating well with buttermilk.

2 Sift flour into a bowl. Using a slotted spoon, transfer onions to the flour. Thoroughly dredge onions in the flour.

3 Heat oil in a deep saucepan and fry onions until golden brown. Keep onions warm in oven at 150°C/300°F/Gas 2. Serve onions with a chilli sauce or chutney.

Serves 4

ingredients

¹/₂ cup buttermilk
2 chillies, chopped
2 large onions, peeled cut into ¹/₂cm/¹/₄in rings
2 cups plain flour
2 tablespoons chilli sauce or chutney
oil for deep frying

Oven temperature 150°C/300°F/Gas 2

mussels
au gratin

Method:

1 Combine mussels and I cup water in a saucepan, bring to the boil, cook mussels until shells open (about 3 minutes).
2 Remove mussels from water, open shells, discard top shell and loosen mussel meat in shells.
3 In a small bowl combine remaining ingredients, top each mussel with a tablespoon of mixture. Grill for 5 minutes until toppings are golden.

Serves 4

ingredients

24 mussels, cleaned
I tablespoon fresh basil, chopped
³/₄ cup freshly grated Parmesan cheese
60g/2oz butter, melted
I cup stale breadcrumbs
2 cloves garlic, crushed

*tuna with wasabi butter and
baby spinach tarts*

elegant
at home
party

These recipes are ideal for more

*These recipes are ideal for more formal entertaining.
Your guests will be impressed when you serve them
such delicacies as Tuna with Wasabi Butter or Smoked
Salmon Mini-Quiches.*

tuna
with wasabi butter

Photograph page 31

ingredients

250g/8oz tuna steaks, cut 1cm/¹/₂in thick
20 small rounds pumpernickel bread

Ginger marinade
2 teaspoons sesame oil
1 tablespoon soy sauce
1 clove garlic, crushed
2 teaspoons grated fresh ginger

Wasabi butter
75g/2¹/₂oz butter, softened
¹/₂-1 teaspoon wasabi paste or wasabi
powder mixed with water to form a paste
2 tablespoons chopped fresh coriander

Method:
1 *To make marinade, place oil, soy sauce, garlic and ginger in a bowl and mix to combine. Cut tuna into thin slices. Add to marinade and toss to coat. Cover and set aside to marinate for 1 hour. Drain.*
2 *To make Wasabi Butter, place butter, wasabi paste and coriander in a small bowl and beat until smooth.*
3 *Spread pumpernickel rounds with Wasabi Butter, then top with tuna slices. Cover and chill until ready to serve.*
   Note: *If fresh tuna is unavailable use fresh salmon fillet*
   Makes 20

baby
spinach tarts

Photograph page 31

ingredients

Pastry
1¹/₂ cups/185g/6oz flour
4 tablespoons grated Parmesan cheese
100g/3¹/₂oz butter, chopped
2-3 tablespoons iced water

Spinach filling
2 teaspoons olive oil
2 spring onions, chopped
1 clove garlic, crushed
8 spinach leaves, shredded
125g/4oz ricotta cheese, drained
2 eggs, lightly beaten
¹/₃ cup/90mL/3fl oz milk
¹/₂ teaspoon grated nutmeg
4 tablespoons pine nuts

Method:
1 *To make pastry, place flour, Parmesan cheese and butter in a food processor and process until mixture resembles fine breadcrumbs.*
2 *With machine running, slowly add enough water to form a soft dough. Turn dough onto a lightly floured surface and knead briefly. Wrap dough in plastic food wrap and refrigerate for 30 minutes.*
3 *Roll out pastry to 3mm/¹/₈in thick. Using an 8cm/3¹/₂in fluted pastry cutter, cut out twenty pastry rounds. Place pastry rounds in lightly greased patty tins. Pierce base and sides of pastry with a fork and bake for 5-10 minutes or until lightly golden.*
4 *To make filling, heat oil in a frying pan over a medium heat. Add spring onions, garlic and spinach and cook, stirring, until spinach is wilted. Remove pan from heat and set aside to cool.*
5 *Place spinach mixture, ricotta cheese, eggs, milk and nutmeg in a bowl and mix to combine. Spoon filling into pastry cases and sprinkle with pine nuts. Reduce oven temperature to 180°C/350°F/Gas 4 and bake for 15-20 minutes or until tarts are golden and filling is set.*
   Makes 20

crispy
parmesan artichokes

Method:

1 *Remove and discard the tough outer leaves from artichokes (about the first 2 layers). Place artichokes in a saucepan of boiling, lightly salted water, then reduce heat and simmer for 30 minutes or until tender when pierced with a fork.*

2 *Drain artichokes and set aside until cool enough to handle. Remove leaves from artichokes and reserve, leaving hearts intact. Cut hearts into quarters.*

3 *Place Parmesan cheese and breadcrumbs in a shallow dish and mix to combine. Dip bottom halves of leaves and all the hearts into beaten egg, then roll in crumb mixture to coat.*

4 *Heat oil in a saucepan until a cube of bread dropped in browns in 50 seconds and deep-fry leaves and hearts, in batches, for 2 minutes or until golden and crisp. Drain on absorbent kitchen paper.*

Serves 6

ingredients

3 globe artichokes
125g/4 oz grated Parmesan cheese
1 cup/60g/2oz breadcrumbs, made
from stale bread
4 eggs, lightly beaten
1 cup/250mL/8fl oz olive oil

Oven temperature 220°C, 425°C, Gas 7

curried
onion puffs

Method:

1 *To make puffs, place butter, water and salt in a saucepan over a medium heat and bring to the boil. Remove from heat, add flour all at once and, using a wooden spoon, beat until mixture is smooth.*

2 *Return pan to heat and cook, stirring constantly, for 3-4 minutes or until mixture leaves the sides of the pan. Remove from heat and beat in eggs, a little at a time, then continue beating until paste is smooth and shiny.*

3 *Place teaspoons of paste on greased baking trays and bake for 10 minutes. Reduce oven temperature to 180°C/350°F/Gas 4 and bake for 10 minutes or until puffs are crisp and golden.*

4 *Melt butter in a saucepan over a medium heat, add onions and cook, stirring, for 5 minutes or until onions are golden. Stir in flour and curry powder and cook for 1 minute. Remove pan from heat and slowly stir in cream and black pepper to taste. Return to heat and cook, stirring constantly, until sauce boils and thickens.*

5 *Make a slit in the side of each puff and spoon filling into cavity. Place filled puffs on a baking tray and bake for 10 minutes or until heated through. Serve immediately.*

Makes 24 puffs

ingredients

30g/1oz butter
2 onions, finely chopped
2 teaspoons flour
2 teaspoons curry powder
1/2 cup/125mL/4fl oz cream (heavy)
freshly ground black pepper

Choux puffs
45g/1 1/2oz butter, cut into pieces
1/2 cup/125mL/4fl oz water
pinch salt
1/2 cup/60g/2oz flour
2 large eggs, beaten

almond
and cheese grapes

Method:
1 Place cream and blue cheeses and cream in a bowl and beat until smooth. Add grapes to cheese mixture and mix gently to coat.
2 Place almonds in a shallow dish. Using a teaspoon, scoop out grapes, one at a time, place in almonds and roll to coat. Place grapes on a plate, cover and refrigerate until firm.

Makes about 30

ingredients

125g/4oz cream cheese, softened
60g/2oz blue cheese, crumbled
2 tablespoons cream (heavy)
250g/8oz large seedless green grapes
125g/4oz toasted slivered almonds,
finely chopped

devilled
mixed nuts

Method:

1 *Place nuts and pretzels in a baking dish and mix to combine. Melt butter in a saucepan over a medium heat. Remove pan from heat and stir in garlic, curry and chilli powders and Worcestershire sauce.*

2 *Drizzle butter mixture over nut mixture and mix to coat. Bake at 210°C/420°F, stirring occasionally, for 10 minutes or until mixture is heated through. Serve hot, warm or cold.*

Makes 500g/1 lb

ingredients

375g/12oz mixed nuts
125g/4oz pretzels
60g/2oz butter
2 cloves garlic, crushed
2 teaspoons curry powder
$\frac{1}{2}$ teaspoon chilli powder
2 teaspoons Worcestershire sauce

Oven temperature 210°C/420°F/Gas 6

almond
meringue cream filled cookies

Method:

1 In a medium bowl, and using electric mixer, beat egg whites with sugar until soft peaks form. Fold in ground almonds and cream of tartar.

2 Cover 2 baking trays with greaseproof paper. Drop teaspoons of the mixture, 4cm /1 ¹/₂in apart on baking trays, smooth the tops and place an almond half on top of biscuit.

3 Bake in moderately slow oven for 20 minutes. Remove from oven and leave to cool on trays for 3 minutes before using a spatula to slide cookies onto a rack to cool.

4 Continue to cook cookies as above, making 25 cookie tops with the almond half on top, and 25 plain cookies for the bases.

5 Whip cream until thick and pipe a circle of cream on top of each base. Top with almond topped cookie.

Makes 25

ingredients

³/₄ **cup sugar**
4 egg whites
³/₄ **cup ground almonds**
¹/₂ **teaspoons cream of tartar**
25 blanched almond halves
1 cup cream

Oven temperature 200°C, 400°F, Gas 6

vegetable
samosa

Method:

1 Heat oil in a large frying pan over a medium heat. Add curry powder, onion, mustard seeds and cumin seeds and cook, stirring, for 3 minutes.

2 Add potatoes and stock to pan and cook, stirring occasionally, for 5 minutes or until potatoes are tender.

3 Add carrot and peas to pan and cook for 2 minutes longer. Remove pan from heat and set aside to cool completely.

4 Roll out pastry to 5mm/¹/₄in thick and, using a 10cm/4in pastry cutter, cut out twelve rounds. Place spoonfuls of filling on one half of each pastry round, brush edges with egg, fold uncovered half of pastry over filling and press to seal.

5 Place pastries on lightly greased baking trays, brush with remaining egg and bake for 12-15 minutes or until samosa are puffed and golden.

Makes 12

ingredients

**2 teaspoons vegetable oil
1 tablespoon curry powder
1 onion, finely chopped
1 tablespoon black mustard seeds
2 teaspoons cumin seeds
2 potatoes, finely diced
¹/₂ cup/125mL/4fl oz vegetable stock
1 carrot, finely diced
125g/4oz fresh or frozen peas
500g/1 lb prepared puff pastry
1 egg, lightly beaten**

shrimp
with creamy pesto dip

Method:

1 *To make dip, place pesto and mayonnaise in a bowl and mix to combine.*
2 *To serve, place dip in a small bowl on a large serving platter and surround with shrimp, carrots, snow peas (mangetout) and red pepper.*

Serves 8

ingredients

1 kg/2 lb cooked medium shrimp, shelled and deveined, tails left intact
2 carrots, cut into thick strips
200g/6¹/₂oz snow peas (mangetout), blanched
1 red pepper, cut into thick strips

Creamy pesto dip
¹/₂ cup/125g/4oz ready-made pesto
¹/₂ cup/125mL/4fl oz whole egg mayonnaise

sweet
chilli parcels

ingredients

**200g/6¹/₂oz pork ground
4 spring onions, chopped
1 carrot, grated
2 tablespoons soy sauce
3 tablespoons crunchy peanut butter
24 spring roll or wonton wrappers,
each 12¹/₂cm/5in square
vegetable oil for deep-frying
sweet chilli sauce**

Method:

1 *Heat a nonstick frying pan over a high heat, add pork and cook, stirring, for 5 minutes or until browned.*

2 *Add spring onions, carrot, soy sauce and peanut butter to pan and cook, stirring, for 2 minutes longer. Remove pan from heat and set aside to cool completely.*

3 *Place spoonfuls of mixture in the centre of each spring roll or wonton wrapper, then draw the corners together and twist to form small bundles.*

4 *Heat oil in a large saucepan until a cube of bread dropped in browns in 50 seconds. Cook bundles a few at a time for 3-4 minutes or until golden. Drain and serve with sweet chilli sauce.*

Makes 16

pickled
quail eggs

ingredients

**8 cups/2 litres/70fl oz white vinegar
2 dried red chillies
12 whole cardamom pods
¹/₃ cup/45g/1¹/₂oz coriander seeds
10 cloves
1 teaspoon tumeric
8 cloves garlic
1 teaspoon salt
1 large onion
36 quail eggs**

Method:

1 *Combine vinegar and chillies in a large saucepan, add cardamom, coriander, cloves, turmeric, garlic and salt, bring mixture to a boil, reduce heat, cover and simmer 5 minutes. Take off the heat and cool. Strain*

2 *Slice onion thinly. Hard boil eggs, about 3 minutes, and plunge into cold water straight away. Shell and place in 1.5 litre/6 cup parfait jar with onion. Pour vinegar over, make sure eggs are completely covered. Cover jar and keep in dark place 1 week before using.*

Makes 36

curry
puffs with minted yogurt

Method:

1 Place cumin and coriander in a nonstick frying pan and cook over a high heat, stirring, for 1 minute. Add curry paste and onions and cook, stirring for 2 minutes longer.

2 Add lamb or beef and cook, stirring, for 4 minutes or until browned. Remove pan from heat and set aside to cool.

3 Roll out pastry to 3mm/^{1}/$_8$in thick and, using a 5cm/2in round pastry cutter, cut out sixteen circles. Place a spoonful of meat mixture on one half of each pastry circle. Fold pastry over to encase meat mixture, then press edges together with a fork to seal.

4 Place pastries on a lightly greased baking tray and bake for 10-12 minutes or until golden brown.

5 To make Minted yogurt, place yogurt, mint and cumin in a small bowl and mix to combine. Serve with warm Curry Puffs.

Makes 16

ingredients

1 teaspoon ground cumin
1 teaspoon ground coriander
2 teaspoons mild curry paste
2 onions, chopped
250g/8oz ground lamb or beef
500g/1 lb prepared puff pastry

Minted yogurt
1 cup/200g/6^1/$_2$oz natural yogurt
4 tablespoons chopped fresh mint
1 teaspoon ground cumin

Oven temperature 180°C, 350°F, Gas 4

featherlight
scones

Method:

1 Place flour, sugar and salt in a bowl and mix to combine. Using fingertips, rub in butter until mixture resembles fine breadcrumbs. Add milk and water all at once and, using a rounded knife, mix lightly and quickly to make a soft, sticky dough.
2 Turn dough onto a lightly floured surface and knead lightly until smooth. Press out to make 3cm/1¼in thick rectangle and using 5cm/2in scone cutter, cut out rounds.
3 Place scones, just touching, in a greased shallow 18x28cm/7x11in baking tin. Brush with milk and bake for 12-15 minutes or until scones are well risen and golden. Transfer to wire racks to cool.
4 To serve, split scones and top with jam or lemon butter (curd) and cream, if desired.

Makes about 20

ingredients

4 cups/500 g/1 lb self-rising flour, sifted
2 tablespoons superfine sugar
¼ teaspoon salt
60g/2oz butter
1 cup/250mL/8fl oz buttermilk
¾ cup/185mL/6fl oz water
milk for glazing
jam or lemon butter (curd)
whipped cream (optional)

smoked
salmon mini quiches

Method:

1 Roll out pastry to 3mm/⅛in thick and using a 6cm/2½in pastry cutter, cut out twenty-four rounds. Press pastry rounds into shallow, greased patty pans (tartlet tins).
2 To make filling, place eggs, cream, nutmeg and black pepper to taste in a bowl and whisk to combine. Stir in salmon and dill.
3 Divide filling between pastry cases and bake for 10-15 minutes or until quiches are puffed and golden.
Makes 24

ingredients

185g/6oz prepared puff pastry

Salmon cream filling
6 eggs, lightly beaten
1½ cups/375mL/12fl oz cream (heavy)
¼ teaspoon ground nutmeg
freshly ground black pepper
125g/4oz smoked salmon, chopped
2 teaspoons chopped fresh dill

Oven temperature 190°C, 375°F, Gas 5

43

chocolate
pecan brownies

Method:

1 *Place corn or golden syrup and sugar in a saucepan over a medium heat and cook, stirring, until sugar dissolves and mixture boils. Remove pan from heat, stir in chocolate and butter and continue stirring until mixture is smooth. Beat in eggs and rum.*

2 *Place pecans and flour in a bowl and mix to combine. Add chocolate mixture and mix to combine.*

3 *Spread mixture into a greased and lined 18x28cm/7x11in shallow cake tin and bake for 25-30 minutes or until brownies are set.*

4 *Stand brownies in tin for 10 minutes, then turn onto a wire rack to cool. To serve, dust brownies with icing sugar, cut into small squares and top each with a strawberry half.*

Makes 24

ingredients

¹/₂ cup/125mL/4fl oz **dark corn or golden syrup**
¹/₄ cup/60g/2oz **sugar**
90g/3oz **dark chocolate, chopped**
45g/1¹/₂oz **butter**
2 **eggs, lightly beaten**
1 tablespoon **dark rum**
185g/6oz **pecan nuts, finely chopped**
¹/₂ cup/60g/2oz **flour**
1 tablespoon **icing sugar**
12 **strawberries, halved**

Oven temperature 180°C, 350°F, Gas 4

Oven temperature 220°C/425°F/Gas 7

cheese
and chive cookies

Method:
1 *Place flour, butter, blue and Parmesan cheeses and chives in a food processor and process until ingredients cling together. Turn onto a lightly floured surface and knead lightly. Shape dough into a ball, wrap in plastic food wrap and chill for 30 minutes.*
2 *Roll heaped teaspoons of mixture into balls, then roll in sesame seeds to coat. Place balls on lightly greased baking trays, flatten slightly with a fork and bake for 10 minutes at 220°C/425°F or until golden. Stand on trays for 3 minutes, then tranfer to wire racks to cool. Store cookies in an airtight container.*

Makes 30

ingredients

**1 cup/125g/4oz self-rising flour, sifted
125g/4oz butter, cut into pieces
60g/2oz hard blue cheese, crumbled
2 tablespoons grated Parmesan cheese
3 tablespoons snipped fresh chives
4 tablespoons sesame seeds**

bacon wrapped shrimp

summer
lunch
party

In the midst of a hot summer day,

these wonderful nibbles will be enjoyed by one and all.

pistachio
cheese balls

Method:
1 Combine butter, cream cheese, curry powder, tabasco, soy, mustard and Worcestershire in food processor. Blend until smooth. Add salt and freshly ground black pepper to taste. Spoon into a bowl, cover and refrigerate until stiff.
2 Shape into balls the size of a walnut, roll in chopped pistachios. Refrigerate until ready to serve.

Makes about 60

ingredients
1/2 cup/120g/4oz butter
250g/8oz cream cheese
1 teaspoon mild curry powder
1 teaspoon tabasco sauce
1 teaspoon light soy sauce
1 teaspoon mustard powder
1 tablespoon Worcestershire sauce
1 cup/10g/4oz finely chopped pistachio
nuts
salt
pepper

bacon
wrapped shrimp

Photograph page 47

Method:
1 To make marinade, place oregano, garlic, oil and vinegar in a bowl and whisk to combine. Add prawns and toss to coat. Cover and refrigerate for at least 1 hour or overnight.
2 Drain shrimp and reserve marinade. Cut each bacon rasher into three pieces, wrap a piece of bacon around each shrimp and secure with a wooden toothpick or cocktail stick.
3 Cook shrimp under a preheated medium grill or on the barbecue, turning occasionally and brushing with reserved marinade for 5 minutes or until bacon is crisp and shrimp are cooked.

Makes about 24

ingredients

750g/1 1/2 lb large uncooked shrimp (shrimp), shelled and deveined, tails left intact
8 rashers bacon, rind removed

Herb marinade
2 tablespoons chopped fresh oregano
2 cloves garlic, crushed
1/2 cup/125mL/4fl oz olive oil
2 tablespoons white wine vinegar

marinated
mushrooms

Method:
1 Trim stalks from mushrooms and wipe with a clean damp teatowel. Place mushrooms in a bowl, pour over boiling water and lemon juice and stand for 5 minutes.
2 To make marinade, place parsley, thyme, garlic, oil, vinegar and black pepper to taste in a screwtop jar and shake to combine.
3 Drain mushrooms, return to bowl, pour over marinade, cover and marinate in the refrigerator for at least 2 hours or overnight.

Makes about 30

ingredients

500g/1 lb button mushrooms
1 cup/250mL/8fl oz boiling water
2 tablespoons lemon juice

Mushroom marinade
1 tablespoon chopped fresh parsley
2 teaspoons chopped fresh thyme
2 cloves garlic, crushed
¹/₃ cup/90mL/3fl oz olive oil
2 tablespoons white wine vinegar
freshly ground black pepper

Oven temperature 150°C/300°F/Gas 2

coconut
lemon wedges

Method:

1 Combine macaroons, coconut and Cointreau, press evenly over base of a 23cm/9in springform pan.

2 Cream butter, lemon rind and sugar in small bowl with electric mixer until light and fluffy. Beat in eggs, one at a time (mixture may curdle but is not a problem). Stir in lemon juice and coconut. Spread over macaroon base.

3 Bake in slow oven (150°C/300°F/Gas 2, for about 40 minutes or until golden brown, cool. Remove sides of pan, cut into wedges to serve.

Makes about 15 wedges

ingredients

¹/₃ **cup crushed coconut macaroons**
³/₄ **cup coconut**
¹/₄ **cup Cointreau Liqueur**
90g/3oz butter
2 teaspoons grated lemon rind
¹/₂ **cup castor sugar**
2 eggs
2 tablespoons lemon juice
1 ¹/₄ **cups coconut**

snow peas
with herb cheese filling

Method:

1 Cook snow peas (mangetout) in boiling water for 20 seconds, drain, and rinse under cold water. Split snow peas along the curved side, leaving the straight side intact.

2 Blend or process combined cream cheese, parsley, dill, garlic and pepper until smooth. Spoon into a piping bag fitted with a small star pipe.

3 Pipe herb mixture into snow peas, refrigerate until firm. Garnish with chilli.

Makes 24

guacamole

Method:
1 *Cut avocados in half, remove seeds and skin. Mash avocados roughly with a fork.*
2 *Plunge tomatoes into boiling water for 30 seconds, remove. Peel off skin, cut into quarters, remove and discard seeds. Cut tomatoes into small dice.*
3 *Combine avocado, tomato, onion, chilli, coriander and lemon juice. Serve with corn chips for dipping.*
Serves 8

ingredients

3 avocados
2 small tomatoes
1 small onion, very finely chopped
3 red chillies, chopped
2 tablespoons chopped fresh coriander
2 tablespoons lemon juice
2 x 200g/6¹/₂oz pkts corn chips

crunchy
split pea snacks

Method:

1 Wash peas under cold running water, drain. Place peas in a bowl, cover with cold water, stir in soda, stand overnight.
2 Drain peas, wash thoroughly under cold, running water, drain well. Drain again on absorbent paper.
3 Deep fry in 4 batches in heated oil, until golden brown, drain on absorbent paper.
4 Combine peas in a bowl with curry, cumin, chilli, and allow to cool.

Makes about 3 cups

ingredients

¹/₂ **cup green split peas**
¹/₂ **cup yellow split peas**
2 **teaspoons bicarbonate of soda**
oil for deep frying
1 **teaspoon curry powder**
1 **teaspoon ground cumin**
¹/₂ **teaspoon chilli powder**

hazelnut
bread

Method:

1 *Beat egg whites in a small bowl with electric mixer until soft peaks form. Gradually add sugar 1 tablespoon at a time, beat until dissolved between additions.*

2 *Fold in flour and hazelnuts, spread evenly into a greased and lined bar pan 7cmx25cm/ 2³/₄inx10in.*

3 *Bake in moderate oven 180°C/350°/Gas 4 for 30 minutes or until light golden brown. Turn onto wire rack to cool. Wrap in foil, stand overnight.*

4 *Using an electric knife or very sharp knife, slice loaf thinly. Bake slices on an oven tray in a slow oven for 45 minutes or until dry and crisp. Store in airtight container for up to 1 month.*

Makes about 48 slices

ingredients

3 egg whites
¹/₂ cup superfine sugar
1 cup plain flour
150g/5oz roasted hazelnuts

Oven temperature 180°C/350°F/Gas 4

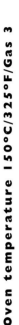

carpaccio

Method:

1 Ask your butcher to cut the fillet into paper thin slices

2 Cut breadstick into 1cm/¹/₂in slices, place in single layer on a baking tray, bake in moderate slow oven 150°C/325°F/Gas 3 for 10 minutes or until bread is crisp but not dry, cool.

3 Spread thinly with combined butter, cheese and rind.

4 Place a slice of beef fillet onto each bread slice, top with a little tartare sauce, anchovy and capers, garnish with parsley.

Makes about 60

ingredients

500g/1lb piece beef eye fillet
2 breadsticks
90g/3oz butter
2 tablespoons grated Parmesan cheese
2 teaspoons grated lemon rind
¹/₃ cup tartare sauce
1 tablespoon chopped anchovy fillets
2 tablespoons chopped capers
parsley to garnish

artichoke
bread savories

Method:

1 Drain artichokes, cut in half.
2 Cut bread slices into circles using a 4cm/
1 1/2in cutter. Deep-fry circles in heated oil
until golden brown, drain.
3 Combine mayonnaise, cream and chives.
4 To assemble place 1 or 2 artichoke halves
(depending on their size) onto bread circles.
Drizzle with a little mayonnaise mixture,
garnish with chopped pimento and dill.

Makes 12

ingredients

240g/8oz can artichoke hearts
12 slices bread
oil for deep-frying
1/4 cup mayonnaise
1 tablespoon thickened cream
1 tablespoon chopped chives
2 tablespoons chopped pimento
dill for garnish

taramosalata

Method:

1 *Peel and chop potatoes, cook in boiling water until tender, drain, cool.*
2 *Remove crusts from bread, combine in a bowl with 1 cup water, stand 2 minutes, strain, press out excess water.*
3 *Place potatoes, bread, tarama, onion and pepper in a blender or processor, blend until smooth.*
4 *With blender running, gradually pour in combined olive oil and lemon juice, blend until combined.*
5 *Split pita bread in half, cut each half into wedges, serve with taramosalata.*

Serves 8

ingredients

250g/¹/₂lb potatoes
6 slices white bread
100g/3¹/₂oz can tarama or 60g/2oz fresh
1 onion, finely grated
freshly ground black pepper
¹/₂ cup olive oil
¹/₂ cup lemon juice
4 slices pita bread

Oven temperature 220°C/440°F/Gas 7

sesame
twists

Method:

1 *Cut pastry sheets in half, brush with melted butter.*
2 *Combine poppy seeds, sesame seeds and cheese, sprinkle over pastry, press firmly into pastry with a rolling pin.*
3 *Using a sharp knife, cut widthwise into strips, 2cm/³/₄in wide and 10cm/4in long. Twist strips slightly.*
4 *Place onto lightly greased baking trays; bake in hot oven 220°C/440°F/Gas 7, for 8 minutes or until puffed and golden brown.*

Makes 48 twists

ingredients

2 sheets ready-rolled puff pastry
60g/2oz butter, melted
2 tablespoons poppy seeds
2 tablespoons sesame seeds
2 tablespoons grated Parmesan cheese

oyster
cases with leek chiffonade

Method:

1. Slice white part of leeks, discard green. Melt butter in a frying pan; add leeks and fennel, stirfry over low heat until tender, about 10 minutes.

2. Add cream, sour cream, salt and pepper, simmer 5 minutes or until reduced and thickened slightly.

3. Spoon mixture into oyster cases, sprinkle with Parmesan cheese, bake in moderate oven 180°C/350°F/Gas 4 for 10 minutes or until heated through.

Makes 16

ingredients

2 leeks
¹/₂ fennel bulb, chopped
30g/1oz butter
¹/₃ cup cream
¹/₃ cup sour cream
salt
pepper
16 puff pastry oyster cases
2 tablespoons grated Parmesan cheese

Oven temperature 180°C/350°F/Gas 4

deep-fried
crab balls

Method:

1 To make sauce, place onion, parsley, basil, gherkins, olives, mustard, mayonnaise and black pepper to taste in a bowl and mix to combine. Cover and refrigerate until required.

2 Place crabmeat, breadcrumbs, butter, mustard, egg yolks, Tabasco sauce and black pepper to taste in a bowl and mix to combine. Cover and chill until mixture is firm.

3 Shape mixture into walnut-sized balls, place on a plate lined with nonstick baking paper, cover and chill for 30 minutes.

4 Heat oil in a large saucepan until a cube of bread dropped in browns in 50 seconds. Roll crab balls in flour to coat, shake off excess and deep-fry in hot oil, in batches, for 2-3 minutes or until golden. Drain on absorbent kitchen paper and serve warm with Tartare Sauce (see below).

Makes about 36

ingredients

**500g/1 lb crabmeat, flaked
½ cup/30g/1oz breadcrumbs,
made from stale bread
60g/2oz butter, softened
1 tablespoon Dijon mustard
2 egg yolks
few drops Tabasco sauce
freshly ground black pepper
vegetable oil for deep-frying
flour for coating**

tartare
sauce

Method:

1 Combine all ingredients.

ingredients

**<u>Sauce tartare</u>
1 teaspoon finely chopped onion
1 teaspoon chopped fresh parsley
1 teaspoon chopped fresh basil
1 teaspoon finely chopped gherkins
1 teaspoon finely chopped green olives
1 teaspoon Dijon mustard
1 cup/250mL/8fl oz good quality egg
mayonnaise**

smoked
salmon bagels

Method:

1 Spread each bagel half with cream cheese and sprinkle with chives. Top bagel halves with salmon, onion, avocado and capers. Sprinkle with lemon juice and serve immediately.

Serving suggestion: *A tomato and onion salad is a delicious side dish. To make salad, arrange sliced tomatoes and very thinly sliced onion on a lettuce lined dish. Sprinkle with chopped fresh basil and drizzle with French dressing. Season to taste with black pepper.*

Serves 4

ingredients

4 bagels, split
125g/4oz cream cheese, softened
2 tablespoons snipped fresh chives
250g/8oz smoked salmon slices
I onion, thinly sliced
I avocado, stoned, peeled and sliced
I tablespoon capers, drained
I tablespoon lemon juice

double
dipped chocolate strawberries

Method:

1 Melt white chocolate with half the copha in a bowl over saucepan of simmering water.
2 Hold strawberries by the stem; dip $^2/_3$ of the strawberry into chocolate. Hold over chocolate to allow excess to run off. Place onto a foil covered tray, refrigerate until set.
3 Melt dark chocolate with remaining copha in a bowl over a saucepan of simmering water.
4 Dip strawberries into chocolate, $^2/_3$ of the way up the white chocolate. Hold over chocolate to allow excess to run off. Place onto foil covered tray, refrigerate until set.

Makes about 52

ingredients

125g/4oz white chocolate
60g/2oz copha (vegetable shortening)
2 x 250g/$^1/_2$lb punnets strawberries
125g/4oz dark chocolate

shrimp
toast

Method:

1 *Peel and devein shrimp, combine in a blender or processor with spring onions, ginger, soy sauce and sesame oil, blend until roughly chopped. Add egg whites, blend until combined.*

2 *Remove crusts from bread slices, spread with prawn mixture.*

3 *Cut each slice into 3 strips. Dip shrimp coated side of each strip into breadcrumbs.*

4 *Deep-fry in heated oil until light golden brown, drain on absorbent paper, serve immediately.*

Makes 18

ingredients

500g/1lb cooked shrimp
6 spring onions (scallions), chopped
2 teaspoons grated fresh ginger
2 teaspoons light soy sauce
¹/₂ teaspoon sesame oil
2 egg whites
6 slices white bread
¹/₂ cup fresh breadcrumbs
oil for deep-frying

barbecue party

*thai barbecue fish cakes and
antipasto skewers*

What better way to entertain than

*with an informal barbecue? On a beautiful and
relaxing day, these tasty recipes will have your guests
coming back for more.*

thai
barbecue fish cakes

Photograph page 65

Method:

1 Place fish, curry paste, lemon grass, coriander, lime leaves and egg white in a food processor and process until smooth.

2 Using wet or lightly oiled hands, take 1 tablespoon of mixture and roll into a ball, then flatten to form a disk. Repeat with remaining mixture. Place fish cakes on a tray lined with plastic food wrap and chill for 30 minutes or until firm.

3 Preheat barbecue to a high heat. Place fish cakes on oiled barbecue plate (griddle) and cook for 1 minute each side or until cooked through. Serve with lime wedges and sweet chilli sauce.

Makes 18

ingredients

**375g/12oz boneless, fine fleshed, white fish
fillets, chopped
2 tablespoons red curry paste
1 stalk fresh lemon grass, chopped or
1/2 teaspoon dried lemon grass,
soaked in hot water until soft
1 tablespoon chopped fresh coriander
4 kaffir lime leaves, finely shredded
1 egg white
lime wedges
sweet chilli sauce**

antipasto
skewers

Photograph page 65

Method:

1 Place rosemary leaves, thyme leaves, vinegar and oil in a bowl and whisk to combine. Cut eggplant (aubergines) and zucchini (courgettes) into cubes. Add to vinegar mixture, then add tomatoes and red pepper (capsicum). Toss to coat vegetables with marinade, cover and marinate for 30-60 minutes.

2 To make dipping sauce, place pesto, sour cream and black pepper to taste in a bowl and mix to combine.

3 Preheat barbecue to a high heat. Roll salami slices tightly. Drain vegetables and reserve marinade. Thread vegetables and salami rolls, alternately, onto small skewers. Cook skewers, brushing frequently with reserved marinade, on oiled barbecue grill for 1-2 minutes each side or until vegetables are tender. Serve skewers warm with dipping sauce.

Makes 12

ingredients

**1 tablespoon fresh rosemary leaves
1 tablespoon fresh thyme leaves
1/4 cup/60mL/2fl oz balsamic vinegar
2 tablespoons olive oil
2 baby eggplant (aubergines),
halved lengthwise
2 zucchini (courgettes),
halved lengthwise
155g/5oz semi-dried tomatoes
1 red pepper (capsicum), diced
250 g/8 oz sliced spicy salami**

Creamy pesto dipping sauce
**1/4 cup/60mL/2fl oz pesto
1/2 cup/125g/4oz sour cream
freshly ground black pepper**

marinated
seared tuna

Method:

1 Preheat barbecue to a high heat.

2 Brush tuna with sesame oil. Place tuna on oiled barbecue grill and cook for 5 seconds each side - the outside of the tuna should be seared only and the centre still uncooked.

3 To make marinade, place spring onions, parsley, ginger, soy sauce, lemon juice in a shallow dish. Place tuna in marinade, turn to coat, cover and marinate in the refrigerator, turning occasionally, for 1-2 hours.

4 To serve, remove tuna from marinade and cut into thin slices. Arrange tuna slices attractively on a serving platter and spoon over a little of the marinade.

Serves 12

ingredients

375g/12oz piece sashimi tuna
2 teaspoons sesame oil

Ginger and lemon marinade
2 spring onions, minced
1 tablespoon finely chopped
flat-leaf parsley
2 teaspoons minced fresh ginger
¼ cup/60mL/2fl oz soy sauce
2 tablespoons lemon juice

barbecue
party

grilled
strawberry kebabs

Method:

1 Preheat barbecue to a high heat.
2 Thread strawberries onto lighlty oiled wooden skewers. Brush strawberries with vinegar, then roll in icing sugar. Cook kebabs on oiled barbecue grill for 10 seconds each side or until icing sugar caramelises. Serve immediately with ice cream.

Note: Remember to soak bamboo or wooden skewers in water before using - this helps to prevent them from burning during cooking. Before threading food onto skewers, lightly oil them so that the cooked food is easy to remove. For this recipe, use a light tasting oil such as canola or sunflower.

Serves 8

ingredients

500g/1 lb strawberries, halved
¹/₄ cup/60 mL/2 fl oz balsamic vinegar
1¹/₂ cups/220g/7oz icing sugar
vanilla ice cream

tomato
salsa on bruschetta

Method:

1 Preheat barbecue to a medium heat. To make the dressing, place garlic cloves on barbecue plate (griddle) and cook for 1-2 minutes each side or until flesh is soft. Squeeze flesh from garlic cloves and mash. Place garlic, vinegar and oil in a screwtop jar and shake to combine.

2 To make salsa, place tomatoes and 2 tablespoons oil in a bowl and toss to coat. Place tomatoes, cut side down, on barbecue plate (griddle) and cook for 1 minute each side. Place tomatoes, cheese, basil and black peppercorns to taste in a bowl, add dressing and toss to combine.

3 Lightly brush bread with oil, place on barbecue grill and toast for 1 minute each side. To serve, pile tomato salsa onto bread and serve immediately.

Makes 12

ingredients

12 slices crusty Italian bread

Grilled tomato salsa
500g/1 lb cherry tomatoes, halved olive oil
6 small bocconcini cheeses, chopped
4 tablespoons torn fresh basil leaves
crushed black peppercorns

Roasted garlic dressing
2 garlic cloves, unpeeled
2 tablespoons balsamic vinegar
1 tablespoon olive oil

lamb
and mango skewers

Method:

1 *To make marinade, place ginger, hoisin and soy sauces, vinegar and oil in a bowl and mix to combine. Add lamb, toss to coat, cover and marinate in the refrigerator for at least 4 hours.*

2 *Thread lamb and mango cubes, alternately, onto oiled skewers. Cook on a preheated hot barbecue for 3-4 minutes each side or until tender.*

Serves 8

ingredients

I kg/2 lb lean lamb, trimmed of visible fat and cut into 2cm/³/₄in cubes
3 mangoes, cut into 2cm/³/₄in cubes

<u>Hoisin Soy Marinade</u>
I tablespoon finely grated fresh ginger
³/₄ cup/185mL/6fl oz hoisin sauce
¹/₄ cup/60mL/2fl oz reduced-salt soy sauce
¹/₄ cup/60mL/2fl oz rice wine vinegar
¹/₄ cup/60mL/2fl oz vegetable oil

spicy
chicken satays

Method:

1 Place onions, lemon rind, ginger, garlic, coriander, cumin and oil in a food processor and process to make a paste. Transfer mixture to a bowl, add chicken and toss to coat. Cover and marinate at room temperature for 1 hour or in the refrigerator overnight.

2 To make sauce, place onion, chillies and peanuts in a food processor or blender and process to make a paste. Heat oil in a saucepan over a medium heat, add onion mixture and cook, stirring, for 5 minutes. Add tamarind sauce and water and bring to the boil. Reduce heat to low and simmer until sauce reduces and thickens.

3 Drain chicken and thread onto oiled skewers. Cook kebabs on a preheated hot barbecue for 5-6 minutes each side or until chicken is tender. Serve with Peanut Sauce.

Serves 8

ingredients

2 onions, chopped
1 tablespoon grated lemon rind
2 teaspoons finely grated fresh ginger
2 cloves garlic, crushed
1 teaspoon ground coriander
1 teaspoon ground cumin
1/4 cup/60mL/2fl oz vegetable oil
6 boneless chicken breast fillets,
cut into 2cm/3/4in cubes

Peanut Sauce
1 onion, chopped
6 fresh red chillies, chopped
155g/5oz peanuts
1/4 cup/60mL/2fl oz vegetable oil
1 tablespoon tamarind sauce
3/4 cup/185mL/6fl oz water

marinated
beef strips

Method:
1 To make marinade, place onion, garlic, parsley, thyme, black peppercorns, wine and oil in a bowl and mix to combine. Add beef, toss to coat, cover and marinate in the refrigerator for at least 4 hours.
2 Drain beef and reserve marinade. Weave beef strips onto oiled skewers, then cook on a preheated hot barbecue grill, brushing frequently with marinade and turning, for 2-3 minutes or until cooked to your liking.
Serves 8

ingredients

**1 kg/2 lb beef rump steak, trimmed
of visible fat and cut into long strips**

**<u>Garlic Wine Marinade</u>
1 large onion, sliced
4 cloves garlic, chopped
4 tablespoons chopped fresh parsley
1 tablespoon fresh thyme leaves
1 tablespoon black peppercorns
1 cup/250mL/8fl oz dry red wine
1/3 cup/90mL/3fl oz olive oil**

tangy
veal skewers

Method:

1 To make marinade, place oil, lemon juice, vinegar, capers and tarragon in a bowl and mix to combine. Add veal, toss to coat, cover and marinate in the refrigerator for at least 4 hours.

2 Cook onions in a saucepan of boiling water for 5 minutes. Drain, cool and cut in half. Drain veal and reserve marinade. Thread veal and onions, alternately, onto oiled skewers.

3 Brush kebabs with reserved marinade and cook on preheated hot barbecue for 2-3 minutes each side or until veal is tender.

Serves 8

ingredients

1 kg/2 lb veal steak, trimmed of visible fat and cut into thin strips
8-12 small pickling onions

Tangy Marinade
¹/₂ cup/125mL/4fl oz olive oil
¹/₄ cup/60mL/2fl oz lemon juice
2 tablespoons white wine vinegar
3 tablespoons drained capers
2 tablespoons chopped fresh tarragon

basil
and shrimp skewers

Method:

1 To make marinade, place basil, peppercorns, oil, wine and lemon juice in a screwtop jar and shake to combine. Place shrimp in a non-reactive bowl, pour over marinade and toss to coat. Cover and marinate in the refrigerator for 2-6 hours.

2 Drain shrimp and reserve marinade. Thread shrimp and lemon slices, alternately, onto oiled skewers. Cook kebabs on a preheated hot barbecue grill, basting with marinade, for 3 minutes each side or until shrimp change colour. Scatter with chopped basil and serve.

Serves 8

ingredients

1 ¹/₂-1 ³/₄ kg/3-3¹/₄ lb medium uncooked shrimp, shelled and deveined, tails left intact
24 slices lemon
3-4 tablespoons chopped fresh basil

Basil Marinade
4-6 tablespoons chopped fresh basil
1 tablespoon crushed black peppercorns
1 cup/250mL/8fl oz olive oil
³/₄ cup/185mL/6fl oz dry white wine
¹/₄ cup/60mL/2fl oz lemon juice

raspberry
marinated chicken wings

Method:

1 Combine oil, vinegar, honey, sesame seeds, cumin, salt and garlic in a screwtop jar, shake until well combined. Pour over chicken wings, cover, refrigerate overnight.

2 Remove from marinade and barbecue until cooked through and crisp, brushing with the marinade and turning from time to time.

Makes 24

ingredients

24 chicken wings

Raspberry marinade
1 cup/250ml/8fl oz olive oil
¹/₃ cup/85ml/3fl oz raspberry vinegar
1 tablespoon honey
1 tablespoon sesame seeds
1 teaspoon cumin
¹/₂ teaspoon salt
2 cloves garlic, crushed

prosciutto
melon

Method:

1 Cut rock melon (cantaloupe) in half lengthwise and scoop out seeds. Cut each half into 8 wedges, remove skin and cut in half, crosswise. Cut each slice of prosciutto or ham, lengthwise into 3 strips and wrap one strip around each piece of melon. Arrange on a serving plate, cover and chill.

Makes 32

ingredients

1 rock melon (cantaloupe)
250g/8oz very thinly sliced prosciutto or lean ham

herb-filled
cherry tomatoes

Method:

1 Cut tops off tomatoes and carefully scoop out seeds. Reserve 2 tablespoons of the pulp. Place tomatoes up side down on absorbent kitchen paper and drain.

2 To make filling, place cream cheese in a food processor and process until light and fluffy. Add reserved tomato pulp, mint, parsley, chives, almonds and black pepper to taste and process briefly to combine.

3 Spoon or pipe filling into tomato shells and arrange on a serving platter. Cover and refrigerate for 1 hour or until firm.

Makes about 36

ingredients

500g/1 lb cherry tomatoes

Herb Cheese Filling
125g/4oz cream cheese, softened
1 tablespoon chopped fresh mint
1 tablespoon chopped fresh parsley
1 tablespoon snipped fresh chives
45g/1¹/₂oz slivered almonds, toasted
freshly ground black pepper

Method:

1 *To make pastry, place flour and icing sugar in a food processor and process to combine. Add butter and process until mixture resembles fine breadcrumbs. With machine running, add egg yolks and water and process to form a rough dough. Turn dough out onto a lightly floured surface and knead until smooth. Wrap dough in plastic food wrap and chill for 20 minutes.*

2 *Roll out dough to 3mm/¹/₈in thick. Using an 8cm/3¹/₄in pastry cutter, cut out eighteen rounds. Place pastry rounds in lightly greased patty pans (tartlet tins). Prick base and sides of pastry with a fork and bake for 10 minutes or until golden. Cool on a wire rack.*

3 *To make custard filling, place sugar, cornflour, eggs and egg yolk in a bowl and whisk until smooth and thick. Heat milk and cream in a saucepan over a medium heat, then gradually whisk in egg mixture. Reduce heat to low and cook, stirring constantly, until mixtures boils and thickens. Remove pan from heat, stir in liqueur, cover and set aside to cool.*

4 *To assemble, place gelatine and boiling water in a bowl and stir until gelatine dissolves. Stir in sieved jam and liqueur and set aside until glaze cools and begins to thicken. Spoon filling into pastry shells, then decorate with fruit and brush tops with gelatine mixture. Chill until firm.*

Makes 18

Oven temperature 190°C, 375°F, Gas 5

fruit
tartlets

ingredients

1 teaspoon gelatine
¹/₃ cup/90mL/3fl oz boiling water
¹/₂ cup/155g/5oz apricot jam, warmed and sieved
2 teaspoons orange-flavoured liqueur
440g/14oz canned apricot halves, drained and sliced
12 strawberries, halved or sliced
125g/4oz seedless green or black grapes, halved
2 peaches, sliced
2 kiwifruit, sliced

Rich pastry
1¹/₂ cups/185g/6oz flour
2 tablespoons icing sugar
125g/4oz butter
2 egg yolks
1 teaspoon water

Custard cream filling
¹/₂ cup/125g/4oz sugar
6 teaspoons cornflour
2 eggs
1 egg yolk
³/₄ cup/185mL/6fl oz milk
¹/₄ cup/6 mL/2fl oz cream (heavy)
1 tablespoon orange-flavoured liqueur

lamb
kebabs tuscany

ingredients

1¹/₂kg/3lb lean lamb, cut into 2¹/₂cm/1in cubes
1 green capsicum (pepper),
cut into 2¹/₂cm/1in cubes
1 red capsicum (pepper),
cut into 2¹/₂cm/1in cubes
2 onions, cut into eighths

<u>Tuscan marinade:</u>
¹/₂ cup tomato paste
¹/₂ cup oil
¹/₄ cup red wine vinegar
3 cloves garlic, crushed
2 teaspoons oregano
¹/₂ teaspoon salt
pepper

Method:

1 *Combine marinade ingredients in a large bowl, mix well. Add lamb, capsicum and onion. Cover, leave at room temperature for at least 3 hours, or refrigerate overnight.*
2 *Thread alternate pieces of lamb, capsicum and onion onto skewers, cook on a lightly greased barbecue, basting and turning frequently, until meat is brown on the outside, still pink inside, about 12 minutes.*
Serves 8

oriental
beef spareribs

ingredients

2kg/4lb beef spareribs, all fat removed
Sambal Badjak*

<u>Oriental Marinade:</u>
¹/₂ cup light soy sauce
100ml/3fl oz freshly squeezed lemon juice
2 cloves garlic
3 tablespoons white wine vinegar
2 tablespoons dark brown sugar
2 tablespoons peanut oil
1 tablespoon grated fresh ginger
2 teaspoons ground coriander
¹/₂ teaspoon ground cumin
¹/₄ teaspoon Tabasco sauce

Method:

1 *In a processor combine all marinade ingredients, puree until smooth. Place spareribs in a dish, pour over marinade, turn ribs to coat well. Cover and refrigerate overnight.*
2 *Remove ribs from marinade, barbecue until dark brown and crisp, turning once, about 6 minutes each side. Serve with Sambal Badjak for dipping.*
Note: **Sambal Badjak is available in Oriental foodstores*
Serves 8

Oven temperature 200°C/400°F/Gas 6

curried
sausage puffs

Method:

1 Cut pastry sheet in half
2 Combine sausage, carrot, spring onion, chutney and curry powder, season to taste with salt and pepper, divide into 4, roll each into a sausage shape the length of the long side of the pastry.
3 Place sausage along pastry, roll up, and seal edge with water. Cut roll into 1cm/ ¹/₂in slices.
4 Place slices onto greased baking trays, bake in moderately hot oven (200°C/400°F/Gas 6 for 15 minutes or until golden brown and puffed.

Makes 24

ingredients

**2 sheet ready-rolled puff pastry
375g/³/₄lb sausage ground
1 small carrot, finely grated
2 spring onions (scallions), chopped
1 tablespoon fruit chutney
1 teaspoon curry powder
salt
pepper**

veal

and cherry with pepper sauce

Method:
1 *Combine marinade ingredients in a bowl. Add veal, toss well to coat, refrigerate overnight.*
2 *Thread alternate pieces o meat, tomato, capsicum and onion on skewers. Barbecue until meat is just cooked through.*
Serves 8

ingredients

1kg/2 lb veal shoulder, trimmed of fat, cubed
16 cherry tomatoes
1 green capsicum(pepper), cubed
1 red capsicum (pepper), cubed
2 large onions, cut into eights

Onion marinade
1 onion, finely chopped
$1/2$ teaspoon cumin
1 teaspoon freshly squeezed lemon juice
$1/2$ teaspoon white wine vinegar
$1/4$ teaspoon chilli flakes
1 clove garlic, crushed

hot

capsicum (pepper) sauce

Method:
1 *Melt butter in a saucepan, add onion and capsicum. Saute until golden. Add tomatoes, chilli and water.*
2 *Bring to a boil, reduce heat, simmer 10 minutes. Season to taste with salt and freshly ground black pepper. Serve hot sprinkled with chopped coriander.*
Makes about 1 cup

ingredients

1 tablespoon butter
1 onion, finely chopped
2 green capsicums (peppers), chopped
2 tomatoes, chopped
$1/4$ teaspoon chilli flakes
$1/3$ cup water
salt
pepper
1 tablespoon chopped coriander

oriental
chicken kebabs

Method:

1 Preheat barbecue to a high heat.

2 To make marinade, place sugar, lime leaves, if using, chilli, soy sauce and lime juice in a bowl and mix to combine.

3 Add chicken, toss to coat and marinate for 20 minutes. Drain chicken. Thread chicken and mushrooms onto lightly oiled skewers and cook on oiled barbecue grill, turning and basting with reserved marinade for 5 minutes or until chicken is tender and cooked.

4 Place snow pea (mangetout) sprouts or watercress, carrots and spring onions in a bowl. Combine sugar and lime juice, pour over salad and toss. Pile salad onto serving plates, then top with chicken kebabs.

Serves 6

ingredients

3 boneless chicken breast fillets, sliced
12 shiitake mushrooms
185g/6oz snow pea (mangetout) sprouts
or watercress
2 carrots, shredded
4 spring onions, chopped
2 teaspoons sugar
2 tablespoons lime juice

Chilli and lime marinade
1 tablespoon brown sugar
3 kaffir lime leaves, shredded (optional)
1 fresh red chilli, chopped
2 tablespoons soy sauce
1 tablespoon lime juice

cakes
and cookies

introduction

introduction

Baking **Secrets**

What happens when you make the cake? This section answers this question and many more. One of the secrets tp producing wonderful cakes and cookies is to understand why certain techniques are used.

Making the **cake**

- Many recipes begin by creaming the butter and sugar. This is an important process as little bubbles of air are trapped in the mixture and it is this air which helps to produce a light-textured cake.

- The butter should be softened for the creaming process and the mixture beaten until it is creamy and fluffy and almost doubled in volume.

- Creaming can be done with a balloon whisk, wooden spoon, electric beater or a food processor.

- After the creaming process an egg or eggs are often added to the mixture. The egg white forms a layer around each bubble of air and as the cake cooks the egg white coagulates and forms a wall around each bubble, preventing the bubbles from bursting and so ruining the cake.

- As the cake cooks, the air bubbles expand and the cake rises.

- As the air bubbles are expanding, the gluten in the flour is also stretching. This will continue until the gluten loses its elasticity.

- Do not open the oven door until at least halfway through the recommended cooking time or the rising process is interrupted. With the sudden drop in temperature the cake stops expanding and it sinks because there is no structure to support it

- The oven should be preheated to the correct temperature before placing the cake in to cook.

- If baking more than one cake, arrange the tins so that they do not touch each other or the sides of the oven.

- Filling the cake tin is an important step towards a successful result. If your batter is soft it can be poured into the cake tin, however a firm batter should be spooned into the tin and spread out evenly using a spatula. For light batters, only half to two-thirds fill the tin; heavy batters can fill as much as three-quarters of the tin.

baking
secrets

Is the cake **cooked?**

- Test the cake just before the end of the recommended cooking time. To test the cake, insert a skewer into the thickest part of the cake. If it comes away clean, your cake is cooked. If there is still cake mixture on the skewer, cook for 5 minutes longer then test again.

- Alternatively, gently press the top of the cake with your fingertips. When cooked, the depression will spring back quickly.

- When the cake starts to leave the side of the tin this is another indication that the cake is cooked.

Cooling the **cake**

- You will find that a freshly baked cake is very fragile. Allow a cake to cool for a short time in the tin before turning onto a wire rack to cool completely.

- Before turning out a cake, loosen the sides with a spatula or palette knife. Then turn the cake onto a wire rack to cool and immediately invert on to a second wire rack so that the top of the cake is not marked with indentations from the rack. If you do not have a second wire rack, invert the cake onto

a clean cloth on your hand then turn it back onto the wire rack.

Storing baked **products**

- Allow cakes to cool completely before placing in an airtight container, or condensation will accumulate in the container and cause the cake to go mouldy.

- Keeping times for cakes vary depending on the ingredients used. A fatless sponge will only stay fresh for 1-2 days while one made with fat will keep fresh for 2-3 weeks and heavy rich fruit cakes will store for a month or more.

- Most undecorated cakes can be frozen successfully. Wrap the cake in freezer wrap or place in a freezer bag and seal. If freezing several cakes, wrap each separately or place freezer wrap or waxed paper between cakes so that they are easy to remove.

- To thaw a frozen cake, leave in package and thaw at room temperature. Large cakes will take 3-4 hours to thaw, layer cakes 1-2 hours and smaller cakes about 30 minutes.

baking
secrets

Preparing the **cake tins**

To grease and flour a cake tin: using a pastry brush lightly brush cake tin with melted butter or margarine, then sprinkle with flour and shake to coat evenly. Invert tin on work surface and tap gently to remove excess flour.

To grease and line a round cake tin: Place cake tin on a large piece of baking paper and using a pencil trace around the base, then cut out a shape. Grease tin and line with paper.

To line a deep cake tin: A deep cake tine should be lined on the bottom and sides. Use a double thickness folded strip of baking paper 5cm/2in higher than the cake tin and long enough to fit around the tin and to overlap by about 2^1/2cm/ 1in. On the folded edge turn up about 2^1/2cm/ 1in and crease, then using scissors snip at regular intervals across the margin as far as the fold. Cut out a piece of baking paper to line the base of the tin previously. Grease the tin and place the strip inside the tin with the snipped margin lying flat on the base of the tin. Ensure that the ends overlap so that the sides are completely covered by the paper.

Place the base piece of baking paper in the tin to cover the snipped margin.

To line a loaf tin: Cut a strip a baking paper the width of the base of the tin and long enough to come up the shorter sides of the tin and overlap by 2^1/2cm/1in. Grease the tin and line with the paper. When the cake is cooked the unlined sides can be loosened with a knife and tha paper ends are used to lift out the cake.

double choc cookies and
quick nut fudge cake

chocolate

For many, chocolate is a delicious

obsession. For the Aztecs, who discovered
it, chocolate was 'food for the gods'.
In its various forms - block chocolate, cocoa
powder and chocolate chips, grated, melted
and chopped - chocolate is one of the
most popular ingredients in cakes, biscuits
and slices.

double
choc cookies

Photograph page 89

Method:

1 Place butter and sugar in a food processor and process until mixture is creamy. Add flour and self-rising flour, eggs and melted chocolate and process until smooth. Stir in chocolate chips.

2 Place spoonfuls of mixture on greased baking trays and bake for 8-10 minutes or until just firm. Stand on trays for 5 minutes before transferring to wire racks to cool completely.
Note: An old-time favourite. Served with a glass of icy cold milk, what better treat is there.
Makes 30

ingredients

75g/2^1/$_2$oz butter, softened
^{1}/$_4$ cup/60g/2oz superfine sugar
1^1/$_2$ cups/155g/5oz flour
^{1}/$_4$ cup/30g/1oz self-rising flour
2 eggs
200g/6^1/$_2$oz milk chocolate, melted and cooled
185g/6oz chocolate chips

Oven temperature 180°C, 350°F, Gas 4

quick nut
fudge cake

Photograph page 89

ingredients

Method:

1 Place butter, brown sugar, eggs and vanilla essence in a large mixing bowl and mix to combine. Stir in cocoa powder, flour and walnuts. Mix well to combine.

2 Spoon batter into a greased and lined 20cm/8in round cake tin and bake for 35-40 minutes or until cake is cooked when tested with a skewer. Stand cake in tin for 5 minutes before turning onto a wire rack to cool.

3 To make icing, place butter in a mixing bowl and beat until light and fluffy. Add chocolate, egg yolks and icing sugar and beat until smooth. Spread icing over cold cake.
Makes a 20cm/8in round cake

125g/4oz butter, melted
1^1/$_2$ cups/250g/8oz soft brown sugar
2 eggs, lightly beaten
1 teaspoon vanilla essence
^{1}/$_4$ cup/30g/1oz cocoa powder, sifted
2 cups/250g/8oz self-rising flour, sifted
60g/2oz chopped walnuts

Chocolate butter icing
125g/4oz butter, softened
100g/3^1/$_2$oz dark chocolate, melted and cooled
2 egg yolks
^{1}/$_2$ cup/75g/2^1/$_2$oz icing sugar, sifted

Oven temperature 180°C, 350°F, Gas 4

chocolate
sandwich cake

Method:

1 Place flour, bicarbonate of soda, cocoa powder, butter, sugar, eggs and sour cream in a large mixing bowl and beat until well combined and mixture is smooth.
2 Spoon batter into two greased and lined 20cm/8in sandwich tins and bake for 25-30 minutes or until cooked when tested with a skewer. Stand cakes in tins for 5 minutes before turning onto a wire rack to cool.
3 Sandwich cold cakes together with whipped cream.
4 To make icing, place chocolate and butter in a small saucepan and cook over a low heat, stirring constantly, until melted. Cool slightly then spread over top of cake.

Makes a 20cm/8in sandwich cake

ingredients

1 cup/125g/4oz self-rising flour, sifted
¹/₄ teaspoon bicarbonate of soda
¹/₂ cup/45g/1 1¹/₂oz cocoa powder, sifted
125g/4oz butter, softened
³/₄ cup/170g/5¹/₂oz superfine sugar
2 eggs, lightly beaten
1 cup/250g/8oz sour cream
¹/₂ cup/125mL/4fl oz cream (heavy), whipped

Chocolate icing
60g/2oz dark chocolate, chopped
30g/1oz unsalted butter

chocolate
shortbread

Photograph page 93

Method:

1 *Place butter and icing sugar in a mixing bowl and beat until mixture is creamy. Sift together flour, cornflour and cocoa powder. Stir flour mixture into butter mixture.*

2 *Turn dough onto a floured surface and knead lightly until smooth. Roll spoonfuls of mixture into balls, place on greased baking trays and flatten slightly with a fork. Bake for 20-25 minutes or until firm. Allow to cool on trays.*

Makes 30

ingredients

250g/8oz butter, softened
¹/₂ cup/75g/2¹/₂oz icing sugar
1 cup/125g/4oz flour
1 cup/125g/4oz cornflour
¹/₄ cup/30g/1oz cocoa powder

Oven temperature 160°C, 325°F, Gas 3

brownies

Photograph page 93

Method:

1 *Place butter, honey, water, eggs, flour, sugar and chocolate in a food processor and process until ingredients are combined.*

2 *Spoon batter into a greased and lined 23cm/9 in square cake tin and bake for 30-35 minutes or until cooked when tested with a skewer. Stand cake in tin for 5 minutes before turning onto a wire rack to cool. Dust cold cake with icing sugar and cut into squares.*

Makes 25

ingredients

155g/5oz butter, softened
¹/₂ cup/170g/5¹/₂oz honey, warmed
2 eggs, lightly beaten
1³/₄ cups/220g/7oz self-rising flour, sifted
²/₃ cup/125g/4oz soft brown sugar
125g/4oz dark chocolate,
melted and cooled
icing sugar

Oven temperature 180°C, 350°F, Gas 4

white choc-chip
chocolate cake

Method:

1 Place butter, sugar and vanilla essence in a mixing bowl and beat until mixture is creamy. Add eggs one at a time beating well after each addition.

2 Sift together flour, cocoa powder and baking powder. Fold flour mixture and milk, alternately, into butter mixture, then fold in chocolate.

3 Spoon batter into a greased and lined 23 cm/9 in round cake tin and bake for 30-35 minutes or until cooked when tested with a skewer. Stand in tin for 5 minutes before turning onto a wire rack to cool completely.

4 To make frosting, place butter in a mixing bowl and beat until light and fluffy. Add chocolate, egg yolks and icing sugar and beat until smooth. Spread frosting over top and sides of cold cake.

Note: A rich chocolate cake studded with white chocolate chips and topped with creamy white chocolate frosting.

Makes a 23cm/9in round cake

ingredients

125g/4oz butter, softened
1 cup/220g/7oz superfine sugar
1 teaspoon vanilla essence
2 eggs
1¹/₃ cups/170g/5¹/₂oz self-rising flour
¹/₄ cup/30g/1oz cocoa powder
¹/₂ teaspoon baking powder
1 cup/250mL/8fl oz milk
200g/6¹/₂oz white chocolate, chopped

White chocolate frosting
125g/4oz butter, softened
100g/3¹/₂oz white chocolate,
melted and cooled
2 egg yolks
¹/₂ cup/75g/2¹/₂oz icing sugar, sifted

chocolate
pinwheels

Method:

1 Place butter, sugar and vanilla essence in a mixing bowl and beat until mixture is creamy. Add egg and beat until well combined.

2 Divide mixture into two equal portions and mix 1 cup/125g/4oz flour into one portion and remaining flour and cocoa powder into the other portion.

3 Roll out each portion between two sheets of greaseproof paper to form a 20 x 30cm/ 8 x 12in rectangle. Remove top sheet of paper from each and invert one onto the other. Roll up from longer edge to form a long roll. Wrap in plastic food wrap and refrigerate for 1 hour.

4 Cut roll into 5mm/¹/₄in slices and place on greased baking trays. Bake for 10-12 minutes or until lightly browned. Cool on wire racks.

Cook's tip: These are ideal last-minute biscuits. The dough can be made in advance and kept in the refrigerator until needed. Layers of plain and chocolate dough are rolled together to make these delicious biscuits.

Makes 30

ingredients

125g/4oz butter
²/₃ cup/140g/4¹/₂oz superfine sugar
1 teaspoon vanilla essence
1 egg
1³/₄cups/220g/7oz flour, sifted
¹/₄ cup/30g/1oz cocoa powder, sifted

Oven temperature 180°C, 350°F, Gas 4

chocolate
date torte

Method:

1 Beat egg whites until soft peaks form. Gradually add sugar and beat until dissolved. Fold in chocolate, dates and hazelnuts.

2 Spoon mixture into two greased and lined 23cm/9in springform pans. Bake for 40 minutes or until firm. Remove from oven and allow to cool in pans.

3 Spread one meringue layer with whipped cream and top with remaining layer. Decorate top with drizzled melted chocolate.

Serves 4

ingredients

6 egg whites
1 cup/220g superfine sugar
200g/6¹/₂oz dark chocolate, grated
160g/5oz pitted dates, chopped
2 cups/280g chopped hazelnuts
1¹/₂ cups/375mL thickened cream, whipped

Topping
100g/3¹/₂oz dark chocolate, melted

Oven temperature 160°C

berry
chocolate mud cake

Method:

1 Place chocolate and butter in a heatproof bowl over a saucepan of simmering water and heat, stirring, until chocolate melts and mixture is smooth. Cool slightly.

2 Beat egg yolks and caster sugar into chocolate mixture, then fold in flour.

3 Place egg whites in a separate bowl and beat until stiff peaks form. Fold egg whites and raspberries into chocolate mixture. Pour into a greased and lined 20cm/8in round cake tin and bake for 1¼ hours or until cooked when tested with a skewer. Turn off oven and cool cake in oven with door ajar.

4 To make coulis, place raspberries in a food processor or blender and process until puréed. Push purée through a sieve to remove seeds. Add sugar to taste. Serve cake with coulis and cream.

Serves 10

ingredients

315g/10oz dark chocolate
250g/8oz butter, chopped
5 eggs, separated
2 tablespoons superfine sugar
¼ cup/30g/1oz self-rising flour, sifted
250g/8oz raspberries
whipped cream, for serving

<u>Raspberry coulis</u>
250g/8oz raspberries
sugar to taste

Oven temperature 120°C, 250°F, Gas ½

chocolate
rolls

Photograph page 99

1 Place egg yolks and sugar in a mixing bowl and beat until mixture is thick and creamy. Beat in chocolate, then fold in flour mixture.

2 Beat egg whites until stiff peaks form and fold into chocolate mixture. Pour into a greased and lined 26x32cm/10¹/₂x12³/₄in Swiss roll tin and bake for 12-15 minutes or until just firm. Turn onto a damp teatowel sprinkled with caster sugar and roll up from the short end. Set aside to cool.

3 To make filling, place chocolate and cream in a small saucepan and cook over a low heat until chocolate melts and mixture is well blended. Bring to the boil, remove from heat and set aside to cool, completely. When cold, place in a mixing bowl over ice and beat until thick and creamy.

4 Unroll cake, spread with filling and reroll. To serve, cut into slices. A chocolate roll filled with chocolate cream makes a special afternoon tea treat or dessert. Irresistibly good to eat, these spectacular cakes are easy to make. Follow these step-by-step instructions for a perfect result every time.

Serves 8

5 eggs, separated
¹/₄ cup/60g/2oz superfine sugar
100g/3¹/₂oz dark chocolate,
melted and cooled
2 tablespoons self-rising flour, sifted with
2 tablespoons cocoa powder

<u>Chocolate filling</u>
60g/2oz dark chocolate
²/₃ cup/170mL/5¹/₂fl oz cream (heavy)

Oven temperature 180°C, 350°F, Gas 4

chocolate

coconut & coffee

austrian coffee cake

The fruit of a tropical palm tree,

coconut is mostly used in its desiccated or shredded form for baking. It adds a distinctive flavour and a moistness to baked goods that usually means they keep well. Toasted or left plain it is a wonderfully easy decoration. Coffee is one of the most popular beverages, and also plays an important role as a flavouring for cakes, biscuits, slices and sweets. If you are using instant coffee powder, dissolve it first in hot water before adding to any mixture.

mocha
fudge

Method:
1 Place chocolate, condensed milk, butter and coffee in a small saucepan and cook, stirring, over a low heat until mixture is smooth. Pour fudge into an aluminium foil-lined 20cm/8in square cake tin and refrigerate for 2 hours or until set. Cut into squares.

Note: This coffee-flavoured chocolate fudge is sure to become a family favourite.

Makes 30 squares

ingredients

500g/1 lb dark chocolate
1 cup/250mL/8fl oz sweetened condensed milk
30g/1oz butter
3 teaspoons instant coffee

---

austrian
coffee cake

Photograph page 101

Method:
1 Place egg yolks and sugar in a bowl and beat until thick and creamy. Beat in almonds, coffee mixture and vanilla essence.

2 Place egg whites in a bowl and beat until stiff peaks form. Sift flour over egg yolk mixture and fold in with egg white mixture. Spoon batter into a greased and lined 20 cm/8 in springform tin and bake for 20-25 minutes or until cooked when tested with a skewer. Stand in tin for 10 minutes, before turning onto a wire rack to cool.

3 To make Coffee Cream, mix sugar, coffee mixture and liqueur into cream. Split cold cake horizontally and use a little of the Coffee Cream to sandwich halves together. Spread remaining Coffee Cream over top and sides of cake. Decorate top of cake with coffee beans or chocolate dots and grated chocolate. Chill and serve cut into slices.

Serves 10

ingredients

4 eggs, separated
1/4 cup/60g/2oz superfine sugar
45g/1 1/2oz ground almonds
3 teaspoons instant coffee powder dissolved in 4 teaspoons boiling water, cooled
1/2 teaspoon vanilla essence
1/4 cup/30g/1oz flour
chocolate-coated coffee beans or chocolate dots
finely grated chocolate

Coffee cream
1 tablespoon superfine sugar
1 teaspoon instant coffee powder dissolved in 2 teaspoons boiling water, cooled
2 tablespoons coffee-flavoured liqueur
1 cup/250mL/8fl oz cream (heavy), whipped

Oven temperature 180°C, 350°F, Gas 4

coconut
cake

Method:

1 Place butter and vanilla essence in a mixing bowl and beat until light and fluffy. Gradually add caster sugar, beating well after each addition until mixture is creamy.

2 Beat in egg whites, one at a time. Fold flour and milk, alternately, into creamed mixture. Divide batter evenly between two greased and lined 23cm/9in sandwich tins and bake for 25-30 minutes or until cakes are cooked when tested with a skewer. Stand in tins for 5 minutes before turning onto a wire rack to cool.

3 To make frosting, place water and sugar in a saucepan and cook over a medium heat, without boiling, stirring constantly until sugar dissolves. Brush any sugar from sides of pan using a pastry brush dipped in water. Bring syrup to the boil and boil rapidly for 3-5 minutes, without stirring, or until syrup reaches the soft ball stage (115°C/239°F on a sweet thermometer). Place egg whites in a mixing bowl and beat until soft peaks form. Continue beating while pouring in syrup in a thin stream a little at a time. Continue beating until all syrup is used and frosting will stand in stiff peaks. Beat in lemon juice.

4 Spread one cake with a little frosting and sprinkle with 2 tablespoons coconut, then top with remaining cake. Spread remaining frosting over top and sides of cake and sprinkle with remaining coconut.

Cook's tip: This cake looks pretty when decorated with edible flowers such as violets, rose petals or borage. This light moist sponge-type cake, covered with a white frosting and topped with shredded coconut is a must for any afternoon tea.

Makes a 23cm/9in round cake

ingredients

125g/4oz butter, softened
1 teaspoon vanilla essence
1 cup/220g/7oz caster sugar
3 egg whites
2 cups/250g/8oz self-rising flour, sifted
³/₄ cup/185mL/6fl oz milk
90g/3oz shredded coconut

Fluffy frosting
¹/₂ cup/125mL/4fl oz water
1¹/₄ cups/315g/10oz sugar
3 egg whites
1 teaspoon lemon juice

Oven temperature 180°C, 350°F, Gas 4

golden
oat cookies

Photograph page 105

Method:

1 Place oats, flour, coconut and sugar in a large mixing bowl. Combine golden syrup, butter, water and bicarbonate of soda.

2 Pour golden syrup mixture into dry ingredients and mix well to combine. Place spoonfuls of mixture 3cm/1¼in apart on greased baking trays and bake for 10-15 minutes or until biscuits are just firm. Stand on trays for 3 minutes before transferring to wire racks to cool.

Note: Golden, crunchy and delicious, these biscuits won't last long.

Makes 30

ingredients

1 cup/90g/3oz rolled oats
1 cup/125g/4oz flour, sifted
90g/3oz desiccated coconut
1 cup/250g/8oz sugar
4 teaspoons golden syrup, warmed
125g/4oz butter, melted
2 tablespoons boiling water
1 teaspoon bicarbonate of soda

Oven temperature 180°C, 350°F, Gas 4

lime
and coconut cookies

Photograph page 105

Method:

1 Place butter, sugar, vanilla essence, egg, flour and self-raising flour, rolled oats, coconut, lime rind and lime juice in a food processor and process until well combined.

2 Place heaped spoonfuls of mixture on greased baking trays and bake for 12-15 minutes or until lightly browned. Cool on wire racks.

Note: The tang of lime and the unique flavour and texture of coconut combine to make these wonderful cookies.

Makes 35

ingredients

125g/4oz butter, chopped
1 cup/170g/5½oz soft brown sugar
1 teaspoon vanilla essence
1 egg
1 cup/125g/4oz flour
½ cup/60g/2oz self-rising flour
1 cup/90g/3oz rolled oats
45g/1½oz desiccated coconut
2 teaspoons finely grated lime rind
2 tablespoons lime juice

Oven temperature 180°C, 350°F, Gas 4

Oven temperature 160°C, 325°F, Gas 3

coffee
sandwich cake

Method:

1 *Place butter and sugar in a food processor and process until creamy. Add eggs, flour and baking powder and process until all ingredients are combined. Spoon batter into two greased and lined 18cm/7in sandwich tins and bake for 30-35 minutes or until golden. Turn onto a wire rack to cool.*

Note: *Layers of light sponge sandwiched together with a liqueur cream and topped with a coffee icing. All this cake needs is a wonderful cup of coffee to accompany it.*

Makes an 18cm/7in sandwich cake

ingredients
250g/8oz butter, softened
1 cup/220g/7oz superfine sugar
6 eggs, lightly beaten
2 cups/250g/8oz self-rising flour, sifted
4 teaspoons baking powder

Coffee icing
60g/2oz butter, softened
³/₄ cup/125g/4oz icing sugar, sifted
¹/₂ teaspoon ground cinnamon
2 teaspoons instant coffee powder
dissolved in 2 teaspoons hot water, cooled

Liqueur cream
1 tablespoon Tia Maria Liqueur
¹/₂ cup/125mL/4fl oz cream (heavy),
whipped

sweet
potato and coconut cake

Method:

1 Place butter, sugar, lime or lemon rind and cinnamon in a bowl and beat until light and fluffy. Gradually beat in egg yolks.

2 Add sweet potato and coconut and mix well. Sift together flour, self-raising flour and bicarbonate of soda. Fold flour mixture into sweet potato mixture.

3 Place egg whites in a clean bowl and beat until stiff peaks form. Fold egg whites into sweet potato mixture.

4 Spoon mixture into two greased and lined 20cm/8in round cake tins and bake for 30 minutes or until cakes are cooked when tested with a skewer. Stand cakes in tins for 5 minutes before turning onto wire racks to cool.

5 To make filling, place cream cheese, icing sugar and lime or lemon juice in a bowl and beat until smooth.

6 To assemble cake, slice each cake in half horizontally. Place one layer of cake on a serving plate and spread with one quarter of the filling. Repeat layers with remaining cake and filling finishing with a layer of filling. Decorate with coconut and candied peel.

Makes a 20cm/8in round cake

ingredients

250g/8oz butter, softened
³/₄ cup/185g/6oz sugar
2 tablespoons finely grated lime or lemon rind
2 teaspoons cinnamon
3 eggs, separated
250g/8oz mashed sweet potato
45g/1¹/₂oz desiccated coconut
1 cup/125g/4oz flour
1 cup/125g/4oz self-raising flour
1 teaspoon bicarbonate of soda
shredded coconut, toasted
candied lime or lemon peel

<u>Cream and citrus filling</u>
250g/8oz cream cheese,
softened and chopped
¹/₄ cup/45g/1¹/₂oz icing sugar
2 tablespoons lime or lemon juice

Oven temperature 160°C, 325°F, Gas 3

coffee
kisses

Photograph page 109

Method:

1 *Place butter and icing sugar in a large mixing bowl and beat until light and fluffy. Stir in coffee mixture and flour.*

2 *Spoon mixture into a piping bag fitted with a medium star nozzle and pipe 2cm/³⁄₄in rounds of mixture 2cm/³⁄₄in apart on greased baking trays. Bake for 10-12 minutes or until lightly browned. Stand on trays for 5 minutes before removing to wire racks to cool completely.*

3 *Join biscuits with a little melted chocolate, then dust with icing sugar.*

Makes 25

ingredients

250g/8oz butter, softened
²⁄₃ cup/100g/3¹⁄₂oz icing sugar, sifted
2 teaspoons instant coffee powder
dissolved in 1 tablespoon hot water, cooled
2 cups/250g/8oz flour, sifted
45g/1¹⁄₂oz dark chocolate, melted
icing sugar

Oven temperature 180°C, 350°F, Gas 4

coconut
and raspberry cake

Method:

1 To make cake, place butter and sugar in a bowl and beat until light and creamy. Add egg yolks one at a time, beating well after each addition. Fold in coconut.

2 Sift flour and baking powder together. Combine vanilla essence and coconut milk. Fold flour mixture and coconut milk mixture, alternately, into butter mixture. Place egg whites in a bowl and beat until stiff peaks form. Fold egg white mixture into batter.

3 Pour batter into two greased and floured 20cm/8in square cake tins and bake for 35-40 minutes or until cake comes away from sides of tin. Stand cakes in tins for 5 minutes before turning onto wire racks to cool.

4 To assemble, top one cake with raspberries, then with remaining cake. Spread top and sides of cake with cream and sprinkle with coconut. Refrigerate until ready to serve.

5 To make coulis, place raspberries and icing sugar in a food processor or blender and process to purée. Press purée through a sieve to remove seeds. Serve with cake.

Makes a 20cm/8in square cake

ingredients

200g/6¹/₂oz fresh or frozen raspberries
1¹/₂ cups/375mL/12fl oz cream (heavy), whipped
90g/3oz shredded coconut, toasted

Coconut cake
185g/6oz butter, softened
1 cup/220g/7oz superfine sugar
4 eggs, separated
90g/3oz desiccated coconut
3 cups/375g/12oz self-rising flour
1 teaspoon baking powder
1 teaspoon vanilla essence
³/₄ cup/185mL/6fl oz coconut milk

Raspberry coulis
500g/1 lb fresh or frozen raspberries
2 tablespoons icing sugar

Oven temperature 180°C, 350°F, Gas 4

Oven temperature 180°C, 350°F, Gas 4

coffee
oat and date cake

Method:

1 *To make topping, place dates, water and caster sugar in a saucepan and cook over a medium heat for 3-4 minutes or until dates are soft and mixture thickens slightly. Remove from heat and set aside to cool. Place oats, sugar and flour in a bowl and stir in butter and walnuts. Set aside.*

2 *Place butter, coffee mixture, sugar, eggs, flour and milk in a large mixing bowl and beat until all ingredients are combined and mixture is smooth. Spoon batter into a greased and lined 23cm/9in square cake tin and top with date mixture, then sprinkle over oat mixture. Bake for 40-45 minutes or until cake is cooked when tested with a skewer. Stand cake in tin for 10 minutes before turning onto a wire rack to cool.*

Note: *Sprinkled with a crunchy topping before baking this cake requires no icing.*

Makes a 23cm/9in square cake

ingredients

125g/4oz butter, softened
4 teaspoons instant coffee powder
dissolved in 4 teaspoons hot water, cooled
³/₄ cup/170g/5¹/₂oz superfine sugar
2 eggs, lightly beaten
1¹/₂ cups/185g/6oz self-rising flour, sifted
¹/₂ cup/125mL/4fl oz buttermilk or milk

<u>Date and oat topping</u>
200g/6¹/₂oz pitted dates, chopped
¹/₃ cup/170mL/5¹/₂fl oz water
1¹/₂ tablespoons caster sugar
3 tablespoons rolled oats
1 tablespoon soft brown sugar
2 tablespoons self-rising flour
30g/1oz butter, melted
1 tablespoon chopped walnuts

fruit, nuts & spice

hazelnut shortbreads and
walnut honey baklava

Fruit and nuts are healthy additions

to any baked product and add flavour, crunch and texture. It's usually safe to substitute your favourite fruit or nuts in a recipe and still end up with a delicious cake, biscuit or slice.

walnut
honey baklava

Photograph page 113

Method:

1 To make filling, combine walnuts, cinnamon, mixed spice and brown sugar in a bowl and set aside.

2 Cut pastry sheets into 18 x 28cm/7 x 11in rectangles. Layer a quarter of the pastry sheets in a greased, shallow 18 x 28cm/ 7 x 11in cake tin, brushing each sheet with butter. Sprinkle pastry with one-third of filling, repeat with remaining pastry and filling, finish with a layer of pastry.

3 Cut pastry into squares using a sharp knife. Brush top with butter and bake for 15 minutes. Reduce oven temperature to 190°C/375°F/Gas 5 and bake for 10 minutes longer or until golden brown.

4 To make syrup, place water, sugar, honey, orange juice and lemon juice in a small saucepan and cook over a medium heat, stirring constantly, until sugar dissolves. Bring to the boil, then remove from heat and pour over hot baklava. Set aside and allow to cool completely in tin.

Note: The secret to this Middle Eastern specialty is to pour the hot syrup over the hot pastry.

Makes 20

ingredients

375g/12oz filo pastry
155g/5oz butter, melted

Walnut filling
250g/8oz finely chopped walnuts, toasted
1 teaspoon ground cinnamon
1 teaspoon ground mixed spice
1/3 cup/60g/2oz soft brown sugar

Honey orange syrup
1/2 cup/125mL/4fl oz water
1/3 cup/90g/3oz sugar
1/3 cup/125g/4oz honey
1/3 cup/90mL/3fl oz freshly squeezed orange juice
2 tablespoons lemon juice

Oven temperature 220°C, 425°F, Gas 7

---

hazelnut
shortbreads

Photograph page 113

Method:

1 Place flour, hazelnuts and ground rice in a food processor, add butter and process until mixture resembles coarse bread crumbs. Add sugar and process to combine.

2 Turn mixture onto a floured surface and knead lightly to make a pliable dough. Place dough between sheets of baking paper and roll out to 5mm/1/4in thick. Using a 5cm/2in fluted pastry cutter, cut out rounds of dough and place 3cm/1in apart on greased baking trays. Bake for 20-25 minutes or until lightly browned. Stand on baking trays for 2-3 minutes before transferring to wire racks to cool completely.

3 Place melted chocolate in a plastic food bag, snip off one corner and pipe lines across each biscuit.

Ground hazelnuts give a deliciously different shortbread.

Makes 40

ingredients

1 1/2 cups/185g/6oz flour, sifted
45g/1 1/2oz hazelnuts, ground
1/4 cup/45g/1 1/2oz ground rice
250g/8oz butter, cut into small pieces
1/4 cup/60g/2oz superfine sugar
100g/3 1/2oz chocolate, melted

Oven temperature 160°C, 325°F, Gas 3

fruit, nuts & spice

Oven temperature 180°C, 350°F, Gas 4

apple
and blueberry cake

Method:

1 *Place butter, vanilla essence, sugar, eggs, flour and milk in a mixing bowl and beat well until ingredients are combined and mixture is smooth.*

2 *Spoon half the batter into a greased and lined 20cm/8in round cake tin. Top with half the apple slices and half the blueberries, then remaining batter. Arrange remaining apple and blueberries over top of batter.*

3 *To make topping, combine sugar and cinnamon and sprinkle over cake. Bake for 55-60 minutes or until cake is cooked when tested with a skewer. Stand in tin for 10 minutes before turning onto a wire rack to cool.*

Variation: You may like to try replacing the blueberries in this recipe with canned blackberries.

Makes a 20cm/8in round cake

ingredients

125g/4oz butter, softened
1 teaspoon vanilla essence
³/₄ cup/170g/5¹/₂oz superfine sugar
2 eggs, lightly beaten
1¹/₂ cups/185g/6oz self-rising flour, sifted
¹/₂ cup/125mL/4fl oz buttermilk or milk
220g/7oz canned apple slices
220g/7oz canned blueberries, well drained

Cinnamon topping
4 teaspoons superfine sugar
1 teaspoon ground cinnamon

thumbprint
cookies

Photograph page 117

Method:

1 *Place butter, icing sugar and vanilla essence in a bowl and beat until light and fluffy. Sift together flour, self-raising flour and custard powder. Fold flour mixture and milk, alternately, into butter mixture.*

2 *Roll tablespoons of mixture into balls and place on greased baking trays. Make a thumbprint in the centre of each cookie.*

3 *Fill thumbprint hole with a teaspoon of jam, lemon curd or chocolate. Bake for 12 minutes or until cookies are golden. Transfer to wire racks to cool.*

Note: *Wrap the dough in plastic food wrap and chill at least 30 minutes to make it easier to shape into balls. For a subtle toasty nut flavour, roll the balls in sesame seeds before making the thumbprint and filling.*

Makes 30

ingredients

185g/6oz butter, softened
1/3 cup/45g/1 1/2oz icing sugar, sifted
1 teaspoon vanilla essence
1/2 cup/60g/2oz flour
1 cup/125g/4oz self-rising flour
1/2 cup/60g/2oz custard powder
1/4 cup/60mL/2fl oz milk
jam, lemon curd or chopped chocolate

Oven temperature 190°C, 375°F, Gas 5

monte carlo
cookies

Photograph page 117

Method:

1 *Place butter, brown sugar and vanilla essence in a bowl and beat until light and fluffy. Add egg, flour, self-raising flour, coconut and rolled oats and mix well to combine.*

2 *Roll tablespoons of mixture into balls, place on greased baking trays and flatten slightly with a fork. Bake for 12 minutes or until biscuits are golden. Transfer to wire racks to cool.*

3 *To make Butter Cream, place butter, icing sugar and vanilla essence in a bowl and beat until light and fluffy. Spread half the biscuits with raspberry jam and top with Butter cream. Top with remaining biscuits.*

Note: *When shaping the biscuits ensure that all are of uniform size and appearance so that each pair is perfectly matched when sandwiched together.*

Makes 20

ingredients

125g/4oz butter, softened
1 cup/170g/5 1/2oz brown sugar
2 teaspoons vanilla essence
1 egg, lightly beaten
1 cup/125g/4oz flour, sifted
1/2 cup/60g/2oz self-rising flour, sifted
90g/3oz desiccated coconut
3/4 cup/75g/2 1/2oz rolled oats
1/2 cup/155g/5oz raspberry jam
Butter cream
60g/2oz butter, softened
1/2 cup/75g/2 1/2oz icing sugar
1 teaspoon vanilla essence

Oven temperature 190°C, 375°F, Gas 5

Oven temperature 180°C, 350°F, Gas 4

spiced
ginger drops

Method:

1 Place flour, ground ginger, mixed spice, cinnamon and bicarbonate of soda in a large mixing bowl. Rub in butter until mixture resembles fine bread crumbs. Stir in sugar, golden syrup and glacé ginger.

2 Turn dough onto a lightly floured surface and knead to form a soft dough. Roll rounded teaspoons of mixture into balls and place 3cm/1¹/₄in apart on greased baking trays. Bake for 10-15 minutes or until golden. Transfer biscuits to wire racks to cool.

Note: Ginger lovers won't be able to get enough of these spicy cookies.

Makes 30

ingredients

1 cup/125g/4oz flour, sifted
¹/₄ teaspoon ground ginger
¹/₄ teaspoon ground mixed spice
¹/₄ teaspoon ground cinnamon
¹/₂ teaspoon bicarbonate of soda
60g/2oz butter, cut into pieces
¹/₂ cup/90g/3oz soft brown sugar
2¹/₂ tablespoons golden syrup, warmed
**1¹/₂ tablespoons finely chopped glacé
ginger or stem ginger in syrup**

sticky
carrot and peach cake

Method:

1 Sift together flour and bicarbonate of soda into a bowl. Add carrot and peaches and mix to combine. Set aside.

2 Place brown sugar, oil and eggs in a bowl and beat until thick and creamy.

3 Fold egg mixture into flour mixture. Spoon mixture into a greased 23cm/9in round tin and bake for 45 minutes or until cake is cooked when tested with a skewer.

4 To make syrup, place peach juice, sugar, brandy and ginger in a saucepan and heat over a low heat, stirring constantly, until sugar dissolves. Bring syrup to the boil, then reduce heat and simmer for 5 minutes or until slightly thickened.

5 Turn cake onto a serving platter, slowly pour hot syrup over hot cake. Serve hot or warm.

Makes a 23cm/9in round cake

ingredients

1½ cups/185g/6oz self-rising flour
1 teaspoon bicarbonate of soda
185g/6oz finely grated raw carrot
440g/14oz canned sliced peaches, drained and chopped, juice reserved
½ cup/125mL/4fl oz vegetable oil
2 eggs

Sticky peach syrup
1 cup/250mL/8fl oz reserved peach juice
1 cup/250g/8oz sugar
1 tablespoon brandy
½ teaspoon ground ginger

Oven temperature 180°C, 350°F, Gas 4

gingerbread
men

Method:

1 Place butter and sugar in a bowl and beat until light and fluffy. Gradually beat in golden syrup and egg.

2 Sift together flour, ginger, cinnamon and bicarbonate of soda. Add flour mixture to butter mixture and mix to form a soft dough. Divide dough into two portions, wrap in plastic food wrap and refrigerate for 1 hour or until firm.

3 Roll out dough on a lightly floured surface to 5mm/1/4in thick. Using a gingerbread man cutter, cut out cookies and place on lightly greased and floured baking trays. Using a small knife and a drinking straw, make indents to form eyes, mouth and buttons. Bake for 10 minutes or until just golden. Stand on trays for 5 minutes before transferring to wire racks to cool.

Makes 24

ingredients

185g/6oz butter, softened
3/4 cup/125g/4oz brown sugar
1/4 cup/90mL/3fl oz golden syrup
1 egg
2 3/4 cups/350g/11oz flour, sifted
2 teaspoons ground ginger
1 teaspoon ground cinnamon
1/2 teaspoon bicarbonate of soda

Oven temperature 180°C, 350°F, Gas 4

spicy
apple cake

Method:

1 Combine oil and sugar in a large bowl. Whisk in eggs and vanilla. Combine flour and spice in one bowl and apples, lemon rind and sultanas in another. Fold flour mixture and apple mixture alternately into beaten egg mixture.

2 Spoon mixture into a greased and lined 20cm/8in square ring pan and bake at 180°C/350°F/Gas 4 for 30-35 minutes or until cooked. Stand 5 minutes before turning out on a wire rack to cool.

Serves 12

ingredients

3 tablespoons polyunsaturated oil
³/₄ cup/190g superfine sugar
2 eggs, lightly beaten
1 teaspoon vanilla essence
1 cup/125g self-rising flour, sifted
1¹/₂ teaspoons ground mixed spice
410g/13oz canned unsweetened sliced apples, drained
1 teaspoon grated lemon rind
¹/₂ cup/80g sultanas (yellow raisins)

banana nut
upside-down cake

Method:
1 To make topping, place butter and brown sugar in a saucepan and cook over a low heat, stirring constantly, until sugar dissolves and mixture thickens to a syrup.
2 Pour mixture over the base of a greased 23cm/9in round cake tin. Top with banana slices and nuts and set aside.
3 To make cake, place butter and sugar in a bowl and beat until light and fluffy. Gradually beat in eggs.
4 Sift together flour, baking powder and ginger. Fold flour mixture into butter mixture with milk.
5 Spoon mixture over topping in tin and bake for 50 minutes or until cake is cooked when tested with a skewer. Stand cake in tin for 5 minutes before turning out. Serve hot or warm.

Makes a 23cm/9in round cake

ingredients

Nutty topping
60g/2oz butter
³/₄ cup/125g/4oz brown sugar
3 bananas, sliced lengthwise
100g/3¹/₂oz macadamia or brazil nuts, roughly chopped

Ginger cake
100g/3¹/₂oz butter, softened
¹/₂ cup/125g/4oz sugar
2 eggs, lightly beaten
2 cups/250g/8oz flour
1 teaspoon baking powder
1 teaspoon ground ginger
¹/₂ cup/125mL/4fl oz milk

Oven temperature 180°C, 350°F, Gas 4

Oven temperature 180°C, 350°F, Gas 4

apricot
ripple cake

Method:
1 Place apricots and water in a bowl and set aside to soak for 30 minutes.
2 Place butter and sugar in a bowl and beat until light and fluffy. Gradually beat in eggs.
3 Sift together flour and cinnamon and fold into butter mixture. Spoon half the mixture into a 23cm/9in fluted ring tin.
4 Top mixture with apricots and remaining cake mixture. Bake for 45 minutes or until cake is cooked when tested with a skewer. Stand cake in tin for 5 minutes before turning onto a wire rack to cool.

Makes a 23cm/9in ring cake

ingredients

125g/4oz dried apricots, chopped
¹/₂ cup/125mL/4fl oz hot water
125g/4oz butter, softened
¹/₂ cup/125g/4oz sugar
2 eggs, lightly beaten
1¹/₂ cups/185g/6oz self-rising flour, sifted
1 teaspoon ground cinnamon

raspberry
truffle cakes

Photograph page 125

raspberry truffle cakes

ingredients

¹/₂ cup/45g/1¹/₂oz cocoa powder, sifted
1 cup/250mL/8fl oz boiling water
1³/₄ cups/400g/12¹/₂oz superfine sugar
125g/4oz butter
1¹/₂ tablespoons raspberry jam
2 eggs
1²/₃ cups/200g/6¹/₂oz self-rising flour, sifted
410g/13oz dark chocolate, melted
raspberries for garnishing

Raspberry cream
125g/4oz raspberries, puréed and sieved
¹/₂ cup/125mL/4fl oz cream (heavy), whipped

Chocolate sauce
125g/4oz dark chocolate
¹/₂ cup/125mL/4fl oz water
¹/₄ cup/60g/2oz superfine sugar
1 teaspoon brandy (optional)

Method:

1 Dissolve cocoa powder in boiling water, then cool.

2 Place sugar, butter and jam in a bowl and beat until light and fluffy. Beat in eggs one at a time, adding a little flour with each egg. Fold remaining flour and cocoa mixture, alternately, into butter mixture.

3 Spoon mixture into eight lightly greased ¹/₂ cup/125mL/4fl oz capacity ramekins or large muffin tins. Bake for 20-25 minutes or until cakes are cooked when tested with a skewer. Stand cakes in tins for 5 minutes then turn onto wire racks to cool. Turn cakes upside down and scoop out centre leaving a 1 cm/¹/₂in shell. Spread each cake with chocolate to cover top and sides, then place right way up on a wire rack.

4 To make cream, fold raspberry purée into cream. Spoon cream into a piping bag fitted with a large nozzle. Carefully turn cakes upside down and pipe in cream to fill cavity. Place right way up on individual serving plates.

5 To make sauce, place chocolate and water in a saucepan and cook over a low heat, stirring, for 4-5 minutes or until chocolate melts. Add sugar and continue cooking, stirring constantly, until sugar dissolves. Bring just to the boil, then reduce heat and simmer, stirring, for 2 minutes. Cool for 5 minutes, then stir in brandy, if using. Cool sauce to room temperature and serve with cakes.

Serves 8

ginger
pear cakes

Method:

1 Place sugar, oil, egg and vanilla essence in a bowl and beat to combine. Sift together flour, bicarbonate of soda, ginger and nutmeg. Mix flour mixture into egg mixture, then fold in pears and chopped ginger.

2 Spoon batter into six lightly greased large muffin tins and bake for 20 minutes. Reduce oven temperature to 160°C/325°F/Gas 3 and bake for 15-20 minutes longer, or until cakes are cooked when tested with a skewer.

3 To make Ginger Cream, place cream, sour cream and honey in a bowl and beat until soft peaks form. Add brandy and ground ginger and beat to combine. Fold in chopped ginger. Serve cakes hot or warm accompanied by Ginger cream.

Serves 6

ingredients

¹/₂ cup/125g/4oz raw sugar
¹/₄ cup/60mL/2fl oz vegetable oil
1 egg, lightly beaten
1 teaspoon vanilla essence
1 cup/125g/4oz flour
1 teaspoon bicarbonate of soda
¹/₂ teaspoon ground ginger
¹/₂ teaspoon ground nutmeg
2 pears, cored, peeled and finely diced
155g/5oz glacé ginger or stem ginger in syrup, chopped

Ginger cream
1 cup/250mL/8fl oz cream (heavy)
¹/₄ cup/60g/2oz sour cream
1 tablespoon honey
1 tablespoon brandy
¹/₄ teaspoon ground ginger
1 tablespoon finely chopped glacé ginger or stem ginger in syrup

Oven temperature 180°C, 350°F, Gas 4

flaky
passion fruit gateau

Method:

1 To make filling, place passion fruit pulp, lime juice, butter, eggs and caster sugar in a heatproof bowl set over a saucepan of simmering water and cook, stirring constantly, until mixture thickens. Remove bowl from pan and set aside to cool.

2 On a lightly floured board, roll out pastry to 3mm/^{1}/$_8$in thick and cut out three 20cm/8in rounds. Place on lightly greased baking trays, brush with a little milk and sprinkle with sugar. Bake for 12 minutes or until pastry is puffed and golden. Tranfer to wire racks to cool.

3 To assemble gâteau, split pastry rounds in half horizontally. Place one pastry layer on a serving plate, spread with some of the cream and drizzle with some of the filling. Repeat layers, finishing with a layer of cream.

4 Decorate top of gâteau with passion fruit pulp and lime rind strips. Serve immediately.

Makes a 20cm/8in round cake

ingredients

440g/14oz prepared puff pastry milk
2 tablespoons sugar
2 cups/500mL/16fl oz cream (heavy), well chilled and whipped
2 tablespoons passion fruit pulp
1 tablespoon thin lime rind strips

Passion fruit filling
^{1}/$_2$ cup/125mL/4fl oz passion fruit pulp
2 tablespoons lime juice
60g/2oz butter
2 eggs
^{1}/$_3$ cup/75g/2^1/$_2$oz superfine sugar

Oven temperature 200°C, 400°F, Gas 6

127

fig pinwheel
cookies

Photograph page 129

fig pinwheel cookies

ingredients

170g/5¹/₂oz butter
1 cup/170g/5¹/₂oz soft brown sugar
1 egg
¹/₂ teaspoon vanilla essence
3 cups/375g/12oz flour
¹/₂ teaspoon bicarbonate of soda
¹/₄ teaspoon ground cinnamon
¹/₄ teaspoon ground nutmeg
2 tablespoons milk

Fig and almond filling
250g/8oz dried figs, finely chopped
¹/₄ cup/60g/2oz sugar
¹/₂ cup/125ml/4fl oz water
¹/₄ teaspoon ground mixed spice
30g/1oz almonds, finely chopped

Oven temperature 180°C, 350°F, Gas 4

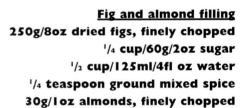

Method:

1 *To make filling, place figs, sugar, water and mixed spice in a saucepan and bring to the boil. Reduce heat and cook, stirring, for 2-3 minutes or until mixture is thick. Remove from heat and stir in almonds. Set aside to cool.*

2 *Place butter in a large mixing bowl and beat until light and fluffy. Gradually add sugar, beating well after each addition until mixture is creamy. Beat in egg and vanilla essence.*

3 *Sift together flour, bicarbonate of soda, cinnamon and nutmeg. Beat milk and half the flour mixture into butter mixture. Stir in remaining flour mixture. Turn dough onto a lightly floured surface and knead lightly. Roll into a ball, wrap in plastic food wrap and refrigerate for 30 minutes.*

4 *Divide dough into two portions. Roll one portion out to a 20 x 28cm/8 x 11in rectangle and spread with filling. Roll up from the long side, like a Swiss roll. Repeat with remaining dough and filling. Wrap rolls in plastic food wrap and refrigerate for 15 minutes or until you are ready to cook the biscuits.*

5 *Cut rolls into 1cm/¹/₂in slices. Place slices on greased baking trays and cook for 10-12 minutes. Stand biscuits on trays for 1 minute before removing to a wire rack to cool completely.*

Freeze it: *The uncooked rolls can be frozen if you wish. When you have unexpected guests or the cookie barrel is empty, these cookies are great standbys.*

Pinwheel cookies always look impressive and are very easy to make. Just follow the step-by-step instructions for making these delicious cookies that wrap a spiced dough around a wonderful fig and almond filling.

Makes 50

citrus flavors

orange and almond gateau

As an ingredient or decoration,

the freshly grated zest of oranges, lemons or limes adds a distinctive taste to any cookie, biscuit or slice. Aromatic citrus fruits have found their way into every aspect of cooking - sweet and savoury. Using these delicious recipes fill your tins and jars with unforgettable goodies.

orange
and almond gateau

Photograph page 131

Method:

1 To make cake, place superfine sugar, eggs, orange juice and rind in a bowl and beat until thick and creamy. Sift together flour, cornflour, baking powder and bicarbonate of soda. Place sour cream and butter in a bowl and whisk lightly to combine. Fold flour and sour cream mixtures, alternately, into egg mixture.

2 Spoon batter into three lightly greased and lined 23cm/9in sandwich tins and bake for 15-20 minutes or until cooked when tested with a skewer.

3 **To make syrup:** Five minutes before cakes complete cooking, place sugar, orange juice and liqueur in a saucepan and cook over a medium heat, stirring constantly, until sugar dissolves.

4 Turn cakes onto wire racks and, using a skewer, pierce surface of cakes to make holes that reach about halfway through the cakes. Spoon hot syrup over hot cakes and cool.

5 To make butter cream, place sugar and water in a saucepan and cook over a medium heat, stirring constantly, until sugar dissolves. Bring syrup to the boil and cook until mixture reaches the soft-ball stage (115°C/239°F on a sugar thermometer). Place egg yolks in a bowl, then beat to combine and continue beating while slowly pouring in sugar syrup. Beat for 5 minutes longer or until mixture cools and is of a thick mousse-like consistency. In a separate bowl beat butter until light and creamy, then gradually beat into egg yolk mixture. Beat in orange rind and juice and liqueur.

6 To assemble, sandwich cakes together with a little butter cream, then spread remaining butter cream over top and sides of cake. Press almonds around sides of cake.

Note: The secret to this spectacular cake is to pour the hot sugar syrup over the cooked cakes while they are still hot. Do not pour cold syrup over hot cakes or hot syrup over cold cakes or the cakes will become soggy.

Serves 10

ingredients

75g/2¹/₂oz flaked almonds, toasted

Sour cream orange cake
1 cup/220g/7oz superfine sugar
3 eggs
4 teaspoons orange juice
1 tablespoon finely grated orange rind
1³/₄ cups/220g/7oz flour
¹/₄ cup/30g/1oz cornflour
1¹/₂ teaspoons baking powder
1 teaspoon bicarbonate of soda
1 cup/250g/8oz sour cream, lightly beaten
250g/8oz butter, melted and cooled

Orange Syrup
¹/₂ cup/125g/4oz sugar
¹/₄ cup/60mL/2fl oz orange juice
¹/₄ cup/60mL/2fl oz orange-flavoured liqueur

Orange butter cream
¹/₂ cup/125g/4oz sugar
¹/₂ cup/125mL/4fl oz water
4 egg yolks
250g/8oz unsalted butter, softened
2 teaspoons finely grated orange rind
¹/₄ cup/60mL/2fl oz orange juice
2 tablespoons orange-flavored liqueur

Oven temperature 180°C, 350°F, Gas 4

easy
lemon and almond cake

Method:

1 Place butter, sugar, lemon butter, eggs, flour, ground almonds and milk in a large mixing bowl and beat well to combine all ingredients.

2 Spoon mixture into a greased and lined 20cm/8in round cake tin and bake for 40 minutes or until cooked when tested with a skewer. Stand cake in tin for 5 minutes before turning onto a wire rack to cool.

3 To make frosting, place cream cheese, lemon rind, icing sugar and lemon juice in a food processor and process for 1 minute or until frosting is of a spreadable consistency. Spread frosting over top of cold cake, then sprinkle with flaked almonds.

Makes a 20cm/8in round cake

ingredients

185g/6oz butter, softened
$^1/_2$ cup/100g/3$^1/_2$oz superfine sugar
$^1/_2$ cup/185g/4oz prepared lemon
butter (curd)
3 eggs, lightly beaten
1$^1/_4$ cups/155g/5oz self-rising flour, sifted
30g/1oz ground almonds
$^1/_2$ cup/125mL/4fl oz milk
3 tablespoons flaked almonds, toasted

Lemon frosting
125g/4oz cream cheese
1 teaspoon finely grated lemon rind
1$^1/_2$ cups/220g/7oz icing sugar
2 teaspoons lemon juice

Oven temperature 180°C, 350°F, Gas 4

lemon
syrup cake

Method:

1 *Place butter, superfine sugar and lemon rind in a bowl and beat until light and fluffy. Gradually beat in eggs.*

2 *Stir flour and coconut into butter mixture. Add sour cream and milk and mix until combined. Spoon mixture into a greased 23 cm/9 in fluted ring tin and bake for 1 hour or until cooked when tested with a skewer.*

3 *To make syrup, place lemon juice, sugar and water in a saucepan and cook over low heat, stirring constantly, until sugar dissolves. Bring to the boil and simmer for 4 minutes or until syrup thickens slightly.*

4 *Pour half the hot syrup over the hot cake and stand in tin for 4 minutes. Turn cake onto a serving plate and pour over remaining syrup.*

Makes a 23cm/9in round cake

ingredients

125g/4oz butter, softened
1 cup/220g/7oz superfine sugar
2 teaspoons finely grated lemon rind
2 eggs, lightly beaten
1¹/₂ cups/185g/6oz self-rising flour, sifted
45g/1¹/₂oz desiccated coconut
1¹/₄ cups/315g/10oz sour cream
¹/₃ cup/90mL/3fl oz milk

Lemon syrup
¹/₃ cup/90mL/3fl oz lemon juice
³/₄ cup/185g/6oz sugar
¹/₄ cup/60mL/2fl oz water

Oven temperature 180°C, 350°F, Gas 4

Oven temperature 180°C, 350°F, Gas 4

orange
liqueur layer cake

Method:

1 Place eggs in a bowl and beat until thick and creamy. Gradually add sugar, beating well after each addition until mixture is creamy.

2 Fold flour and milk into egg mixture. Pour mixture into two greased and lined 26 x 32cm/10¹/₂ x 12³/₄in Swiss roll tins and bake for 10-12 minutes or until cake is cooked. Stand cakes in tins for 5 minutes before turning onto wire racks to cool. Cut each cake into three equal pieces.

3 To make filling, place cream, liqueur, icing sugar and orange rind in a bowl and beat until thick.

4 To assemble, place a layer of cake on a serving plate and spread with filling. Repeat layers, finishing with a layer of filling. Spread remaining filling over sides of cake and decorate with candied orange peel.

Serves 6-8

ingredients

6 eggs
I cup/220g/7oz superfine sugar
I¹/₂ cups/185g/6oz self-rising flour, sifted
¹/₃ cup/90mL/3fl oz warm milk
candied orange peel, to decorate

Orange filling
2 cups/500 mL/16fl oz cream (heavy)
¹/₄ cup/60mL/2fl oz orange-flavoured liqueur
2 tablespoons icing sugar
2 teaspoons finely grated orange rind

orange
and lime cheesecake

Method:

1 Place biscuits and butter in a bowl and mix to combine. Press biscuit mixture over base and up sides of a well-greased 23cm/9in flan tin with a removable base. Bake for 5-8 minutes, then cool.
2 To make filling, place cream cheese, sugar, orange and lime rinds and orange and lime juices in a bowl and beat until creamy. Beat in egg, then mix in condensed milk and fold in cream.
3 Spoon filling into prepared biscuit case and bake for 25-30 minutes or until just firm. Turn oven off and cool cheesecake in oven with door ajar. Chill before serving. Serve cheesecake decorated with toasted coconut.

Serves 8

ingredients

155g/5oz plain sweet biscuits, crushed
90g/3oz butter, melted
desiccated coconut, toasted

Orange and lime filling
185g/6oz cream cheese, softened
2 tablespoons brown sugar
1 1/2 teaspoons finely grated orange rind
1 1/2 teaspoons finely grated lime rind
3 teaspoons orange juice
3 teaspoons lime juice
1 egg, lightly beaten
1/2 cup/125mL/4fl oz sweetened
condensed milk
2 tablespoons cream (heavy), whipped

Oven temperature 180°C, 350°F, Gas 4

lemon
and pistachio pancakes

Method:

1 Place flour and sugar in a bowl and mix to combine. Whisk in yogurt, egg, milk, lemon rind and pistachio nuts and continue whisking until batter is smooth.

2 Cook dessertspoonfuls of mixture in a heated, greased, heavy-based frying pan for 1-2 minutes or until bubbles form on the surface, then turn and cook for 1-2 minutes longer or until golden. Serve immediately.

Serves 6

ingredients

1 cup/125g/4oz self-rising flour
¼ cup/60g/2oz sugar
250g/8oz natural yogurt
1 egg, lightly beaten
⅓ cup/90 mL/3fl oz milk
1 tablespoon finely grated lemon rind
60g/2oz chopped pistachio nuts

choc-chip
orange cake

Method:

1 *Place butter, orange rind, sugar, eggs, flour, orange juice, yogurt and milk in a large mixing bowl and beat until all ingredients are combined and batter is smooth. Fold in grated chocolate.*

2 *Spoon batter into a greased 20cm/8in ring cake tin and bake for 45-50 minutes or until cake is cooked when tested with a skewer. Stand cake in tin for 5 minutes before turning onto a wire rack to cool.*

3 *To make icing, place butter and orange rind in a mixing bowl and beat until creamy. Add icing sugar, cocoa and orange juice and beat until combined. Add a little more orange juice if necessary. Place in a heatproof bowl over a saucepan of simmering water and cook, stirring constantly, for 2-3 minutes or until mixture is smooth and runny. Pour icing over cold cake.*

Makes a 20cm/8in ring cake

ingredients

125g/4oz butter, softened
2 teaspoons grated orange rind
$^3/_4$ cup/170g/5$^1/_2$oz superfine sugar
2 eggs, lightly beaten
1$^1/_2$ cups/185 g/6 oz self-rising flour, sifted
2 tablespoons freshly squeezed orange juice
$^1/_2$ cup/100g/3$^1/_2$oz natural yogurt
$^1/_4$ cup/60mL/2fl oz milk
100g/3$^1/_2$oz roughly grated chocolate

Chocolate icing
45g/1$^1/_2$oz butter, softened
$^1/_2$ teaspoon grated orange rind
$^3/_4$ cup/125g/4oz icing sugar, sifted
1$^1/_2$ tablespoons cocoa powder, sifted
4 teaspoons freshly squeezed orange juice

Oven temperature 180°C, 350°F, Gas 4

Oven temperature 190°C, 375°F, Gas 5

lemon
and lime bars

Method:
1 Place butter, flour and icing sugar in a food processor and process to form a soft dough. Turn dough onto a lightly floured surface and knead lightly. Press dough into a greased and lined shallow 18 x 28 cm/7 x 11 in cake tin and bake for 20 minutes or until firm. Allow to cool in tin.

2 To make topping, place eggs, sugar, flour, lemon juice, lime juice and lemon rind in a mixing bowl and mix until combined. Pour over cooked base and cook for 25-30 minutes longer or until firm. Refrigerate until cold, then cut into bars. Just prior to serving, dust with icing sugar.

Makes 30

ingredients

125g/4oz butter
1 cup/125g/4oz flour
½ cup/75g/2½oz icing sugar
icing sugar, to dust

<u>**Lemon and lime topping**</u>
2 eggs, lightly beaten
1 cup/220g/7oz superfine sugar
4 teaspoons flour
4 teaspoons lemon juice
2 tablespoons lime juice
1 teaspoon finely grated lemon rind

139

lemon
yogurt cake

Method:

1 *Place butter, sugar, lemon rind and vanilla essence in a bowl and beat until light and creamy. Add eggs one at a time, beating well after each addition.*

2 *Add flour, lemon juice and yogurt and mix to combine. Pour batter into a greased 23cm/9in fluted ring tin and bake for 1 hour or until cake is cooked when tested with a skewer.*

3 *To make syrup, place sugar and lemon juice in a saucepan and cook over a low heat, stirring constantly, until sugar dissolves. Bring to the boil and cook, without stirring, for 4 minutes or until mixture thickens slightly. Pour hot syrup over hot cake in tin. Stand for 5 minutes before turning onto a serving plate.*

ingredients

185g/6oz butter
³/₄ cup/185g/6oz sugar
1 tablespoon finely grated lemon rind
1 teaspoon vanilla essence
2 eggs, lightly beaten
2¹/₄ cups/280g/9oz self-rising flour, sifted
¹/₄ cup/60mL/2fl oz lemon juice
1 cup/200g/6¹/₄oz natural yogurt

Lemon syrup
1 cup/250g/8oz sugar
¹/₂ cup/125 mL/4fl oz lemon juice

lemon
marshmallow slice

Method:

1 Place crushed cookies, butter and coconut in a bowl and mix well to combine. Press mixture into a greased and lined shallow 18 x 28cm/ 7 x 11in cake tin. Refrigerate until firm.

2 To make filling, place marshmallows, gelatine, milk, lemon juice and rind in a saucepan and cook, stirring, over a low heat until mixture is smooth and gelatine dissolves. Remove from heat and allow to cool, stirring every 3-5 minutes. Pour over biscuit base and refrigerate until firm.

Lime Marshmallow Slice: Replace lemon juice and rind with lime juice and rind.

Note: A fluffy marshmallow topping combines with a crunchy coconut base to make this delicious no-bake slice.

Makes 30

ingredients

100g/3¹/₂oz plain sweet cookies, crushed
60g/2oz butter, melted
30g/1oz desiccated coconut

<u>Lemon Marshmallows toppings</u>
400g/9¹/₂oz white marshmallows
4 teaspoons gelatine
²/₃ cup/170mL/5¹/₂fl oz milk
¹/₃ cup/90mL/3fl oz lemon juice
¹/₂ cup/90g/3oz finely grated lemon rind

ham and mustard scrolls

something savory

Who could resist a slice of savory

bread fresh from the oven? These recipes
make perfect accompaniments for soups
and salads, as well as being tasty meals
on their own,

mexican
cornbread

Photograph page 143

Oven temperature 180°C, 350°F, Gas 4

Method:
1 *Place cornmeal (polenta), flour, tasty cheese (mature Cheddar), Parmesan cheese, olives, sun-dried tomatoes, sweet corn and green peppers in a bowl and mix to combine.*
2 *Combine eggs, milk, yogurt and oil. Add egg mixture to dry ingredients and mix until just combined.*
3 *Pour mixture into a greased 20cm/8in springform pan and bake for 1 hour or until bread is cooked when tested with a skewer. Serve warm or cold.*
Makes a 20cm/8in round loaf

ingredients

2 cups/350g/11oz cornmeal (polenta)
2 cups/250g/8oz self-rising flour, sifted
**125g/4oz grated tasty cheese
(mature Cheddar)**
60g/2oz grated Parmesan cheese
12 pitted black olives, sliced
12 sun-dried tomatoes, chopped
**100g/3¹/₂oz canned sweet corn kernels,
drained**
**3 bottled hot green peppers,
chopped finely**
2 eggs, lightly beaten
1 cup/250mL/8fl oz milk
³/₄ cup/155g/5oz yogurt
¹/₄ cup/60mL/2fl oz vegetable oil

ham
and mustard scrolls

Photograph page 143

Oven temperature 220°C, 425°F, Gas 7

Method:
1 *Place flour, baking powder and butter in a food processor and process until mixture resembles coarse breadcrumbs. With machine running, slowly add egg and milk and process to form a soft dough. Turn dough onto a lightly floured surface and press out to make a 1cm/¹/₂in thick rectangle.*
2 *To make filling, place ham, ricotta cheese, tasty cheese (mature Cheddar) and mustard into a bowl and mix to combine. Spread filling over dough and roll up from short side.*
3 *Using a serrated edged knife, cut roll into 2cm/³/₄in thick slices and place on a lightly greased and floured baking tray. Bake for 15-20 minutes or until puffed and golden.*

ingredients

2 cups/250g/8oz self-rising flour, sifted
1 teaspoon baking powder, sifted
60g/2oz butter, chopped
1 egg, lightly beaten
¹/₂ cup/125mL/4fl oz milk

Ham and mustard filling
4 slices smoked ham, chopped
¹/₂ cup/125g/4oz ricotta cheese, drained
**60g/2oz grated tasty cheese
(mature Cheddar)**
2 tablespoons wholegrain mustard

Makes 18

potato
and cheese pancake

Method:

1 Rinse potatoes in a colander under cold running water, then turn onto a clean teatowel or absorbent kitchen paper and pat dry.
2 Place potatoes, eggs, onions, flour, coriander, Cheddar cheese and black pepper to taste in a bowl and mix to combine.
3 Heat oil in a large nonstick frying pan over a medium heat, spread potato mixture over base of pan and cook for 15 minutes. Place pan under a preheated medium grill and cook for 10 minutes or until top is golden and pancake is cooked through. Serve cut into wedges and topped with yogurt.

Serves 6-8

ingredients

1 kg/2 lb potatoes, grated
2 eggs, lightly beaten
2 onions, grated
2 tablespoons flour
1 teaspoon finely chopped fresh coriander
60g/2oz reduced-fat Cheddar cheese, grated
freshly ground black pepper
2 tablespoons olive oil
6 tablespoons low-fat natural yogurt

basil
beer bread

Photograph page 147

Oven temperature 160°C, 325°F, Gas 3

Method:
1 *Place flour, sugar, basil, peppercorns and beer in a bowl and mix to make a soft dough.*
2 *Place dough in a greased and lined 11x21cm/ 4¹/₂ x 8¹/₂in loaf tin and bake for 50 minutes or until bread is cooked when tested with a skewer.*
3 *Stand bread in tin for 5 minutes before turning onto a wire rack to cool. Serve warm or cold.*
Makes an 11x 21cm/4¹/₂x8¹/₂in loaf

ingredients

3 cups/375g/12oz self-rising flour, sifted
¹/₄ cup/60g/2oz sugar
6 tablespoons chopped fresh basil
1 teaspoon crushed black peppercorns
1¹/₂ cups/375mL/12fl oz beer, at room temperature

olive
soda bread

Photograph page 147

Oven temperature 200°C, 400°F, Gas 6

ingredients

Method:
1 *Place butter, sugar and egg in a food processor and process until smooth. Add wholemeal flour, flour, bicarbonate of soda and milk and process to form a soft dough.*
2 *Turn dough onto a lightly floured surface and knead in olives. Shape dough into a 20cm/8in round and place on a lightly greased and floured baking tray. Using a sharp knife, cut a cross in the top. Sprinkle with fennel seeds and salt and bake for 45 minutes or until cooked.*
Makes a 20cm/8in round loaf

125g/4oz butter, softened
¹/₄ cup/60g/2oz sugar
1 egg
3 cups/470g/15oz wholemeal self-rising flour
1¹/₂ cups/185g/6oz flour
1¹/₂ teaspoons bicarbonate of soda
1¹/₂ cups/375mL/12fl oz buttermilk or milk
125g/4oz black olives, chopped
2 teaspoons fennel seeds
1 teaspoon coarse sea salt

rock cakes and carrot cake

healthy alternative

Good tastes that are full of goodness

Enjoy these cakes, cookies and slices anytime of the day for snacks or treats.

rock
cakes

Photograph page 149

ingredients

2 cups/250g/8oz self-rising flour, sifted
¹/₄ cup/60g/2oz superfine sugar
90g/3oz butter
125g/4oz mixed dried fruit, chopped
1 teaspoon finely grated lemon rind
1 teaspoon finely grated orange rind
1 egg, lightly beaten
¹/₃ cup/90mL/3fl oz milk
¹/₂ teaspoon cinnamon mixed with
2 tablespoons caster sugar

Method:

1 Place flour and sugar in a mixing bowl. Rub in butter, using fingertips, until mixture resembles fine bread crumbs. Stir in mixed fruit, lemon rind and orange rind. Add egg and milk and mix to form a soft dough.

2 Place tablespoons of mixture on greased baking trays and dust lightly with cinnamon sugar mixture. Bake for 12-15 minutes or until golden. Transfer to wire racks to cool.

Makes 30

carrot
cake

Photograph page 149

ingredients

2 cups/375g/2oz ground rice, sifted
2 teaspoons ground mixed spice
2 teaspoons bicarbonate of soda
1 cup/170g/5¹/₂oz soft brown sugar
125g/4oz margarine, softened
4 small carrots, grated
125g/4oz pecans, chopped
170g/5¹/₂oz sultanas (golden raisins)
2 cups/400g/12¹/₂oz natural low-fat yogurt
1 teaspoon vanilla essence
icing sugar

Method:

1 Place ground rice, mixed spice, bicarbonate of soda, brown sugar, margarine, carrots, pecans, sultanas, yogurt and vanilla essence in a large mixing bowl and mix well to combine all ingredients.

2 Spoon mixture into a greased and lined 20 cm/8 in square cake tin and bake for 45-50 minutes or until cooked when tested with a skewer. Stand cake in tin for 10 minutes before turning onto a wire rack to cool. Dust with icing sugar.

Note: A gluten-free cake that is suitable for anyone who has a wheat intolerance.

Makes a 20cm/8in square cake

Oven temperature 190°C, 375°F, Gas 5

apricot
date slice

Method:

1 Place apricots in a small bowl and add boiling water to cover. Set aside to soak for 10 minutes. Drain.

2 Sift together flour and sugar into a large mixing bowl. Add coconut, dates and apricots, pour in melted butter and mix to combine. Press mixture into a greased and lined, shallow 18 x 28cm/7 x 11in cake tin and bake for 25 minutes or until firm. Allow to cool in tin.

3 To make icing, place butter in a mixing bowl and beat until creamy. Add icing sugar and lemon juice and beat until icing is of a spreadable consistency. Add a little more lemon juice if necessary.

Note: Spread icing over cold slice and sprinkle with coconut. Cut into bars.

Makes 30

ingredients

90g/3oz dried apricots, chopped
boiling water
2 cups/250g/8oz self-rising flour, sifted
1 cup/170g/5¹/₂oz soft brown sugar
75g/2¹/₂oz desiccated coconut
60g/2oz dates, chopped
185g/6oz butter, melted

Lemon icing
90g/3oz butter, softened
1¹/₂ cups/220g/7oz icing sugar, sifted
2 tablespoons lemon juice
15g/¹/₂oz desiccated coconut, toasted

pineapple
and muesli cookies

Method:

1 *Place muesli, flour, sugar and pineapple in a bowl. Add butter and egg and mix well to combine.*
2 *Place spoonfuls of mixture on greased baking trays and bake for 12-15 minutes or until golden brown. Stand on trays for 5 minutes before removing to wire racks to cool.*

Makes 30

ingredients

2 cups/250g/8oz toasted muesli
I cup/125g/4oz self-raising flour, sifted
¹/₂ cup/125g/4oz demerara (brown) sugar
45g/1¹/₂oz glacé pineapple, chopped
125g/4oz butter, melted
I egg, lightly beaten

Oven temperature 180°C, 350°F, Gas 4

Oven temperature 180°C, 350°F, Gas 4

honey
oat loaf

Method:

1 Sift together flour and self-rising flour, salt and baking powder into a large mixing bowl. Stir in rolled oats.

2 Combine butter, eggs, water and honey and mix into flour mixture until just combined. Pour into a greased and lined 11 x 21cm/ 4¹/₂ x 8¹/₂in loaf tin and bake for 40-45 minutes or until cooked when tested with a skewer. Stand in tin for 5 minutes before turning onto a wire rack to cool completely. Plain, or spread with a little butter and jam, this loaf tastes delicious.

Makes an 11 x 21cm/ 4¹/₂x8¹/₂in loaf

ingredients

¹/₂ cup/60g/2oz flour
1 cup/125g/4oz self-rising flour
1 teaspoon salt
1¹/₂ teaspoons baking powder
1 cup/90g/3oz rolled oats
45g/1¹/₂oz butter, melted
2 eggs, lightly beaten
¹/₄ cup/60mL/2fl oz water
¹/₂ cup/170g/5¹/₂oz honey, warmed

fruity
cereal slice

Photograph page 155

ingredients

3 cups/90g/3oz unsweetened
puffed rice cereal
I cup/45g/I¹/₂oz bran flakes, crumbled
125g/4oz slivered almonds, toasted
125g/4oz dried apricots, chopped
100g/3¹/₂oz glacé pineapple, chopped
100g/3¹/₂oz glacé ginger or stem ginger
in syrup, chopped
90g/3oz raisins, chopped
170g/5¹/₂oz sultanas (golden raisins)
125g/4oz butter
¹/₂ cup/125mL/4fl oz cream (heavy)
¹/₂ cup/170g/5¹/₂oz honey
¹/₃ cup/90g/3oz demerara (brown) sugar

Method:

1 Place rice cereal, bran flakes, almonds, apricots, pineapple, ginger, raisins and sultanas in a large mixing bowl and set aside.

2 Combine butter, cream, honey and sugar in a saucepan and cook over a low heat, stirring constantly, until sugar dissolves and butter melts. Bring to the boil, then reduce heat and simmer for 5 minutes or until mixture thickens slightly.

3 Pour honey mixture into dry ingredients and mix well to combine. Press mixture into a greased and lined shallow18x28cm/ 7x11in cake tin. Refrigerate until firm, then cut into squares.

Note: Dried fruit, rice bubbles, coconut, nuts and honey – just reading the ingredients you know that this slice is going to be delicious.

Makes 30

date bars

Photograph page 155

ingredients

³/₄ cup/185mL/6fl oz evaporated milk
125g/4oz pitted dates, chopped
125g/4oz butter, softened
¹/₂ cup/100g/3¹/₂oz superfine sugar
I teaspoon vanilla essence
I cup/125g/4oz self-rising flour, sifted
60g/2oz pecans, chopped

Method:

1 Place evaporated milk in a saucepan and cook over a low heat until just boiling, then remove pan from heat. Place dates in a bowl, pour hot milk over and set aside to cool.

2 Combine butter, sugar and vanilla essence in a large mixing bowl and beat until light and fluffy. Mix flour and date mixture, alternately, into butter mixture, then fold in pecans. Spoon mixture into a greased and lined 23cm/9in square cake tin and bake for 25-30 minutes or until firm. Stand in tin 5 minutes before turning onto a wire rack to cool. Cut into bars.

Note: Studded with dates and pecans, this slice is a great lunch box filler.

Makes 30

Oven temperature 180°C, 350°F, Gas 4

icing
on the cake

The icing on the cake

This selection of easy icings, fillings and toppings will dress up any plain cake to make it into something really special.

Chocolate ripple cream

Cream well chilled, with chocolate folded through as soon as it is melted - the secret to this wonderful topping or filling for a chocolate cake or sponge.

Enough to fill and top a 20cm/8in cake

100g/3¹/₂oz dark chocolate
1 cup/250mL/8fl oz cream (heavy),
well chilled and whipped

Melt chocolate in a small bowl over a saucepan of simmering water, or melt in the microwave oven on HIGH (100%) for 45 seconds to 1 minute. Fold melted chocolate through chilled cream.

Butterscotch frosting

Enough to cover a 20cm/8in cake

1¹/₂ cups/250g/8oz soft brown sugar
¹/₄ cup/60mL/2fl oz milk
30g/1oz butter
1 cup/155g/5oz icing sugar

Place sugar, milk and butter in a small saucepan and cook, stirring constantly, over a low heat until sugar dissolves. Bring to the boil and boil for 3-4 minutes. Remove from heat and set aside to cool until just warm, then beat in icing

sugar until frosting is of a spreadable consistency. Use immediately.

Vanilla butter icing

Enough to cover a 20cm/8in cake or 18 biscuits

1¹/₂ cups/220g/7oz icing sugar, sifted
60g/2oz butter
2 tablespoons boiling water
¹/₄ teaspoon vanilla essence
few drops of food colouring (optional)

Place icing sugar and butter in a bowl and add boiling water. Mix to make a mixture of spreadable consistency, adding a little more water if necessary. Beat in vanilla essence and food colouring if using.

Chocolate Butter Icing

Add ¹/₄ cup/30g/1oz cocoa powder to icing sugar.

Coffee Butter Icing:

Add 1 tablespoon instant coffee powder to boiling water.

Lemon Butter Icing:

Omit vanilla essence and add 1-2 teaspoons fresh lemon juice to icing sugar mixture.

Passion Fruit Icing:

Replace vanilla essence with 2-3 tablespoons passion fruit pulp. A little more icing sugar may be required to make an icing of spreadable consistency.

icing
on the cake

Mock *cream*

Enough to fill a 20cm/8in cake

60g/2oz butter
¹/₄ cup/60g/2oz superfine sugar
¹/₄ cup/60mL/2fl oz boiling water
¹/₄ teaspoon vanilla essence

Place butter and sugar in a small bowl and add boiling water. Beat, using an electric mixer, until creamy. Beat in vanilla essence.
Cook's tip: If the mixture curdles, place over a pan of simmering water and continue beating.

Chocolate *fudge topping*

Enough to fill and cover a 20cm/8in cake

³/₄ cup/185g/6oz superfine sugar
¹/₃ cup/90mL/3fl oz evaporated milk
125g/4oz dark chocolate,
broken into pieces
45g/1¹/₂oz butter
¹/₄ teaspoon vanilla essence

1 *Place sugar and evaporated milk in a heavy-based saucepan and cook, stirring, over a low heat until sugar melts. Bring mixture to the boil and simmer stirring constantly for 4 minutes.*

2 *Remove pan from heat and stir in chocolate. Continue stirring until chocolate melts, then stir in butter and vanilla essence.*

3 *Transfer frosting to a bowl and set aside to cool. Cover with plastic food wrap and chill until frosting thickens and is of spreadable consistency.*

Marshmallow *frosting*

Enough to fill and cover a 20cm/8in cake

1 egg white
2 teaspoons gelatine dissolved in
¹/₂ cup/125mL/4fl oz hot water, cooled
1 cup/155g/5oz icing sugar
flavouring of your choice
few drops of colouring (optional)

Beat egg white until stiff peaks form, then continue beating while gradually adding gelatine mixture. Beat in icing sugar and flavouring. Continue beating until frosting is thick.

quick
cooking

introduction

Quick cooking

More often than not fast food is associated with large food chains which turn out hamburgers, pizzas and fried chicken almost before you have had time to order!

Here you will find a wonderful selection of recipes that prove you can create great food at home and it need not take you hours. This book is for all those who yearn to eat real food, but do not have time to cook. A quick look at the recipes and ingredients will show you that it can be just as quick to cook at home as it is to stop at a takeaway food shop, with the added advantage that you know exactly what you are eating.

Every kitchen-tested recipe is superbly photographed and captures the flavour and diversity of modern cooking, using readily available ingredients and short cuts. You will find recipes for all occasions appetising ideas for fast dinners when running late, easy exotic stir-fries, tempting entrees and treats for the barbecue.

Photograph page 161 and recipe page 180 (Thigh Steaks with Fruity Salsa)

camembert surprise in
banana sauce

succulent
starters

Starters are far too good to be reserved

for special occasions, however being light and easily
digestible, they make perfect lunch or supper dishes.
Simply adjust the quantities or reduce the number of
servings if more substantial portions are required.

satay
style oysters

Method:

1 Place peanut butter, sour cream and Tabasco sauce to taste in a bowl and mix to combine.
2 Place oysters in a baking tin, place a spoonful of mixture onto each oyster and sprinkle with bacon. Cook under a preheated hot grill for 2-3 minutes or until oysters are golden. Sprinkle with parsley or coriander and serve.

Note: Serve as an entrée with a squeeze of fresh lemon or lime juice and buttered fresh brown bread.

ingredients

2 tablespoons smooth peanut butter
$^1/_3$ cup/90g/3oz sour cream
Tabasco sauce
12 fresh oysters, on the half shell
2 rashers bacon, chopped
chopped fresh parsley or coriander

camembert
surprise in banana sauce

Photograph page 163

Method:

1 Halve Camemberts horizontally. Sprinkle banana slices with lemon juice and arrange on four of the Camembert halves. Sprinkle with coconut and top with remaining cheese halves. Press together firmly.
2 Combine egg and milk. Dip each Camembert in flour, egg mixture and breadcrumbs. Repeat crumbing process. Chill until firm.
3 Cook in hot oil until golden. Drain on absorbent paper and serve with sauce.
4 To prepare sauce, peel and roughly chop bananas. Place into the bowl of a food processor, add coconut cream, cream, spice and lemon juice. Process until smooth. Serve sauce separately or spooned over Camembert.

Cook's tip: Use a toothpick to hold each Camembert together while preparing and cooking. Remove toothpick before serving.

Serves 4

ingredients

4 x 125g Camembert cheese
2 ripe bananas, peeled and sliced
lemon juice
2 teaspoons desiccated coconut
plain flour
1 egg, beaten
3 tablespoons milk
3 cups/375g dry breadcrumbs
polyunsaturated oil for cooking

Banana sauce
2 ripe bananas
$^1/_2$ cup/125 ml coconut cream
2 tablespoons cream
$^1/_4$ teaspoon ground mixed spice
1 teaspoon lemon juice

chicken
and corn chowder

Method:

1 *Heat oil in a saucepan over a medium heat, add onion and cook, stirring, for 4-5 minutes or until onion is soft. Add chicken and cook for 2 minutes longer or until chicken just changes colour.*

2 *Add potatoes and stock and bring to the boil. Reduce heat and simmer for 10 minutes or until potatoes are almost cooked. Stir sweet corn, milk, bay leaf and black pepper to taste into stock mixture and bring to the boil. Reduce heat and simmer for 3-4 minutes or until potatoes are cooked. Remove bay leaf. Stir in lemon juice, parsley, chives and black pepper to taste. Just prior to serving, sprinkle with Parmesan cheese.*

Note: *To chop the sweet corn, place in a food processor or blender and process using the pulse button until the sweet corn is coarsely chopped. Creamed sweet corn can be used in place of the kernels if you wish. If using creamed sweet corn there is no need to chop it.*

Serves 6

ingredients

1 tablespoon vegetable oil
1 small onion, diced
250g/8oz boneless chicken breast
fillets, shredded
3 potatoes, chopped
3¹/₂ cups/875mL/1¹/₂pt chicken stock
315g/10oz canned sweet corn kernels,
drained and coarsely chopped
1¹/₄ cups/315mL/10fl oz milk
1 bay leaf
freshly ground black pepper
1 tablespoon lemon juice
2 tablespoons chopped fresh parsley
1 tablespoon snipped fresh chives
60g/2oz grated Parmesan cheese

vegetable
bean soup

Method:

1 Heat oil in a large saucepan over a medium heat, add onions and cook, stirring, for 5 minutes or until onions are lightly browned.

2 Add carrots, potatoes and stock and bring to the boil. Reduce heat, cover and simmer for 30 minutes or until vegetables are tender.

3 Stir in beans, milk, dill, parsley and black pepper to taste and cook, stirring frequently, for 3-4 minutes or until heated through.

Serves 4

ingredients

2 tablespoons vegetable oil
3 onions, diced
3 carrots, diced
3 potatoes, diced
3 cups/750mL/1¹/₄pt vegetable stock
315g/10oz canned cannellini beans,
drained and rinsed
¹/₂ cup/125mL/4 fl oz milk
2 tablespoons chopped fresh dill
1 tablespoon chopped fresh parsley
freshly ground black pepper

Oven temperature 200°C/400°F/Gas 6

french
onion flans

Method:

1 Line six individual flan tins with pastry. Melt butter in a frypan and cook onions until golden. Divide into six portions and spread over base of flans.

2 Combine eggs, sour cream, nutmeg and horseradish. Pour into flans. Top with cheese and bake at 200°C/400°F/Gas 6 for 20 minutes or until firm.

Cook's tip: If fresh dill is unavailable, substitute 1 teaspoon dried dill leaves or ¼ teaspoon ground dill.

Serves 6

ingredients

3 sheets prepared puff pastry, thawed
6 onions, sliced
60g/2oz butter
3 eggs, beaten
1³/₄ cups/435g sour cream
1 teaspoon ground nutmeg
1¹/₂ teaspoons horseradish relish
1¹/₂ cups/175g grated tasty cheese

scampi
with basil butter

Method:
1 Cut scampi or yabbies in half, lengthwise.
2 To make Basil Butter, place butter, basil, garlic and honey in a small bowl and whisk to combine.
3 Brush cut side of each scampi or yabbie half with Basil Butter and cook under a preheated hot grill for 2 minutes or until they change colour and are tender. Drizzle with any remaining Basil Butter and serve immediately.

Serves 8

ingredients

8 uncooked scampi or yabbies, heads removed

Basil butter
90g/3oz butter, melted
2 tablespoons chopped fresh basil
1 clove garlic, crushed
2 teaspoons honey

brushetta

Method:

1 Brush bread slices with oil, place under a preheated hot grill and toast both sides until golden. Rub one side of toasts with cut side of garlic cloves.

2 For Tomato and Basil Topping, top half the toast slices with some tomato, onion and basil, and grill for 1-2 minutes or until topping is warm.

3 For Eggplant and Feta Topping, brush eggplant (aubergine) slices with oil and cook under preheated hot grill for 3-4 minutes each side or until lightly browned. Top remaining toasts with eggplant (aubergine) slices and sprinkle with feta cheese and black pepper to taste. Cook under a preheated hot grill for 1-2 minutes or until topping is warm.

Makes 16-20

ingredients

**1 French bread stick, cut into
1 cm/¹/₂ in slices
2 tablespoons olive oil
2 cloves garlic, halved**

**<u>Tomato and basil topping</u>
2 tomatoes, sliced
1 red onion, sliced
2 tablespoons shredded basil leaves**

**<u>Eggplant and feta topping</u>
2 baby eggplant (aubergines), sliced
1 tablespoon olive oil
125g/4oz feta cheese, crumbled
freshly ground black pepper**

asparagus and salmon salad

simple salads

Fine food comes in many guises,

but seldom is it simpler to prepare, more flavorsome or more packed with goodness than when it is gathered from the garden or garnered from the greengrocer.

chicken
and orange salad

Method:
1 *Combine chicken, celery, water chestnuts, orange segments and onion in a salad bowl. Mix all the remaining ingredients in a screwtop jar. Close the lid tightly, shake the dressing until well mixed and pour it over the salad.*
Serves 4

ingredients

500g/1lb cooked chicken, cut into bite-size pieces
2 sticks celery, sliced
90g/3oz drained canned water chestnuts, halved
2 oranges, peeled and neatly segmented
1 red onion, finely chopped
1 tblspn chopped fresh parsley
3 tablespoons salad oil
1 small garlic clove, crushed
1 tablespoon tarragon vinegar

asparagus
and salmon salad

Photograph page 171

Method:
1 *Boil, steam or microwave asparagus until tender. Drain, refresh under cold running water, drain again and chill. Arrange lettuce leaves, asparagus and salmon on serving plates.*
2 *To make sauce, place yogurt, lemon rind, lemon juice, dill and cumin in a small bowl and mix to combine.*
3 *Spoon sauce over salad. Sprinkle with black pepper, cover and chill until required.*
Note: *If fresh asparagus is unavailable, green beans or snow peas (mangetout) are good alternatives for this recipe.*
Serves 6

ingredients

750g/1 1/2 lb asparagus spears, trimmed
lettuce leaves of your choice
500g/1 lb smoked salmon slices
freshly ground black pepper

Lemon yogurt sauce
1 cup/200g/6 1/2oz natural low-fat yogurt
1 tablespoon finely grated lemon rind
1 tablespoon lemon juice
1 tablespoon chopped fresh dill
1 teaspoon ground cumin

mediterranean
chickpea salad

Method:

1 *Heat oil in a frying pan over a medium heat, add garlic, chickpeas and rosemary and cook, stirring, for 5 minutes. Remove pan from heat and set aside to cool slightly.*

2 *Place chickpea mixture, sun-dried tomatoes, eggplant (aubergines), olives, feta cheese and rocket or watercress in a bowl and toss to combine. Sprinkle with olive oil and vinegar.*

Serving suggestion: *Serve with thick slices of fresh wholemeal bread. Canned ratatouille can be used in place of the marinated eggplant (aubergines) if you wish.*

Serves 4

ingredients

1 tablespoon olive oil
2 cloves garlic, crushed
2 x 440g/14oz canned chickpeas, drained
2 tablespoons chopped fresh rosemary
90g/3oz sun-dried tomatoes, sliced
125g/4oz marinated eggplant (aubergines), sliced
125g/4oz pitted marinated olives
250g/8oz feta cheese, crumbled
125g/4oz rocket (lettuce) or watercress
1 tablespoon olive oil
3 tablespoons balsamic or red wine vinegar

rainbow
salad

Method:

1 Cook bacon under a preheated hot grill for 5 minutes or until very crisp. Drain on absorbent kitchen paper and when cool break into bite-sized pieces.

2 Place spinach, carrots, yellow pepper, red pepper, snow peas (mangetout) and bacon in a salad bowl and toss to combine. Scatter with feta cheese and walnuts.

3 To make dressing, place chives, mayonnaise, vinegar and black pepper to taste in a bowl and whisk to combine. Drizzle dressing over salad and serve immediately.

Note: This salad looks great served on a bed of mixed lettuce leaves on a large serving platter.

Serves 6

ingredients

4 rashers bacon
1 bunch English spinach, leaves shredded
2 carrots, cut into thin strips
1 yellow pepper, cut into thin strips
1 red pepper, cut into thin strips
125g/4oz snow peas (mangetout),
cut into thin strips
185g/6oz feta cheese, crumbled
125g/4oz walnuts, chopped

Chive dressing
1 tablespoon snipped fresh chives
¹/₂ cup/125mL/4fl oz mayonnaise
2 tablespoons tarragon vinegar
freshly ground black pepper

Oven temperature 180°C, 350°F, Gas 4

green
seed salad

Method:

1 Rub bread with cut side of garlic, brush both sides lightly with olive oil and cut into 2cm/³/₄in cubes. Place bread cubes on a non-stick baking tray and bake for 10 minutes or until bread is golden and crisp. Cool slightly.

2 Place sunflower, pumpkin and sesame seeds on a non-stick baking tray and bake for 3-5 minutes or until golden. Cool slightly.

3 Place salad leaves, avocados, tomatoes, tofu and oranges in a salad bowl and toss. Sprinkle with croûtons and toasted seeds.

4 To make dressing, place oil, lemon juice, chilli sauce, soy sauce and sesame oil in a bowl and whisk to combine. Drizzle dressing over salad and serve immediately.

Note: Sunflower, pumpkin and sesame seeds are available from health food shops or the health food section of larger supermarkets.

Serves 6

ingredients

3 slices wholemeal bread, crusts trimmed
1 clove garlic, halved
¹/₄ cup/60mL/2fl oz olive oil
3 tablespoons sunflower seeds
2 tablespoons pumpkin seeds
2 tablespoons sesame seeds
500g/1 lb assorted salad leaves
2 avocados, stoned, peeled and sliced
250g/8oz cherry tomatoes, halved
250g/8oz firm tofu, chopped
2 oranges, segmented

Chilli sesame dressing
¹/₄ cup/60 mL/2 fl oz vegetable oil
2 tablespoons lemon juice
1 tablespoon sweet chilli sauce
1 teaspoon soy sauce
1 teaspoon sesame oil

pesto
pasta salad

Method:

1 Cook pasta in boiling water in a large saucepan following packet directions. Drain, rinse under cold running water and set aside to cool completely.

2 Place pasta, tomatoes, snow pea (mangetout) sprouts or watercress and green pepper (capsicum) in a salad bowl and toss to combine.

3 To make dressing, place basil leaves, 3 tablespoons pine nuts, Parmesan cheese, garlic, mayonnaise and water in a food processor or blender and process until smooth. Spoon dressing over salad and sprinkle with remaining pine nuts.

Note: This salad looks pretty when made with attractive pasta shapes such as bows, spirals or shells. Choose the pasta to suit the other dishes you are serving, for example, if serving the salad with fish, shells would be the perfect choice.

Serves 6

ingredients

375g/12oz pasta of your choice
250g/8oz cherry tomatoes
125g/4oz snow pea (mangetout) sprouts
or watercress
1 green pepper (capsicum), chopped
2 tablespoons pine nuts

Pesto dressing
1 bunch fresh basil
3 tablespoons pine nuts
3 tablespoons grated Parmesan cheese
1 clove garlic, crushed
$^1/_2$ cup/125mL/4fl oz mayonnaise
2 tablespoons water

waldorf
salad

Method:

1 Place green apples, red apple, celery, walnuts and parsley in a bowl and toss to combine.

2 Place sour cream, mayonnaise and black pepper to taste in a small bowl and mix to combine. Add mayonnaise mixture to apple mixture and toss to combine. Cover and chill.

Note: This salad can be made in advance, but if making more than 2 hours ahead toss apples in 1 tablespoon lemon juice to prevent them from browning.

Serves 6

ingredients

2 large green eating apples, cored and diced
1 large red eating apple, cored and diced
3 stalks celery, diced
60g/2oz walnut pieces
1 tablespoon chopped fresh parsley
¹/₄ cup/60g/2oz sour cream
¹/₄ cup/60mL/2fl oz mayonnaise
freshly ground black pepper

chicken and vegetable stir-fry

everyday
meals

Just because you're busy doesn't mean

you can't prepare stylish and tasty meals. With these recipes you can have a delicious dinner on the table in no time at all.

thigh
steaks with fruity mint salsa

Photograph page 161

Method:

1 Pound thigh fillets on both sides with a meat mallet to flatten. Sprinkle with salt (if using), pepper and oregano.

2 Heat a non-stick frying pan and lightly spray with oil, place in the thigh steaks and cook for 3 minutes on each side. Remove to a heated plate and keep hot. Add diced pear, banana, lemon juice, mint and chilli sauce to the pan. Scrape up pan juices and stir to heat fruit.

3 Pile hot fruit salsa on top of thigh steaks. Serve immediately with mashed potatoes or rice.

Serves 3-4

ingredients

500g/1 lb chicken thighs
Canola oil spray
salt, pepper to taste (optional)
$^1/_2$ teaspoon dried oregano
1 pear, peeled and diced
1 banana, peeled and diced
2 tablespoons lemon juice
3 tablespoons finely chopped mint
2 teaspoons sweet chilli sauce

chicken
and vegetable stir-fry

Photograph page 179

Method:

1 Heat oil in a wok, add garlic, ginger and spring onions and stirfry for 1 minute then add chicken and stirfry until cooked through. Remove the chicken and spring onions from the wok.

2 Mix together the oyster sauce, stock powder and water and add to the wok. Add snow peas (mangetout) and capsicum (pepper) and cook, lifting vegetables from the bottom and turning over continuously for 2 minutes. Add drained vegetables and continue stirring for one minute.

3 Return the chicken and spring onions to the pan and toss through vegetables to reheat for 2 minutes. Pile onto a platter and serve immediately.

Serves 4-5

ingredients

2 tablespoons canola oil
1 clove garlic, crushed
1 teaspoon finely chopped
fresh ginger
6 spring onions, sliced into 1cm/$^1/_s$in
lengths on diagonal
500g/1 lb chicken stirfry
2 tablespoons oyster sauce
$^1/_2$ teaspoon chicken stock powder
$^1/_4$ cup/60ml/2fl oz water
200g/7oz snow peas (mangetout), trimmed
1 red capsicum (pepper), seeded
and cut into strips
485g/16oz can mixed vegetables, drained

italian
pork in lemon sauce

Method:

1 Place flour, ¹/₂ teaspoon oregano and black pepper to taste in a shallow dish and mix to combine. Place egg, water and black pepper to taste in a separate shallow dish and whisk to combine. Place breadcrumbs and remaining oregano in a third shallow dish and mix to combine.

2 Coat pork with flour mixture, then dip in egg mixture and finally coat with breadcrumb mixture. Place coated pork on a plate lined with plastic food wrap and chill for 10-15 minutes.

3 Heat 2-3 tablespoons oil in a frying pan over a medium-high heat and cook 1-2 schnitzels (escalopes) at a time for 3 minutes each side or cook steaks for 4 minutes each side. Remove pork from pan, set aside and keep warm.

4 To make sauce, melt butter in same pan, then stir in lemon juice. Spoon sauce over pork and serve immediately.

Note: When cooking the pork it is important not to crowd the pan or the meat will steam and the coating will be soggy.

ingredients

flour
1 teaspoon dried oregano
freshly ground black pepper
1 egg, beaten
1 tablespoon cold water
dried breadcrumbs
8 pork schnitzels (escalopes) or
4 butterfly pork steaks, lightly pounded
vegetable oil

<u>Lemon butter sauce</u>
2 teaspoons butter
1 tablespoon lemon juice

This is also a delicious way of cooking chicken. In place of the pork use boneless chicken breast fillets. Pound the fillets lightly to flatten, then proceed as directed in the recipe. The cooking time for chicken will be 4 minutes each side.

Serves 4

181

italian
meatballs

Method:

1 *Place beef, breadcrumbs, Parmesan cheese, oregano, ground garlic, eggs and black pepper to taste in a bowl and mix to combine. Form mixture into sixteen balls.*

2 *Heat oil in a frying pan over a medium heat, add meatballs and cook, turning frequently, for 10 minutes or until brown on all sides. Remove meatballs from pan and set aside.*

3 *Add red pepper (capsicum), onion and garlic to same pan and cook, stirring, for 3 minutes. Add mushrooms and cook for 4 minutes longer. Stir in pasta sauce, return meatballs to pan, cover and bring to simmering. Simmer, stirring occasionally, for 10 minutes.*

Note: *Serve spooned over hot spaghetti or pasta of your choice. This dish can be made 1-2 days in advance and reheated in the microwave when required. Dried ground garlic also called garlic powder can be found in the spice section of supermarkets. It has a pungent taste and smell and should be used with care.*

Serves 6

ingredients

500g/1 lb lean beef mince
1/2 cup/60g/2oz dried breadcrumbs
2 tablespoons grated Parmesan cheese
1 teaspoon dried oregano
1/2 teaspoon dried ground garlic
2 eggs, beaten
freshly ground black pepper
1 tablespoon olive oil
1 red pepper (capsicum), diced
1 onion, diced
3 large cloves garlic, crushed
8 mushrooms, chopped
500g/16oz bottled tomato pasta sauce

vegetable
cheesecake

Method:

1 Place spinach in a sieve and squeeze to remove as much liquid as possible.
2 Place cream cheese, feta cheese, eggs, zucchini (courgettes), carrot, red pepper, spinach and black pepper to taste in a bowl and mix to combine.
3 Pour egg mixture into a greased 23cm/9in square cake tin, sprinkle with tasty cheese (mature cheddar) and bake for 25 minutes or until set.

Serving suggestion: Serve with wholegrain rolls and a salad of mixed lettuces and chopped fresh herbs. Also delicious cold this cheesecake is a tasty addition to any picnic and leftovers are always welcome in packed lunches.

Serves 4

ingredients

375g/12oz frozen spinach, thawed
250g/8oz cream cheese, softened
125g/4oz feta cheese, crumbled
4 eggs, lightly beaten
2 zucchini (courgettes), grated
I carrot, grated
I red pepper, chopped
freshly ground black pepper
60g/2oz tasty cheese (mature cheddar), grated

pesto
pasta

Method:

1 To make pesto, place basil leaves, parsley, Parmesan or Romano cheese, pine nuts or almonds, garlic and black pepper to taste in a food processor or blender and process to finely chop. With machine running, slowly add oil and continue processing to make a smooth paste.

2 Cook pasta in boiling water in a large saucepan following packet directions. Drain and divide between serving bowls, top with pesto, toss to combine and serve immediately.

Note: Spinach pesto makes a tasty alternative when fresh basil is unavailable. To make, use fresh spinach in place of the basil and add 1 teaspoon dried basil.

Serves 4

ingredients

500g/1 lb fettuccine or other pasta of your choice

Basil and garlic pesto
1 large bunch fresh basil
1/2 bunch fresh parsley, broken into sprigs
60g/2oz grated Parmesan or Romano cheese
30g/1oz pine nuts or almonds
2 large cloves garlic, quartered freshly ground black pepper
1/3 cup/90mL/3fl oz olive oil

tandoori
beef burgers

Method:

1 To make dressing, place yogurt, coriander, cumin and chilli powder to taste in a bowl and mix to combine. Cover and chill until required.

2 To make patties, place beef, garlic, breadcrumbs, egg, Tandoori paste and soy sauce in a bowl and mix to combine. Divide beef mixture into four portions and shape into patties.

3 Heat a little oil in a frying pan over a medium-high heat, add patties and cook for 4-5 minutes each side or until cooked to your liking.

4 Top bottom half of each roll with a lettuce leaf, some tomato slices, 2 cucumber slices, a pattie and a spoonful of dressing. Place other halves on top.

Note: These burgers are also delicious made using lamb mince in place of beef.

Serves 4

ingredients

**4 wholemeal bread rolls,
split and toasted
4 lettuce leaves
2 tomatoes, sliced
8 slices cucumber**

Tandoori patties
**500g/1 lb lean beef mince
2 cloves garlic, crushed
2 tablespoons dried breadcrumbs
1 egg
1¹/₂ tablespoons Tandoori paste
1 tablespoon soy sauce
vegetable oil**

Spiced yogurt dressing
**¹/₂ cup/100g/3¹/₂oz natural yogurt
1 tablespoon chopped fresh coriander
¹/₂ teaspoon ground cumin
pinch chilli powder**

quick
chicken satay

Method:

1 Place oil, soy sauce, garlic and ginger in a bowl and mix to combine. Add chicken and marinate for 15 minutes.

2 Drain chicken, thread onto lightly oiled skewers and cook under a preheated medium grill or on a barbecue for 15-20 minutes or until chicken is cooked.

3 To make sauce, heat oil in a saucepan over a medium heat, add garlic and ginger and cook, stirring, for 2 minutes. Stir in stock, coconut milk and soy sauce, bring to simmering and simmer for 5 minutes.

4 Add peanut butter and simmer for 5 minutes longer. Just prior to serving, stir in chilli sauce. Serve sauce with chicken.

Note: The sauce can be made in advance and stored in a sealed container in the refrigerator for 5-7 days. Reheat over a low heat before serving. If sweet chilli sauce is not available mix ordinary chilli sauce with a little brown sugar.

Serves 4

ingredients

1 tablespoon vegetable oil
1 tablespoon soy sauce
1 large clove garlic, crushed
¹/₂ teaspoon finely grated fresh ginger
500g/1 lb boneless chicken thigh or breast fillets, skinned and cut into 2¹/₂ cm/1in cubes

Satay sauce
1 teaspoon vegetable oil
2 large cloves garlic, crushed
2 teaspoons finely grated fresh ginger
1 cup/250mL/8fl oz chicken stock
1 cup/250mL/8fl oz coconut milk
1 tablespoon soy sauce
2 tablespoons crunchy peanut butter
2 teaspoons sweet chilli sauce

lamb
and almond pilau

Method:

1 Heat olive and vegetable oils together in a large saucepan over a low heat, add onions and cook, stirring frequently, for 10 minutes or until onions are golden. Remove from pan and set aside.

2 Increase heat to high and cook lamb in batches for 4-5 minutes or until lamb is well browned. Remove lamb from pan and set aside.

3 Wash rice under cold running water until water runs clears. Drain well. Add rice to pan and cook, stirring constantly, for 5 minutes. Slowly stir boiling stock into pan. Add thyme, oregano and black pepper to taste, then reduce heat, cover pan with a tight-fitting lid and simmer for 20 minutes or until all liquid is absorbed. Return lamb and onions to pan, cover and cook for 5 minutes longer.

4 Remove pan from heat and using a fork fluff up rice mixture. Sprinkle with raisins and almonds and serve.

Note: When cooking pilau it is important that the lid fits tightly on the pan. If the lid does not fit the pan tightly, first cover with aluminium foil, then with the lid.

Serves 6

ingredients

2 tablespoons olive oil
2 tablespoons vegetable oil
3 onions, quartered
500g/1 lb lean diced lamb
1 cup/220g/7oz long-grain rice
**3 cups/750mL/1 ¼ pt boiling
chicken or beef stock**
1 teaspoon dried thyme
1 teaspoon dried oregano
freshly ground black pepper
125g/4oz raisins
60g/2oz whole almonds, roasted

mongolian
lamb

Photograph page 189

ingredients

2 tablespoons vegetable oil
**500g/1 lb lamb fillet, cut into
paper-thin slices**
2 onions, cut into 8 wedges
4 spring onions, chopped
3 cloves garlic, crushed
**2 small fresh red chillies, seeded
and chopped**
1 tablespoon chopped fresh coriander

<u>Mongolian sauce</u>
2¹/₂ teaspoons cornflour
1¹/₂ tablespoons light soy sauce
1 tablespoon oyster sauce
¹/₂ cup/125mL/4fl oz chicken stock

Method:

1 *To make sauce, place cornflour in a small bowl, then stir in soy sauce, oyster sauce and stock. Set aside.*

2 *Heat oil in a wok or frying pan over a medium heat, add lamb and stir-fry for 3-4 minutes or until it just changes colour. Remove lamb from pan and set aside.*

3 *Add onions to pan and stir-fry for 2-3 minutes. Add spring onions, garlic and chillies and stir-fry for 2 minutes.*

4 *Return lamb to pan, add sauce and cook, stirring, for 2-3 minutes or until mixture thickens slightly. Sprinkle with coriander and serve immediately.*

Note: *When handling fresh chillies do not put your hands near your eyes or allow them to touch your lips. To avoid discomfort you might like to wear rubber gloves. Bottled minced chillies, available from supermarkets and Oriental food shops, are a convenient product that can be substituted for fresh chillies.*

Serves 4

chinese
pork and spring onions

Photograph page 189

ingredients

500g/1 lb pork fillet
3 tablespoons vegetable oil
4 spring onions, thinly sliced
1 red chilli, seeded and diced
1 tablespoon soy sauce
1 teaspoon sherry

<u>Marinade</u>
1 tablespoon cornflour
2 cloves garlic, crushed
1 tablespoon soy sauce
2 teaspoons sugar

Method:

1 *Using a sharp knife, cut pork across the grain into 5mm/¹/₄in thick slices. Place pork between sheets of greaseproof paper and pound lightly to tenderise and flatten.*

2 *To make marinade, place cornflour, garlic, soy sauce and sugar in a bowl and mix to combine. Add pork, toss to coat and marinate at room temperature for 20 minutes.*

3 *Heat oil in a wok or frying pan over a high heat, add pork and stir-fry for 5 minutes or until pork is tender.*

4 *Add spring onions, chilli, soy sauce and sherry and stir-fry for 1-2 minutes. Serve immediately.*

Note: *For a complete meal accompany with steamed vegetables of your choice and boiled rice or Oriental noodles.*

Serves 4

*snapper with lemon
and coriander*

fast food

from the barbecue

Quick cooking on the barbecue to feed

family and friends involves easy preparation with the many new sauces and marinades available today. Food in this chapter are all cooked over direct heat and take 4-16 mins to cook on flat-top barbecues, chargrills or on a hot-plate.

barbecue
lemon sardines

Method:

1 Place sardines in a bowl with salt and black pepper to taste. Add lemon juice and oil and lightly mix to coat. Set aside to marinate for 30 minutes.

2 Drain and roll sardines in breadcrumbs, pressing firmly to coat. Place on a piece of greased aluminium foil on the grill rack or hotplate over hot coals and cook for 2-3 minutes on each side, or until cooked through and golden. Sprinkle with parsley and serve immediately with lemon quarters.

Note: Look for small sardines about 10cm/4in long and cook them whole. If using larger fish, remove the heads, slit the stomach and remove entrails before cooking.

Serves 4

ingredients

**24 fresh sardines, cleaned
salt
freshly ground black pepper
3 tablespoons lemon juice
60ml/2fl oz vegetable or olive oil
60g/2oz breadcrumbs, made from stale bread
chopped fresh parsley for garnish
3 lemons, quartered to serve**

snapper fillets
with lemon and coriander

Photograph page 191

Method:

1 Mix the first 5 ingredients together in a shallow dish. Place the fillets in the dish and turn to coat well. Cover and stand 10-15 minutes.

2 Heat the barbecue to medium/hot and oil the grill bars. Place a sheet of baking paper over the bars and make a few slashes between the grill bars to allow ventilation. Place the fish on the paper and cook for 3-4 minutes each side according to thickness. Brush with marinade during cooking. Remove to plate. Heat any remaining marinade and pour over the fish.

Tip: Fish is cooked, if when tested with a fork, it flakes or the sections pull away. Lingfish, Haddock and Perch may also be used.

Serves 4

ingredients

**1 teaspoon chopped fresh ginger
1 teaspoon crushed garlic
2 tablespoons finely chopped coriander
2 tablespoon olive oil
1¹/₂ tablespoon lemon juice
500g/1lb snapper fillets (4 portions)**

perfect
t-bone steak

Method:

1 Bring the steaks to room temperate. Mix garlic, oil and salt and pepper together. Rub onto both sides of the steak. Stand for 10-15 minutes at room temperature.

2 Heat the barbecue until hot and oil the grill bars. Arrange the steaks and sear for one minute each side. Move steaks to cooler part of the barbecue to continue cooking over moderate heat, or turn heat down. If heat cannot be reduced then elevate on a wire cake-rack placed on the grill bars. Cook until desired level is achieved. Total time 5-6 minutes for rare, 7-10 minutes for medium and 10-14 minutes for well done. Turn during cooking.

3 Serve on a heated steak plate and top with a dollop of garlic butter. Serve with jacket potatoes.

Note: Many a time this delicious steak has been ruined on the barbecue.

Cook on all barbecues and improvise a hood if using a flat-top barbecue.

Serves 4

ingredients

4 T-bone steaks
2 teaspoons crushed garlic
2 teaspoons oil
salt and pepper

Garlic Butter
60g/2oz butter
1 teaspoon crushed garlic
1 tablespoon parsley flakes
2 teaspoons lemon juice
mix all ingredients together and serve in a pot with a spoon

skewered
chicken liver in coriander

Method:

1 *Place coriander, crushed garlic, chopped ginger oil and lemon juice in a bowl. Cut chicken livers into 2 through centre membrane and carefully stir into the coriander marinade. Cover and refrigerate for I hour or more.*

2 *Cut each bacon strip into 3 approximately 10cm/4in strips. Wrap a strip of bacon around each halved liver and secure with a toothpick.*

3 *Heat the barbecue until hot. Place on overturned wire cake-rack over the grill bars. Arrange the skewered livers on the rack. Cook for 8-10 minutes, turning frequently and brushing with any remaining marinade. Serve as finger food.*

Note: *Cook on any flat-top barbecue or electric barbecue grill.*

**Yields approximately
22 skewers**

ingredients

**2 finely chopped coriander
I teaspoon crushed garlic
I teaspoon chopped
fresh ginger
2 teaspoons oil
I tablespoon lemon juice
250g/8oz chicken livers
6 rashers bacon
toothpicks**

cajun
cutlets

Method:

1. Beat the butter to soften and mix in 1½ teaspoons of the cajun seasoning and the chopped chilli. Place butter along the centre of a piece of plastic wrap or greaseproof paper to one centimetre thickness. Fold plastic wrap over the butter then roll up. Smooth into a sausage shape and twist ends. Refrigerate to firm.

2. Trim the cutlets if necessary and snip the membrane at the side to prevent curling. Flatten slightly with the side of a meat mallet. Mix together 1½ teaspoons of the Cajun Seasoning and olive oil then rub mixture well into both sides of the cutlets. Place in a single layer onto a tray, cover and stand 20 minutes at room temperature, or longer in the refrigerator.

3. Heat the barbecue or electric barbecue grill to high. Place a sheet of baking paper on the grill bars, making a few slashes between the bars for ventilation. Place cutlets on grill and cook for 3 minutes each side for medium and 4 minutes for well-done. When cooked, transfer to a serving plate and top each cutlet with a round slice of Cajun butter. Serve immediately with vegetable accompaniments.

Note: Suitable for all barbecues. Ideal for electric grill/barbecue.

ingredients

125g/4oz butter
3 teaspoons Cajun seasoning
1 small red chilli, seeded and chopped
12 lamb cutlets
1 tablespoon olive oil

skewered
garlic shrimp

Method:

1 Place soy sauce, oil, lemon juice, onion and garlic in a large deep bowl and mix well. Add shrimp, turning to coat in mixture, and marinate for at least 2 hours.

2 Drain shrimp, reserving marinade. Thread onto pre-soaked bamboo skewers alternately with spring onions and little sprigs of herbs. Cook over hot coals, brushing often with marinade, for 5-6 minutes, depending on size of shrimp, or until tender.

Serves 4

ingredients

125ml/4fl oz light soy sauce
125ml/4fl oz vegetable oil
125ml/4fl oz lemon juice
1 small onion, finely chopped
3 cloves garlic, chopped
1kg/2lb uncooked shrimp, shelled and deveined, tails left intact
6 spring onions, cut into 2¹/₂cm/1in lengths
fresh oregano or thyme sprigs

teriyaki
shrimp

Method:

1 Shell and devein shrimp, leaving tail shells intact, or leave them in their shells, split each down the back and remove the vein. Place shrimp in a deep bowl.

2 To make marinade, place soy sauce, oil, garlic, ginger, orange rind, sherry and brandy in a bowl, mix well and pour over prawns. Set aside to marinate for 2-3 hours, turning prawns occasionally.

3 Thread shrimp onto pre-soaked bamboo skewers and cook over hot coals for 3-5 minutes or until they turn red and shells are opaque and crispy. Serve with remaining marinade for dipping.

Note: Shrimp grilled in the shell untilthey turn crunchy are wonderful eaten shell and all. Provide finger bowls and plenty of paper napkins.

Serves 4

ingredients

750g/1¹/₂lb uncooked shrimp

Ginger Sherry Marinade
125ml/4fl oz light soy sauce
60ml/2fl oz peanut oil
2 cloves garlic, crushed
2 tablespoons grated fresh ginger
small strip orange rind, finely shredded
2 tablespoons dry sherry
2 tablespoons brandy

barbecued
lamb pitta breads

Method:

1 *Combine lemon rind, cumin and oil. Rub surface of lamb with oil mixture. Place in a shallow glass or ceramic dish and marinate at room temperature for 30 minutes.*

2 *Preheat barbecue to a medium heat. Place lamb on lightly oiled barbecue grill and cook for 3-5 minutes each side or until lamb is tender and cooked to your liking.*

3 *Warm pitta breads on barbecue for 1-2 minutes each side. Split each pitta bread to make pocket, then spread with hummus and fill with endive, tabbouleh and sliced lamb.*

Note: *For extra flavor serve with a spoonful of your favourite chutney.*

Serves 6

ingredients

1 tablespoon finely grated lemon rind
1 teaspoon ground cumin
1 tablespoon olive oil
750g/1¹/₂lb lamb fillets
6 pitta bread rounds
6 tablespoons ready made hummus
1 bunch curly endive
250g/8oz ready-made tabbouleh

toasted
steak sandwiches

Method:

1 Cut the topside steak into 4 or 5 pieces and pound with a meat mallet until thin. Place in a non-metal container. Mix the lemon juice, garlic, salt, pepper and oil together and pour over the steaks. Turn to coat both sides and marinate for 30 minutes at room temperature, or longer in the refrigerator.

2 Soften the butter and spread a thin coating on both sides of the bread. If desired mix a little garlic into the butter.

3 Heat barbecue until hot and oil the grill bars and hotplate. Place onions on the hotplate. Toss and drizzle with a little oil as they cook. When beginning to soften, push to one side and turn occasionally with tongs. Place toast on hotplate and cook until golden on both sides. Place steaks on grill bars and cook 2 minutes on each side.

4 Assemble sandwiches as food cooks by placing steak and onions on one slice of toast, topping with a good squirt of steak sauce and closing with second slice of toast.

Note: A great favorite for backyard barbecue gatherings or fun family meals. Flat-top barbecues, hot-plates or kettle barbecues are best. May also be cooked on electric barbecue grills. For each sandwich allow 90g/3oz of raw steak per serve.

Yields 5 sandwiches

ingredients

500g/1lb topside steak
2 tablespoons lemon juice
1 teaspoon crushed garlic
salt and pepper
1 tablespoon oil
butter for spreading
10 slices toasted bread
2 large onions, thinly sliced
1 tablespoon oil
steak sauce of choice

barbecued
chicken and mushroom patties

Method:

1 Place ground chicken meat in a large bowl and add remaining ingredients except oil. Mix well to combine ingredients, then knead a little with one hand to make the meat fine in texture. With wet hands, shape into 4 or 5 flat patties.

2 Heat barbecue or grill to medium-high. Spray grill bars or rack with a little oil and place on the patties. Cook for 8 minutes on each side or until cooked through. Patties are cooked when juices run clear after being pricked with a skewer.

Serve hot with vegetable accompaniments.

Note: For quick preparation place onion, parsley and mushrooms in a food processor and chop together. May be cooked on flat-top barbecue, electric table grill or conventional gas or electric grill.

ingredients

500g/1lb ground chicken meat
$^1/_2$ cup dried breadcrumbs
1 medium onion, chopped
$^1/_2$ teaspoon salt
$^1/_2$ teaspoon pepper
2 tablespoons lemon juice
2 tablespoons chopped parsley
$^1/_2$ cup finely chopped mushrooms
vegetable oil

chicken nut stir-fry

wok cooking

As the wok has become almost standard

in many Western kitchens, so its uses have changed. The recipes in this book reflect these changes and tempt the cook with a selection of interesting and exciting tastes.

indonesian
chilli beef

Method:

1 Place vermicelli in a bowl, pour over enough hot water to cover and soak for 10 minutes. Drain, set aside and keep warm.

2 Heat oil in a large frying pan or wok over a medium heat, add beef, onion, chilli, garlic and black pepper to taste and stir-fry for 5 minutes, or until beef is cooked through.

3 Arrange vermicelli on serving plates and sprinkle with cucumber. Spoon meat over cucumber, sprinkle with peanuts and serve.

Note: Rice vermicelli (or cellophane noodles) do not require cooking after soaking, as the soaking is sufficient to rehydrate and tenderise.

Serves 4

ingredients

200g/6¹/₂oz rice vermicelli
1 tablespoon peanut oil
250g/8oz rump steak, thinly sliced
1 onion, quartered
1 fresh red chilli, finely chopped
2 cloves garlic, crushed
freshly ground black pepper
¹/₂ cucumber, peeled, seeded and diced
45g/1¹/₂oz roasted peanuts

chicken
and nut stir-fry

Photograph page 201

Method:

1 To make sauce, place marmalade, stock and lime juice in a bowl and mix to combine. Set aside.

2 Heat oil in a wok over a medium heat, add onion and ginger and stir-fry for 3 minutes or until onion is golden. Increase heat to high, add chicken and stir-fry for 5 minutes or until chicken is brown. Remove chicken mixture from wok, set aside and keep warm.

3 Add pear to wok and stir-fry for 3 minutes or until golden. Return chicken mixture to wok, add sauce and stir-fry for 3 minutes or until sauce thickens slightly. Season to taste with black pepper. Scatter with nuts and coriander and serve immediately.

Note: This stir-fry can be made using other nut oils and nuts. You might like to try walnut oil and walnuts or almond oil and almonds. Nut oils are available from larger supermarkets and specialty delicatessens.

Serves 4

ingredients

1 tablespoon macadamia or vegetable oil
1 onion, cut into eighths
2 tablespoons finely grated fresh ginger
4 boneless chicken breast fillets, thinly sliced
1 pear, peeled, cored and cut into thick slices
freshly ground black pepper
60g/2oz macadamias or Brazil nuts, chopped
2 tablespoons fresh coriander leaves

Ginger lime sauce
1 tablespoon ginger lime marmalade
¹/₂ cup/125mL/4fl oz chicken stock
1 tablespoon lime juice

warm
thai lamb salad

Method:

1 *To make dressing, place coriander, sugar, soy and chilli sauces, lime juice and fish sauce in a bowl and mix to combine. Set aside.*
2 *Arrange lettuce leaves and cucumber on a serving platter and set aside.*
3 *Heat oil in a wok over a high heat, add lamb and stir-fry for 2 minutes or until brown. Place lamb on top of lettuce leaves, drizzle with dressing and serve immediately.*
   Note: *This salad is also delicious made with pork fillet. Use a vegetable peeler to make long thin slices of cucumber - simply peel off lengthwise strips.*

Serves 4

ingredients

250g/8oz assorted lettuce leaves
I cucumber, sliced lengthwise into thin strips
2 teaspoons vegetable oil
500g/I lb lamb fillets, trimmed of all visible fat, thinly sliced

Coriander and chilli dressing
2 tablespoons chopped fresh coriander
I tablespoon brown sugar
¹/₄ cup/60mL/2fl oz soy sauce
2 tablespoons sweet chilli sauce
2 tablespoons lime juice
2 teaspoons fish sauce

wilted
arugula (rocket) cheese salad

Method:

1 Heat 2 tablespoons oil in a wok over a medium heat, add bread and stir-fry for 3 minutes or until golden. Drain on absorbent kitchen paper.

2 Heat remaining oil in wok, add spring onions and garlic and stir-fry for 2 minutes. Add zucchini (courgettes), red pepper (capsicum) and raisins and stir-fry for 3 minutes or until vegetables are just tender. Remove from wok and set aside.

3 Add arugula (rocket) to wok and stir-fry for 2 minutes or until rocket just wilts. Place arugula (rocket) on a serving platter or divide between individual bowls or plates, top with vegetable mixture and scatter with croûtons and blue cheese. Drizzle with balsamic vinegar and serve immediately.

Note: If arugula (rocket) is unavailable this salad is also delicious made with English spinach or watercress.

Serves 4

ingredients

3 tablespoons olive oil
4 slices white bread, crusts removed and cut into cubes
3 spring onions, sliced diagonally
2 cloves garlic, crushed
2 zucchini (courgettes), cut lengthwise into thin strips
1 red pepper (capsicum), thinly sliced
1/2 cup/90g/3oz raisins
2 bunches/250g/8oz arugula (rocket)
125g/4oz blue cheese, crumbled
2 tablespoons balsamic vinegar

bacon
and herb omelette

Method:

1 Heat oil in a wok over a medium heat, add leeks and bacon and stir-fry for 5 minutes or until bacon is crisp. Transfer leek mixture to a bowl, add parsley, basil and oregano and mix to combine. Set aside.

2 Place eggs, milk, cheese and black pepper to taste in a bowl and whisk to combine. Pour one-quarter of the egg mixture into wok and swirl so mixture covers base and sides. Top with one-quarter of the leek mixture and cook for 1 minute or until set. Remove from wok, roll up and place on a slice of toast. Repeat with remaining mixture to make 4 omelettes.

Note: Fresh mint can be used in place of the oregano if you wish. For a vegetarian version omit the bacon and replace with well-drained cooked spinach. Squeeze as much moisture as possible from the spinach before making the omelette.

Serves 4

ingredients

2 teaspoons vegetable oil
2 leeks, chopped
6 rashers bacon, chopped
2 tablespoons chopped fresh parsley
2 tablespoons chopped fresh basil
2 tablespoons chopped fresh oregano
6 eggs, lightly beaten
1/2 cup/125mL/4fl oz milk
60g/2oz grated tasty cheese (mature Cheddar)
freshly ground black pepper
4 thick slices wholemeal or grain bread, toasted

balsamic
pork stir-fry

Method:

1 Heat oil in a wok over a high heat, add garlic and stir-fry for 1 minute or until golden. Add pork and stir-fry for 3 minutes or until brown. Add red pepper (capsicum), green pepper (capsicum), orange juice and vinegar and stir-fry for 3 minutes or until pork is cooked. Season to taste with black pepper.

2 Divide rocket or watercress between serving plates, then top with pork mixture. Serve immediately.

Note: Balsamic vinegar is a dark red wine vinegar. Once a delicatessen item, in recent years it has become increasingly popular and can now be purchased from many supermarkets.

Serves 4

ingredients

2 teaspoons olive oil
2 cloves garlic, crushed
500g/1 lb pork fillet, trimmed of all
visible fat, cut into 1cm/¹/₂in thick slices
1 red pepper (capsicum), chopped
1 green pepper (capsicum), chopped
¹/₂ cup/125mL/4fl oz orange juice
¹/₄ cup/60mL/2fl oz balsamic vinegar
freshly ground black pepper
1 bunch/125g/4oz rocket
or watercress leaves

plum
and chilli beef stir fry

Method:

1 Trim beef of any excess fat. Slice into thin strips across the grain. Put large saucepan of water on to boil for noodles.
2 Heat oil in a wok of frypan. Stir fry garlic and onion 1 minute. Add beef in two batches, stir fry 2-3 minutes. Add zucchini (courgette) and capsicum (pepper) stir fry 2 minutes.
3 Add combined ground ginger, chilli sauce, plum sauce and cornflour to beef vegetables and corn. Cook 2-3 minutes.
4 Meanwhile, cook noodles in boiling water 2-3 minutes.
5 Serve beef stir fry with noodles

Serves 4-6

ingredients

750g/1 1/2lb lean steak
2 teaspoons olive oil
2 teaspoons freshly crushed garlic
1 onion, cut in wedges, petals separated
1 large zucchini (courgette),
sliced diagonally
1 red capsicum (pepper), cut into
2 1/2cm/1 in cubes
1/4 teaspoon ground ginger
1-2 teaspoons hot chilli sauce
1/2 cup plum sauce
2 teaspoons cornflour
440g/14oz can baby corn, drained
375g/12oz rice noodles

stir-fry
chilli shrimp

Method:

1 *Heat vegetable and sesame oils together in a wok over a medium heat, add garlic and chillies and stir-fry for 1 minute. Add shrimp and stir-fry for 2 minutes or until they change colour.*

2 *Stir in sugar, tomato juice and soy sauce and stir-fry, for 3 minutes or until sauce is heated through.*
   Note: *For a complete meal, serve shrimp with boiled rice or noodles of your choice and stir-fried vegetables.*
   Serves 4

ingredients

1 teaspoon vegetable oil
1 teaspoon sesame oil
3 cloves garlic, crushed
3 fresh red chillies, chopped
1 kg/2 lb uncooked medium shrimp,
shelled and deveined
1 tablespoon brown sugar
$^1/_3$ cup/90mL/3fl oz tomato juice
1 tablespoon soy sauce

stir-fry
lime wings

Method:

1 Place chicken wings in a flat non-metal container. Combine lime juice, vinegar, sugar and soy sauce and pour over the wings, turn into coat. Marinate for 30 minutes or longer.

2 Heat the wok, add oil and heat. Remove wings from marinade and stir-fry about 15 minutes until brown and tender. Add shallots and stir-fry one minute then pour in the marinade. Stir to coat and heat through. Remove to a platter.

3 Add the lime slices and water to the wok. Allow to simmer to tenderise the slices. Stir in the sugar and vinegar and cook until the slices are coated with a thick syrup. Remove and arrange over and between the wings. Pour over any remaining syrup. Serve as finger food or as a meal with rice and vegetables.

Yields 12 pieces

ingredients

1kg/2lb chicken wings, tips removed
$^1/_4$ cup lime juice
1 tablespoon white wine vinegar
2 tablespoons brown sugar
2 teaspoons soy sauce

Soy sauce
2 tablespoons canola oil
$^1/_4$ cup sliced shallots

Garnish
2 limes, thinly sliced
$^1/_2$ cup water
$^1/_4$ cup white sugar
$^1/_2$ teaspoon white wine vinegar

*fish fillets with yoghurt
marinade*

microwave
cooking

In this chapter you will find recipes

*that save you time and dishes that are every bit
as good as if they were cooked conventionally – in
fact most are better. It is also all about showing
you how to make the most of your microwave and
use it to its full potential.*

couscous
marrakesh

Method:

1 *Place couscous in a microwavable bowl, pour over stock and toss with a fork. Cover and stand for 5 minutes or until liquid is absorbed.*

2 *Place spring onions and oil in a separate microwavable bowl, cover with a microwavable plate and set aside.*

3 *Place squash or zucchini (courgettes) in a clean microwavable plastic bag. Twist neck of bag and fold under vegetables to seal. Place bag on plate on top of bowl and cook on High (100%) for 5 minutes.*

4 *Add spring onions, squash or zucchini (courgettes), prunes, nuts, orange rind and orange juice to couscous and mix to combine. Cover and cook on Medium (50%) for 4 minutes or until heated through.*

Note: *The microwave is handy for heating savoury couscous dishes through before serving ensuring they are hot, but not dry or burnt. Serve with a lamb or chicken casserole, roast meat or as a vegetable dish for a vegetarian meal.*

Serves 4

ingredients

1 cup/185g/6oz couscous
1 cup/250mL/8fl oz boiling chicken or vegetable stock, made with stock cubes
3 spring onions, sliced
1 tablespoon olive oil
125g/4oz yellow squash, cut into wedges or zucchini (courgettes), sliced
12 dessert prunes, pitted and quartered
60g/2oz pistachio nuts, coarsely chopped
2 teaspoons finely grated orange rind
2 tablespoons orange juice

fish
fillets with yogurt marinade

Photograph page 211

Method:

1 *To make marinade, place yogurt, chilli sauce, coriander and chilli in a bowl and mix to combine. Place fish fillets in a shallow glass or ceramic dish, spoon over marinade, cover and marinate in the refrigerator for at least 3 hours.*

2 *Place fish in a shallow microwavable dish, with thickest parts of fillets towards edge of dish. Spoon over any remaining marinade, cover and cook on Medium (50%) for 4 minutes. To serve, place fillets on serving plates, stir sauce and spoon over fish.*

Note: *Delicious served with savory couscous, snow peas (mangetout) and carrots.*

Serves 2

ingredients

2 fillets cod or similar fish, skinned

Yogurt chilli marinade
2/3 cup/140g/4 1/2oz natural yogurt
2 tablespoons sweet chilli sauce
2 tablespoons chopped fresh coriander
1 fresh red chilli, seeded and finely chopped

tandoori
shrimp rolls

Method:

1 Place tandoori paste and 1 tablespoon yogurt in a bowl and mix to combine. Add shrimp and toss to coat. Cover and marinate in the refrigerator for at least 1 hour or up to 24 hours.

2 Place shrimp, like numbers on a clock face with the thickest part towards the edge, on a microwave dinner plate and cook on High (100%) for 1 minute, then on Medium (50%) for 1-2 minutes or until shrimp change color and are cooked.

3 Heat naan bread on Defrost (30%) for 1 minute. Place 6 shrimp along centre of each naan bread, top with cucumber and 2 tablespoons yogurt, roll up and serve immediately.

Note: A delicious snack, perfect for a weekend lunch or supper on the run. The longer you marinate the shrimp the more robust the flavor. Take care not to overcook the shrimp or they will become tough.

Serves 2

ingredients

3 tablespoons tandoori paste
natural yogurt
12 large uncooked shrimp,
shelled and deveined
2 naan bread
4 tablespoons coarsely chopped
cucumber

peanut
beef curry

Method:

1 Place oil, onion, garlic and chilli in a microwavable casserole dish, cover and cook on High (100%) for 3 minutes.
2 Stir in beef, satay sauce, coconut milk and lemon juice, cover and cook for 5 minutes.
3 Add green beans and red pepper (capsicum), stir, cover and cook on Medium (50%) for 5 minutes or until vegetables are tender crisp.

Note: For a complete meal serve with brown or white rice or Oriental noodles.

Serves 4

ingredients

1 tablespoon peanut (groundnut) oil
1 onion, finely chopped
2 cloves garlic, crushed
1 teaspoon finely chopped fresh red chilli
500g/1 lb rump steak or silverside,
cut into thin strips
220g/7oz bottled satay stir-fry sauce
1/2 cup/125mL/4fl oz coconut milk
2 tablespoons lemon juice
250g/8oz green beans, halved
1 red pepper (capsicum), thinly sliced

Method:

1 Place eggplant (aubergine), garlic and dressing in a bowl and mix to combine.

2 Place veal around edge of a microwavable casserole dish and place eggplant (aubergine) in the centre, cover and cook on High (100%) for 3 minutes.

3 Stir in sauce, cover and cook on Medium (50%) for 5 minutes, stir, then cook for 5 minutes longer or until veal is cooked. Scatter with olives and serve immediately.

Note: This is a quick version of a classic recipe which uses a good quality processed sauce to save time. For a complete meal serve with pasta, noodles or rice and a tossed green salad.

Serves 4

veal
cacciatore

ingredients

**1 eggplant (aubergine), cut into
1cm/¹/₂in cubes
1 clove garlic, crushed
¹/₃ cup/90mL/3fl oz French dressing
4 thin slices veal steak or schnitzel
(escalopes), cut into thin strips
500mL/16fl oz jar cacciatore or similar
tomato pasta sauce
8 green olives, sliced**

hot
potato salad

Method:

1 Using a sharp knife score around the circumference of each potato.

2 Place potatoes evenly around edge of turntable and cook on High (100%) for 5 minutes, turn over and cook for 3-5 minutes longer or until potatoes are cooked. Set aside until cool enough to handle, then remove skin and cut potatoes into 1cm/1/2in cubes.

3 Place onion and bacon in a microwavable bowl, cover and cook on High (100%) for 3 minutes, stir, then cook for 2 minutes longer.

4 Stir in cornflour, stock and vinegar, cover and cook for 4 minutes. Add mustard, cream and potatoes and mix gently to combine. Cover and cook on Medium (50%) for 2 minutes or until hot. Season to taste with black pepper and sprinkle with chives. Serve warm.

Note: This is a good hot dish to serve at a salad buffet or barbecue. Flat oval-shaped potatoes seem to cook the most evenly in the microwave.

Serves 6

ingredients

**4 red-skinned potatoes, about 750g/1¹/₂ lb
1 onion, diced
2 rashers bacon, chopped
2 tablespoons cornflour
1 cup/250mL/8fl oz vegetable stock
¹/₄ cup/60mL/2fl oz cider or tarragon vinegar
2 tablespoons wholegrain mustard
¹/₃ cup/90mL/3fl oz cream (heavy)
freshly ground black pepper
snipped fresh chives**

Method:

1 To make stuffing, place butter and spring onions in a small microwavable bowl, cover with a piece of absorbent kitchen paper and cook on High (100%) for 2 minutes. Add spinach, breadcrumbs and black pepper to taste and mix to combine. Unroll loin and spread with stuffing. Reroll and tie securely with kitchen string.

2 To make glaze, place mustard, barbecue sauce and tomato sauce in a bowl, mix to combine and brush over lamb.

3 Heat a microwave browning dish on High (100%) for 3 minutes. Place lamb in centre of dish and roll to brown outside and to seal. Cook on HIGH (100%) for 3 minutes, then on Medium (50%) for 9 minutes. Alternatively, brown meat in a frying pan then transfer to a microwavable dish and cook as directed.

4 Cover lamb with aluminium foil and stand for 5 minutes.

Note: Select symetrically shaped joints without bones for even cooking and trim off as much fat as possible. A marinade or glaze helps to give the meat an appetising appearance. Serve lamb with mint jelly or sauce, carrots and creamy mashed potatoes.

Serves 2-3

stuffed
loin of lamb

ingredients

500g/1 lb boned and rolled loin of lamb, trimmed of all visible fat

Spinach stuffing
15g/¹/₂oz butter
8 spring onions, thinly sliced
125g/4oz cooked spinach, well drained
1 slice wholemeal bread, crumbed
freshly ground black pepper

Mustard glaze
1 tablespoon wholegrain mustard
1 tablespoon barbecue sauce
1 tablespoon tomato sauce

chocolate
shortcake

Method:

1 Melt chocolate in a microwavable bowl on Defrost (30%) for 2 minutes, stir, then heat for 2 minutes longer. Continue in this way for 6-8 minutes longer or until chocolate is completely melted.

2 Stir shortbread into chocolate, then add sour cream or cream, almonds or hazelnuts and liqueur, if using, and mix well to combine.

3 Press mixture in a base-lined and buttered 18cm/7in diameter round cake tin and chill until firm.

Note: This is a quick and slick treat for chocoholics who don't want to spend a lot of time in the kitchen. Serve cut into wedges for morning coffee or afternoon tea or with sugared berries for a simple dessert.

Makes an 18cm/7in round cake

ingredients

200g/6¹/₂oz dark cooking chocolate, broken into small pieces
100g/3¹/₂oz shortbread finger biscuits, cut into chunky pieces
¹/₂ cup/125g/4oz sour cream or
¹/₂ cup/125mL/4fl oz cream (heavy)
¹/₂ cup/60g/2oz ground almonds or hazelnuts
I tablespoon orange-flavoured or whiskey liqueur (optional)

rhubarb
and strawberry crumble

Method:

1 Place rhubarb into a microwavable dish, sprinkle with sugar, cover and cook on High (100%) for 3 minutes, stir, then cook for 2 minutes longer. Scatter strawberries over cooked rhubarb.

2 To make topping, place flour and butter in a food processor and process for 30 seconds or until mixture resembles fine breadcrumbs. Add muesli, wheat germ, burghul (cracked wheat) and nutmeg and using the pulse process briefly to combine.

3 Sprinkle topping over fruit and cook on Medium (50%) for 5 minutes.

Note: Stewed rhubarb and fresh strawberries are a delicious and colorful combination in this superb dessert. Serve crumble hot with thick cream, vanilla ice cream or mascarpone.

Serves 6

ingredients

500g/1 lb rhubarb, trimmed and pink parts only cut into ¹/₂cm/1 in pieces
¹/₄ cup/45g/1¹/₂oz brown sugar
250g/8oz strawberries, quartered or halved

Muesli crumble topping
¹/₂ cup/75g/2¹/₂oz wholemeal flour
60g/2oz unsalted butter, cubed
¹/₂ cup/100g/3¹/₂oz toasted muesli
1 tablespoon wheat germ
1 tablespoon burghul (cracked wheat)
¹/₂ teaspoon ground nutmeg

microwave
essentials

The microwave is great for all those little jobs that are time consuming when done conventionally. Use these hints and tips to make the most of your microwave and to save time when preparing meals.

Jam or honey:
Melt for use in cooking. Remove lid from jar. Place jar in microwave and cook on HIGH (100%) for 20-30 seconds or until melted. The jam or honey can now be easily measured.

Ice cream:
To soften hard ice cream for serving, place ice cream container in microwave and cook on MEDIUM (50%) for 1 minute. Remove from microwave and allow to stand for a few minutes before removing scoops.

Butter or cream cheese:
To soften butter or cream cheese, cook on DEFROST (30%) for 40-60 seconds.

Pastry Cream and Hollandaise Sauce:
Egg-based sauces are easy to make in the microwave. Cook on MEDIUM (50%), stirring frequently during cooking until sauce thickens slightly. Remove sauce when cooking is almost complete. The sauce will finish cooking if you allow it to stand.

Stale bread:
Freshen stale bread by wrapping in absorbent kitchen paper and cooking on HIGH (100%) for 20-30 seconds.

Even cooking:
Arrange food so that the thicker portions are on the outside of turntable and thinner portions towards the centre. You will find that the food will cook more evenly.

Covering:
To cover or not to cover. Generally, food that requires covering for conventional cooking will also need to be covered for microwave cooking. Most food requires covering when reheating.

Defrosting:
Pack meat or chicken cuts in single layers to freeze. Thaw in the microwave on DEFROST (30%). Remove thawed cuts, then continue to microwave until remaining cuts are defrosted.

Instant Hot Dog:
Make three slashes across frankfurt and place in a buttered roll. Wrap roll in absorbent kitchen paper and cook on HIGH (100%) for 30 seconds.

Plump up dried fruits:
When cooking cakes and puddings use the microwave to plump up the fruit. For 500g dried fruit, place fruit in a large microwave-safe dish, add 1 cup (250 mL) water, cover and cook on HIGH (100%) for 3-4 minutes, or until fruit is no longer dried. Stir and set aside to stand for 30 minutes or until cool enough to complete recipe.

Melting chocolate:
Break chocolate into small pieces and place in a microwave-safe jug. Cook on HIGH (100%) for 1-2 minutes per 200g of chocolate. Stir frequently during cooking.

Plastic containers and plastic food wrap:
Only use containers and plastic food wraps marked microwave safe.

Peeling tomatoes:
Score skin of tomatoes with a sharp knife, then cook on HIGH (100%) for 10-15 seconds per tomato.

Microwaved vegetables:
Vegetables cooked in the microwave retain more of their colour and nutrients, because of the quicker cooking time and small quantity of water used.

Stale potato chips:
Revive these by placing on absorbent kitchen paper and cooking on HIGH (100%) for 30 seconds, set aside and allow to cool.

Speedy roast dinner:
To shorten the cooking time of a roast dinner but still achieve a crispy result, start the cooking in the microwave, then transfer to the oven to complete. For a 1.5 kg chicken, cook in the microwave on HIGH (100%) for 15 minutes, then bake in oven at 220°C for 30 minutes or until golden. For 8 potatoes, cook in the microwave on HIGH (100%) for 6 minutes, then bake in oven at 220°C for 20-30 minutes or until tender and crisp.

Juicier fruit:
Get more juice from your fruit by warming on HIGH (100%) for 30 seconds per piece of fruit. Set aside to stand for 5 minutes then squeeze.

Standing time:
Larger portions of food, such as whole chickens or roasts require standing time after cooking time is completed. For best results, cover with aluminium foil and stand for 10-15 minutes before slicing. This allows the juices to settle and the heat to equalise.

Quicker cooking:
Food that is at room temperature will cook faster than refrigerated foods. Lighter foods cook more rapidly than dense food; for example, potatoes and pumpkin will take longer to cook than broccoli or eggs.

Toasting of coconut and nuts:
This can be achieved quickly and efficiently in the microwave. For coconut, spread it over a microwave-safe dish and cook on HIGH (100%) for 5-6 minutes, stirring frequently during cooking until golden. Remember coconut can still burn in the microwave if overcooked. To toast nuts, place in a single layer in a microwave-safe dish and cook on HIGH (100%) for 5-6 minutes or until golden. Stir frequently during cooking to prevent burning.

rum raisin nut brownies

quick bakes

The aroma of a freshly baked cake,

the taste of a still warm biscuit and the compliments of family and friends is what quick bakes is all about. Baking has never been simpler, quicker or more fun than with this selection of easy cakes and bakes.

chewy
cookie bars

Method:

1 Place butter and cookie crumbs in a bowl and mix to combine. Press into the base of an 18x28cm/7x11in shallow cake tin and set aside.

2 To make topping, place condensed milk, chocolate chips, coconut, pecans and orange rind in a bowl and mix to combine.

3 Pour topping over base and bake for 30 minutes or until golden. Cool in tin, then cut into bars.

Note: The keeping quality of nuts depends on the amount of oil in them. Always check that nuts are fresh before you buy them; check the use-by date and if possible, buy whole shelled nuts and grind them as needed, keeping the remainder in an airtight container in the refrigerator or freezer.

Makes 24

ingredients

125g/4oz butter, melted
1¹/₂ cups/185g/6oz sweet cookie crumbs

Chewy nut topping
410g/13oz sweetened condensed milk
1¹/₄ cups/220g/7oz chocolate chips
100g/3¹/₂oz shredded coconut
155g/5oz chopped pecans
1 tablespoon finely grated orange rind

Oven temperature 160°C/325°F/Gas 3

rum raisin
nut brownies

Photograph page 223

Method:

1 Place raisins and brandy in a bowl and set aside to soak for 15 minutes or until raisins soften.

2 Place chocolate and butter in a heatproof bowl set over a saucepan of simmering water and heat, stirring constantly, until mixture is smooth. Remove bowl from pan and set aside to cool slightly.

3 Place eggs and brown sugar in a bowl and beat until thick and creamy. Add chocolate mixture, flour, nuts and raisin mixture and mix to combine.

4 Pour mixture into a greased 20 cm/8 in square cake tin and bake for 35 minutes or until firm. Cool brownies in tin. Then cut into squares and dust with icing sugar and drinking chocolate.

Note: For a dinner party dessert top these irresistibly rich and moist brownies with thick cream, a chocolate sauce or berry coulis and a garnish of fresh fruit.

Makes 16

ingredients

75g/2¹/₂oz raisins
¹/₄ cup/60mL/2fl oz brandy
100g/3¹/₂oz dark chocolate, chopped
125g/4oz unsalted butter
2 eggs
³/₄ cup/125g/4oz brown sugar
1 cup/125g/4oz flour, sifted
155g/5oz macadamia or brazil nuts, chopped
icing sugar, sifted
drinking chocolate, sifted

Oven temperature 180°C, 350°F, Gas 4

hazelnut
shortbread

Method:

1 Place butter, flour, hazelnuts and ground rice in a food processor and process until mixture resembles coarse breadcrumbs. Add sugar and process to combine.

2 Turn mixture onto a floured surface and knead lightly to make a pliable dough. Place dough between sheets of baking paper and roll out to 5mm/¹/₄in thick. Using a 5cm/2in fluted cutter, cut out rounds of dough and place 2¹/₂cm/1in apart on greased baking trays. Bake for 20-25 minutes or until lightly browned. Stand on baking trays for 2-3 minutes before transferring to wire racks to cool.

3 Place melted chocolate in a plastic food bag, snip off one corner and pipe lines across each biscuit.

Note: The consistency of chopped or ground nuts is important to the success of a recipe. Ground nuts should be a powder not a paste. Particular care should be taken when using a food processor or grinder as they chop very quickly. When using a food processor use the pulse button and only chop about 60g/2oz at a time. This helps avoid overworking the nuts.

Makes 40

ingredients

250g/8oz butter, chopped
1¹/₂ cups/185g/6oz flour, sifted
45g/1¹/₂oz hazelnuts, ground
¹/₄ cup/45g/1¹/₂oz ground rice
¹/₄ cup/60g/2oz caster sugar
100g/3¹/₂oz chocolate, melted

Oven temperature 160°C/325°F/Gas 3

Oven temperature 180°C, 350°F, Gas 4

easy
banana loaf

ingredients

Method:

1 *Place butter, sugar, brown sugar, eggs, vanilla essence, lemon rind, flour and banana in a bowl and beat for 5 minutes or until mixture is light and smooth.*

2 *Pour mixture into a greased and lined 11x21cm/4¹/₂x8¹/₂in loaf tin and bake for 45 minutes or until loaf is cooked when tested with a skewer. Stand loaf in tin for 5 minutes before turning onto a wire rack to cool.*

Note:*When grating lemon or orange rind, take care not to grate the white pith beneath the skin as it has a bitter unpleasant taste. Grate the rind on a fine-textured grater or use a metal 'zester' tool which consists of a row of tiny holes that cuts and curls fine, long slivers of rind.*

Makes an 11x21cm/4¹/₂x 8¹/₂in loaf

250g/8oz butter, softened
¹/₂ cup/125g/4oz sugar
¹/₂ cup/90g/3oz brown sugar
3 eggs, lightly beaten
I teaspoon vanilla essence
2 teaspoons finely grated lemon rind
2 cups/250g/8oz self-raising flour, sifted
2 ripe bananas, mashed

shaggy
dog lamingtons

Method:

1 Cut cake into 5cm/2in squares. Split each square horizontally and set aside.

2 To make filling, place cream and chocolate in a heatproof bowl set over a saucepan of simmering water and heat, stirring, until chocolate melts and mixture is smooth. Remove bowl from pan and set aside to cool. Beat filling until light and fluffy.

3 Spread filling over bottom half of cake squares and top with remaining cake squares.

4 To make icing, sift icing sugar and cocoa powder together in a bowl, add butter and mix to combine. Stir in enough milk to make an icing with a smooth coating consistency.

5 Dip cake squares in icing to coat completely. Roll in coconut and dust with drinking chocolate. Refrigerate until ready to serve.

Note: To make coating the cake easier, place coconut and icing in two shallow dishes or cake tins. Use tongs or two forks to dip the cake in the icing, then place on a wire rack set over a sheet of paper and allow to drain for 2-3 minutes before rolling in the coconut.

Makes 12

ingredients

1x18x28 cm/7x11in butter or sponge cake
185g/6oz shredded coconut
drinking chocolate, sifted

Chocolate cream filling
1¼ cups/315mL/10fl oz cream (heavy)
200g/6½oz dark chocolate, chopped

Chocolate icing
2 cups/315g/10oz icing sugar
2 tablespoons cocoa powder
30g/1oz butter, softened
¼ cup/60mL/2fl oz milk

apricot
oatmeal slice

Photograph page 229

ingredients

**2 cups/315g/10oz wholemeal flour
1 teaspoon bicarbonate soda
2¹/₂cups/235g/7¹/₂oz rolled oats
1 cup/170g/5¹/₂oz brown sugar
200g/6¹/₂oz butter, melted
icing sugar for dusting**

**Apricot filling
250g/8oz dried apricots
²/₃ cup/170mL/5¹/₂fl oz water
2 tablespoons apricot jam**

Method:

1 To make filling, place apricots, water and jam in a saucepan and cook over a low heat, stirring, until jam melts. Bring to the boil, then reduce heat and simmer for 5 minutes or until mixture thickens. Remove from heat and set aside to cool.

2 Sift flour and bicarbonate of soda together in a bowl. Return husks to bowl. Add rolled oats, sugar and butter and mix well to combine.

3 Press half the oat mixture over the base of a greased and lined 18x28cm/7x11in shallow cake tin. Spread with filling and sprinkle with remaining oat mixture.

4 Bake for 35 minutes or until slice is cooked. Cool in tin, then cut into bars and sprinkle with icing sugar.

Note: This slice is delicious made using any dried fruit. For something different why not try dried dates or figs.

Makes 28

Oven temperature 180°C, 350°F, Gas 4

peanut
butter cookies

Photograph page 229

ingredients

**250g/8oz butter, softened
1 cup/265g/8¹/₂oz peanut butter
1 cup/170g/5¹/₂oz brown sugar
2 eggs, lightly beaten
2¹/₄cups/280g/9oz flour, sifted
2 teaspoons bicarbonate of soda, sifted**

Method:

1 Place butter, peanut butter and sugar in a bowl and beat until light and fluffy. Gradually beat in eggs.

2 Stir flour and bicarbonate of soda together. Add to egg mixture and mix well. Roll tablespoons of mixture into balls, place on lightly greased baking trays and flatten slightly.

3 Bake for 15 minutes or until cookies are golden and crisp. Stand on trays for 3 minutes before transferring to wire racks to cool.

Note: For a traditional look to these biscuits, flatten the dough balls with a fork so that the tines of the fork leave a chequerboard imprint.

Makes 36

Oven temperature 180°C, 350°F, Gas 4

chocolate
cream hearts

Method:

1 Place butter, sugar and vanilla essence in a bowl and beat until light and fluffy. Add egg and beat well.

2 Sift together flour, cocoa powder and baking powder over butter mixture and fold in with milk.

3 Knead mixture lightly to form a ball, then wrap in plastic food wrap and refrigerate for 30 minutes. Roll out dough on a lightly floured surface to 3mm/¹/₈in thick.

4 Using a heart-shaped cutter, cut out biscuits, place on greased baking trays and bake for 10 minutes. Transfer biscuits to wire racks to cool.

5 To make Chocolate Cream, place chocolate and butter in a heatproof bowl set over a saucepan of simmering water and heat, stirring constantly, until mixture is smooth. Remove bowl from pan and set aside to cool slightly.

6 Spread half the biscuits with Chocolate Cream and top with remaining biscuits.
Note: Decorate the top of these biscuits by piping crisscross lines of melted dark or white chocolate – or both!

Makes 20

ingredients

**125g/4oz butter, softened
1 cup/250g/8oz sugar
1 teaspoon vanilla essence
1 egg, lightly beaten
2¹/₂ cups/315g/10oz flour
¹/₄ cup/30g/1oz cocoa powder
1¹/₂ teaspoons baking powder
¹/₂ cup/125mL/4fl oz milk**

Chocolate cream
**125g/4oz dark chocolate, chopped
100g/3¹/₂oz butter**

Oven temperature 180°C, 350°F, Gas 4

hazelnut
coconut slice

Method:

1 Place flour, sugar and butter in a food processor and process until mixture forms a soft dough.
2 Press dough into the base of a 20cm/8in square tin and bake for 10 minutes. Set aside to cool.
3 To make topping, combine hazelnuts, coconut, brown sugar and flour in a bowl. Add eggs and mix to combine.
4 Spread topping over base. Increase oven temperature to 190°C/375°F/Gas 5 and bake for 20 minutes longer or until topping is golden. Cool slice in tin, then cut into squares.

Note: Fat or shortening in whatever form makes a baked product tender and helps to improve its keeping quality. In most baked goods, top quality margarine and butter are interchangeable.

Makes 16

ingredients

1 cup/125g/4oz flour
¹/₄ cup/60g/2oz sugar
100g/3¹/₂oz butter, softened

Nutty topping
155g/5oz hazelnuts, roughly chopped
45g/1¹/₂oz desiccated coconut
2 cups/350g/11oz brown sugar
¹/₄ cup/30g/1oz flour
2 eggs, lightly beaten

Oven temperature 180°C/350°F/Gas 4

caramel
hazelnut cake

Photograph page 233

caramel hazelnut cake

ingredients
4 eggs
1 cup/220g/7oz superfine sugar
1 1/4 cups/155g/5oz self-rising flour, sifted
1/3 cup/45g/1 1/2oz ground hazelnuts
1/2 cup/125mL/4fl oz milk, warmed
15g/1/2oz butter, melted
60g/2oz whole hazelnuts

Caramel and cream filling
2 cups/500mL/16fl oz cream (heavy)
1 tablespoon icing sugar, sifted
375g/12oz soft caramels

Oven temperature 180°C, 350°F, Gas 4

Method:

1 *Place eggs in a bowl and beat until thick and creamy. Gradually add superfine sugar, beating well after each addition, until mixture is creamy.*

2 *Combine flour and ground hazelnuts. Fold flour mixture, milk and butter into egg mixture. Pour mixture into two greased and lined 20cm/8in round cake tins and bake for 25 minutes or until cakes are cooked when tested with a skewer. Turn onto wire racks to cool.*

3 *To make filling, place cream and icing sugar in a bowl and beat until thick. Place caramels in a saucepan and cook, stirring, over a low heat until caramels melt and mixture is smooth. Remove from heat and set aside to cool slightly.*

4 *To assemble, split each cake in half horizontally using a serrated edged knife. Place one layer of cake on a serving plate,*

spread with cream mixture, drizzle with caramel and top with a second layer of sponge. Repeat layers, finishing with a layer of filling and drizzling with caramel. Decorate top of cake with whole hazelnuts.

Note: *Caramelised hazelnuts make an elegant garnish for this European-style dessert cake. To make, gently melt a little granulated sugar in a frying pan until it turns a pale golden colour. Remove from heat, quickly drop in whole toasted hazelnuts and stir briskly with a wooden spoon until well coated. Cool on an oiled baking sheet or on baking paper.*

Makes a 20cm/8in round cake

tasty low fat cooking

introduction

introduction

be healthy, **stay slim**

Good food and enjoyable meals are truly one of life's great pleasures. Yet today, with the multitude of diet books and food 'scares' that regularly appear in the media, food has become a source of concern and unhappiness for many people. This book aims to counter the myths and fallacies surrounding food, dieting and nutrition. It is not just for people who are watching their weight, but also for anyone interested in healthy eating.

All recipes are low in fat, low in sugar, with no added salt. And they will give your meals a boost of all-important fibre, nature's own appetite suppressant.

Not only are they good for you and your waistline, they are also delicious, quick and easy to prepare, and suitable for all the family. When you're eating our dishes, you won't feel as if you're on a diet! Each recipe has a nutritional analysis, so you can see exactly how many calories, fibre, cholesterol or fat you are eating. Because weight control is more than just a diet plan, we've included information on nutrition, exercise, and body shape, latest research on obesity, eating out and help of overweight children. There is also a fat counter of common foods, as cutting down fats (including polyunsaturated fats) is currently considered the best way to stay slim and healthy. If you don't want to give up your favourite dishes, look for our tips on how to adapt recipes to be loser in fat, cholesterol and salt.

how to adapt your recipes – **Limiting fat**

Grill, dry-roast, stir-fry, microwave, casserole or poach in stock. A non-stick frypan or 'dry frypan' with a tight-fitting lid is a must for low-fat cookery. Also look for silicon-coated paper pan liners which line your frypan and transfer the heat to food direct - no fat needed at all!

- To brown meat or vegetables, brush your pan with oil (don't pour it in) and cook over moderate heat to avoid sticking.
- Use small quantities of butter, margarine, oil, cream, mayonnaise and cooking fats.
- Substitute low-fat dairy foods for full-cream products. Low-fat unflavoured yogurt makes an excellent substitute for cream (do not boil after adding it). Use fat-reduced and skin milks instead of full-cream milk and ricotta, cottage cheese and fat-reduced cheeses for regular cheeses.

Reducing **salt** -

Don't use salt in cooking. Experiment with herbs and spices as seasoning and your palate will gradually adapt the 'real' flavor of foods, which are often masked by salt. Double quantities of garlic, onion, chilli, basil, dill, lemon juice lift the flavour.

- Salt substitutes (potassium chloride or a mixture of salt and potassium chloride) are helpful. Use low-salt and salt-free food products from the supermarket. Over 50% of sodium intake comes from commercial foods like bread, butter, margarine, cheese, and luncheon meats which do not taste 'salty'. Stock cubes or powder, soy sauce, meat seasonings, garlic salt, Worcestershire and similar sauces all add salt.

Limiting **sugar** -

Gradually reduce the quantity of sugar and honey that you use.

- Offer substitutes for whipped cream for puddings - low-fat ice cream, vanilla custard, thick unflavoured yogurt, or a blend of ricotta and yogurt flavoured with vanilla essence and lemon rind.

Increasing **fibre intake** -

Where possible, do not peel vegetables, but cook with the skin on.

- Try brown rice more often. It adds an interesting nutty flavour. Try buckwheat and barley, two high-fibre grains.
- Add cooked or canned soybeans or kidney beans to casseroles; throw a handful of lentils into soups.
- For coatings or toppings use wholemeal breadcrumbs and crushed wheat biscuits (breakfast biscuits). Alternatively, try oat bran or a mixture of oat and wheat brans.

Sample recipes showing how to adapt to suit your new lifestyle

Before

Pork with **tarragon**

4 pork chops, about 200g/7 oz each
4 tablespoons plain flour
1 teaspoon salt
freshly ground black pepper
90g/3 oz butter
1 onion, chopped
$^1/_2$ cup/125ml/4fl oz dry white wine
$^1/_2$ cup/125ml/4fl oz chicken stock
1 tablespoon plain flour
1 cup/250ml/8fl oz cream
3 tablespoons fresh or 1 teaspoon dried
chopped tarragon

1   *Coat pork with seasoned flour. Heat butter in a frypan and brown chops, turning each until golden in colour. Transfer to a shallow casserole dish and keep warm. Reduce heat to low.*
2   *Reduce heat in frypan to low. Add onion and cook for 2-3 minutes. Add wine and stock; pour over pork. Cover and simmer for 30 minutes or until pork is cooked.*
3   *Remove pork, Mix in flour with a little cream and tarragon. Pour sauce over pork and serve.*

After

Pork with **tarragon**

2 lean pork fillets, about 250g/8 oz each
or 4 pork medallions, fat removed
a little plain flour
freshly ground black pepper
1 tablespoon oil
1 onion, chopped
$^1/_2$ cup/125ml/4fl oz dry white wine
$^1/_2$ cup/125ml/4fl oz homemade chicken
stock, without fat
2 tablespoons fresh or $^1/_2$ teaspoon dried
tarragon
1 tablespoon plain flour
3 tablespoons cream
$^1/_2$ cup/125ml/4fl oz thick plain yoghurt
1 tablespoon fresh chopped tarragon
(extra)

1   *Combine flour and pepper and coat pork. Place in an oiled baking dish and bake in a moderate oven 180°C/350°F for 15 minutes until just cooked.*
2   *Heat oil in a small saucepan and cook onion for 1-2 minutes or until golden. Add wine, stock and tarragon, cook for another 1-2 minutes, scraping sides of pan.*
3   *Mix flour with cream until smooth and stir into pan with yoghurt (do not boil). Keep warm until needed.*
4   *To serve, slice pork fillet and place 3-4 rounds on each plate. Spoon a little sauce over each; serve and garnish with extra tarragon.*

herbs
and spices

There are many flavor-packed ingredients with little or no calories which you can use to improve the flavor of a dish. Garlic, lemon rind, curry powder, soy sauce are familiar examples, as well as aromatic herbs (both fresh and dried). Start using these in place of butter, cream, bacon and other high-fat ingredients, which often feature in traditional cookery. If you're cutting back on salt, herbs and spices become even more important. Fresh and pure dried herbs and spices contain virtually no sodium (salt chemically is sodium chloride), but be sure to check the label of herb mixtures. Some, such as 'celery salt', 'garlic salt' or 'herb seasoning' often contain salt as an ingredient.

Enhance the *flavour of your favourite foods:*

Fish - *Bay leaf, chives, dill, fennel, horseradish, oregano, parsley, tarragon*

Chicken, turkey - *Garlic, pepper, rosemary, sage, tarragon, thyme*

Beef, veal - *Cumin, garlic, horseradish, marjoram, oregano, pepper, thyme*

Lamb, mutton - *Coriander, mint, rosemary, sorrel*

Pork - *Savory, ginger, caraway, paprika, garlic, sage, thyme*

Vegetables - *Basil, borage, caraway, chervil, chives, coriander, fennel, dill, garlic, mint, mustard, nasturtium, oregano, parsley, pepper, sage, salad burnett, savory, thyme*

Eggs - *Basil, caraway, chervil, chives, sage*

Fruit - *Allspice, aniseed, cinnamon, cloves, ginger, nutmeg, vanilla more about herbs*

Fresh herbs can be dried or frozen for winter use. Basil, thyme, marjoram and nasturtium can be used as a pepper substitute. Herbs can be used to replace salt intake: try lovage, thyme and marjoram. Scatter edible flowers of borage all look fantastic used this way. Fresh herbs should be chopped only at the last moment so that the full flavour of the aromatic oils is captured in the dish. Basil and savory are a boon to people on low-salt diets. Fresh is best. Many fresh herbs such as caraway, chervil, lemon balm, salad burnet, savory and sorrel are not readily available from the local fruit and vegetable market but can all be grown easily and quickly in your garden or on the kitchen windowsill.

basil

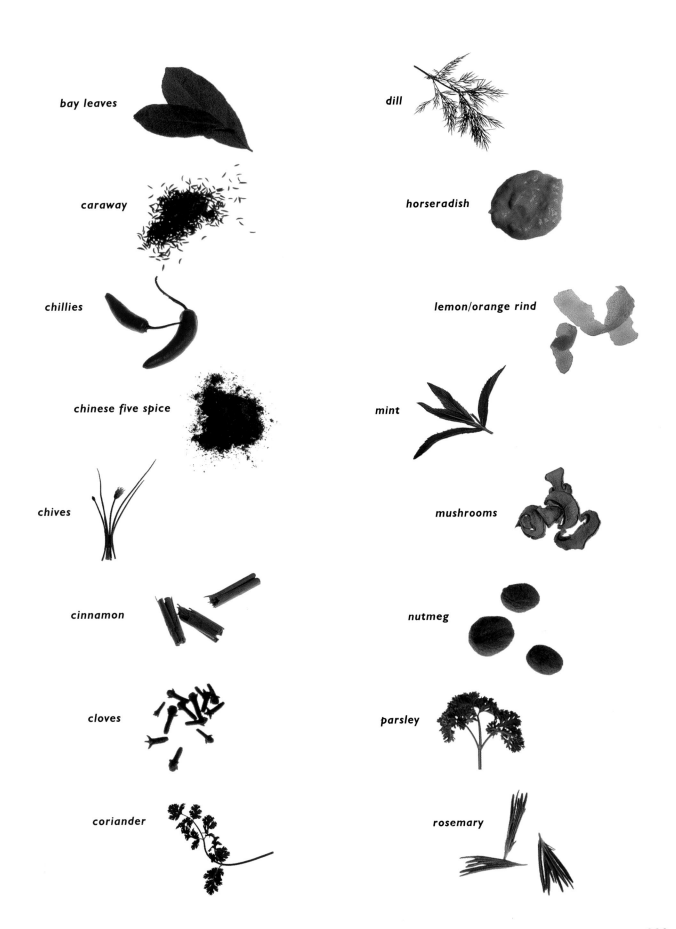

bay leaves

dill

caraway

horseradish

chillies

lemon/orange rind

chinese five spice

mint

chives

mushrooms

cinnamon

nutmeg

cloves

parsley

coriander

rosemary

puffed nut granola

start
the
day

It's time to consider the vitality

---

and goodness you gain from eating breakfast - it only

takes a few minutes! A balanced breakfast keeps you

going until lunch and there is less temptation to snack.

mighty
muesli

ingredients

4 cups/380g rolled oats
2 tablespoons shredded coconut
3 tablespoons oat bran
3 tablespoons wheat germ
I cup/40g oat flakes
3 tablespoons sunflower kernels
4 tablespoons chopped dried peaches
3 tablespoons chopped dried pears
3 tablespoons currants

Method:

1 Place rolled oats and coconut in a baking dish and bake for 15-20 minutes, or until oats and coconut are toasted. Stir several times during cooking to ensure even toasting. Remove from oven and set aside to cool.

2 Place cooled rolled oats and coconut, oat bran, wheat germ, oat flakes, sunflower kernels, dried peaches, dried pears and currants in a bowl. Mix well to combine.

Serving suggestion: Sprinkle with banana chips if desired and top with icy cold milk or juice.

Makes 20 servings

125 calories per serve
Fat Medium   **Fibre** Medium

Oven temperature 180°C, 350°F, Gas 4

puffed
nut granola

Photograph page 241

ingredients

90g/3oz puffed corn
I cup/90g/3oz rolled oats
¹/₂ cup/30g/Ioz bran cereal
90g/3oz Brazil nuts, roughly choppd
30g/Ioz flaked coconut
I teaspoon ground cinnamon
¹/₃ cup/90mL/3fl oz unsweetened apple juice
2 tablespoons honey
125g/4oz dried apricots, chopped
125g/4oz dried pears, chopped
90g/3oz pitted fresh or dried dates, chopped

Method:

1 Place puffed corn, rolled oats, bran cereal, nuts, coconut, cinnamon, apple juice and honey in a bowl and mix well to combine.

2 Place mixture in a shallow ovenproof dish, spread out evenly and bake, stirring occasionally, for 20-30 minutes or until golden.

3 Set aside to cool slightly. Add apricots, pears and dates and toss to combine. Set aside to cool completely. Store in an airtight container.

Serves 10

259 calories per serve -
Fat low   **Fibre** high

Oven temperature 180°C, 350°F, Gas 4

fruit
and yogurt porridge

ingredients

Method:
1 *Place milk, rolled oats, apples, sultanas and cinnamon in a saucepan and mix to combine. Cook over a medium heat, stirring, for 5-7 minutes or until oats are soft. Spoon porridge into serving bowls and serve topped with a spoonful of yogurt.*
Serves 2

382 calories per serve
***Fat** medium* ***Fibre** high*

2 cups/500mL/16fl oz low-fat milk
³/₄ cup/75g/2¹/₂oz rolled oats
3 tablespoons chopped dried apples
3 tablespoons sultanas
(golden raisins)
1 teaspoon ground cinnamon
2 tablespoons low-fat natural
or diet fruit yogurt

summer
fruit breakfast

Method:

1 Place nectarines, peaches, raspberries and blueberries in a bowl and toss to combine. Divide fruit between serving bowls.

2 Place yogurt, wheat germ and maple syrup into a bowl and mix to combine. Spoon yoghurt mixture over fruit and serve.

Serves 4

155 calories per serve -
Fat low **Fibre** high

ingredients

3 nectarines, sliced
3 peaches, sliced
125g/4oz raspberries
125g/4oz blueberries
I cup/200g/6¹/₂oz low-fat
vanilla-flavoured yogurt
45g/I¹/₂oz wheat germ
I tablespoon maple syrup

wholemeal
nutty pancakes

Method:

1 Place flour and sugar in a bowl and mix to combine. Add yogurt, milk and egg and whisk to combine. Fold in blueberries and nuts.

2 Heat a nonstick frying pan over a low heat, pour 2 tablespoons of batter into pan and cook for 2 minutes or until bubbles appear on the surface. Turn pancake over and cook for 2 minutes longer or until golden on second side. Remove pancake from pan and repeat with remaining batter.

Serves 4

456 calories per serve -
Fat medium   **Fibre** high

ingredients

1 cup/155g/5oz wholemeal
self-rising flour
$^1/_2$ cup/90g/3oz brown sugar
250g/8oz low-fat natural yogurt
$^1/_3$ cup/90mL/3fl oz reduced-fat milk
1 egg, lightly beaten
250g/8oz blueberries
90g/3oz macadamia nuts,
roughly chopped

mixed
mushroom frittata

Method:

1 *Place eggs, milk, mustard, dill and black pepper to taste in a bowl and whisk to combine.*

2 *Heat a nonstick frying pan over a medium heat, spray with polyunsaturated cooking oil spray, add spring onions and cook, stirring, for 2 minutes. Add oyster, field and button mushrooms and cook, stirring, for 3 minutes longer or until mushrooms are tender.*

3 *Pour egg mixture into pan and cook over a low heat for 5 minutes or until frittata is almost set.*

4 *Place pan under a preheated medium grill and cook for 3 minutes or until top is golden.*

Serves 4

114 calories per serve -
Fat *low*   **Fibre** *medium*

ingredients

4 eggs, lightly beaten
¹/₂ cup/125mL/4fl oz reduced-fat milk
1 tablespoon Dijon mustard
2 tablespoons chopped fresh dill
freshly ground black pepper
4 spring onions, chopped
125g/4oz oyster mushrooms
125g/4oz field mushrooms, sliced
125g/4oz button mushrooms, sliced

turkey
muffins

Method:

1 *Place tomato slices on muffin halves.
Top with turkey slices, cheese and black
pepper to taste. Place under a preheated
grill until heated through.*

Serves 2

250 calories per serve
Fat *low*   **Fibre** *medium*

ingredients

2 muffins, halved and toasted

Topping
1 tomato, sliced
2 slices cooked turkey breast
**3 tablespoons grated low-fat
tasty cheese**
freshly ground black pepper

muesli cakes

need a snack

Snacks aren't necessarily to blame

for a failed attempt at weight loss. When well-planned, snacks can be part of a healthy eating plan. However, remember some snacks contribute little except fat, salt and lots of unwanted calories!

248

crispy
pizza rolls

ingredients

2 large wholemeal pitta bread rounds, split
4 tablespoons tomato paste (purée)
¹/₂ green capsicum (pepper), chopped
2 slices reduced-fat ham, chopped
2 spring onions, chopped
60g/2oz grated reduced-fat
Cheddar cheese

Method:
1 Spread each bread round with I tablespoon tomato paste (purée) leaving a 2cm/³/₄in border. Sprinkle with green capsicum (pepper), ham, spring onions and cheese.
2 Roll up bread rounds and cut in half. Secure with a wooden toothpick or cocktail stick. Place rolls on baking trays and bake for 20 minutes or until bread is crisp. Serve hot or cold.
Makes 8

102 calories per roll -
Fat *low* **Fibre** *low*

Oven temperature 180°C, 350°F, Gas 4

muesli
cakes

Photograph page 249

ingredients

1³/₄ cups/280g/9oz wholemeal
self-rising flour
¹/₃ cup/90g/3oz sugar
75g/2¹/₂oz polyunsaturated margarine,
chopped
³/₄ cup/90g/3oz untoasted natural muesli
¹/₄ cup/45g/1¹/₂oz sultanas (golden raisins)
¹/₂ teaspoon mixed spice
¹/₂ cup/125mL/4fl oz low-fat milk
or buttermilk
¹/₄ cup/45g/1¹/₂oz low-fat natural yogurt
I egg, lightly beaten

Method:
1 Place flour, sugar and margarine in a food processor and process until mixture resembles breadcrumbs.
2 Transfer flour mixture to a bowl, add muesli, sultanas, mixed spice, milk, yogurt and egg and mix to form a soft, slightly sticky dough.
3 Take 2 tablespoons of mixture and drop onto a nonstick baking tray. Repeat with remaining mixture and bake for 15 minutes or until cakes are cooked and golden. Transfer to wire racks to cool.
Makes 20

113 calories per cake -
Fat *low* **Fibre** *medium*

Oven temperature 190°C, 375°F, Gas 5

pancake
sandwiches

Method:
1 Place flour and sugar in a bowl and mix to combine. Make a well in centre of flour mixture, add egg and milk and mix until smooth.
2 Heat a nonstick frying pan over a medium heat, drop tablespoons of batter into pan and cook for 1 minute each side or until golden. Remove pancake, set aside and keep warm. Repeat with remaining batter to make 12 pancakes.
3 To make filling, place ricotta cheese, lemon juice and sugar in a food processor or blender and process until smooth.
4 To assemble, top half the pancakes with filling, then with remaining pancakes.
Makes 6

136 calories per serve -
Fat *low* **Fibre** *low*

ingredients

³/₄ **cup/90g/3oz self-raising flour**
1 tablespoon sugar
1 egg, lightly beaten
³/₄ **cup/185mL/6fl oz low-fat milk**
or buttermilk

Lemon ricotta filling
¹/₂ **cup/125g/4oz ricotta cheese**
2 tablespoons lemon juice
1 tablespoon sugar

curried
pumpkin soup

Method:

1 *Heat oil in a large saucepan. Cook onion, coriander, cumin and chilli powder until onion softens.*

2 *Cut pumpkin into cubes and add to saucepan with stock. Cook pumpkin for 20 minutes or until tender, then cool slightly. Transfer soup in batches to a food processor or blender and process until smooth.*

3 *Return soup to a rinsed saucepan and heat. Season to taste with pepper.*

Serves 4

144 calories per serve
Fat *low* **Fibre** *medium*

ingredients

1 tablespoon polyunsaturated oil
1 large onion, chopped
$\frac{1}{2}$ teaspoon ground coriander
$\frac{1}{2}$ teaspoon ground cumin
$\frac{1}{2}$ teaspoon chilli powder
1 kg/2lb pumpkin, peeled and seeds removed
4 cups/1 litre chicken stock
freshly ground black pepper

herb
and cheese loaf

Method:

1 In a bowl combine flour, rolled oats, bran, low fat and Parmesan cheeses, chives and parsley. Make a well in the centre of the dry ingredients. Add milk and oil. Mix to combine.

2 Beat egg whites until stiff peaks form. Lightly fold through dough.

3 Spoon into a 23x12cm/9x5in non-stick loaf pan. Bake at 180°C/350°F/Gas 4 for 40 minutes.

Serves 12

161 calories per serve
Fat medium **Fibre** high

1 ¼ cups/170g self-rising wholemeal flour
1 cup/90g rolled oats
1 cup/45g unprocessed bran
½ cup/60g grated low fat cheese
1 tablespoon grated Parmesan cheese
2 tablespoons chopped chives
2 tablespoons chopped fresh parsley
1 cup/250mL low fat milk
4 tablespoons sunflower oil
3 egg whites

Oven temperature 180°C, 350°F, Gas 4

spicy rice
tomato and vegetables

Method:

1 Heat oil in a large saucepan. Cook onion, capsicum and chilli for 3-4 minutes. Add rice, mix well and cook for 3-4 minutes.

2 Add tomatoes to the pan with stock or water. Bring to the boil and simmer for 30 minutes or until liquid is absorbed and rice is tender. Season with pepper.

Serves 4

182 calories per serve
Fat *low*   **Fibre** *high*

ingredients

1 tablespoon olive oil
1 onion, sliced
1 green capsicum (pepper), diced
1 red chilli, seeded and finely chopped
³/₄ cup/170g white rice
³/₄ cup/170g quick-cooking brown rice
400g/13oz canned peeled tomatoes, undrained and roughly chopped
1¹/₂ cups/375mL vegetable stock or water
freshly ground black pepper

lasagne

Method:

1 Heat oil in a frypan. Cook onion and garlic for 2-3 minutes. Add beef and cook over medium heat until well browned. Combine soy beans, tomatoes, tomato paste, 2 teaspoons basil, oregano and sugar. Drain pan of any juices and stir in tomato mixture. Simmer, uncovered, for 15 minutes or until sauce thickens slightly.

2 Spread half the meat mixture over the base of a 15x25cm/6x10in ovenproof dish. Top with three lasagne sheets, placed side by side. Repeat with remaining meat mixture and lasagne sheets.

3 Place ricotta cheese, cottage cheese and egg white in a food processor or blender and process until smooth. Spread cheese mixture over lasagne in dish. Top with Parmesan cheese and remaining basil. Bake at 200°C/ 400°F/Gas 6 for 35-40 minutes or until tender.

How We've Cut Fat and Calories

We have used lean ground beef for the filling. We alternated a layer of vegetable with the meat to keep the fibre high and the calories low.

Instead of the usual rich Bechamel cheese sauce on top, we made a lighter version based on skim milk and cornflour.

Serves 4

262 calories per serve
Fat low   **Fibre** high

ingredients

2 teaspoons olive oil
1 onion, chopped
1 clove garlic, crushed
155g/5oz lean ground beef
315g/10oz canned soy beans, drained
440g/14oz canned peeled tomatoes, undrained and mashed
1 tablespoon tomato paste
1 1/2 tablespoons chopped fresh basil
1/4 teaspoon dried oregano leaves
1/4 teaspoon sugar
6 sheets instant spinach lasagne noodles
1/2 cup/125g ricotta cheese
1/2 cup/125g cottage cheese
1 egg white
1 tablespoon grated Parmesan cheese

Oven temperature 200°C, 400°F, Gas 6

salmon in pepper and mint

keep fit
with fish

Seafood is good news for slimmers.

*All seafood is low in calories, with fewer calories than
even the leanest meat or chicken. And, of course, with
seafood you don't need to trim any fat. Just grill,
barbeque, bake, steam, poach or microwave seafood
to keep a low calorie count.*

crispy
potatoes

Method:
1 Cut potatoes into wedges. Place on a very lightly greased baking tray and spray lightly with polyunsaturated cooking oil spray.
2 Sprinkle potatoes with salt and rosemary and bake, turning occasionally, for 35-45 minutes or until potatoes are crisp and golden.
Serves 6

Note: *Nothing like crispy potato chips to compliment your fish dish.*

66 calories per serve -
Fat *low*   **Fibre** *low*

ingredients

6 potatoes, scrubbed
sea salt
1 tablespoon chopped fresh rosemary

Oven temperature 200°C, 400°F, Gas 6

salmon
with pepper and mint

Photograph page 257

Method:
1 To make marinade, place wine, lime juice, mint and black pepper in a large shallow glass or ceramic dish and mix to combine.
2 Add salmon to marinade and set aside to marinate for 10 minutes. Turn once. Drain and cook on a preheated hot barbecue or under a grill for 2-3 minutes each side or until salmon flakes when tested with a fork. Serve immediately.
Serves 4

216 calories per serve -
Fat *medium*   **Fibre** *low*

ingredients

4 salmon cutlets

Pepper and mint marinade
3 tablespoons dry white wine
2 tablespoons lime juice
2 tablespoons chopped fresh mint
2 teaspoons crushed black peppercorns

marinated
trout fillets

Method:

1 To make marinade, place lime juice, thyme, mustard seeds, bay leaves and black pepper to taste in a shallow glass or ceramic dish.

2 Add trout fillets to marinade and set aside to marinate, turning several times, for 15 minutes. Drain trout well.

3 Heat a nonstick frying pan over a medium heat. Add trout and cook for 2-3 minutes each side or until fish flakes when tested with fork. Serve immediately.

Serves 6

324 calories per serve -
***Fat** low* ***Fibre** low*

ingredients

12 small trout fillets

Lime and thyme marinade
2 tablespoons lime juice
2 tablespoons fresh lemon thyme or thyme or 1 teaspoon dried thyme
1 tablespoon yellow mustard seeds
2 bay leaves
freshly ground black pepper

spiced
fish kebabs

Method:

1 Thread fish onto lightly oiled skewers. Place paprika, black pepper, cumin and chilli powder in a bowl and mix to combine. Sprinkle spice mixture over kebabs.

2 Cook kebabs under a preheated hot grill or on a barbecue for 2-3 minutes each side or until fish is cooked.

3 To make sauce, place yogurt, lemon juice, thyme and black pepper to taste in a bowl and mix to combine. Serve with kebabs.

Serves 4

242 calories per serve -
Fat *medium* **Fibre** *low*

ingredients

750g/1¹/₂ lb firm white fish fillets, cut into 2¹/₂cm/1in cubes
1 tablespoon ground paprika
2 teaspoons crushed black peppercorns
1 teaspoon ground cumin
¹/₂ teaspoon chilli powder

Lemon yoghurt sauce
¹/₂ cup/100g/3¹/₂oz low-fat natural yogurt
1 tablespoon lemon juice
1 tablespoon chopped fresh lemon thyme or ¹/₂ teaspoon dried thyme
freshly ground black pepper

fish cutlets
with italian sauce

Method:

1 *Brush fish cutlets with lemon juice. Place under a preheated griller and cook for 4-5 minutes each side. Remove from griller and keep warm.*

2 *Place shallots, garlic, tomatoes, mushrooms, wine, basil, oregano and pepper to taste in a saucepan. Bring to the boil. Reduce heat and simmer gently for 8-10 minutes.*

3 *Arrange fish cutlets on serving plates. Spoon sauce over and top with Parmesan cheese.*

Serves 4

206 calories per serve
Fat *low* **Sodium** *medium*

ingredients

4x150g/5oz white fish cutlets
2 tablespoons lemon juice
6 shallots, finely chopped
1 clove garlic, crushed
400g/13oz canned tomatoes (no added salt)
200g/6¹/₂oz button mushrooms, sliced
¹/₂ cup/125mL red wine
2 teaspoons finely chopped fresh basil
¹/₂ teaspoon dried oregano
freshly ground black pepper
2 tablespoons grated Parmesan cheese

salmon
souffles

Method:

1 Combine salmon, oysters, capers, dill, Tabasco and cottage cheese in a bowl. Season to taste with pepper.

2 Beat egg whites until stiff peaks form and fold lightly through salmon mixture. Spoon into four lightly greased individual soufflé dishes and bake at 200°C/400°F/Gas 6 for 30-35 minutes.

Serves 4

132 calories per serve
Fat low **Fibre** low

ingredients

220g/7oz canned red salmon, no-added-salt, drained and flaked
100g/3½oz bottled oysters, drained, rinsed and chopped
2 teaspoons finely chopped capers
1 teaspoon finely chopped fresh dill
2-3 dashes Tabasco sauce
1 cup/250g low fat cottage cheese
freshly ground black pepper
4 egg whites

teriyaki
fish

Method:

1 Place fish fillets in a single layer in a shallow dish. To make marinade, combine teriyaki sauce, honey, sherry, ginger and garlic and pour over fish. Cover and marinate for 1 hour.

2 Toss sesame seeds in a frypan and cook over medium heat until golden brown, stirring frequently.

3 Remove fish from marinade and grill for 2-3 minutes, each side. Baste occasionally with marinade during cooking. Serve sprinkled with sesame seeds.

Serves 4

270 calories per serve
Fat low   **Fibre** low

ingredients

4 large white fish fillets
2 teaspoons sesame seeds

Marinade
3 tablespoons teriyaki sauce
1 tablespoon honey
1 tablespoon dry sherry
¼ teaspoon grated fresh ginger
1 clove garlic, crushed

keep fit
with fish

lemon
fish parcels

Method:

1 *Lightly grease four sheets of aluminium foil and place a fish fillet in the centre of each sheet.*

2 *Top each fillet with a teaspoon of capers. Pour over lemon juice and season with pepper. Place two asparagus spears over each fillet and dust lightly with paprika.*

3 *Fold up edges of aluminium foil and completely encase fish. Place parcels on an oven tray and bake at 180°C/350°F/Gas 4 for 15-20 minutes, or until fish flakes when tested with a fork. Remove from parcels to serve.*

Serves 4

125 calories per serve
Fat *low*   **Fibre** *low*

ingredients

4 large white fish fillets
I tablespoon finely chopped capers
¹/₂ cup/125mL lemon juice
freshly ground black pepper
8 asparagus spears (fresh or canned)
¹/₂ teaspoon paprika

Oven temperature 180°C, 350°F, Gas 4

steamed
spiced fish with nuts

Method:

1 Pat fish dry with absorbent kitchen paper and set aside.

2 Place coriander, chives, garlic, ginger, cumin, paprika, turmeric, cayenne pepper and lime juice in a shallow glass or ceramic dish and mix to combine. Add fish, cover and marinate in the refrigerator for 2 hours.

3 Cut four circles of aluminium foil large enough to completely enclose the fillets. The foil should be at least 10cm/4in larger than the fillets on all sides. Fold foil in half lengthwise and cut a half-heart shape. Open out foil.

4 Place a fillet on one half of each foil heart, near the centre line, then sprinkle with pistachio nuts. Fold foil over fish and roll edges to seal. Place parcels on a rack set in a baking dish. Add ¹/₂ cup/125mL/4fl oz hot water to baking dish and bake for 15 minutes or until fish flakes when tested with a fork.

Serves 4

289 calories per serve - **Fat** medium
Fibre medium

ingredients

**4 firm white fish fillets
2 tablespoons chopped fresh coriander
2 tablespoons snipped fresh chives
2 cloves garlic, crushed
2¹/₂ cm/1in piece fresh ginger,
finely chopped
2 teaspoons ground cumin
2 teaspoons paprika
1 teaspoon ground turmeric
¹/₄ teaspoon cayenne pepper
2 tablespoons lime juice
90g/3oz pistachio nuts, toasted and
roughly chopped**

chicken mango pockets

it's
lunch

With the exception of breakfast,

lunch is the meal most often missed. It is, however, the
pitstop most needed to get you through the daily
trauma of work at the office or at home. It also stops
the snack attack which, if one succumbs, can result in
a diet blow-out.

layered
lunch loaf

Method:

1 Cut bread horizontally into four even layers.
2 For sprouts layer, place tomato paste (purée), yogurt and coriander in a bowl and mix to combine. Place alfalfa sprouts, bean sprouts and snow pea (mangetout) sprouts or watercress on bottom layer of bread. Top with yogurt mixture and second bread layer.
3 For beef layer, spread bread with mustard, then top with roast beef, lettuce and red pepper (capsicum) and third bread layer.
4 For salad layer, top bread with tomatoes, gherkins and cucumber and final bread layer. Serve cut into wedges.

Serves 4

342 calories per serve -
Fat *low*   **Fibre** *high*

1 round rye or wholegrain cottage loaf

Mixed sprouts layer
2 teaspoons tomato paste (purée)
4 tablespoons low-fat natural yogurt
1 teaspoon ground cilantra (coriander)
90g/3oz alfalfa sprouts
60g/2oz bean sprouts
**90g/3oz snow pea (mangetout) sprouts
or watercress**

Roast beef layer
3 teaspoons French mustard
4 slices lean rare roast beef
4 lettuce leaves of your choice
1/2 red capsicum (pepper), chopped

Tomato salad layer
2 tomatoes, sliced
3 gherkins, sliced
1/2 cucumber, sliced

chicken
mango pockets

Method:

1 Make a slit in the top of each pitta bread round. Set aside.
2 Place ricotta cheese, cucumber, mint and cumin in a bowl and mix to combine. Spread the inside of each pitta bread with ricotta mixture, then fill with onion, alfalfa sprouts, chicken and chutney.

Serves 4

449 calories per serve - **Fat** *medium*
Fibre *medium*

Photograph page 267

4 wholemeal pitta bread rounds
90g/3oz ricotta cheese
1 small cucumber, chopped
2 tablespoons chopped fresh mint
1 teaspoon ground cumin
1 red onion, thinly sliced
90g/3oz alfalfa sprouts
**500g/1 lb cooked chicken, skin
removed and flesh shredded**
4 tablespoons mango chutney

greek
tuna focaccia

Method:
1 Split focaccia bread horizontally and toast lightly under a preheated medium grill.
2 Top each piece of bread with feta cheese, rocket or watercress, tuna, sun-dried tomatoes, capers and onion rings. Sprinkle with dill.

Serves 4

445 calories per serve -
Fat *low* **Fibre** *high*

ingredients

2x10cm/4in squares focaccia bread
90g/3oz marinated or plain feta cheese, crumbled
1/2 bunch rocket or watercress, broken into sprigs
440g/14oz canned tuna in brine or springwater, drained
60g/2oz sun-dried tomatoes in oil, drained and sliced
1 tablespoon capers, drained
1 onion, thinly sliced into rings
1 tablespoon chopped fresh dill

chicken
and asparagus rolls

Method:

1 Boil, steam or microwave asparagus until just tender. Drain and set aside to cool.
2 Place chicken and chutney in a bowl and mix to combine. Top pitta bread with chicken mixture, asparagus, cucumber and green capsicum (pepper). Roll up.

Serves 2

465 calories per roll -
Fat medium   **Fibre** high

ingredients

250g/8oz asparagus spears
125g/4oz chopped cooked chicken, all skin and visible fat removed
1 tablespoon tomato chutney
2 large wholemeal pitta bread rounds
¹/₂ cucumber, sliced
¹/₂ green capsicum (pepper), sliced

grilled
ricotta focaccia

Method:

1 Spread each piece of focaccia bread with mustard, then top with tomatoes, green capsicum (pepper) and mushrooms.
2 Place ricotta cheese, rosemary and black pepper to taste in a bowl and mix to combine. Top vegetable mixture with ricotta mixture and cook under a preheated hot grill for 3 minutes or until heated through and slightly brown.

Serves 2

355 calories per serve -
Fat medium **Fibre** high

ingredients

2x12¹/₂cm/5in squares focaccia bread,
split and toasted
2 tablespoons wholegrain mustard
2 tomatoes, sliced
¹/₂ green capsicum (pepper), sliced
4 mushrooms, sliced
4 tablespoons ricotta cheese
2 teaspoons chopped fresh rosemary
freshly ground black pepper

roasted
garlic and tomato soup

Photograph page 273

Method:

1 Place tomatoes and garlic in a lightly greased shallow ovenproof dish, brush lightly with oil and sprinkle with salt and black pepper to taste. Bake for 30 minutes or until garlic is golden and tomatoes are soft. Cool slightly.
2 Place tomatoes, garlic and stock in batches into food processor or blender and process until smooth.
3 Place soup mixture and onion in a saucepan, bring to simmering and simmer for 10 minutes or until heated through. Stir in basil and serve.

Serves 6

71 calories per serve -
***Fat** low* ***Fibre** medium*

ingredients

**1 kg/2 lb plum (egg or Italian) tomatoes, halved
5 cloves garlic, peeled
1 tablespoon olive oil
sea salt
freshly ground black pepper
6 cups/1 ¹/₂ litres/2¹/₂pt vegetable stock
1 large red onion, finely chopped
3 tablespoons chopped fresh basil**

Oven temperature 190°C, 375°F, Gas 5

leek
and parsnip soup

Photograph page 273

ingredients

**1 tablespoon olive oil
30g/1oz butter
2 leeks, sliced
750g/1¹/₂lb parsnips, peeled and sliced
1 teaspoon finely grated orange rind
4 cups/1 litre/1³/₄pt chicken stock
2 cups/500mL/16fl oz water
freshly ground black pepper
2 tablespoons snipped fresh chives**

Method:

1 Heat oil and butter in a saucepan over a medium heat, add leeks and cook for 5 minutes or until leeks are golden.
2 Add parsnips, orange rind and 1 cup/250mL/8fl oz stock to pan, cover, cook over a low heat for 15 minutes or until parsnips are soft.
3 Stir in remaining stock, water and black pepper to taste, bring to simmering and simmer for 30 minutes longer. Remove pan from heat and set aside to cool slightly.
4 Place soup in batches into food processor or blender and process until smooth. Return soup to a clean pan, bring to simmering and simmer for 5 minutes or until heated through. Sprinkle with chives and serve.

Serves 6

141 calories per serve -
***Fat** low* ***Fibre** medium*

pesto
potato salad

Photograph page 275

ingredients

10 small potatoes, chopped
2 spring onions, chopped

Pesto dressing
$^1/_3$ cup/60g/2oz low-fat natural yogurt
4 tablespoons chopped fresh basil
2 tablespoons grated Parmesan cheese
I clove garlic, crushed
freshly ground black pepper

Method:

1 *Boil, steam or microwave potatoes until tender. Drain and set aside to cool.*
2 *To make dressing, place yogurt, basil, Parmesan cheese, garlic and black pepper to taste in a food processor or blender and process to combine.*
3 *Place potatoes and spring onions in a bowl. Spoon over dressing and toss to combine. Cover and refrigerate until required.*
   Serves 4

135 calories per serve -
Fat *low* **Fibre** *medium*

lebanese
salad

Photograph page 275

ingredients

**$^1/_3$ cup/60g/2oz burghul
(cracked wheat)**
**125g/4oz canned chickpeas,
rinsed and drained**
2 tomatoes, chopped
$^1/_2$ bunch fresh parsley, chopped
3 tablespoons chopped fresh mint
I$^1/_2$ tablespoons lemon juice
freshly ground black pepper
wholemeal flatbread

Creamy chickpea dressing
3 tablespoons hummus
3 tablespoons low-fat natural yogurt
$^1/_2$ teaspoon chilli powder
$^1/_2$ teaspoon ground cumin

Method:

1 *Place burghul (cracked wheat) in a bowl, cover with boiling water and set aside to stand for 10-15 minutes or until soft. Drain.*
2 *Place burghul (cracked wheat), chickpeas, tomatoes, parsley, mint, lemon juice and black pepper to taste in a bowl and toss to combine.*
3 *To make dressing, place hummus, yogurt, chilli powder and cumin in a bowl and mix to combine. Spoon dressing over salad and pack into containers. Serve with flat bread.*
   Note: *If canned chickpeas are unavailable, use cold cooked chickpeas instead. To cook chickpeas, soak overnight in cold water. Drain. Place in a saucepan, cover with cold water and bring to the boil over a medium heat. Boil for 10 minutes, then reduce heat and simmer for 45-60 minutes or until chickpeas are tender. Drain and cool. Cooked chickpeas freeze well, so cook more than you need and freeze what you do not use.*
   Serves 2

285 Calories per serve -
Fat *medium to high* **Fibre** *high*

steamed
ginger chilli mussels

Method:

1. To make sauce, place ginger, garlic, lemon grass, chillies, spring onions, coriander, wine, vinegar, fish sauce and sesame oil in a bowl and mix to combine. Set aside.

2. Place mussels in a large steamer, set over a saucepan of boiling water, cover and steam for 5 minutes or until mussels open. Discard any mussels that do not open after 5 minutes cooking. Spoon sauce over mussels and heat for 1 minute longer. Serve immediately.

Note: It may be necessary to steam the mussels in batches. For a complete meal serve with boiled brown or white rice and steamed vegetables of your choice.

Serves 4

104 calories per serve -
Fat *low* ***Fibre*** *low*

ingredients

**1 kg/2 lb mussels, scrubbed
and beards removed**

Ginger chilli sauce
**5cm/2in piece fresh ginger,
finely chopped**
3 cloves garlic, crushed
**1 stalk lemon grass, finely chopped or
1 teaspoon dried lemon grass soaked
in hot water until soft**
3 small fresh red chillies, finely sliced
3 spring onions, diagonally sliced
4 tablespoons coriander leaves
¹/₄ cup/60mL/2fl oz white wine
2 tablespoons rice vinegar
1 tablespoon fish sauce
2 teaspoons sesame oil

chicken
spinach parcels

Method:

1 Place spinach in a steamer set over a saucepan of boiling water and cook for 3 minutes or until spinach wilts. Remove from steamer and cool slightly. Squeeze to remove as much moisture as possible, chop roughly and place in a bowl. Add butter, garlic and sage to spinach and mix to combine.

2 Make a deep slit in the side of each chicken fillet to form a pocket. Fill pocket with spinach mixture then secure with wooden toothpicks or cocktail sticks.

3 Wrap each fillet loosely in aluminium foil and place in a steamer set over a saucepan of boiling water. Cover and steam for 30 minutes or until chicken is tender. Remove steamer from pan, set aside and keep warm.

4 To make sauce, place stock, wine and mustard in a saucepan and bring to the boil. Reduce heat and simmer until mixture is reduced by half. Pour stock mixture into a bowl and cool for 5 minutes. Stir in yogurt and chives and serve with chicken.

Serves 4

226 calories per serve -
Fat low   **Fibre** medium

ingredients

1 bunch English spinach
15g/¹/₂oz butter, softened
2 cloves garlic
2 tablespoons chopped fresh sage or
1 teaspoon dried sage
4 boneless chicken breast fillets, skinned
and trimmed of all visible fat

Creamy sauce
¹/₂ cup/125mL/4fl oz chicken stock
¹/₂ cup/125mL/4fl oz dry white wine
1 tablespoon wholegrain mustard
¹/₄ cup/45g/1¹/₂oz low-fat natural yogurt
1 tablespoon snipped fresh chives

lettuce roll ups

green cuisine

Fresh vegetables are one of the

mainstays of a healthy diet, providing essential vitamins, minerals, fibre and are virtually non-existent in fat. When you tempt your tastebuds with our light, refreshing and spicy selection of vegetable and salad recipes, you can safely come back for a second helping.

lettuce
roll-ups

Photograph page 279

ingredients

6 large lettuce leaves
I cup/60g bean sprouts
2 mangoes, peeled and chopped
**260g/9oz canned sliced water
chest-nuts, drained**
2 teaspoons finely chopped preserved ginger
2 teaspoons finely chopped mint leaves
3 tablespoons low fat mayonnaise
I tablespoon low fat unflavoured yogurt

Method:

1 *Tear lettuce leaves in half lengthways. Toss together sprouts, mangoes, water chestnuts, ginger and mint.*
2 *Combine mayonnaise and yogurt. Fold through mango mixture.*
3 *Place a spoonful of mixture on each lettuce leaf. Roll up tightly and secure with a toothpick.*
Serves 6

141 calories per serve
Fat *low*   **Fibre** *high*

french
bean salad

ingredients

500g/I lb green beans, trimmed and sliced
I clove garlic, crushed
I teaspoon ground fenugreek
**2 tablespoons finely chopped
fresh mint leaves**
I teaspoon red wine vinegar
I tablespoon olive oil
2 teaspoons toasted sesame seeds

Method:

1 *Boil, steam or microwave beans until just tender. Drain and place in a salad bowl.*
2 *Combine garlic, fenugreek and mint. Toss with warm beans. Set aside and allow to cool slightly.*
3 *Blend together vinegar and olive oil, pour over beans and refrigerate for 1-2 hours. Sprinkle with sesame seeds and serve.*
Serves 4

66 calories per serve
Fat *medium*   **Fibre** *high*

stir-fried
greens

Method:

1 Place sesame seeds and garlic in a nonstick frying pan and stir-fry over a medium heat for 2 minutes or until golden.

2 Add snow peas (mangetout), Chinese greens, bean sprouts, soy sauce, oyster sauce and chilli sauce to pan and stir-fry for 3 minutes or until vegetables are tender. Serve immediately.

Note: Ordinary cabbage is a suitable alternative to the Chinese greens in this recipe.

Serves 4

89 calories per serve -
Fat low   **Fibre** high

ingredients

**2 tablespoons sesame seeds
I clove garlic, crushed
185g/6oz snow peas (mangetout)
185g/6oz Chinese greens such as bok choy, Chinese broccoli and Chinese cabbage, chopped
155g/5oz bean sprouts
2 tablespoons sweet soy sauce
I tablespoon oyster sauce
I tablespoon sweet chilli sauce**

Method:

1 Place squid (calamari), chilli sauce, vinegar and coriander in a bowl and toss to combine. Cover and marinate at room temperature for 30 minutes or in the refrigerator overnight.

2 Drain squid (calamari) and cook on a preheated hot barbecue plate (griddle) for 2 minutes or until squid (calamari) is tender.

3 Arrange lettuce leaves, snow pea (mangetout) sprouts or watercress and tomatoes attractively on a platter, top with warm squid (calamari) and serve immediately.

Note: To clean squid (calamari), pull tentacles from the squid (calamari), carefully taking with them the stomach and ink bag. Next cut the beak, stomach and ink bag from the tentacles and discard. Wash tentacles well. Wash 'hood' and peel away skin. Cut hood in rings.

Serves 4

65 calories per serve -
Fat low   **Fibre** medium

warm
squid salad

ingredients

2 squid (calamari) tubes, cut into rings
3 tablespoons sweet chilli sauce
2 tablespoons red wine vinegar
2 tablespoons chopped fresh coriander
250g/8oz assorted lettuce leaves
125g/4oz snow pea (mangetout) sprouts
or watercress
250g/8oz cherry tomatoes, halved

spaghetti
with asparagus sauce

Method:

1 Cook spaghetti in boiling water in a large saucepan following packet directions.

2 To make sauce, steam, boil or microwave asparagus until tender. Drain and refresh under cold running water. Cut into 3cm/1¼in pieces and set aside. Heat oil in a frypan, add breadcrumbs and cook over low heat for 2 minutes, stirring all the time. Stir in milk and asparagus, and cook over medium heat for 5 minutes. Mix in cheese and continue to cook until melted. Season to taste with pepper.

3 Place spaghetti on a warmed serving platter, spoon over sauce and toss gently to combine. Sprinkle with Parmesan cheese and serve immediately.

Serves 6

237 calories per serve
Fat medium   **Fibre** medium

ingredients

**500g/1lb spaghetti
2 tablespoons grated Parmesan cheese**

**<u>Asparagus sauce</u>
500g/1lb fresh asparagus spears, trimmed
1 tablespoon olive oil
1 thick slice wholegrain bread, crumbed
1 cup/250mL evaporated skim milk
60g/2oz grated mozzarella cheese
freshly ground black pepper**

stir-fried
broccoli with almonds

Method:

1 Boil, steam or microwave carrots and broccoli until they just change colour. Drain and refresh under cold running water.

2 Heat oil in wok or frypan. Add onion, garlic and ginger and stir-fry for 4-5 minutes. Add carrots, broccoli and soy sauce, and stir-fry for 3-4 minutes longer, or until vegetables are heated through. Just prior to serving toss through almonds.

Serves 4

92 calories per serve
Fat low   **Fibre** high

ingredients

2 carrots, cut into matchsticks
500g/1 lb broccoli, cut into florets
2 teaspoons peanut oil
1 onion, sliced
1 clove garlic, crushed
2 teaspoons grated fresh ginger
2 teaspoons low salt soy sauce
2 tablespoons toasted almonds

mixed
pepper and onion tart

Method:

1 Place stock and brown sugar in a nonstick frying pan and cook over a medium heat for 3-4 minutes or until sugar dissolves. Add onions and cook, stirring, for 15 minutes or until onions start to caramelise.

2 Layer pastry sheets, brushing between each layer with water. Brush top sheet of pastry with oil and use layered pastry to line a lightly greased 18x28cm/7x11in shallow cake tin. Roll pastry edges to neaten.

3 Place ricotta cheese, basil and black pepper to taste in a bowl and mix to combine. Spread ricotta mixture over pastry, then top with onions and roasted capsicums (peppers) and bake for 20 minutes or until pastry is crisp and golden.

Serves 6

156 calories per serve –
Fat *low* **Fibre** *low*

ingredients

$^1/_4$ **cup/60mL/2fl oz chicken stock**
2 teaspoons brown sugar
3 onions, thinly sliced
8 sheets filo pastry
$^1/_4$ **cup/60mL/2fl oz water**
1 tablespoon oil
200g/6$^1/_2$oz ricotta cheese, drained
2 tablespoons chopped fresh basil
freshly ground black pepper
1 red capsicum (pepper), roasted
and cut into thin strips
1 green capsicum (pepper), roasted
and cut into thin strips

Oven temperature 180°C, 350°F, Gas 4

herby
vegetable salad

Method:

1 Boil, steam or microwave cauliflower, broccoli, carrot and snow peas (mangetout) until just tender. Drain, refresh under cold water.

2 Drain vegetables well. Toss in a salad bowl with capsicum (pepper), lemon juice, cilantra (coriander) and rosemary. Season to taste with pepper. Refrigerate until required.

3 To make vinaigrette, combine all ingredients in a screwtop jar. Shake well to combine. Pour over salad just prior to serving.

Serves 4

82 calories per serve
Fat low   **Fibre** medium

tingredients

¹/₄ **cauliflower, broken into florets**
I head broccoli, broken into florets
I large carrot, cut into thin strips
150g/5oz snow peas (mangetout), trimmed
I red capsicum (pepper), cut into thin strips
3 tablespoons lemon juice
2 teaspoons finely chopped fresh cilantra (coriander)
2 teaspoons finely chopped fresh rosemary
freshly ground black pepper

<u>Lemon Viniagrette</u>
2 tablespoons lemon juice
I tablespoon olive oil
I clove garlic, crushed
I teaspoon wholegrain mustard

spinach
and salmon timbales

Method:

1 Boil, steam or microwave spinach until just wilted. Drain and allow to cool.
2 Select the largest spinach leaves and use to line four very lightly greased individual ramekins of about 1 cup/250mL capacity. Leave some of the leaves overhanging the top.
3 To make filling, squeeze as much liquid as possible from remaining spinach and chop finely. In a food processor or blender, combine salmon, ricotta, chives, parsley and egg. Process until smooth. Mix in chopped spinach and season with pepper.
4 Spoon mixture into prepared ramekins. Fold spinach leaves over the top. Bake at 180°C/350°C/Gas 4 for 30 minutes or until set.

Serves 4

156 calories per serve
Fat low   **Fibre** high

ingredients

**1 bunch spinach
(about 1 kg/2lb), washed**

<u>**Filling**</u>
**220g/7oz canned salmon, drained
100g/3¹/₂oz ricotta cheese
2 tablespoon finely chopped chives
2 tablespoons finely chopped fresh parsley
1 egg, lightly beaten
freshly ground black pepper**

Oven temperature 180°C, 350°F, Gas 4

cajun chicken with
pawpaw salsa

dinner
winners

This tasty selection of dinner menus

for everyday family meals will fit into your eating
plan and leave the rest of the family feeling satisfied
and healthy.

cajun
chicken with pawpaw salsa

Photograph page 289

Oven temperature 180°C, 350°F, Gas 4

ingredients

**4 boneless chicken breast fillets,
skinned and trimmed of all visible fat
2 cloves garlic, crushed
I tablespoon onion salt
I tablespoon ground white pepper
I tablespoon cracked black pepper
2 teaspoons cayenne pepper
I tablespoon paprika
I tablespoon dried mixed herbs**

**<u>Pawpaw salsa</u>
I small pawpaw, diced
I cucumber, diced
2 tablespoons mint leaves
2 tablespoons low-fat natural yogurt
2 tablespoons lime juice**

Method:

1 *Rub chicken with crushed garlic. Place onion salt, white pepper, black pepper, cayenne pepper, paprika and mixed herbs in a bowl and mix to combine.*

2 *Rub spice mixture over chicken, place on a nonstick baking tray and bake for 25-30 minutes or until chicken is tender. Cover and stand for 5 minutes before serving.*

3 *To make salsa, place pawpaw, cucumber, mint, yogurt and lime juice in a bowl and mix to combine. Serve with chicken.*

Note: *After rubbing spice mixture onto chicken wash your hands and do not touch your face or lips as the cayenne pepper causes burning.*

Serves 4

223 calories per serve –
Fat *low* **Fibre** *medium*

pasta
with goat's cheese

ingredients

**500g/I lb tagliatelle
2 teaspoons olive oil
2 cloves garlic, crushed
I cup/60g/2oz wholemeal breadcrumbs,
made from stale bread
250g/8oz cherry tomatoes, halved
I bunch rocket
90g/3oz goat's cheese**

Method:

1 *Cook pasta in boiling water in a saucepan following packet directions. Drain, set aside and keep warm.*

2 *Heat oil in a nonstick frying pan over a medium heat, add garlic and cook, stirring, for 2 minutes or until golden. Add breadcrumbs and cook, stirring, for 5 minutes or until breadcrumbs are crisp and golden. Remove from pan and set aside.*

3 *Add tomatoes and rocket to pan and cook, stirring occasionally, for 5 minutes or until tomatoes are soft and rocket wilts. Add tomato mixture, breadcrumb mixture and cheese to pasta and toss to combine.*

Serves 4

223 calories per serve –
Fat *low* **Fibre** *medium*

spicy
seafood stir-fry

Method:

1 Make a single cut down length of each squid (calamari) tube and open out. Using a sharp knife, cut parallel lines down the length of the squid (calamari), taking care not to cut right through the flesh. Make more cuts in the opposite direction to form a diamond pattern. Cut each piece into 2¹/₂cm/1in squares. Set aside.

2 Heat oil in a wok or frying pan over a high heat, add onion, ginger, garlic and chilli paste (sambal oelek) and stir-fry for 2 minutes or until onion is golden. Add red capsicum (pepper), yellow capsicum (pepper), lime juice and honey and stir-fry for 2 minutes longer.

3 Add squid (calamari), shrimp and scallops and stir-fry for 5 minutes or until prawns just change colour. Add beans, snow peas (mangetout) and coconut milk and cook for 2 minutes or until seafood is cooked.

Serves 4

291 calories per serve -
Fat *low* ***Fibre*** *medium*

ingredients

2 squid (calamari) tubes (bodies)
1 tablespoon sesame oil
1 onion, cut into wedges and layers separated
2 teaspoons finely chopped fresh ginger
1 clove garlic, crushed
2 teaspoons chilli paste (sambal oelek)
1 red capsicum (pepper), chopped
1 yellow capsicum (pepper), chopped
2 tablespoons lime juice
1 tablespoon honey
315g/10oz medium uncooked shrimp, shelled and deveined
90g/3oz scallops, cleaned
125g/4oz green beans, cut into 2¹/₂cm/1in pieces
125g/4oz snow peas (mangetout)
¹/₄ cup/60mL/2fl oz coconut milk

pumpkin
and artichoke risotto

Method:

1 *Place stock and wine in a saucepan and bring to the boil over a medium heat. Reduce heat and keep warm.*

2 *Heat oil in a saucepan over a medium heat, add onion, cumin and nutmeg and cook, stirring, for 3 minutes or until onion is soft. Add pumpkin and cook, stirring, for 3 minutes.*

3 *Add rice and cook, stirring, for 5 minutes. Pour 1 cup/250mL/8fl oz hot stock mixture into rice and cook over a medium heat, stirring constantly, until stock is absorbed. Continue cooking in this way until all the stock is used and rice is tender.*

4 *Add artichokes, sun-dried tomatoes, sage and black pepper to taste to rice mixture. Mix gently and cook for 2 minutes or until heated through. Remove pan from heat, gently stir in Parmesan cheese and serve.*

Note: *Arborio or risotto rice is traditionally used for making risottos. It absorbs liquid without becoming soft and it is this special quality that makes it so suitable for risottos. A risotto made in the traditional way, where liquid is added gradually as the rice cooks, takes 20-30 minutes to cook.*

Serves 4

487 calories per serve -
Fat *low* ***Fibre*** *high*

ingredients

3 cups/750mL/1¹/₄pt vegetable stock
1 cup/250 mL/8fl oz white wine
1 tablespoon olive oil
1 onion, chopped
2 teaspoons ground cumin
¹/₂ teaspoon nutmeg
185g/6oz pumpkin, chopped
**1¹/₂ cups/330g/10¹/₂ oz Arborio
or risotto rice**
**440g/14oz canned artichoke hearts,
drained and chopped**
90g/3oz sun-dried tomatoes, chopped
2 tablespoons chopped fresh sage
freshly ground black pepper
30g/1oz grated Parmesan cheese

fish
and wedges

Method:

1 Pat fish dry with absorbent kitchen paper and set aside.
2 Place garlic, dill, wine and lemon juice in a shallow glass or ceramic dish and mix to combine. Add fish, cover and marinate in the refrigerator for 2 hours.
3 Place potatoes on a nonstick baking tray, brush lightly with oil and bake, turning several times, for 30-45 minutes or until potatoes are crisp and golden.
4 Drain fish well and cook under a preheated medium grill for 5 minutes or until fish flakes when tested with a fork. Serve immediately with potato wedges.

Serves 4

346 calories per serve –
Fat low   **Fibre** high

ingredients

4 firm white fish fillets
I clove garlic, crushed
I tablespoon chopped fresh dill
¹/₄ cup/60mL/2fl oz white wine
2 tablespoons lemon juice
4 large potatoes, cut into wedges
I tablespoon olive oil

Oven temperature 220°C, 425°F, Gas 7

pork
with mango couscous

Photograph page 295

pork with mango couscous

ingredients

**1¹/₂ kg/3 lb boneless pork loin, rind removed
and trimmed of all visible fat**

Mango couscous stuffing
¹/₂ cup/90g/3oz couscous
¹/₂ cup/125mL/4fl oz boiling water
¹/₂ mango, chopped
2 spring onions, chopped
3 tablespoons chopped fresh cilantra (coriander)
2 teaspoons finely grated lime rind
¹/₂ teaspoon garam masala
1 egg white, lightly beaten
1 tablespoon lime juice

Creamy wine sauce
¹/₂ cup/125mL/4fl oz chicken stock
¹/₂ cup/125mL/4fl oz white wine
2 tablespoons low-fat natural yogurt

Method:

1 *To make stuffing, place couscous in a bowl, pour over boiling water and toss with a fork until couscous absorbs all the liquid. Add mango, spring onions, cilantra (coriander), lime rind, garam masala, egg white and lime juice and mix to combine.*

2 *Lay pork out flat and spread stuffing evenly over surface. Roll up firmly and secure with string. Place pork on a wire rack set in a roasting tin, pour in 2¹/₂cm/1in water and bake for 1¹/₂ hours or until pork is cooked to your liking. Place pork on a serving platter, set aside and keep warm.*

3 *To make sauce, skim excess fat from pan juices, stir in stock and wine and bring to the boil over a medium heat. Reduce heat and*

simmer for 10 minutes or until sauce reduces by half. Remove tin from heat and whisk in yogurt. Slice pork and serve with sauce.

Note: *On completion of cooking, remove meat from oven, cover and stand in a warm place for 10-15 minutes before carving. Standing allows the juices to settle and makes carving easier.*

Serves 8

351 calories per serve -
***Fat** medium* ***Fibre** low*

red
wine steaks

Method:

1 To make marinade, place wine, Worcestershire sauce, mustard and black pepper to taste in a shallow dish and mix to combine.

2 Add steaks to marinade and set aside to marinate for at least 30 minutes. Cook steaks on a preheated hot barbecue or under a grill for 3-5 minutes each side or until cooked to your liking.

Serves 4

264 calories per serve -
Fat *medium* **Fibre** *low*

ingredients

4 lean boneless sirloin steaks

<u>Red wine marinade</u>
¼ cup/60mL/2fl oz red wine
2 tablespoons Worcestershire sauce
2 teaspoons French mustard
freshly ground black pepper

spicy
marinated lamb kebabs

Method:

1 To make marinade, combine honey, soy, garlic, cinnamon and sesame oil in a glass bowl. Add meat and marinate for 30 minutes.

2 Remove meat from marinade and thread meat onto eight bamboo skewers, alternating with capsicum (pepper), mushrooms and courgettes (zucchini). Grill under medium heat for 8-10 minutes, turning frequently and basting with marinade.

Serves 4

339 calories per serve
Fat medium   **Fibre** medium

ingredients

500g/1lb lean lamb, cubed
1 large green capsicum (pepper), cubed
16 button mushrooms
2 medium courgettes (zucchini),
sliced into 2cm/³/₄in widths

Marinade
2 tablespoons honey
1 tablespoon low-salt soy sauce
1 clove garlic, crushed
¹/₂ teaspoon ground cinnamon
2 teaspoons sesame oil

herbed
ham and pineapple pizza

Method:

1 To make dough, place sugar, yeast and $^1/_4$ cup/60mL/2fl oz water in a bowl and whisk with a fork until yeast dissolves. Set aside in a warm draught-free place for 5 minutes or until mixture is foamy.

2 Sift wholemeal flour and flour together into a bowl. Return husks to bowl. Stir in oil, yeast mixture and remaining water and mix to make a soft dough. Turn onto a lightly floured surface and knead for 10 minutes or until dough is smooth and glossy.

3 Place dough in a lightly oiled bowl, cover with plastic food wrap and set aside in a warm draught-free place for 1 hour or until doubled in volume. Punch dough down and divide into two equal portions.

4 On a lightly floured surface roll out dough to form two 30cm/12in rounds. Place pizza bases on lightly greased baking trays and spread with tomato paste (purée). Then spread with pasta sauce and top with pineapple pieces, ham and red capsicum (pepper). Sprinkle with spring onions, cheese and parsley and bake for 20 minutes or until bases are crisp and cooked.

Serves 8

335 calories per serve -
Fat low   **Fibre** high

ingredients

Wholemeal pizza dough
3 teaspoons sugar
7g/$^1/_4$oz active dry yeast
1 cup/250mL/8fl oz warm water
2 cups/315g/10oz wholemeal flour
1$^1/_4$ cups/155g/5oz flour
$^1/_4$ cup/60mL/2fl oz vegetable oil

Ham and pineapple topping
2 tablespoons tomato paste (purée)
1 cup/250mL/8fl oz bottled tomato pasta sauce
440g/14oz canned pineapple pieces in natural juices, drained
125g/4oz lean ham, chopped
1 red capsicum (pepper), sliced
4 spring onions, chopped
60g/2oz reduced-fat grated mozzarella cheese
2 tablespoons chopped fresh parsley

Oven temperature 220°C, 425°F, Gas 7

lamb
with roast capsicum (pepper) purée

Method:

1 Place garlic, wine, vinegar, mustard and honey in a shallow glass or ceramic dish and mix to combine. Add lamb, cover and marinate in the refrigerator for 3-4 hours or overnight.

2 To make purée, place red and yellow capsicum (peppers), skin side up, under a preheated hot grill and cook for 10-15 minutes or until skins are blistered and charred. Place peppers in a plastic food bag or paper bag and set aside until cool enough to handle, then remove skins. Place capsicum (peppers) and yogurt in a food processor or blender and process to make a purée. Stir in mint and set aside.

3 Drain lamb and cook under a preheated medium grill or on a barbecue for 3-5 minutes each side or until lamb is cooked to your liking. Serve with purée.

Serves 4

294 calories per serve -
Fat *medium*   **Fibre** *low*

ingredients

1 clove garlic, crushed
¼ cup/60mL/2fl oz white wine
2 tablespoons tarragon vinegar
2 tablespoons wholegrain mustard
1 tablespoon honey
8 lamb cutlets, trimmed of
all visible fat

<u>Roast capsicum (pepper) purée</u>
1 red capsicum (pepper),
seeded and quartered
1 yellow capsicum (pepper),
seeded and quartered
½ cup/100g/3½oz low-fat yogurt
2 tablespoons chopped fresh mint

orange
chicken

Photograph page 301

Method:

1 To make marinade, combine orange juice, rind, mustard, nutmeg and curry powder in a shallow glass dish. Season to taste with pepper. Add chicken and marinate for 1-2 hours.

2 Transfer chicken and a little of the marinade to a baking dish. Bake at 180°C/350°C/Gas 4 for 30 minutes or until chicken is tender. Place remaining marinade and cornflour mixture in a saucepan. Cook over medium heat until sauce boils and thickens. Spoon over chicken and serve.

Serves 4

215 calories per serve
Fat *low* **Fibre** *low*

ingredients

4 boneless chicken breasts, skinned
2 teaspoons cornflour blended with
3 tablespoons chicken stock

Marinade
³/₄ cup/190mL orange juice
1 tablespoon grated orange rind
¹/₂ teaspoon French mustard
¹/₂ teaspoon ground nutmeg
¹/₂ teaspoon curry powder
freshly ground black pepper

Oven temperature 180°C, 350°F, Gas 4

pork
with prunes and apricots

Photograph page 301

Method:

1 Heat oil in a frypan. Cook pork, onion, sage and thyme until meat changes colour and is just tender.

2 Puree apple juice, six prunes and vinegar in a food processor or blender and pour onto meat in pan. Stir in apricots and remaining prunes. Cook, covered, for 15 minutes, stirring occasionally. Serve sprinkled with almonds.

Serves 4

269 calories per serve
Fat *low* **Fibre** *high*

ingredients

2 tablespoons polyunsaturated oil
500g/1lb lean pork, cubed
1 onion, cut into eighths
¹/₂ teaspoon ground sage
¹/₂ teaspoon ground thyme
1 cup/250mL apple juice
10 large pitted prunes
1 teaspoon cider vinegar
8 dried apricots
2 tablespoons slivered almonds, toasted

Oven temperature 180°C, 350°F, Gas 4

tropical rice pudding

sweet treats

Our light, luscious and refreshing

Our light, luscious and refreshing selection of dessert recipes will satisfy any cravings for something sweet and keep you slim and healthy.

berry
peach parfaits

Method:

1 Place ricotta cheese, yogurt, maple syrup and liqueur in a bowl and beat until smooth.
2 Place a layer of ricotta mixture into the base of a parfait glass, top with a layer of mixed berries, then a second layer of ricotta mixture, a layer of peaches and a final layer of ricotta mixture. Decorate with strawberries and coconut. Repeat with remaining fruit and ricotta mixture to make six desserts.

Serves 6

216 calories per serve -
Fat *low* **Fibre** *high*

ingredients

**200g/6¹/₂oz ricotta cheese
1 cup/200g/6¹/₂oz low-fat natural yogurt
¹/₄ cup/60mL/2fl oz maple syrup
1 tablespoon orange-flavored liqueur
500g/1 lb mixed berries of your choice, such as blueberries and raspberries or strawberries and blackberries
440g/14oz canned peach slices in natural juice, drained
6 strawberries, halved
¹/₂ cup/45g/1¹/₂oz shredded coconut, toasted**

tropical
rice pudding

Photograph page 303

Method:

1 Place rice, reduced-fat milk, coconut milk, orange rind, cinnamon stick and vanilla bean (pod) in a saucepan and bring to the boil. Reduce heat, cover and simmer over a low heat for 15 minutes or until rice is tender and liquid is absorbed. Remove pan from heat, discard cinnamon stick and vanilla bean (pod) and cool slightly.
2 Stir brown sugar, egg yolks and rum into rice mixture and mix well.
3 Place egg whites in a clean bowl and beat until stiff peaks form. Fold egg whites into rice mixture. Spoon mixture in a lightly greased 23cm/9in fluted ring tin. Place ring tin in a baking dish, add enough hot water to come halfway up the sides of the tin and bake for 40 minutes or until set.
4 Remove tin from baking dish and set aside to cool. Turn mould onto a serving dish, fill centre with fruit and drizzle mould and fruit with passion fruit pulp.

Serves 8

313 calories per serve -
Fat *low* **Fibre** *medium*

ingredients

**1 cup/220g/7oz basmati rice
2¹/₂ cups/600 mL/1pt reduced-fat milk
¹/₂ cup/125mL/4fl oz coconut milk
1 tablespoon finely grated orange rind
1 cinnamon stick
1 vanilla bean (pod), split
1 cup/170g/5¹/₂oz brown sugar
3 eggs, separated
2 tablespoons dark rum
500g/1 lb tropical fruit of your choice, such as sliced guavas, tamarillos, kiwifruit, starfruit, mangoes, pawpaw and pineapple
6 passion fruit**

Oven temperature 190°C, 375°F, Gas 5

raspberry
and yogurt mousse

Method:

1 Place raspberries in a food processor or blender and process to make a purée. Press purée through a sieve to remove seeds. Stir in icing sugar.

2 Place ricotta cheese, yogurt, sugar, vanilla essence and lime or lemon juice in a food processor or blender and process until smooth.

3 Divide mixture into two equal portions. Stir raspberry purée into one portion. Alternate spoonfuls of plain and raspberry mixtures in serving glasses and swirl to give a ripple pattern. Refrigerate for at least 1 hour.

Note: To make thick yogurt, line a sieve with a double thickness of muslin or absorbent kitchen paper and place over a bowl. Place yogurt in sieve and set aside to drain for 2-3 hours at room temperature or overnight in the refrigerator.

Serves 6

155 calories per serve -
Fat medium   **Fibre** medium

315g/10oz fresh or frozen raspberries
2 teaspoons icing sugar
350g/11oz ricotta cheese
1 cup/200g/6¹/₂oz thick low-fat
natural yogurt
2 tablespoons caster sugar
2 teaspoons vanilla essence
2 teaspoons lime or lemon juice

passion fruit
souffle

Method:

1 Place ricotta cheese, passion fruit pulp, egg yolks, liqueur and half the caster sugar in a bowl and beat for 5 minutes or until mixture is smooth.

2 Place egg whites and cream of tartar in a clean bowl and beat until soft peaks form. Gradually beat in remaining caster sugar until stiff peaks form.

3 Fold one-third egg white mixture into passion fruit mixture, then fold in remaining egg white mixture.

4 Pour soufflé mixture into a greased 20cm /8in soufflé dish and bake for 20 minutes or until soufflé is well risen. Sprinkle with icing sugar and serve.

Serves 4-6

167 calories per serve -
Fat *low* **Fibre** *high*

ingredients

60g/2oz ricotta cheese
1¹/₂ cups/375mL/12fl oz passion fruit pulp
2 egg yolks
1 tablespoon orange-flavored liqueur
¹/₃ cup/75g/2¹/₂oz caster sugar
6 egg whites
pinch cream of tartar
icing sugar, sifted

Oven temperature 180°C, 350°F, Gas 4

apple
and date ricotta slice

Method:

1 Place flour and butter in a food processor and process until mixture resembles fine breadcrumbs. Add sugar and process to combine. With machine running, slowly add enough water to form a rough dough. Turn dough onto a lightly floured surface and knead briefly. Wrap dough in plastic food wrap and refrigerate for 20 minutes.

2 Roll out dough to 5mm/¼in thick and large enough to line the base of a lightly greased and lined 23cm/9in square cake tin.

3 For topping, arrange apples and dates over pastry.

4 Place ricotta cheese, sugar, flour, milk, eggs and brandy in a bowl and beat until smooth. Spoon ricotta mixture over fruit, spread out evenly and bake for 1 hour or until topping is set. Cool in tin, then cut into squares.

Makes 36

*92 calories per serve -
low fibre; low fat*

ingredients

1½ cups/235g/7½oz wholemeal
self-rising flour
60g/2oz butter or margarine
½ cup/100g/3½oz superfine sugar
¼-⅓ cup/60-90mL/2-3fl oz iced water

Apple date topping
440g/14oz canned pie apple, drained
90g/3oz fresh or dried dates,
pitted and halved
500g/1 lb ricotta cheese, drained
½ cup/100g/3½oz superfine sugar
2 tablespoons flour
½ cup/125mL/4fl oz reduced-fat milk
2 eggs, lightly beaten
1 tablespoon brandy

creamy
cheesecake

Method:

1 To make base, combine biscuit crumbs, nuts and butter. Spread over the base of a lightly greased 20cm/8in springform pan and set aside.

2 To make filling, place ricotta, cottage cheese, semolina, buttermilk and egg yolks in a food processor or blender and process until smooth.

3 Beat egg whites until soft peaks form. Add sugar a spoonful at a time, beating well after each addition until whites are thick and glossy.

4 Fold cheese mixture into egg whites, then lightly fold through lemon rind and sultanas. Spoon mixture into prepared pan and bake at 180°C/350°F/Gas 4 for 50-55 minutes or until firm. Cool in pan.

Serves 8

334 calories per serve
Fat medium   **Fibre** low

ingredients

Base
125g/4oz sweet biscuit crumbs
1 tablespoon ground hazelnuts
60g/2oz butter, melted

Filling
250g/8oz ricotta cheese
125g/4oz cottage cheese
1 tablespoon fine semolina
2 tablespoons buttermilk
3 eggs, separated
³/₄ cup/190g/6oz superfine sugar
2 teaspoons grated lemon rind
3 tablespoons sultanas (golden raisins)

Oven temperature 180°C, 350°F, Gas 4

Oven temperature 200°C, 400°F, Gas 6

fruit
brulee

Method:

1 Place apple, sultanas and cinnamon in a bowl and mix to combine. Divide mixture between four 1 cup/250mL/8fl oz capacity ramekins.

2 To make topping, place yogurt, ricotta cheese and vanilla essence in a food processor or blender and process until smooth. Spread topping over fruit, sprinkle with sugar and bake for 25 minutes or until fruit is heated through and top is golden.

Serves 4

158 calories per serve -
Fat *low* ***Fibre*** *medium*

ingredients

**440g/14oz canned unsweetened
apple pie filling
4 tablespoons sultanas (golden raisins)
1 teaspoon ground cinnamon**

Yogurt topping
**¹/₂ cup/100g/3¹/₂oz low-fat
natural yogurt
¹/₂ cup/125g/4oz ricotta cheese
1 teaspoon vanilla essence
1¹/₂ tablespoons brown sugar**

fast simple family meals

introduction

introduction

introduction

Fast simple *family meals*

There's a great deal of nostalgia for honest-to-goodness family cooking: hearty soups, pastas and satisfying family favourites, complete with desserts and an array of fresh vegetables.

Everyday Family Meals includes all the old favorites, but because we live in an era where the cooking is likely to be shared by the whole family, and time is often a commodity more sought after than rare spices, the book also contains plenty of ideas for speedy snacks, salads both simple and sumptuous, and recipes for pasta and pizzas that can be made at home in less time than it takes to telephone for a takeaway.

We all aim to eat less meat and more fresh fruit and vegetables, but it isn't always easy to persuade the family to eat up their greens. The first step to a solution is provided by the chapter on salads and sides, where convenience foods are combined with fresh produce to provide a mouthwatering selection of side dishes.

Photograph page 313 also appears on recipe page 332 (Spaghetti with tuna and olives)

shrimp bisque

soups
&
snacks

The door bangs, bags are dropped

in the hall, and the cry goes up: "What is there to eat?
Where starving!" Stave off post-school starvation with
this selection of soups and snacks.

leek
and mushroom soup

ingredients

45g/1¹/₂oz butter
2 leeks, thinly sliced
1 tablespoon yellow mustard seeds
250g/8oz button mushrooms, sliced
2 tablespoons chopped fresh thyme or
2 teaspoons dried thyme
4 cups/1 litre/1³/₄pt vegetable stock
125g/4oz risoni pasta
¹/₂ cup/125mL/4fl oz cream (heavy)

Method:

1 Melt butter in a large saucepan over a medium heat, add leeks and mustard seeds and cook, stirring, for 5 minutes or until leeks are soft and golden.

2 Add mushrooms and thyme to pan and cook for 5 minutes longer. Add stock and pasta, bring to the boil, then reduce heat and simmer for 15 minutes or until pasta is tender. Stir in cream and simmer for 5 minutes longer.

Serves 4

shrimp
bisque

Photograph page 315

ingredients

315g/10oz cooked shrimp,
shelled and deveined
¹/₂ onion, diced
¹/₂ cup/125mL/4fl oz tomato paste (purée)
2¹/₂ cups/600mL/1pt chicken stock
¹/₃ cup/90mL/3fl oz cream (heavy)
¹/₄ teaspoon paprika
freshly ground black pepper
1-2 tablespoons dry sherry

Method:

1 Place shrimp, onion and tomato paste (purée) in a food processor or blender and process to make a purée. With machine running, slowly add stock and process to combine.

2 Place shrimp mixture in a saucepan and cook over a low heat, stirring frequently, for 10 minutes or until the mixture comes to the boil.

3 Stir in cream, paprika and black pepper to taste and cook for 2 minutes or until heated through. Stir in sherry and serve immediately.

Serves 6

mexican
corn chowder

Method:

1 Melt butter in a large saucepan and cook bacon, onion, celery and chilli for 4-5 minutes or until onion softens.

2 Add stock, cumin and thyme, bring to the boil and simmer for 10 minutes.

3 Stir in flour mixture, then milk and corn kernels, stir continuously until boiling, then reduce heat and simmer for 3 minutes. Season to taste with pepper.

ingredients

10g/¹/₃oz butter
2 rashers bacon,
rind removed and chopped
1 onion, finely chopped
2 stalks celery, chopped
1 small red chilli, finely chopped
2 cups/500mL chicken stock
1 teaspoon ground cumin
1 teaspoon dried thyme
2 tablespoons flour blended with
3 tablespoons milk
1³/₄ cups/440mL milk
440g/14oz canned sweet corn kernels,
drained
freshly ground black pepper

hot ham
sandwiches

Photograph page 319

ingredients

**2 x 10cm/4in squares focaccia bread or
2 small French bread sticks
185g/6oz ricotta cheese, drained
250g/8oz smoked ham, sliced
60g/2oz sun-dried tomatoes, sliced
3 tablespoons chopped fresh basil
30g/1oz fresh Parmesan cheese
shavings**

Method:

1 Split focaccia bread or French bread sticks horizontally and spread each half with ricotta cheese. Top with ham, sun-dried tomatoes, basil and Parmesan cheese shavings. Place under a preheated hot grill and cook for 3-4 minutes or until cheese melts and is golden.

Serving suggestion: Serve with a fresh mushroom salad. To make mushroom salad, place sliced button mushrooms and chopped red pepper in a bowl. Toss with lemon juice, olive oil, chopped fresh parsley or chives, minced garlic and a pinch of chilli powder. Set aside to marinate while preparing and cooking the sandwiches.

Note: Cottage cheese can be used in place of ricotta cheese if you wish and fresh tomatoes or sliced black olives are good alternatives to the sun-dried tomatoes. To make Parmesan cheese shavings.

Serves 4

grilled
banana sandwiches

Photograph page 319

ingredients

**8 slices rye or Granary bread
2 bananas, sliced
1 avocado, sliced
8 slices Gruyère cheese**

Method:

1 Place bread under a preheated hot grill and cook for 2-3 minutes or until toasted on one side. Top untoasted side with bananas, avocado and cheese. Place under grill and cook for 3-4 minutes longer or until cheese melts and is golden.

Serving suggestion: Serve with a cos lettuce and bacon salad. To make salad, grill 1-2 rashers bacon and break into pieces. Separate leaves of 1 cos lettuce, tear into large pieces and place in a salad bowl. Sprinkle with bacon pieces, 2-3 tablespoons croûtons and 2-3 tablespoons grated Parmesan cheese. Drizzle salad with a creamy dressing.

Serves 4

hot chicken
sandwiches

Photograph below

Method:

I Spread toast with mayonnaise and top with chicken, asparagus, black pepper to taste and cheese. Place under a preheated hot grill and cook for 3-4 minutes or until cheese melts and is golden.

Serving suggestion: Accompany with a bowl of canned soup and a salad of mixed lettuces and chopped fresh herbs tossed with a French dressing.

Note: Dress up canned soup by sprinkling with croûtons or fresh herbs. Prepared croûtons are available from supermarkets and are a useful ingredient to keep in your pantry for garnishing soups and salads.

Serves 4

ingredients

8 slices wholemeal or white bread, toasted
4 tablespoons mayonnaise
500g/1 lb cooked chicken, skin removed and flesh shredded
440g/14oz canned asparagus spears, drained
freshly ground black pepper
8 slices Swiss cheese, such as Emmental or Gruyère

crusty
chicken salad rolls

Photograph page 321

Method:

1 To make salad, place mayonnaise, dressing and mustard in a bowl and mix to combine. Add chicken, apples, eggs, celery, spring onions and parsley. Season to taste with black pepper and toss to combine.

2 Cut rolls in half and spread bases with mayonnaise. Top with salad, then place other halves on top.

Note: *For a tropical chicken salad, add 125g/4oz canned diced mangoes or peaches. In summer fresh peaches or mangoes are also delicious additions.*

Serves 4

ingredients

4 large crusty bread rolls
4 tablespoons mayonnaise

Chicken salad
$^1/_2$ cup/125mL/4fl oz mayonnaise
2 tablespoons vinaigrette dressing
1 teaspoon French mustard
**1 cooked chicken, skinned,
boned and cut into small pieces**
2 eating apples, peeled, cored and diced
2 hard-boiled eggs, diced
2 stalks celery, sliced thinly
2 spring onions, shredded
1 tablespoon chopped fresh parsley
freshly ground black pepper

smoked
salmon crossiants

Photograph page 321

Method:

1 To make filling, place cream cheese and sour cream into a bowl and beat until smooth. Add salmon, spring onion, dill, capers and lime or lemon juice and mix to combine.

2 Top bottom half of each croissant with filling, then place other halves on top.

Serves 4

ingredients

4 croissants, split

Smoked salmon filling
155g/5oz cream cheese, softened
$^1/_4$ cup/60g/2oz sour cream
155g/5oz sliced smoked salmon, chopped
1 spring onion, thinly sliced
3 teaspoons chopped fresh dill
2 teaspoons capers, drained and chopped
2 teaspoons lime or lemon juice

cheesy noodles

faster pasta

Simple and speedy to prepare,

*inexpensive, satisfying and extremely versatile –
there can be few ingredients with so much to offer
as pasta. As the recipes in this chapter prove,
pasta is equally happy when topped with a simple
sauce or as the basis for a hearty family bake.*

spaghetti
with pesto

Method:

1 Combine basil, pine nuts, garlic, sugar and salt in a blender or food processor. Process briefly to mix. With motor running, gradually add oil through lid or feeder tube, as when making mayonnaise. The mixture will form a thick sauce. Scrape pesto into a bowl or jug, cover and set aside.

2 Bring a large saucepan of lightly salted water to the boil. Add spaghetti and cook until just tender.

3 Drain spaghetti and tip it into a heated bowl. Add pesto and toss until all the spaghetti is evenly coated. Serve at once, garnished with fresh basil.

Serves 6

ingredients

60g/2oz fresh basil leaves, plus basil sprigs for garnish
3 tablespoons pine nuts
4 cloves garlic, crushed
$1/4$ teaspoon sugar
$1/2$ teaspoon salt
5 tablespoon mild olive oil
375g/12oz spaghetti

cheesy
noodles

Photograph page 323

ingredients

2 x 90g/3oz packets quick-cooking noodles
4 tablespoons sour cream
freshly ground black pepper
60g/2oz tasty cheese (mature cheddar), grated

Method:

1 Prepare noodles according to packet directions. Drain, add sour cream and black pepper to taste and toss to combine.

2 Divide noodle mixture between two heatproof serving dishes and sprinkle with cheese. Place under a preheated hot grill and cook for 3-4 minutes until cheese melts and is golden.

Serving suggestion: Accompany with a salad made of the lettuce or lettuces of your choice, cherry tomatoes, chopped or sliced red or green peppers and chopped or sliced cucumber tossed with a French dressing.

Note: Mixtures of fresh salad greens are available from many greengrocers and supermarkets. These are an economical and easy alternative to buying a variety of lettuces and making your own salads of mixed lettuce leaves.

Serves 2

curried
vegetable salad

Method:

1. Cook pasta in boiling water in a large saucepan following packet directions. Drain, rinse under cold running water and cool completely.

2. Boil, steam or microwave broccoli and carrots separately until just tender. Drain and refresh under cold running water. Drain again and place in a serving bowl. Add zucchini (courgettes), red pepper, spring onions and pasta and toss to combine.

3. To make dressing, place mayonnaise, mustard, lemon juice, curry powder and black pepper to taste in a bowl and mix to combine. Spoon dressing over salad and toss to combine. Serve at room temperature.

Note: This dish makes a great vegetarian main meal when served with a tossed green salad and crusty bread or serve it as an accompaniment to grilled chicken or meat.

ingredients

250g/8oz macaroni
250g/8oz broccoli,
cut into small florets
2 carrots, cut into matchsticks
2 zucchini (courgettes),
cut into matchsticks
I red pepper, cut into thin strips
2 spring onions, thinly sliced

Curry dressing
4 tablespoons mayonnaise
I tablespoon French mustard
I tablespoon lemon juice
$1/2$ teaspoon curry powder
freshly ground black pepper

creamy
pea and ham pasta

Photograph page 327

Method:

1 Cook pasta in boiling water in a large saucepan following packet directions. Drain, set aside and keep warm.

2 Boil, steam or microwave peas until just cooked.

3 Place pasta, peas, ham and cream in a frying pan and heat over a medium heat, stirring frquently, for 5 minutes or until heated through. Season to taste with black pepper. Sprinkle with Parmesan cheese and serve immediately.

Note: Fresh Parmesan cheese is available from Continental delicatessens and some supermarkets. It is best purchased in a piece, then grated as required. Fresh Parmesan cheese has a milder and better flavour than the grated powder that comes in packets.

Serves 4

ingredients

500g/1 lb linguine, spaghetti or other thin pasta of your choice
155g/5oz shelled fresh or frozen peas
250g/8oz diced ham
1 cup/250mL/8fl oz cream (heavy)
freshly ground black pepper
grated fresh Parmesan cheese

speedy
lasagne

Photograph page 327

Method:

1 Heat oil in frying pan over a medium heat, add beef and cook, stirring constantly, to break up, for 5 minutes or until beef is brown. Drain off excess fat and stir in pasta sauce. Bring to simmering and simmer, stirring occasionally, for 10 minutes.

2 Place ricotta cheese, parsley, egg and black pepper to taste in a bowl and mix well to combine.

3 Spread one-third of the meat sauce over base of a lightly greased ovenproof dish, top with one-third lasagne sheets, cutting to fit as necessary, and one-third ricotta cheese mixture, then sprinkle with one-third mozzarella cheese and one-third Parmesan cheese. Repeat layers, to use all ingredients, finishing with a layer of cheese. Bake for 25 minutes or until top is golden and lasagne is hot.

Note: If fresh lasagne is unavailable instant (no precooking required) lasagne can be used instead. When using this type of lasagne dip the lasagne sheets in warm water before assembling.

For a complete meal serve with garlic bread and a fresh green salad.

Serves 6

ingredients
2 tablespoons olive oil
250g/8oz lean ground beef
3 cups/750mL/1¼pt bottled tomato pasta sauce
500g/1 lb ricotta cheese, drained
2 tablespoons chopped fresh parsley
1 egg
freshly ground black pepper
500g/1 lb fresh lasagne sheets
500g/1 lb grated mozzarella cheese
125g/4oz grated Parmesan cheese

Oven temperature 180°C, 350°F, Gas 4

Method:

1 Place hot pasta and 125g/4oz cheese in a lightly greased ovenproof dish, mix to combine and set aside.

2 Cook ham in a nonstick frying pan for 3-4 minutes. Add mushrooms and cook for 3 minutes longer. Spoon ham mixture over pasta and top with pasta sauce and basil. Combine breadcrumbs and remaining cheese. Sprinkle cheese mixture over pasta and bake for 20 minutes.

Serving suggestion: Accompany with a broccoli and cauliflower salad. To make salad, combine 2 tablespoons lemon juice, 2 teaspoons Dijon mustard, 3 tablespoons olive oil, 1 tablespoon finely chopped fresh parsley and black pepper to taste and toss with cooked broccoli and cauliflower florets.

Note: For quicker preparation, buy products that are partly prepared - cubed meat, grated cheese, instant (no precooking required) lasagne and boned chicken. Many supermarkets and greengrocers also sell fresh salads and vegetable mixes for soups and casseroles.

Serves 4

cheesy
pasta bake

ingredients

**500g/1 lb pasta of your choice, cooked
220g/7oz tasty cheese
(mature cheddar), grated
8 slices ham, shredded
250g/8oz button mushrooms, sliced
750g/1 ½ lb jar tomato pasta sauce
2 tablespoons chopped fresh basil
30g/1oz breadcrumbs,
made from stale bread**

Oven temperature 200°C, 400°F, Gas 6

pasta
puttanesca

Method:

1 Cook pasta in boiling water in a large saucepan following packet directions. Drain, set aside and keep warm.

2 To make sauce, heat oil in a saucepan over a low heat, add garlic and cook, stirring, for 2 minutes. Add tomatoes and bring to the boil, then stir in anchovies, black olives, capers, oregano and chilli powder and simmer for 3 minutes longer. Spoon sauce over hot pasta, sprinkle with parsley and Parmesan cheese and serve.

Note: With practice the sauce can be made in 20 minutes. The reserved juice from the tomatoes can be frozen and used in a casserole or soup at a later date.

Serves 6

ingredients

500g/1 lb linguine or thin spaghetti

Puttanesca sauce
2 tablespoons olive oil
5 cloves garlic, crushed
4 x 440g/14oz cans peeled Italian plum tomatoes, drained and chopped
6 anchovy fillets, coarsely chopped
60g/2oz stoned black olives
2 tablespoons capers, drained and chopped
1 teaspoon dried oregano
$^1/_4$ teaspoon chilli powder
$^1/_2$ bunch flat-leaved parsley, coarsely chopped
30g/1oz grated Parmesan cheese

fettuccine
with mushrooms

Method:

1 Cook pasta in boiling water in a large saucepan following packet directions. Drain, add 15g/¹/₂oz butter, toss, set aside and keep warm.

2 Heat oil and remaining butter in a frying pan over a medium heat, add mushrooms and cook, stirring, for 5 minutes or until the mushrooms start to give up their juices. Season to taste with black pepper. Sprinkle with parsley and cook for 1 minute longer.

3 Spoon mushrooms and pan juices over pasta, toss and sprinkle with Parmesan cheese.

Serves 4

ingredients

500g/1 lb fettuccine
30g/1oz butter
2 tablespoons olive oil
315g/10oz mushrooms, thinly sliced
freshly ground black pepper
3 tablespoons chopped flat-leaved parsley
4 tablespoons grated Parmesan cheese

creamy
mushroom gnocchi

Method:

1 Place potatoes in a bowl and mash. Add flour, butter, half the Parmesan cheese and black pepper to taste and mix to make a stiff dough. Turn dough onto a lightly floured surface and knead until smooth. Shape dough into 2½cm/1in ovals and press with the back of a fork.

2 Cook gnocchi, in batches, in boiling water in a large saucepan for 3 minutes or until they rise to the surface. Using a slotted spoon, remove gnocchi from pan and place in a greased shallow, ovenproof dish.

3 To make sauce, melt butter in a frying pan over a medium heat, add mushrooms and cook, stirring, for 5 minutes. Stir in mustard and cream and bring to the boil, reduce heat and simmer for 10 minutes or until sauce reduces and thickens.

4 Spoon sauce over gnocchi. Sprinkle with tasty cheese (mature cheddar) and Parmesan cheese and bake for 10-15 minutes or until cheese melts.

Note: For a delicious alternative, shred 250g/8oz spinach and blanch in boiling water for 1 minute. Drain well and squeeze to remove as much liquid as possible, then stir into potato mixture. Serve gnocchi with crusty bread and a salad of crisp vegetables and mixed lettuces.

Serves 4

ingredients

500g/1 lb potatoes, cooked
2 cups/250g/8oz flour, sifted
30g/1oz butter, melted
30g/1oz grated Parmesan cheese
freshly ground black pepper

<u>Mushroom sauce</u>
30g/1oz butter
125g/4oz button mushrooms, sliced
2 tablespoons wholegrain mustard
1 cup/250mL/8fl oz cream (heavy)
**60g/2oz grated tasty cheese
(mature cheddar)**
30g/1oz grated Parmesan cheese

Oven temperature 180°C, 350°F, Gas 4

331

spaghetti
with tuna and olives

Method:

1 Cook spaghetti in boiling water in a large saucepan following packet directions. Drain and set aside to keep warm.

2 To make sauce, heat reserved oil from tuna in a frypan and cook onion, pepper and garlic for 3-4 minutes or until onion is soft. Stir in tomato puree, tomato paste and wine and cook for 3-4 minutes.

3 Add tuna to sauce and cook, stirring gently, for 4-5 minutes. Spoon sauce over spaghetti and toss to combine. Garnish with black pepper, parsley and olives.

Serves 4

ingredients

1 lb/500g tubular spaghetti

Tuna sauce
14 oz/440g canned tuna in oil, drained & oil reserved
1 large onion, chopped
1 green pepper, sliced
1 teaspoon minced garlic
1 1/2 cups/375g tomato puree
1 tablespoon tomato paste
1/2 cup/125mL white wine
1 tablespoon cracked black pepper
2 tablespoons finely chopped fresh parsley
8 pitted black olives, halved

fettuccine
bacon and cream

Method:

1 Cook fettuccine in boiling water in a large saucepan following packet directions. Drain and set aside to keep warm.

2 To make sauce, cook bacon in a large frypan for 4-5 minutes or until crisp. Add shallots, and cook for 1 minute longer. Stir in cream and stock, bring to the boil then reduce heat and simmer until reduced and thickened. Stir in sun-dried tomatoes and toss fettuccine in cream sauce. Sprinkle with Parmesan cheese and serve.

Serving suggestion: A crisp salad and crusty bread is all that is needed to finish this course.

Serves 4

ingredients

500g/1lb dried fettuccine
4 tablespoons grated Parmesan cheese

Bacon and cream sauce
2 rashers of bacon, trimmed and chopped
4 green shallots, chopped
¹/₂ cup/125 mL cream
¹/₂ cup/125mL chicken stock
3 tablespoons chopped sun-dried tomatoes (optional)

kingfish potato casserole

simple
seafood

Fish is one of the healthiest main meal

foods that you can eat and one of the quickest to cook.

The recipes in this section range from simple Salmon

Croquettes to a terrific Tuna and Macaroni Bake.

speedy
bouillabaisse

Method:

1 Heat oil in a large frying pan over a medium heat, add onions, garlic and chilli and cook, stirring, for 4 minutes or until onions are soft.

2 Add shrimp and cook for 1 minute. Add mussels, scallops, soup and stock and bring to simmering.

3 Stir in squid (calamari) and herbs and cook for 1 minute longer or until seafood is cooked.

Serving suggestion: Serve with quick-cooking brown rice or pasta.

Serves 4

kingfish
potato casserole

Photograph page 335

Method:

1 Preheat oven to moderate temperature 200°C/400°/Gas 6.

2 Boil potatoes. When cooked, mash with butter and hot milk. Spread potato into the bottom of a large, shallow, greased casserole dish.

3 Spread one third of the sour cream over the potatoes, and spoon chopped onion over.

4 Arrange fish on top. Sprinkle with combined breadcrumbs and cheese. Spread remaining sour cream over crumb mixture, and sprinkle with paprika.

5 Bake in the moderately hot preheated oven for 30 minutes.

Serves 6

ingredients

6 medium potatoes
30g/1oz butter
85mL/2¹/₂fl oz hot milk
300mL/10fl oz sour cream
1 small onion (finely chopped)
6 kingfish fillets
65g/2oz dry breadcrumbs
2 tablespoons cheese (grated)
ground paprika

Oven temperature 200°C, 400°F, Gas 6

salmon
croquettes

Method:

1 Combine potato, onion, salmon, mustard, mayonnaise and egg, season to taste. Shape mixture into croquettes and roll in cookie crumbs to coat.

2 Heat oil in a frypan. Cook croquettes over medium heat until golden brown. Drain on absorbent paper.

Serves 4

ingredients

3 large potatoes, cooked and mashed
1 onion, grated
440g/14oz canned pink salmon, drained and flaked
1 teaspoon Dijon-style mustard
2 tablespoons mayonnaise
1 egg, beaten
220g/7oz cheese flavoured cookies, crushed
polyunsaturated oil for cooking

barbequed
shark and vegetables
with orange vinaigrette

Photograph page 339

*barbequed shark and
vegetables with orange
vinaigrette*

ingredients

**1kg/2lb fresh shark steaks (cut into
chunks about 2¹/₂cm/1in-thick)
2 red or yellow pepper (capsicums)
(pierced once with a knife)
12 small red-skinned potatoes
(washed)
orange vinaigrette (see below)
3 zucchini (ends trimmed)
1 head radicchio (red chicory)**

Method:

1 Cut the shark into 6 even pieces. Set aside.

2 Heat a barbecue (until coals are medium-hot). Pierce capsicums with a knife and place on the hottest part of the grill. The skin should blister and char slightly after 12 minutes. Place in an airtight plastic lock bag. Allow to steam and cool. When cool enough to handle, peel away the skin and discard it.

3 If desired, thread all the potatoes on metal skewers. Place them over the hottest part of the fire. Cook for 25-30 minutes (turning occasionally, and basting with the orange vinaigrette).

4 Add zucchini, and cook (until slightly blackened, but tender). Baste occasionally with orange vinaigrette. (Zucchini will require about 8-10 minutes total cooking time.)

5 Add the shark steaks, and cook (for 6 minutes per side). Baste occasionally with orange vinaigrette. Slice radicchio in half lengthwise, and add to grill. Baste with vinaigrette. Cook for 4-5 minutes, until leaves are wilted and slightly charred. Remove all vegetables and fish from grill. Keep warm.

6 Transfer remaining orange vinaigrette to a microwave-safe container. Cook on high (100%) power for 2 minutes, stirring occasionally (until mixture boils). Drizzle over hot vegetables and fish, and serve.

Serves 6

ORANGE VINAIGRETTE

**Ingredients
2 tablespoons olive oil
1 teaspoon chopped ginger
1 tablepoon soy sauce
1 teaspoon orange rind
250mL/8fl oz orange juice
2 tablespoons balsamic vinegar
pinch cayenne pepper
1 teaspoon dry mustard**

Method

1 Combine all ingredients. Blend well. Transfer to a container with an air-tight lid. Shake vigerously before serving.

2 Dressing can be made up to one week in advance

tomato
basil trout

Method:

1 Heat oil in a large frying pan, add spring onions and garlic and cook for 1 minute. Add trout to pan, pour over wine and top with tomatoes, basil and black pepper to taste. Cover and simmer for 10 minutes or until fish flakes when test with a fork.

Serving suggestion: Vegetables and crispy potato wedges are the perfect accompaniment to this dish. To make potato wedges, cut small potatoes into wedges and boil or microwave until tender. Drain and pat dry. Toss potatoes with 1/4 teaspoon chilli powder, 1 teaspoon ground turmeric, 1/2 teaspoon garam masala, 1 teaspoon ground coriander and 1/2 teaspoon ground ginger to coat. Shallow-fry for 5-10 minutes or until potatoes are crisp.

Note: Trout freezes well and keeping a few trout in your freezer ensures that you always have a basis for a tasty meal.

Remember when freezing any fish or shellfish that it has a shorter freezer life than meat or chicken because of the higher proportion of polyunsaturated fats in it. Frozen fish is best used within 3 months of freezing and should be cooked directly from frozen, this ensures that it holds its shape and retains its flavour and texture.

Serves 4

ingredients

2 teaspoons vegetable oil
4 spring onions, chopped
1 clove garlic, crushed
4 small trout, cleaned
3/4 cup/185mL/6fl oz red wine
4 tomatoes, chopped
4 tablespoons chopped fresh basil
freshly ground black pepper

parmesan
crusted fish

Method:

1 Pat fish dry. Combine flour, paprika and black pepper to taste. Combine breadcrumbs and Parmesan cheese. Coat fillets with flour mixture. Dip in egg, then coat with breadcrumb mixture. Heat oil in a frying pan over a medium heat, add fillets and cook for 2-3 minutes each side or until cooked.

2 To make Lemon Thyme Butter, heat butter, lemon rind, lemon juice and thyme in a saucepan over a medium heat for 1 minute or until butter melts. Serve with fish fillets.

Serving suggestion: *Accompany with potato crisps and vegetables. To make crisps, using a vegetable peeler, peel thin slices from potatoes. Dry slices and deep-fry for 7-10 minutes or until cooked. Drain and sprinkle with salt.*

Serves 4

ingredients

4 firm white fish fillets
¹/₂ cup/60g/2oz flour
1 teaspoon paprika
freshly ground pepper
1 cup/125g/4oz dried breadcrumbs
90g/3oz grated Parmesan cheese
1 egg, lightly beaten
2 tablespoons olive oil

<u>Lemon thyme butter</u>
60g/2oz butter
1 tablespoon grated lemon rind
1 tablespoon lemon juice
1 tablespoon chopped fresh thyme
or lemon thyme

unbelievable
salmon quiche

Photograph page 343

Method:

1 *Place flour, eggs and butter in a food processor and process to combine.*
2 *Pour egg mixture into a pie plate. Top with salmon, onion and black pepper to taste, then sprinkle with cheese and bake for 35-40 minutes or until mixture is set and top is brown.*

Note: *As this quiche cooks a crust forms on the bottom of it.*

For variety, canned tuna, cooked bacon, ham or chopped cooked chicken or turkey can be used in place of the salmonto make this magic recipe.

Serves 4

ingredients

¹/₂ cup/60g/2oz flour
5 eggs
60g/2oz butter, softened
**220g/7oz canned red salmon,
drained and flaked**
I onion, diced
freshly ground black pepper
**60g/2oz grated tasty cheese
(mature cheddar)**

Oven temperature 180°C, 350°F, Gas 4

tuna
and macaroni bake

Photograph page 343

Method:

1 *Melt butter in a saucepan over a medium heat, stir in flour and cook for I minute. Remove pan from heat, add mustard and slowly stir in milk and lemon juice. Return pan to heat and cook, stirring constantly, for 5 minutes or until sauce boils and thickens.*
2 *Stir in tuna, pasta, half the cheese and black pepper to taste. Spoon mixture into a greased shallow ovenproof dish, sprinkle with remaining cheese and bake for 20 minutes or until cheese melts and top is golden.*

Note: *A great way to use up leftover pasta, this traditional family favourite is also delicious made with canned salmon, ham leftover cooked chicken or turkey in place of the tuna.*

Serves 4

ingredients

60g/2oz butter
2 tablespoons flour
I teaspoon dry mustard
I¹/₂ cups/375mL/12fl oz milk
2 teaspoons lemon juice
**220g/7oz canned tuna,
drained and flaked**
**90g/3oz elbow macaroni or other small
pasta, cooked**
**125g/4oz grated tasty cheese
(mature cheddar)**
freshly ground black pepper

Oven temperature 180°C, 350°F, Gas 4

chicken tacos

family favorites

It's great to come home to the

*mouthwatering aroma of a home made pizza. This chapter
also includes vegetarian dishes and tasty grilled chicken that is
bound to become a family favorite.*

ginger
beef with cashews

Method:
1 Using a sharp knife, slice meat thinly across the grain.
2 Heat oil in a wok or frying pan over a medium heat, add garlic and ginger and stir-fry for 1 minute. Increase heat to high, add beef and stir-fry for 2-3 minutes or until meat is brown.
3 Add cabbage, red pepper, bean sprouts and soy sauce and stir-fry for 2 minutes or until cabbage just starts to wilt.
4 Divide noodles between serving plates, top with beef mixture and scatter with cashews.
Serves 4

ingredients

500g/1 lb lean sirloin or rump steak
1 tablespoon vegetable oil
2 cloves garlic, crushed
1 teaspoon finely grated fresh ginger
$\frac{1}{2}$ Chinese cabbage (pak choi), shredded
$\frac{1}{2}$ red pepper (capsicum), sliced thinly
30g/1oz bean sprouts
1$\frac{1}{2}$ tablespoons soy sauce
3 x 75g/2$\frac{1}{2}$oz packets quick-cooking noodles, cooked and kept warm
60g/2oz raw cashews, roasted

chicken tacos

Photograph page 345

Method:
1 To make filling, heat oil in a frying pan, add onion, spring onions and tomatoes and cook, stirring, for 4 minutes. Add chicken, taco seasoning mix and salsa and cook, stirring, for 2 minutes longer or until heated through.
2 Spoon filling into taco shells and top with lettuce, red pepper, cheese, avocado and sour cream.
Serving suggestion: Accompany with a celery salad and crusty bread. To make salad, combine 2 tablespoons olive oil, 2 tablespoons white wine vinegar, 1 teaspoon Dijon mustard and freshly ground black pepper to taste, spoon over sliced celery and toss to combine.
Note: Remember to make turning the oven on the first step when you are preparing a meal that requires you to cook in it.
Serves 4

ingredients

12 taco shells, warmed
8 lettuce leaves, shredded
1 red pepper (capsicum), thinly sliced
125g/4oz tasty cheese (mature cheddar), grated
1 avocado, stoned, peeled and sliced
$\frac{1}{2}$ cup/125g/4oz sour cream

Chicken filling
2 teaspoons vegetable oil
1 onion, chopped
2 spring onions, chopped
3 tomatoes, chopped
1 kg/2 lb cooked chicken, skin removed and flesh shredded
2 tablespoons taco seasoning mix
4 tablespoons bottled tomato salsa

burgers
with a lot

Method:

1 Place ground beef, breadcrumbs, egg and parsley in a bowl and mix to combine. Shape mixture into six patties.

2 Heat oil in a frying pan over a medium heat, add patties and cook for 3 minutes each side or until cooked to your liking.

3 Cut rolls in half and toast under a preheated medium grill for 2-3 minutes each side or until golden. Spread bottom halves of rolls with tomato relish and top each with a pattie, a lettuce leaf, some alfalfa sprouts, some beetroot, a slice of cheese and top half of roll.

Serving suggestion: Accompany with oven fries and coleslaw. To make coleslaw, place finely shredded cabbage, grated carrot, chopped celery, chopped red pepper (capsicum) and grated tasty cheese (mature cheddar) in a large bowl, add 3-4 tablespoons creamy or coleslaw dressing and toss to combine. Sprinkle with chopped fresh parsley.

Note: Many fresh salads are available from supermarkets and delicatessans. When time is really short these salads are a great timesaver.

Serves 6

ingredients

500g/1 lb lean ground beef
³/₄ cup/45g/1¹/₂oz wholemeal breadcrumbs, made from stale bread
1 egg, lightly beaten
1 tablespoon chopped fresh parsley
1 tablespoon vegetable oil
6 wholegrain rolls
4 tablespoons tomato relish
6 lettuce leaves
60g/2oz alfalfa sprouts
1 raw beetroot, peeled and grated
6 slices Swiss cheese such as Emmental

fish
and chips

Method:

1 To make batter, place flour in a bowl and make a well in the centre. Add egg whites, beer and 1 tablespoon vegetable oil and mix until smooth.

2 Cook oven fries according to packet directions.

3 Heat 5cm/2in oil in a frying pan over a medium heat until a cube of bread dropped in browns in 50 seconds. Dip fish into batter, add to pan and cook for 3 minutes each side or until golden brown. Drain on absorbent kitchen paper. Serve with oven fries.

Serving suggestion: Accompany with a salad or vegetables of your choice.

Note: Get to know your supermarket and write shopping lists according to the layout of the shelves.

Serves 4

ingredients

500g/1 lb oven fries
vegetable oil for shallow-frying
4 boneless firm white fish fillets

Beer batter
1 cup/125g/4oz flour
2 egg whites
³/₄ cup/185mL/6fl oz beer
1 tablespoon vegetable oil

super
steak sandwiches

Method:

1 Heat oil in a frying pan over a high heat, add onions and cook, stirring, for 2-3 minutes or until onions are soft. Push onions to side of pan, add steaks and pineapple rings and cook for 2 minutes each side or until steak is cooked to your liking.

2 Top 4 slices of toast each with a slice of cheese, 2 slices tomato, a lettuce leaf, a steak, some onions, a pineapple ring, a spoonful of tomato or barbecue sauce and remaining toast slices. Serve immediately.

Serving suggestion: Serve with oven fries or potatoes and coleslaw.

Note: Steak sandwiches can also be cooked on the barbecue; rather than cooking in a frying pan cook on a lightly oiled preheated medium barbecue plate (griddle).

Serves 4

ingredients

2 teaspoons vegetable oil
2 onions, chopped
4 small lean rump steaks
4 canned pineapple rings, drained
8 thick slices wholemeal bread, toasted
4 slices tasty cheese (mature cheddar)
8 slices tomato
4 lettuce leaves
tomato or barbecue sauce

mixed
vegetable omelette

Method:

1 Melt 60g/2oz butter in a frypan, add leek, vegetables, garlic and mustard seed. Stir over medium heat for 5 minutes or until vegetables are just tender, remove from pan and keep warm.

2 Beat eggs and water together until fluffy, season to taste. Melt remaining butter in pan. Pour in half the egg mixture and cook until set. Spoon half the vegetable mixture onto omelette and fold over. Repeat with remaining egg mixture and vegetables.

Timesaver: Using some of the frozen mixed vegetable varieties for this recipe cuts down on preparation time as the chopping of the vegetables is eliminated. The cooking will remain the same.

ingredients

90g/3oz butter
I leek, washed and sliced
I ¹/₂ cups/375g finely chopped
mixed vegetables of your choice
I clove garlic, crushed
I teaspoon mustard seed
6 eggs
3 tablespoons water

350

Serves 2

vegetarian
pie

Method:

1 Combine rice, cheeses, shallots, zucchini, carrot, asparagus, pine nuts, eggs and yogurt. Season with pepper.
2 Spoon mixture into a deep well-greased 23cm/9in springform pan. Bake at 190°C/ 370°C/Gas 5 for 40 minutes or until firm. Cut into wedges to serve.

Serves 6

ingredients

2 cups/300g cooked brown rice
1²/₃ cups/225g grated tasty cheese
4 tablespoons grated Parmesan cheese
2 shallots, chopped
2 zucchini, grated
1 carrot, peeled and grated
1 cup/150g canned asparagus cuts, drained
3 tablespoons pine nuts, toasted
3 eggs, lightly beaten
220g/7oz unflavoured yogurt
freshly ground black pepper

Oven temperature 190°C, 370°F, Gas 5

351

fast
lamb curry

Method:

1 Heat oil in a wok or frying pan over a medium heat, add curry paste and cumin and cook, stirring, for 1 minute. Add lamb and stir-fry for 3 minutes or until lamb changes colour and is tender. Remove lamb mixture from pan and set aside.

2 Add red pepper (capsicum), zucchini (courgettes), broccoli and cauliflower to pan and stir-fry for 2 minutes. Stir in coconut milk and stock, bring to simmering and simmer for 4 minutes. Return lamb to pan and cook for 2 minutes longer or until heated through.

Serving suggestion: Serve with rice or noodles and poppadums.

Serves 4

ingredients

2 teaspoons vegetable oil
1 tablespoon curry paste
1 teaspoon ground cumin
500g/1 lb lean lamb fillets, cut into strips
1 red pepper (capsicum), cut into strips
2 zucchini (courgettes), sliced
250g/8oz broccoli florets
**250g/8oz cauliflower,
broken into small florets**
1 cup/250mL/8fl oz coconut milk
1/2 cup/125mL/4fl oz beef stock

grilled
chicken in pesto

Method:

1 Heat oil in a char-grill or frying pan over a high heat. Add chicken and cook for 4-5 minutes each side or until cooked through. Set aside and keep warm.

2 Add red pepper (capsicum), green peppe (capsicum)r, zucchini (courgettes) and eggplant (aubergines) to pan and cook for 2 minutes each side or until soft.

3 To make sauce, place pesto, mayonnaise, vinegar and black pepper to taste in bowl and mix to combine. To serve, arrange vegetables on serving plates, top with chicken and a spoonful of sauce.

Serving suggestion: Accompany with crusty bread.

Note: This recipe is ideal for cooking on the barbecue. Instead of cooking the chicken and vegetables in a char-grill or frying pan, simply cook on a lightly oiled preheated medium barbecue grill.

ingredients

2 teaspoons vegetable oil
4 boneless chicken breast fillets
1 red pepper (capsicum), quartered
1 green pepper (capsicum), quartered
2 zucchini (courgettes), halved lengthwise
2 baby eggplant (aubergines), halved lengthwise

Pesto sauce
1/2 cup/125g/4oz ready-made pesto
1/2 cup/125g/4oz mayonnaise
2 tablespoons balsamic or red wine vinegar
freshly ground black pepper

chicken
parcels

Method:

1 Melt butter in a frying pan, add mushrooms and spring onions and cook for 3 minutes. Remove pan from heat, add chicken, sour cream and black pepper to taste and set aside.

2 Roll out pastry to 5mm/¹/₄in thick and cut out four 18cm/7in rounds. Divide chicken mixture into four portions and place one portion on one half of each pastry round. Fold over other half of pastry and press edges to seal. Place parcels on a baking tray, brush with egg and bake for 15 minutes or until pastry is golden.

Serving suggestion: Delicious served with a salad of spinach and grilled bacon. To make salad, tear spinach leaves into pieces and place in a bowl. Scatter with grilled bacon pieces and chopped sun-dried tomatoes. Combine 2 tablespoons olive oil, 2 tablespoons balsamic or red wine vinegar and freshly ground black pepper to taste, spoon over salad and toss.

Serves 4

ingredients

15g/¹/₂oz butter
375g/12oz button mushrooms, halved
3 spring onions, chopped
1 kg/2 lb cooked chicken, skin removed and flesh chopped
³/₄ cup/185g/6oz sour cream
freshly ground black pepper
500g/1 lb prepared shortcrust pastry
1 egg, lightly beaten

mustard
crusted steaks

Method:

1 To make crust, place mustard, garlic, honey and mayonnaise in a small bowl and mix to combine. Spread mustard mixture over steaks.

2 Heat oil in a frying pan over a high heat, add steaks and cook for 2 minutes each side or until cooked to your liking.

Serving suggestion: *An unusual accompaniment is broccoli with browned garlic. To make, divide a large head of broccoli into small florets, then boil, steam or microwave it until just tender. Refresh under cold running water. Divide a head of garlic into individual cloves and peel each clove. Heat 3 tablespoons olive oil in a frying pan, add garlic and cook, stirring, for 5-7 minutes or until garlic is brown. Take care that the garlic does not burn. Add broccoli to pan and cook, stirring, for 2-3 minutes or until heated. To complete the meal add mashed potatoes and finish with Caramel Chip Ice Cream.*

Serves 4

ingredients

4 lean beef fillet steaks
2 teaspoons vegetable oil

Mustard crust
4 tablespoons wholegrain mustard
1 clove garlic, crushed
1 tablespoon honey
2 tablespoons mayonnaise

355

Oven temperature 230°C, 450°F, Gas 8

pizzas

Method:

1 *To assemble pizzas, spread bases with pasta sauce or tomato paste (purée).*
2 *For Supreme pizza, top a prepared pizza base with ham, salami, green peppe (capsicum)r, pineapple pieces, mushrooms and olives, if using.*
3 *For Hawaiian pizza, top a prepared pizza base with ham, pineapple pieces and red pepper (capsicum).*
4 *For Vegetarian pizza, top a prepared pizza base with mushrooms, red pepper (capsicum), broccoli and onion.*
5 *Sprinkle pizzas with cheese, place on baking trays and bake for 20 minutes at 230°C/450°F/Gas 8 or until base is crisp and golden.*
Serving suggestions: *All that pizzas require to make a complete meal is a tossed green salad.*
Serves 4-6

ingredients

3 large purchased pizza bases
1¹/₂ cups/375mL/12fl oz pasta sauce or tomato paste (purée)
375g/12oz mozzarella cheese or tasty cheese (mature cheddar), grated

Supreme topping
8 slices ham, chopped
6 slices spicy salami
¹/₂ green pepper (capsicum), chopped
125g/4oz canned pineapple pieces, drained
125g/4oz button mushrooms, sliced
60g/2oz pitted olives (optional)

Hawaiian topping
10 slices ham, shredded
185g/6oz canned pineapple pieces, drained
¹/₂ red pepper (capsicum), chopped

Vegetarian topping
250 g/8 oz button mushrooms, sliced
1/2 red pepper (capsicum), chopped
155g/5oz broccoli, broken into small florets
1 small onion, sliced

family favorites

pork steaks
with red wine marinade

Method:

1 To make marinade, place garlic, red wine, sugar and black pepper to taste in a shallow glass or ceramic dish. Add steaks, turn to coat and marinate for 5 minutes. Turn over and marinate for 5 minutes longer. Drain steaks and reserve marinade.

2 Heat oil in a frying pan over a high heat, add steaks and cook for 1-2 minutes each side or until cooked to your liking. Remove steaks from pan, set aside and keep warm. Add reserved marinade to pan and boil until reduced by half. Spoon sauce over steaks and serve immediately.

Serving suggestion: Serve with peppered fettuccine and vegetables. For fettuccine, toss hot fettucine with 1 tablespoon olive oil and 1 tablespoon coarsely crushed black peppercorns.

Serves 4

ingredients

4 veal or pork steaks
2 teaspoons vegetable oil

<u>Red wine marinade</u>
2 cloves garlic, crushed
³/₄ cup/185mL/6fl oz red wine
3 tablespoons brown sugar
freshly ground black pepper

chicken and penne salad

simple
salads

Salads are becoming increasingly

Salads are becoming increasingly popular as main courses. These substantial salads are one-dish meals. You might like to try a Tuna and bean salad, Italian potato salad or a Salad nicoise. Accompany with crusty French bread or wholemeal rolls for for a complete meal.

358

carrot
and sultana salad

Method:
1 *Place carrots and sultanas in a serving bowl.*
2 *To make dressing, place orange juice and honey in a small bowl and whisk to combine. Spoon dressing over carrot mixture and toss to combine. Sprinkle with nuts, cover and refrigerate until required.*
Serves 10

ingredients
6 carrots, grated
125g/4oz sultanas (golden raisins)
60g/2oz chopped nuts

Orange dressing
¼ cup/60mL/2fl oz orange juice
2 tablespoons honey

chicken
and penne salad

Photograph page 359

Method:
1 *Arrange penne, chicken, green pepper (capsicum), chives, sweet corn, celery, tomatoes and endive on a large serving platter or in a large salad bowl. Spoon dressing over salad and serve immediately.*
Serving suggestion: *This salad is delicious served with chilli toast cheese. To make toast cheese, trim crusts from slices of white or wholemeal bread and cook under a preheated medium grill for 2-3 minutes or until toasted on one side. Top untoasted side with grated cheese and a pinch of chilli powder and cook for 2-3 minutes longer or until cheese melts and is golden.*
Serves 4

ingredients

500g/1 lb penne, cooked
1 kg/2 lb cooked chicken, skin removed and flesh shredded
1 green pepper (capsicum), chopped
3 tablespoons snipped fresh chives
440g/14oz canned sweet corn kernels, drained
2 stalks celery, chopped
250g/8oz yellow teardrop or red cherry tomatoes
250g/8oz curly endive
¾ cup/185mL/6fl oz creamy salad dressing

warm
seafood salad

Method:

1 Arrange watercress and lettuce leaves on individual dinner plates.

2 In a non-stick frypan, heat oil and cook onion and garlic until soft. Add scallops, shrimp and fish and cook for 5-6 minutes or until prawns turn pink and fish is just cooked. Season with pepper. Arrange fish mixture over lettuce leaves.

3 To make dressing, combine lime juice, oil, pepper and dill in a screwtop jar and shake well to combine. Sprinkle over fish, garnish with dill sprigs and serve immediately.

Note: Our warm seafood salad makes a marvellous light meal in spring or autumn when there is a slight chill in the air.

Serves 6

ingredients

¹/₂ **bunch watercress**
mignonette lettuce leaves
butter lettuce leaves
I tablespoon olive oil
I onion, thinly sliced
I clove garlic, crushed
315g/10oz scallops, cleaned
220g/7oz shrimp, shelled and deveined
250g/8oz firm white fish fillets
freshly ground black pepper
fresh dill sprigs for garnish

<u>Dressing</u>
¹/₂ **cup/125mL lime juice**
I tablespoon olive oil
freshly ground black pepper
**I tablespoon finely chopped
fresh dill**

nutty
rice salad

Method:

1 Cook rice in boiling water in a large saucepan following packet directions or see instructions at the beginning of this chapter. Drain well and set aside to cool.

2 Boil, steam or microwave asparagus until just tender. Drain and refresh under cold running water. Set aside to cool completely. Cut into 5cm/2in pieces.

3 Heat oil in a frying pan over a medium heat. Add onions and cook, stirring occasionally, for 10 minutes or until onions are soft and golden. Set aside to cool.

4 Place rice, asparagus, onions, spring onions, tomatoes, pecans and sultanas in a salad bowl and toss to combine.

5 To make dressing, place garlic, mustard, orange juice and oil in a bowl and whisk to combine. Pour dressing over salad and toss to combine.

Serves 6

ingredients

**2 cups/440g/7oz brown rice
250g/8oz asparagus spears, trimmed
1 tablespoon olive oil
3 onions, peeled and sliced
3 spring onions, sliced
3 tomatoes, chopped
60g/2oz chopped pecans
3 tablespoons sultanas (golden raisins)**

**<u>Orange dressing</u>
1 clove garlic, peeled and crushed
1 teaspoon Dijon mustard
¹/₄ cup/60mL/2fl oz orange juice
1 tablespoon olive oil**

potato
salad

Method:

1 Place potatoes in a saucepan, cover with cold water and bring to the boil. Reduce heat and simmer for 10-15 minutes or until potatoes are tender. Drain and set aside to cool.

2 Place eggs in a saucepan, cover with cold water and bring to the boil over a medium heat, then simmer for 10 minutes. Drain and cool under cold running water. Cool completely. Remove shells and cut into quarters.

3 Place bacon in a nonstick frying pan and cook over a medium heat, stirring occasionally, for 10 minutes or until crisp. Drain on absorbent kitchen paper.

4 Place potatoes, eggs, bacon, onion, spring onions, dill and mint in a salad bowl and toss gently to combine.

5 To make dressing, combine mayonnaise, yogurt, mustard and black pepper to taste in a bowl. Spoon dressing over salad and toss to combine.

Serves 6

ingredients

1 kg/2 lb potatoes, peeled and cut into cubes
3 eggs
4 rashers bacon, rind removed, chopped
1 onion, peeled and finely chopped
2 spring onions, chopped
2 tablespoons chopped fresh dill
1 tablespoon chopped fresh mint

Mustard dressing
1 cup/250mL/8fl oz mayonnaise
3 tablespoons natural yogurt
1 tablespoon Dijon mustard
freshly ground black pepper

italian
green bean salad

Photograph page 365

Method:

1 *Boil, steam or microwave beans until just tender. Refresh under cold running water.*
2 *Place beans, shallots, tomatoes and olives in a salad bowl.*
3 *To make dressing, place oil, lemon juice, garlic, parsley, chives, rosemary and thyme in a screwtop jar. Shake well to combine and pour over salad. Season with pepper and toss.*

Serves 4

ingredients

500g/1lb green beans, topped and tailed
6 shallots, finely chopped
3 tomatoes, peeled and chopped
8 black olives, stoned
freshly ground black pepper

Dressing
1 tablespoon olive oil
3 tablespoons lemon juice
1 clove garlic, crushed
1 tablespoon chopped fresh parsley
1 tablespoon finely chopped fresh chives
1 teaspoon finely chopped fresh rosemary
1 teaspoon finely chopped fresh thyme

tomato
and basil salad

Photograph page 365

Method:

1 *Arrange tomato slices overlapping on a serving platter and sprinkle with basil leaves.*
2 *To make dressing, place garlic, oil and vinegar in a screwtop jar. Shake well to combine and sprinkle over tomatoes. Just before serving, sprinkle tomato salad with Parmesan cheese. Season with pepper.*

Note: *You might like to try a combination of cherry tomatoes and little yellow teardrop tomatoes to make this aromatic tomato salad look even more attractive.*

Serves 6

ingredients

750g/1¹/₂lb ripe tomatoes, peeled, sliced
4 tablespoons finely chopped fresh basil
2 tablespoons grated Parmesan cheese
freshly ground black pepper

Dressing
1 clove garlic, crushed
1 tablespoon olive oil
3 tablespoons white wine vinegar

sweet
potato chip salad

Method:

1 *Preheat barbecue to a high heat. Brush sweet potato slices with oil. Cook sweet potatoes, in batches, on barbecue plate (griddle) for 4 minutes each side or until golden and crisp. Drain on absorbent kitchen paper.*

2 *Place spinach and rocket leaves, tomatoes, onions, olives and parmesan cheese shavings in a bowl and toss to combine. Cover and chill until required.*

3 *To make dressing, place oregano leaves, sugar, vinegar and black pepper to taste in a screwtop jar and shake to combine.*

4 *To serve, add sweet potato chips to salad, drizzle with dressing and toss to combine.*

Serves 8

ingredients

1 kg/2 lb sweet potatoes, thinly sliced
3-4 tablespoons olive oil
185g/6oz baby spinach leaves
185g/6oz rocket leaves
3 tomatoes, chopped
2 red onions, sliced
4 tablespoons pitted black olives
60g/2oz parmesan cheese shavings

Sweet oregano dressing
2 tablespoons fresh oregano leaves
1 ¹/₂ tablespoons brown sugar
¹/₃ cup/90mL/3fl oz balsamic vinegar
freshly ground black pepper

marinated
zucchini salad

Method:

1 Place zucchini (courgettes) and onion in a bowl.
2 To make dressing, place dill, parsley, garlic, vinegar, oil, lemon juice and black pepper to taste in bowl and whisk to combine. Pour over zucchini (courgette) mixture and toss. Cover and chill for at least 1 hour before serving.

Serves 8

ingredients

6 zucchini (courgettes), sliced
1 onion, sliced

<u>Fresh herb dressing</u>
2 tablespoons chopped fresh dill
1 tablespoon chopped fresh parsley
1 clove garlic, crushed
$^1/_4$ cup/60mL/2fl oz white vinegar
2 tablespoons olive oil
1 tablespoon lemon juice
freshly ground black pepper

cauliflour parmesan

on the side

A sensational side dish can add

color, flavor and variety to an otherwise simple meal. Many of these side dishes can also double as light meals. Delight the family by serving one of following dishes in this chapter, it's sure to be a success.

rosemary
potatoes

Method:

1 Bring a large saucepan of water to boil. Add potatoes. When water boils again, remove pan from heat and drain potatoes in a colander. Pat dry with paper towels.

2 Melt butter in a large frying pan over moderate heat. Add garlic, potato slices and rosemary.

3 Sauté potatoes until lightly golden and cooked through. Shake pan frequently to prevent them from sticking, and turn them over occasionally with a spatula. Serve at once, in a heated dish.

Serves 4

ingredients

500g/1lb potatoes, peeled and thinly sliced
60g/2oz butter
1 clove garlic, crushed
1 tablespoon finely chopped fresh rosemary

cauliflour
parmesan

Photograph page 369

Method:

1 Boil, steam or microwave cauliflower until just tender. Drain well and place in a lightly buttered shallow baking dish.

2 Melt butter in a saucepan over a medium heat, add breadcrumbs and cook, stirring, for 4-5 minutes or until golden. Remove pan from heat, add Parmesan cheese and black pepper to taste and mix to combine.

3 Sprinkle breadcrumb mixture over cauliflower and cook under a preheated hot grill for 3-5 minutes or until top is golden. Sprinkle with parsley and serve.

Note: For something different make this easy side dish using broccoli in place of the cauliflower or use a combination of broccoli and cauliflower.

Serves 6

ingredients

1 small cauliflower, broken into florets
60g/2oz butter
3/4 cup/90g/3oz dried breadcrumbs
60 g/2 oz grated Parmesan cheese
freshly ground black pepper
2 tablespoons chopped flat-leaved parsley

braised
artichokes and beans

Method:

1 Melt butter in a frying pan over a medium heat, add garlic and onions and cook, stirring, for 3 minutes or until onions are soft.

2 Add carrots, beans, artichokes and stock and bring to the boil. Reduce heat and simmer for 10 minutes or until vegetables are tender. Season to taste with black pepper.

Serves 6

ingredients

30g/1oz butter
2 cloves garlic, crushed
2 onions, sliced
2 carrots, sliced
250g/8oz fresh broad beans, shelled or
125g/4oz frozen broad beans
440g/14oz canned artichoke hearts, drained
1 cup/250mL/8fl oz vegetable stock
freshly ground black pepper

beans
with cumin vinaigrette

Photograph page 373

Method:

1 *Boil, steam or microwave beans until just tender. Drain, refresh under cold running water and drain again.*
2 *Place beans and tomatoes in a salad bowl.*
3 *To make vinaigrette, place spring onions, mustard, cumin, oil, vinegar and black pepper to taste in a screwtop jar and shake well. Spoon dressing over bean mixture and toss to combine.*

Note: *Do not refrigerate this dish after making - the flavors will develop if it is left to stand at room temperature for a while.*

Serves 4

ingredients

500g/1 lb green beans, halved
12 cherry tomatoes, cut in half

<u>Cumin vinaigrette</u>
2 spring onions, finely chopped
1 teaspoon dry mustard
1/2 teaspoon ground cumin
1/2 cup/125mL/4fl oz olive oil
2 tablespoons wine vinegar
freshly ground black pepper

ratatouille

Photograph page 373

Method:

1 *Heat oil in a large saucepan over a medium heat, add onions and cook, stirring, for 5 minutes or until onions are lightly browned. Add green peppers (capsicums), and garlic and cook, stirring occasionally, for 5 minutes longer.*
2 *Add zucchini (courgettes), eggplant (aubergines), tomatoes, oregano, basil and marjoram and bring to the boil. Reduce heat and simmer, stirring occasionally, for 30 minutes or until mixture reduces and thickens and vegetables are well cooked. Season to taste with black pepper. Serve hot, warm or at room temperature.*

Note: *Red peppers, mushrooms and fresh herbs are all tasty additions to this popular side dish. With the addition of canned beans this becomes a great main meal for vegetarians. Drain and rinse the beans and add to the vegetable mixture in the last 5 minutes of cooking.*

Serves 6

ingredients

1/4 cup/60mL/2fl oz vegetable oil
2 onions, chopped
2 green peppers (capsicums), diced
2 cloves garlic, crushed
4 zucchini (courgettes), diced
2 eggplant (aubergines), diced
2 x 440g/14oz canned tomatoes, undrained and mashed
1 teaspoon dried oregano
1 teaspoon dried basil
1 teaspoon dried marjoram
freshly ground black pepper

potato
gratin

Method:

1 Layer potatoes, onions, chives and black pepper to taste in six lightly greased individual ovenproof dishes.

2 Place yogurt and cream in a bowl and mix to combine. Carefully pour yogurt mixture over potatoes and sprinkle with Parmesan cheese. Bake for 45 minutes or until potatoes are tender and top is golden.

Serves 6

ingredients

1 kg/2 lb potatoes, thinly sliced
2 large onions, thinly sliced
2 tablespoons snipped fresh chives
freshly ground black pepper
1¼ cup/250g/8oz low-fat natural yogurt
1 cup/250mL/8fl oz cream (heavy)
60g/2oz grated Parmesan cheese

asparagus
in prosciutto

Method:
1 *Preheat barbecue to a high heat.*
2 *Top each prosciutto slice with a basil leaf and an asparagus spear. Wrap prosciutto around asparagus to enclose.*
3 *Brush asparagus parcels with lemon juice and sprinkle with black pepper to taste. Place asparagus parcels on oiled barbecue and cook, turning frequently, until prosciutto is crisp and asparagus is tender.*
4 *To make dipping sauce, place mayonnaise, lemon juice and chopped basil in a bowl and mix to combine. Serve with asparagus parcels.*

Serves 12

ingredients

250g/8oz prosciutto slices
fresh basil leaves
500g/1 lb fresh asparagus spears
¹/₃ cup/90mL/3fl oz lemon juice
freshly ground black pepper

Basil dipping sauce
³/₄ cup/185mL/6fl oz whole egg mayonnaise
2 tablespoons lemon juice
2 tablespoons chopped fresh basil

dijon
mushrooms

Method:

1 Melt butter in a nonstick frying pan over a medium heat, add onions or shallots and garlic and cook, stirring, for 2-3 minutes or until onions or shallots are soft.

2 Add mushrooms and cook, stirring occasionally, for 5 minutes or until mushrooms are cooked. Remove mushrooms from pan, set aside and keep warm.

3 Stir wine, mustard and coriander into pan and bring to the boil. Reduce heat and simmer for 10 minutes or until liquid reduces by half. Remove pan from heat, stir in yogurt and season to taste with black pepper. Return pan to a low heat, and cook for 2-3 minutes or until heated through. Spoon sauce over mushrooms, sprinkle with parsley and serve.

Serves 4

ingredients

30g/1oz butter
4 pickling onions or shallots, finely chopped
1 clove garlic, crushed
500g/1 lb mushrooms
³/₄ cup/185mL/6fl oz dry white wine
1 tablespoon Dijon mustard
1 teaspoon finely chopped fresh coriander
1 ¹/₄ cup/250g/8oz low-fat natural yogurt
freshly ground black pepper
2 tablespoons chopped fresh parsley

barbecued
potato skins

Method:

1 Bake potatoes in the oven for 1 hour or until tender. Remove from oven and set aside until cool enough to handle. Cut potatoes in half and scoop out flesh leaving a 5mm/¼in thick shell. Reserve potato flesh for another use. Cut potato skins into large pieces and brush with oil.

2 Preheat barbecue to a medium heat. Cook potato skins on lightly oiled barbecue grill for 5-8 minutes each side or until crisp and golden.

Serving suggestion: Potato skins are delicious served with a dip of your choice.

Cook's tip: The reserved potato flesh can be used to make a potato salad to serve at your barbecue. It could also be used to make a potato curry, as a topping on a cottage pie, or to make croquettes.

Serves 4

ingredients

6 large potatoes, scrubbed
olive oil

Oven temperature 200°C, 400°F, Gas 6

sticky date pudding

short
& sweet

A little something sweet and satisfying

for dessert is a favourite with everyone, but it needn't
take all day to prepare. Simply scrumptious sweets like
the recipes featured in this chapter can be assembled
using canned or fresh fruit, and look as though you've
spent hours in the kitchen.

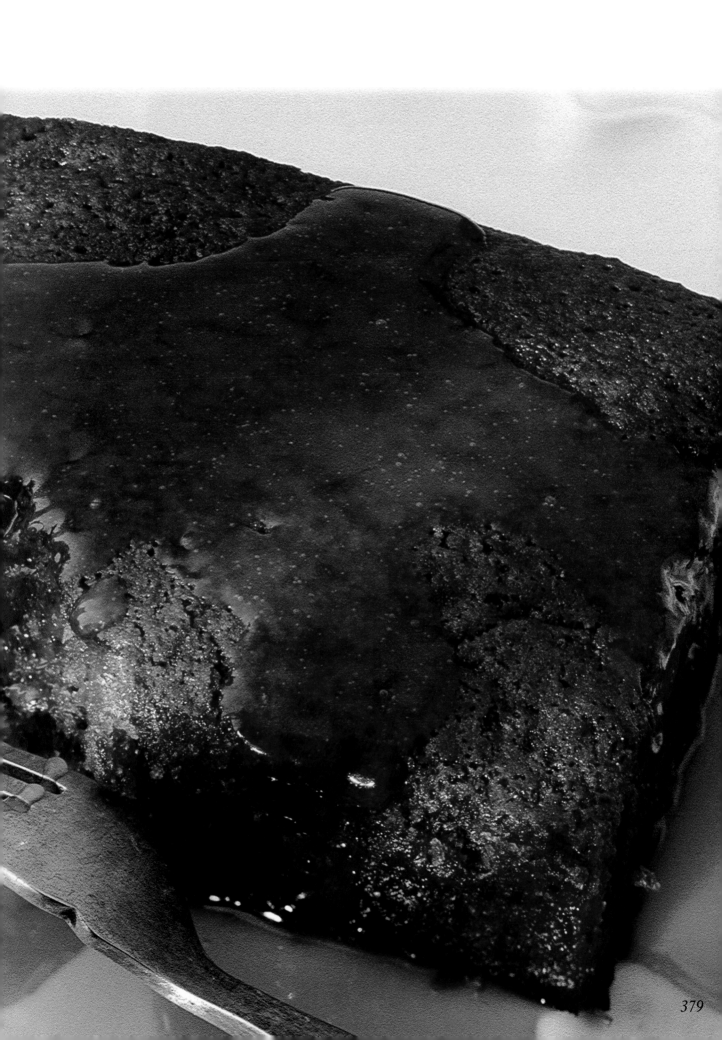

apple
and apricot crumble

Method:

1 Place apricots, apples, sugar and cinnamon in a bowl and mix to combine. Spoon fruit mixture into a greased ovenproof dish.

2 To make topping, place rolled oats or muesli, coconut, butter and honey in bowl and mix to combine. Sprinkle topping over fruit mixture and bake for 30 minutes or until fruit is hot and topping is crisp and golden.

Note: Any canned fruit is delicious used in this dessert. For something different you might like to try plums and apples or pears and peaches.

Serves 6

ingredients

2 x 440g/14oz canned apricot
halves, drained
440g/14oz canned sliced apples, drained
2 tablespoons brown sugar
¹/₄ teaspoon ground cinnamon

Crumble topping
2 cups/185g/6oz rolled oats or muesli
30g/1oz shredded coconut
125g/4oz butter, melted
2 tablespoons honey

Oven temperature 180°C, 350°F, Gas 4

sticky
date pudding

Photograph page 379

Method:

1 Place dates and water in a saucepan and bring to the boil over a medium heat. Reduce heat and simmer for 5 minutes or until dates are soft. Remove pan from heat and stir in bicarbonate of soda. Set aside.

2 Place butter and sugar in a bowl and beat until light and creamy. Beat in eggs, one at a time, beating well after each addition. Fold in flour. Add date mixture and mix to combine.

3 Pour mixture into a lightly greased 18x28cm/ 7x11in cake tin and bake for 25 minutes or until cooked when tested with a skewer.

4 To make sauce, place butter and sugar in a saucepan and cook over a low heat, stirring constantly, for 4-5 minutes or until butter melts and ingredients are combined. Stir in cream, bring to simmering and simmer, stirring constantly, for 5 minutes or until sauce thickens. Pour sauce over hot pudding and serve immediately.

Serves 8

ingredients

155g/5oz pitted dates, chopped
2 cups/500mL/16fl oz water
1 teaspoon bicarbonate of soda
60g/2oz butter, softened
1¹/₄ cups/220g/7oz brown sugar
2 eggs, lightly beaten
³/₄ cup/90g/3oz self-rising flour, sifted

Toffee cream sauce
60g/2oz butter
¹/₂ cup/90g/3oz brown sugar
³/₄ cup/185mL/6fl oz cream (heavy)

Oven temperature 180°C, 350°F, Gas 4

Method:

1 Place milk, butter and eggs in a bowl and whisk to combine.

2 Sift together flour and cocoa powder into a separate bowl. Add sugar and mix to combine. Make a well in the centre of the dry ingredients and pour in milk mixture. Beat for 5 minutes or until mixture is smooth.

3 Pour mixture into a greased 20cm/8in round cake tin and bake for 40 minutes or until cooked when tested with a skewer. Stand cake in tin for 5 minutes before turning onto a wire rack to cool.

4 To make icing, sift icing sugar and cocoa powder together into a bowl. Stir in milk and mix until smooth. Spread icing over cold cake.

Makes a 20cm/8in round cake

easy
chocolate cake

ingredients
1 cup/250mL/8fl oz milk
125g/4oz butter, softened
2 eggs, lightly beaten
1 1/3 cups/170g/5 1/2oz self-rising flour
2/3 cup/60g/2oz cocoa powder
1 cup/220g/7oz caster sugar

Chocolate icing
1 cup/155g/5oz icing sugar
2 tablespoons cocoa powder
2 tablespoons milk

Oven temperature 180°C, 350°F, Gas 4

raspberry
mousse

Method:

1 Place raspberries in a food processor or blender and process to make a purée. Push purée through a sieve to remove seeds and set aside. Stir gelatine mixture into purée and set aside.

2 Place ricotta or curd cheese in a food processor or blender and process until smooth. Set aside.

3 Place egg yolks and sugar in a heatproof bowl, set over a saucepan of simmering water and beat until a ribbon trail forms when beater is lifted from mixture. Remove bowl from heat. Whisk egg yolk mixture, then ricotta or curd cheese into raspberry purée. Cover and chill until just beginning to set.

4 Place egg whites in a bowl and beat until stiff peaks form. Fold egg white mixture into fruit mixture. Spoon mousse mixture into four lightly oiled ¹/₂ cup/125mL/4fl oz capacity moulds or ramekins, cover and chill until set.

5 To serve, garnish with chocolate curls.

Serves 4

ingredients

500g/1 lb fresh or frozen raspberries
2 teaspoons gelatine dissolved in
2 tablespoons hot water, cooled
125g/4oz ricotta or curd cheese, drained
4 eggs, separated
¹/₄ cup/60g/2oz superfine sugar
whipped cream
chocolate curls, to garnish (optional)

plum
clafoutis

Method:

1 Arrange plums, cut side down, in a lightly greased 25cm/10in flan dish.
2 Sift flour into a bowl and make a well in the centre. Break eggs into well, add caster sugar and milk and mix to form a smooth batter.
3 Pour batter over plums and bake for 45 minutes at 190°C/375°F or until firm and golden. Serve hot, warm or cold, sprinkled with icing sugar.

Serves 6

ingredients

500g/1 lb dark plums, halved and stoned, or 440g/14oz canned plums, well drained
1 cup/125g/4oz self-rising flour
3 eggs
1/2 cup/100g/3 1/2oz superfine sugar
1/2 cup/125mL/4fl oz reduced-fat milk
1 tablespoon icing sugar, sifted

new orleans
style bananas

Method:

1 Melt butter in a heavy-based saucepan over a medium heat, add sugar and cinnamon and cook, stirring, until sugar melts and mixture is combined.

2 Stir in liqueur or orange juice and half the rum and cook for 5 minutes or until mixture is thick and syrupy.

3 Add bananas and toss to coat with syrup. Add remaining rum, swirl pan and ignite immediately. Baste bananas with sauce until flame goes out.

4 To serve, divide bananas and ice cream between serving plates and drizzle sauce from pan over ice cream.

ingredients

60g/2oz unsalted butter
¼ cup/60g/2oz brown sugar
½ teaspoon ground cinnamon
¼ cup/60mL/2fl oz banana-flavoured liqueur or orange juice
½ cup/125mL/4fl oz dark rum
4 bananas, halved lengthwise
4 scoops vanilla ice cream

caramel
cherries

Method:

1 Place cherries in a shallow ovenproof dish.
2 Place cream and liqueur or sherry in a bowl and beat until soft peaks form. Spoon cream mixture over cherries, sprinkle thickly with brown sugar and cook under a preheated hot grill for 3-4 minutes or until sugar melts. Serve immediately.

Serves 6

ingredients

**440g/14oz canned, pitted sweet
cherries, drained
1 ¼ cups/315mL/10fl oz cream
(heavy), whipped
1 teaspoon liqueur of your choice or sherry
brown sugar**

chicken
for all seasons

introduction

introduction

The chicken has always been a valuable food source. From the earliest recorded history, it has appeared on the tables of ancient Egypt, Greece, Rome and Asia.

The ancestor of the chicken of today is thought to be the Indian Jungle Fowl which was domesticated by the Indus Valley civilization in about 2500 BC. It is not known how the bird travelled to other areas, but travel it did. The chicken has been used by almost all cultures throughout the world in their cooking pots, with each adding aspects of their culinary heritage to this versatile meat. With our rich diversity of cultures our repertoire of chicken dishes has expanded to new dimensions, and continues to expand. Ethnic dishes from other countries, such as Tandoori Chicken, Chicken Cacciatore and Hawaiian Chicken are just as popular in the world as the traditional roast chicken.

Through the pages of this book you will experience the new flavor combinations which have resulted from our culinary cultural exchange, presented in simple and quick-to-prepare recipes.

Chicken production today has made available not only the bird dressed and ready for the pot, but also each cut portioned out so you can buy as needed. Gone are the days when the favourite part of the family chicken, usually the breast, was the most popular piece.

Nutritional Value

Chicken is high in first class protein, which means it has all of the essential amino acids. Vitamins, particularly A and the B group vitamins, are well represented, as are minerals including Iron and Zinc. It is a light, tender meat which makes it easy to chew and easy to digest, so it is especially suitable for infants, children and the elderly. When the skin is removed, chicken is even lower in fat, making it an ideal food for everyone.

Purchasing and Storage of Chicken

Chicken may be purchased fresh or frozen, whole or in pieces. The choice is for the individual to make, depending on how and when one wishes to prepare and eat the chicken.

Fresh Chicken:

• When purchasing fresh chicken, make it the last purchase on your shopping trip. It is advisable to take along an insulated bag to place the chicken in to keep it cold on the trip home.

- When arriving home with your chicken purchase, remove from package (if any), rinse and wipe dry with a paper towel. Cover loosely with plastic wrap and refrigerate immediately. Fresh chicken may be kept in the refrigerator for 3 days. Place in the coldest part of the refrigerator, below 4°C/39°F.

- If chicken needs to be stored longer, it is better to buy ready frozen chicken than to buy fresh and freeze at home.

- If the chicken pieces are to be purchased and frozen for future use, make sure they are fresh. Wipe dry with paper towel then pack flat in plastic freezer bags. Extract air by pushing out towards the opening, and tape bag closed. Label and date packages.

Frozen chicken

- When purchasing frozen chicken, check that the packages are not torn.

- Place in freezer immediately you return home.

- Thaw frozen chicken thoroughly before cooking to avoid toughening the texture and to reduce the chance of some parts being undercooked. Undercooked parts could harbor food-spoiling bacteria.

- Do not refreeze thawed chicken. It is advisable to cook the thawed chicken and freeze it when cooked.

- To thaw frozen chicken, remove from wrap, place on a rack in a dish to allow liquid to collect beneath the chicken. Do not touch it. Cover loosely with plastic wrap and place in the refrigerator for 24 hours.

This is the safest way to thaw. Thawing on the kitchen bench encourages the growth of bacteria and should be avoided.

preparation

As with all perishable foods, there are simple rules to follow in the preparation and handling of chicken. Adhering to these rules will lessen the likelihood of bacterial growth, and thereby increase the quality, flavor and enjoyment of your dishes. Many of these rules also apply to other perishable foods. They should become a common part of your kitchen routine.

Food producers and retailers maintain high standards of quality assurance and cleanliness so that we can buy safe and wholesome foods with confidence.

Consumers need to ensure that they maintain these quality and safety standards after purchase. Perishable foods, including chicken, need special attention to prevent deterioration and possible food poisoning.

Purchasing and storage instructions are provided in the introduction to this book, and should be followed at all times. The safe handling tips listed below should be employed to avoid encouraging bacterial growth and transfer.

Safe Food Handling Tips:

- Wash hands thoroughly before handling fresh chicken and other foods. Wash again before handling other food.

- Chopping boards, knives and other utensils must be washed with hot soapy water after handling raw chicken and other raw foods to prevent cross-contamination .

- Always keep cold food at 4°C/39°F or below in a refrigerator.

- Never keep raw chicken at room temperature for longer than 1 hour, including preparation time.

- Poultry must be cooked through to the center, not left rare. This ensures that all bacteria have been killed by the heat penetration. To test, insert a skewer into the centre of the chicken or portion - if the juice runs clear the chicken is cooked through.

- Stuffing should be treated with special care. Bacteria from raw poultry can grow in the stuffing. Stuff loosely, only 2/3 full, just before cooking and remove the stuffing immediately after cooking.

- Cool cooked foods quickly by placing them in the refrigerator. Large quantities of food should be divided into smaller portions to allow quicker cooking. This relates particularly to simmered chicken and chicken stock. Do not be afraid to place hot foods in the refrigerator - it is built to take them.

- Store raw and cooked foods separately, with cooked foods at the top and raw foods at the bottom on a tray or plate.

Do not let juices drop onto other foods.

- *Understand that the danger zone for bacterial growth is between 4°C/39°F and 65°C/149°F, so keep foods cold (below 4°C/39°F) or hot (above 65°C/150°F). Food must not be left to stand on the kitchen bench as room temperature is in the danger zone.*

- *When reheating cooked chicken, bring to 75°C/167°F and hold there for a few minutes.*

Tips for Cooking Chicken in the Microwave

Whole Chicken:

1. *The microwave does not brown the chicken as the conventional oven does but a brown appearance can be achieved by either rubbing the surface with paprika, or brushing it over with a glaze.*

2. *Tie legs together with string or a strip of plastic or an elastic band to give a more even cooking shape.*

3. *Calculate the cooking time simply by doubling the size number on the chicken; e.g. No, 15 is cooked for 30 minutes and cook on MEDIUM/HIGH. Larger chickens are more successful if cooked on MEDIUM/HIGH for the first half of the cooking time, then reduce the power to MEDIUM for the remainder adding 5-8 minutes cooking time per kg.*

4. *Remember the starting temperature of the chicken will affect cooking time. A refrigerated chicken will take a few minutes longer than one at room temperature. It is advisable to cook the chicken on HIGH for the first 3-5 minutes to warm the surface then reduce power to MEDIUM/HIGH for remainder of the cooking time.*

Chicken Pieces

1. *Arrange chicken pieces with the thicker part to the outside of the dish or roasting rack for even cooking.*

2. *Rearrange pieces that are in the centre to the outside halfway through cooking.*

3. *Chicken casseroles cook better if chicken is cut into small even pieces; i.e. breast cut into 2 pieces, and thigh separated from drumstick.*

4. *Chicken pieces may be browned in a browning dish before adding to a casserole, or browned in a frying pan before microwaving. You may prefer to remove skins before placing in a casserole as they do tend to become a little rubbery.*

5. *Chicken pieces may be crumbed then cooked on a roasting rack. The result is very successful. Choose a deep-coloured dried bread crumb and add dried herbs, lemon, pepper or toasted sesame seeds. The crumbs will remain crisp.*

Breast fillets

Thigh fillets

Chicken Tenderloin

Chicken Marylard

Thigh - with bone

Chicken breast on the bone - half breast

Stir-fry pieces

Chicken mince

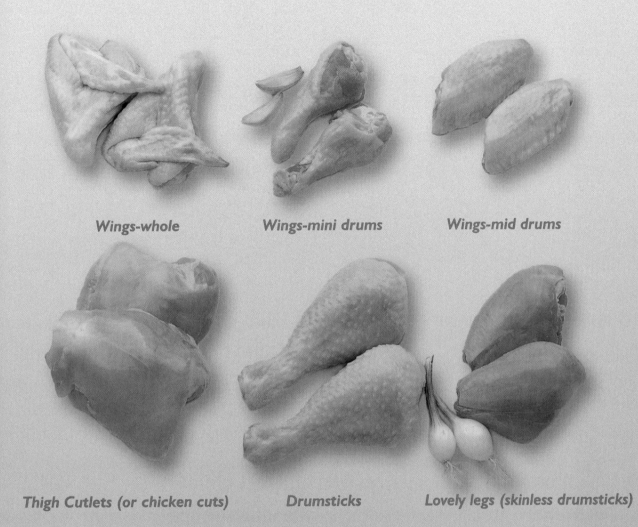

Wings-whole   **Wings-mini drums**   **Wings-mid drums**

Thigh Cutlets (or chicken cuts)   **Drumsticks**   **Lovely legs (skinless drumsticks)**

Casserole pieces

Chicken Cuts
– the way they look

The skinless cuts (breasts, breast fillets, thigh fillets and lovely legs) are extremely low in fat and are a boon to the health conscious and those watching their fat and calorie intake. Stir-fry pieces and ground chicken are sometimes available ready-prepared. If not, use chicken breast fillets or chicken thigh fillets and cut into strips for stir-frying or pass though a mincer or food processor for delicious, low fat ground chicken.

chicken wings moroccan style

autumn delights

With the advent of winter, autumn

gives us the opportunity to use the last of the summer ingredients. Dishes such as Chicken Roasted Pepper. Olive and Feta Pie and a Spicy Corn and Lentil Chowder, allows the use of summer ingredients with winter cookery methods.

chicken
wings moroccan style

Photograph page 395

ingredients

Method:

1 *Heat oil in a wide-based saucepan or lidded skillet, add chicken wings a few at a time and brown lightly on both sides. Remove to a plate as they brown.*

2 *Add onions and fry for 2 minutes. Stir in garlic, ginger and spices. Cook, while stirring for 1 minute, return chicken to the pan, stir and turn the wings to coat with spices.*
Add vinegar and apricot nectar, season to taste. Cover and simmer for 25 minutes.

3 *Add prunes, apricots, honey and lemon juice. Cover and simmer 10 minutes and then remove lid and simmer uncovered for 5 minutes. If a thicker sauce is desired, remove wings and fruit to a serving platter, increase heat and boil until sauce reduces and thickens, stirring occasionally.*
Pour sauce over wings. Serve immediately with steamed couscous or rice.

Serves 3-4

2 tablespoons oil
1kg/2 lb tray chicken wings
1 large onion, finely chopped
1 clove garlic, crushed
1 1/2 teaspoons chopped fresh ginger
1/2 teaspoon ground turmeric
1/2 teaspoon cumin
1/2 cinnamon stick
1/4 cup/60ml/2fl oz cider vinegar
450g/15oz can apricot nectar
salt, pepper
100g/3oz dried prunes, pitted
100g/3oz dried apricots
1 tablespoon honey
1/4 cup/60ml/2fl oz lemon juice
steamed couscous or rice to serve

greek style
chicken rissoles in tomato sauce

ingredients

Rissoles
500g/1 lb ground chicken
1 medium onion (grated)
2 tablespoons parsley (finely chopped)
¹/₂ teaspoon salt
pepper
1 egg
¹/₂ cup/60g/2oz breadcrumbs (dried)
1 tablespoon water
oil (for frying)

Tomato Sauce
1 medium onion (finely chopped)
1 clove garlic (crushed)
1 tablespoon oil
1 x 440g/15oz can tomatoes
1 tablespoon tomato paste
¹/₂ cup/120ml/4fl oz water
¹/₂ teaspoon oregano (dried)
1 teaspoon sugar
salt, pepper
1 tablespoon parsley (chopped)

Method:

1 *Place gound chicken in a bowl, grate onion into the chicken, and add remaining ingredients. Mix well to combine, and knead a little by hand. With wet hands roll into balls. Heat oil (1cm deep) in a frying pan, and sauté the rissoles until they change colour on both sides. Remove to a plate.*

2 *To the pan add the onion and garlic, and sauté a little. Add remaining sauce ingredients, and bring to the boil. Return the rissoles to the pan, reduce heat, and simmer (covered) for 30 minutes.*

3 *Serve over boiled spaghetti or other pasta.*

Serves 4-6

chicken

roasted pepper, olive & feta pie

Photograph page 399

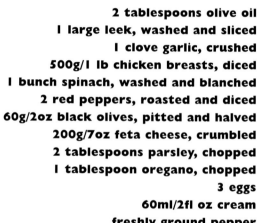

ingredients

2 tablespoons olive oil
1 large leek, washed and sliced
1 clove garlic, crushed
500g/1 lb chicken breasts, diced
1 bunch spinach, washed and blanched
2 red peppers, roasted and diced
60g/2oz black olives, pitted and halved
200g/7oz feta cheese, crumbled
2 tablespoons parsley, chopped
1 tablespoon oregano, chopped
3 eggs
60ml/2fl oz cream
freshly ground pepper
8-16 sheets filo pastry
1 tablespoon olive oil (extra)
1 tablespoon butter, melted
1 tablespoon sesame seeds

*chicken roasted capsicum
(pepper), olive & feta pie*

Method:

1 Pre-heat oven to 180°C/350°F.

2 Heat one tablespoon oil in a large fry pan, add leek and garlic, and cook for five minutes or until soft. Set aside.

3 Heat extra oil, add chicken in batches, and cook for 6-8 minutes.

4 Drain spinach, squeeze out excess water, and chop roughly.

5 In a large bowl, combine chicken, spinach, peppers, olives, feta, parsley, oregano, eggs, cream and pepper. Stir until well combined. Set aside.

6 Lightly grease a 23 x 23cm/9 x 9in square baking dish. Combine the extra oil and butter.

7 Lay out sheets of filo, put two together, and brush with the oil mixture. Put another two on top, and brush again. Continue to repeat this until you have four double sheets. Line the baking dish with the filo, and trim around the edges. Fill with the chicken mixture. Brush the remaining sheets with oil (the same as before, using the same amount). Place the filo on top of the baking dish, tucking the edges inside the baking dish.

8 Brush the top with the oil mixture, sprinkle with sesame seeds, and bake in the oven for 40-45 minutes.

Serves 4-6

399

chicken
and leek roll

Method:

1 *Melt butter in a frying pan over a medium heat, add leeks and cook, stirring, for 4 minutes or until leeks are golden. Add mushrooms and cook for 2 minutes longer or until mushrooms are soft. Remove from pan and set aside to cool.*

2 *Add chicken to pan and cook, stirring, for 5 minutes or until chicken is just cooked. Remove chicken from pan and set aside to cool.*

3 *Place leek mixture, chicken, sour cream, chives and black pepper to taste in a bowl and mix to combine.*

4 *Brush each pastry sheet with oil and layer. Spread filling over pastry leaving a 2cm/³⁄₄in border. Fold in sides and roll up like a Swiss roll. Place roll on a baking tray, brush with oil and sprinkle with poppy seeds. Bake for 20 minutes or until pastry is crisp and golden.*

Serves 4

ingredients

30g/1oz butter
3 leeks, sliced
125g/4oz button mushrooms, sliced
2 boneless chicken breast fillets, sliced
¹⁄₃ cup/90g/3oz sour cream
1 tablespoon snipped fresh chives
freshly ground black pepper
12 sheets filo pastry
2 tablespoons olive oil
1 tablespoon poppy seeds

Oven temperature 200°C, 400°F, Gas 6

chicken
pasta gratin

Method:

1 Brush tomatoes with oil and cook under a preheated hot grill for 10 minutes or until soft and browned. Set aside.

2 Cook pasta in boiling water in a large saucepan following packet directions, drain and set aside.

3 Melt butter in a frying pan over a medium heat, add garlic and onion and cook, stirring, for 3 minutes or until onion is soft and golden. Add chicken and cook, stirring, for 6 minutes longer or until chicken is tender.

4 Stir wine, cream and tarragon into pan and bring to the boil. Reduce heat and simmer for 10 minutes. Remove pan from heat, add tomatoes, pasta, half the tasty cheese (mature Cheddar) and black pepper to taste and mix gently to combine.

5 Spoon mixture into a greased 8 cup/ 2 litre/3¹/₂pt capacity ovenproof dish. Combine remaining tasty cheese (mature Cheddar) and Parmesan cheese and sprinkle over pasta mixture. Bake for 20 minutes or until cheese melts and is golden.

ingredients

6 plum (egg or Italian) tomatoes, halved
1 tablespoon vegetable oil
315g/10oz wholemeal pasta shapes
30g/1oz butter
1 clove garlic, crushed
1 red onion, sliced
2 boneless chicken breast fillets, sliced
¹/₄ cup/60ml/2fl oz white wine
1¹/₄ cups/315ml/10fl oz cream (heavy)
**1 tablespoon chopped fresh tarragon
or 1 teaspoon dried tarragon**
**125g/4oz grated tasty cheese
(mature Cheddar)**
freshly ground black pepper
30g/1oz grated Parmesan cheese

Serves 4

chicken
moussaka

Method:

1 Place eggplant (aubergine) slices in a colander set over a bowl and sprinkle with salt. Set aside to stand for 10 minutes then rinse under cold running water and pat dry with absorbent kitchen paper.

2 Heat 2 tablespoons oil in a frying pan over a medium heat and cook eggplant (aubergine) slices in batches for 2 minutes each side or until golden. Set aside.

3 Heat remaining oil in frying pan, add garlic and onion and cook, stirring, for 3 minutes or until onion is soft and golden. Add chicken and cook, stirring, for 5 minutes or until chicken browns. Stir in tomatoes and bring to the boil. Reduce heat and simmer for 15 minutes, or until mixture reduces and thickens. Remove pan from heat and set aside to cool.

4 To make sauce, melt butter in a saucepan over a medium heat, stir in flour and cook for 1 minute. Remove pan from heat and gradually stir in milk. Return pan to heat and cook, stirring constantly, until sauce boils and thickens. Remove pan from heat and stir in tasty cheese (mature Cheddar).

5 Arrange half the eggplant (aubergine) slices over base of a 10 cup/2¹/₂ litre/4pt capacity ovenproof dish. Top with half the chicken mixture, half the potatoes and half the cheese sauce. Repeat layers to use all ingredients. Combine breadcrumbs and Parmesan cheese and sprinkle over moussaka. Bake for 50 minutes or until top is golden and moussaka is cooked through.

Note: The addition of chicken to this moussaka recipe is a refreshing alternative to a traditional dish which is more often made with lamb or beef mince.

Serves 8

ingredients

4 large eggplant (aubergines),
thinly sliced
salt
3 tablespoons olive oil
2 cloves garlic, crushed
1 onion, chopped
500g/1 lb chicken mince
2 x 440g/14oz canned peeled
tomatoes, undrained and mashed
500g/1 lb potatoes, thinly sliced
¹/₂ cup/30g/1oz breadcrumbs, made
from stale bread
60g/2oz grated Parmesan cheese

Cheese sauce
30g/1oz butter
2 tablespoons flour
1¹/₄ cups/315ml/10fl oz milk
60g/2oz grated tasty cheese
(mature Cheddar)

oriental
chicken pizza

Method:

1 Place pizza base on a lightly greased baking tray. Spread base with teriyaki sauce and top with chicken, snow peas (mangetout), spring onions, tofu and asparagus. Sprinkle with coriander (cilantro) and sesame seeds.

2 Drizzle chilli sauce over pizza and bake for 30 minutes or until base is golden and crisp.
Note: For a complete meal serve this tasty pizza with a selection of your favourite salads. Sweet soy sauce also known as kechap manis can be used instead of teriyaki in this recipe if you wish.

Serves 4

ingredients

1 packaged 30cm/12in pizza base
¹/₄ cup/60ml/2fl oz thick teriyaki sauce
2 boneless chicken breast fillets,
cooked and sliced
125g/4oz snow peas (mangetout),
thinly sliced
4 spring onions, sliced
155g/5oz tofu, chopped
6 asparagus spears, cut into 5cm/2in pieces
3 tablespoons chopped fresh coriander
(cilantro)
3 tablespoons sesame seeds, toasted
2 tablespoons sweet chilli sauce

Oven temperature 200°C, 400°F, Gas 6

italian
chicken in a pan

Method:

1 Place chicken between sheets of greaseproof paper and pound lightly to flatten. Dust with flour, then dip in egg and finally coat with breadcrumbs. Place on a plate lined with plastic food wrap and refrigerate for 15 minutes.

2 Heat oil in a large frying pan over a medium heat, add chicken and cook for 2-3 minutes each side or until golden. Remove from pan and set aside.

3 Add pasta sauce to pan and cook over a medium heat, stirring, for 4-5 minutes or until hot. Place chicken in a single layer on top of sauce, then top each fillet with a slice of prosciutto or ham, a slice of cheese and a sprig of sage. Cover and simmer for 5 minutes or until chicken is cooked through and cheese melts. Serve immediately.

Serves 6

ingredients

6 boneless chicken breast fillets, skinned
seasoned flour
1 egg, beaten
dried breadcrumbs
¹/₄ cup/60ml/2fl oz vegetable oil
500g/1 lb bottled tomato pasta sauce
6 slices prosciutto or ham
6 slices mozzarella cheese
6 sprigs fresh sage

crisp
curried wings

Photograph page 407

ingredients

1kg/2lb chicken wings
2 tablespoons mild curry paste
1¹/₂ cups/330g/110x basmati rice, rinsed
¹/₂ teaspoon salt
3 cups/750ml/24fl oz boiling water
2 tomatoes, blanched
and skinned
1 small cucumber
1 cup/240g/8oz fruit chutney

Method:

1 *Rinse the chicken wings and pat dry with kitchen paper. Rub the curry paste well onto the chicken wings with your fingers, covering all surfaces. Pin back the wing tip to form a triangle. Place in single layer on a tray; stand for 30 minutes in refrigerator, uncovered.*

2 *Meanwhile place the rice in a 8cup/2lt/70fl oz casserole dish; add salt and boiling water. Cover with lid or foil and place on lower shelf of oven, preheated to 180°C/350°F. Cook for 40 minutes. Remove from oven and stand covered 5 minutes.*

3 *Transfer chicken wings to a wire rack placed over a baking tray. Place on top shelf of oven above the rice. Cook for 20 minutes, turning once. When rice has been removed, increase oven temperature to 200°C/400°F for 5 minutes to crisp the wings.*

For the Sambal: Halve the tomatoes and remove the seeds then cut into small dice.

Peel cucumber; slice in half lengthwise, remove the seeds with a teaspoon. Dice the cucumber and mix with the diced tomato. Place in a suitable dish, place chutney in a similar dish. Serve the crisp curried wings with the rice and accompanying sambals.

Tip: Co-ordinate the cooking so that rice and chicken utilise the same oven.

Serves 4-6

chicken and corn chowder

winter
warmers

As winter sets in and the days

become shorter and the nights colder, a steaming soup, aromatic curry or a flavorsome casserole is the perfect remedy for warmth and satisfaction.

chicken
and corn chowder

Photograph page 409

Method:

1 Heat oil in a saucepan over a medium heat, add onion and cook, stirring, for 4-5 minutes or until onion is soft. Add chicken and cook for 2 minutes longer or until chicken just changes colour.

2 Add potatoes and stock and bring to the boil. Reduce heat and simmer for 10 minutes or until potatoes are almost cooked. Stir sweet corn, milk, bay leaf and black pepper to taste into stock mixture and bring to the boil. Reduce heat and simmer for 3-4 minutes or until potatoes are cooked. Remove bay leaf. Stir in lemon juice, parsley, chives and black pepper to taste. Just prior to serving, sprinkle with Parmesan cheese.

Note: To chop the sweet corn, place in a food processor or blender and process using the pulse button until the sweet corn is coarsely chopped. Creamed sweet corn can be used in place of the kernels if you wish. If using creamed sweet corn there is no need to chop it.

Serves 6

ingredients

1 tablespoon vegetable oil
1 small onion, diced
250g/8oz boneless chicken breast fillets, shredded
3 potatoes, chopped
3¹/₂cups/875ml/1¹/₂pt chicken stock
315g/10oz canned sweet corn kernels, drained and coarsely chopped
1¹/₄cups/315ml/10fl oz milk
1 bay leaf
freshly ground black pepper
1 tablespoon lemon juice
2 tablespoons chopped fresh parsley
1 tablespoon snipped fresh chives
60g/2oz grated Parmesan cheese

mulligatawny
soup

Method:

1 Heat oil in a large saucepan over a medium heat, add onions, apple and garlic and cook, stirring, for 5 minutes or until onions are tender. Add lemon juice, curry powder, sugar, cumin and coriander and cook over a low heat, stirring, for 10 minutes or until fragrant.

2 Blend flour with a little stock and stir into curry mixture. Add chicken, rice and remaining stock to pan and stirring constantly, bring to the boil. Reduce heat, cover and simmer for 20 minutes or until chicken and rice are cooked. Season to taste with black pepper.

Note: A dash of chilli sauce and a chopped tomato are delicious additions to this soup. Serve with crusty bread rolls, naan or pita bread.

Serves 4

ingredients

1 tablespoon vegetable oil
2 onions, chopped
1 green apple (cored, peeled and chopped)
1 clove garlic, crushed
2 tablespoons lemon juice
1 tablespoon curry powder
1 teaspoon brown sugar
$\frac{1}{2}$ teaspoon ground cumin
$\frac{1}{4}$ teaspoon ground coriander
2 tablespoons flour
8 cups/2 litres/3$\frac{1}{2}$pt chicken stock
500g/1 lb boneless chicken breast or thigh fillets, cut into 1 cm/$\frac{1}{2}$in cubes
$\frac{1}{3}$ cup/75g/2$\frac{1}{2}$oz rice
freshly ground black pepper

chicken
minestrone

Method:

1 *Lightly spray base of large saucepan with canola oil spray. Add onion and garlic, stirring over heat until they color a little. Add celery and carrot and continue to stir for 1 minute.*

2 *Chop tomatoes and add to the saucepan with the juice. Stir in water, pepper, oregano, spice and parsley. Bring to the boil and add the macaroni. Stir until soup returns to the boil, turn down to a simmer and cook for 15 minutes.*

3 *Stir in cabbage, peas and chicken stirfry. Simmer for 15-20 minutes. Serve hot with crusty bread.*

Tip: *Left-over soup may be frozen for later use.*

Serves 4-6

ingredients

canola oil spray
1 onion, finely chopped
1 clove garlic, chopped
1 stick celery, diced
1 carrot, peeled and diced
420g/14oz can peeled tomatoes
(no added salt)
4 cups/1 litre/35fl oz water
freshly ground black pepper
1 teaspoon dried oregano
1 teaspoon mixed spice
2 tablespoons chopped parsley
½ cup/60g/2oz cut macaroni
¼ cabbage, shredded
150g/5oz frozen baby peas
200g/7oz chicken stir-fry

roasted tomato
red pepper (capsicum) and bread soup

Method:

1 Preheat the oven to 220°C/440°F.
2 Lightly oil a baking dish, place tomatoes in the dish and bake for 20 minutes or until the skins have blistered. Set aside to cool, then remove skins and roughly chop.
3 Heat the oil in a saucepan, add the garlic and the onion, and cook for 5 minutes or until soft. Add cumin and coriander, and cook for 1 minute until well combined. Add tomatoes, capsicums and stock to the saucepan, bring to the boil, and simmer for 30 minutes. Add the bread, balsamic vinegar and salt & pepper, and cook a further 5-10 minutes.
4 Serve with Parmesan cheese (if desired).

Serves 4

ingredients

1kg/2 lb Roma tomatoes, roasted
2 red capsicums (peppers), roasted and roughly chopped
30ml/10z olive oil
2 onions, finely chopped
3 cloves garlic, crushed
2 teaspoons ground cumin
1 teaspoon ground coriander
4cups/1 litre/35fl oz chicken stock
2 slices white bread, crusts removed and torn into pieces
30ml/1 oz balsamic vinegar
salt & freshly ground pepper (to taste)

coq au vin

Method:

1 Toss chicken in flour to coat. Shake off excess flour and set aside.

2 Heat oil in a large, nonstick frying pan over a medium heat and cook chicken in batches, turning frequently, for 10 minutes or until brown on all sides. Remove chicken from pan and drain on absorbent kitchen paper.

3 Add garlic, onions or shallots and bacon to pan and cook, stirring, for 5 minutes or until onions are golden. Return chicken to pan, stir in stock and wine and bring to the boil. Reduce heat, cover and simmer, stirring occasionally, for 1¼ hours or until chicken in tender. Add mushrooms and black pepper to taste and cook for 10 minutes longer.

Serves 6

ingredients

2kg/4lb chicken pieces
1/2 cup/60g/2oz seasoned flour
2 tablespoons olive oil
2 cloves garlic, crushed
12 pickling onions or shallots, peeled
8 rashers bacon, chopped
1 cup/250ml/8fl oz chicken stock
3 cups/750ml/1¼ pt red wine
250g/8oz button mushrooms
freshly ground black pepper

cashew nut
butter chicken

Method:

1 Melt ghee or butter in a saucepan over a medium heat, add garlic and onions and cook, stirring, for 3 minutes or until onions are golden.

2 Stir in curry paste, coriander and nutmeg and cook for 2 minutes or until fragrant. Add chicken and cook, stirring, for 5 minutes or until chicken is brown.

3 Add cashews, cream and coconut milk, bring to simmering and simmer, stirring occasionally, for 40 minutes or until chicken is tender.

To roast cashews, spread nuts over a baking tray and bake at 180°C/350°F for 5-10 minutes or until lightly and evenly browned. Toss back and forth occasionally with a spoon to ensure even browning. Alternatively, place nuts under a medium grill and cook, tossing back and forth until roasted.

ingredients

60g/2oz ghee or butter
2 cloves garlic, crushed
2 onions, minced
1 tablespoon curry paste
1 tablespoon ground coriander
¹/₂ teaspoon ground nutmeg
750g/1¹/₂ lb boneless chicken thigh or breast fillets, cut into 2cm/³/₄ in cubes
60g/2oz cashews, roasted and ground
1¹/₄ cups/315ml/10fl oz cream (heavy)
2 tablespoons coconut milk

Serves 6

moroccan
beans

Method:

1 *Heat oil in a saucepan over a medium heat, add ginger, cinnamon, cumin seeds, and turmeric and cook, stirring, for 1 minute. Add onions and cook for 3 minutes longer or until onions are soft.*

2 *Add red kidney beans, soy beans, chickpeas, chicken (if using), tomato paste (purée) and stock to pan and bring to the boil. Reduce heat and simmer for 10 minutes.*

3 *Add currants and pine nuts and cook for 2 minutes longer.*

Note: *For a complete meal, be sure to serve this delicious mix with a hearty wholegrain bread so that all the essential amino acids are present to build complete protein.*

Serves 4-6

ingredients

1 tablespoon vegetable oil
1 tablespoon grated fresh ginger
1 teaspoon ground cinnamon
1 teaspoon cumin seeds
1/2 teaspoon turmeric
2 onions, chopped
440g/14oz canned red kidney beans,
rinsed and drained
440g/14oz canned soy beans,
rinsed and drained
440g/14oz canned chickpeas,
rinsed and drained
375g/12oz chopped cooked chicken (optional)
440g/14oz canned tomato paste (purée)
1 cup/250ml/8fl oz vegetable stock
75g/2¹/₂oz currants
60g/2oz pine nuts, toasted

smoked
chicken papperdelle

Method:

1 To make Nasturtium Butter, place butter, garlic, lime juice and flowers in a bowl, mix well to combine and set aside.

2 Cook pasta in boiling water in a large saucepan following packet directions. Drain, set aside and keep warm.

3 Heat a nonstick frying pan over a medium heat, add chicken and cook, stirring, for 1 minute. Add wine, cream, chives and black pepper to taste, bring to simmering and simmer for 2 minutes. To serve, top pasta with chicken mixture and Nasturtium Butter.

Note: The perfect accompaniment to this dish is a salad of watercress or rocket tossed in balsamic vinegar and topped with shavings of Parmesan cheese. The Nasturtium butter is also delicious as a sandwich filling when teamed with watercress or rocket.

Serves 6

ingredients

750g/1½lb pappardelle
1½kg/3lb smoked chicken, skin removed and flesh sliced
½ cup/125ml/4fl oz white wine
1 cup/250ml/8fl oz cream
2 tablespoons snipped fresh chives
freshly ground black pepper

Nasturtium Butter
125g/4oz butter, softened
1 clove garlic, crushed
1 tablespoon lime juice
6 nasturtium flowers, finely chopped

apricot
chicken

Photograph page 419

ingredients

**1¹/2kg/ 3lb chicken pieces
1 onion, sliced
45g/1¹/2oz packet French onion or
chicken noodle soup
2 teaspoons curry powder
440g/14oz canned apricot halves in
natural juice
¹/4 cup/60ml/2fl oz white wine
or water**

Method:

1 Arrange chicken pieces in a large ovenproof dish. Scatter with onion, then sprinkle with soup mix and curry powder.

2 Combine apricots with juice and wine or water, pour over chicken and mix to combine. Cover and bake for 1-1¹/4 hours or until chicken is tender.

Note: Chicken can be one of the least expensive bases for a main course, especially if you purchase the more economical chicken pieces such as legs, wings or thigh fillets.

Serves 6

Oven temperature 180°C, 350°F, Gas 4

---

chicken
stroganoff

Photograph page 419

ingredients

**2 tablespoons olive oil
1 onion, sliced
1 clove garlic, crushed
8 chicken thigh fillets or 4 boneless
chicken breast fillets, sliced
125g/4oz button mushrooms, sliced
1¹/4 cups/315g/10oz sour cream
¹/4 cup/60ml/ fl oz tomato paste
(pureé)
¹/2 teaspoon paprika
freshly ground black pepper
2 spring onions, chopped or
chopped fresh parsley**

Method:

1 Heat oil in a frying pan over a medium heat, add onion and garlic and cook, stirring, for 4-5 minutes or until onion is tender. Add chicken and cook, stirring, for 3-4 minutes or until chicken is just cooked. Add mushrooms and cook, stirring, for 2 minutes longer.

2 Stir sour cream, tomato paste (pureé), paprika and black pepper to taste into pan, bring to simmering and simmer for 5 minutes or until sauce thickens. Sprinkle with spring onions or parsley and serve immediately.

Note: Chicken is a cheaper choice for protein and works just as well as red meat in classic dishes such as this. Serve with rice or pasta and a green salad. If you prefer a saucier mixture, add a little chicken stock or a 440g/14oz can of undrained mashed tomatoes at same time as the mushrooms.

Serves 6

419

green
chicken curry

Method:

1 Heat oil in a wok over a medium heat, add onion, lemon grass and lime leaves and stir-fry for 3 minutes or until onion is golden.

2 Add curry paste and shrimp paste (if using) and stir-fry for 3 minutes longer or until fragrant. Stir in coconut milk, fish sauce and sugar, bring to the boil, then reduce heat and simmer, stirring frequently, for 10 minutes.

3 Add chicken, bamboo shoots, sweet corn and basil and cook, stirring frequently, for 15 minutes or until chicken is tender.

Medium: Fresh lemon grass is available from Oriental food shops and some supermarkets and greengrocers. It is also available dried; if using dried lemon grass soak it in hot water for 20 minutes or until soft before using. Lemon grass is also available in bottles from supermarkets, use this in the same way as you would fresh lemon grass.

Serves 6

ingredients

1 tablespoon peanut (groundnut) oil
1 onion, chopped
1 stalk fresh lemon grass, finely chopped or 1 teaspoon dried lemon grass, soaked in hot water until soft
3 kaffir lime leaves, finely shredded
2 tablespoons Thai green curry paste
1 teaspoon shrimp paste (optional)
2 cups/500ml/16fl oz coconut milk
1 tablespoon Thai fish sauce (nam pla)
1 tablespoon sugar
1 kg/2 lb boneless chicken thigh or breast fillets, cut into 2cm/³⁄₄in cubes
220g/7oz canned bamboo shoots, drained
31g/10oz canned baby sweet corn, drained
2 tablespoons chopped fresh basil

green banana
chicken curry

Method:

1 Combine salt and turmeric and rub over bananas.

2 Heat oil in a wok over a medium heat, add bananas and stir-fry for 5 minutes or until brown. Remove bananas from pan and drain on absorbent kitchen paper.

3 Add spring onions, ginger and chillies to pan and stir-fry for 2 minutes or until mixture is soft. Stir in coconut milk, cinnamon, sultanas, cashews and chicken and bring to simmering. Simmer, stirring occasionally, for 20 minutes.

4 Slice bananas, return to pan and simmer, stirring occasionally, for 10 minutes or until chicken is tender. Remove cinnamon stick before serving.

Serves 6

ingredients

salt
1 teaspoon ground turmeric
10 green bananas, peeled
2 tablespoons vegetable oil
3 spring onions, chopped
1 tablespoon finely grated fresh ginger
2 small fresh red chillies,
seeded and chopped
1 1/2 cups/375ml/12fl oz coconut milk
1 cinnamon stick
45g/1 1/2oz sultanas (golden raisins)
30g/1oz roasted cashews
6 chicken breast fillets, cut into
thin strips

stir-fry chicken
with almonds and broccoli

Method:

1 *Place the chicken in a bowl and sprinkle over the cornflour, five spice powder and salt. Mix well and set aside. Heat about 2½cm/1in deep oil in the wok and fry the almonds until golden. Remove and drain, set aside. Add the ginger and garlic and stirfry for one minute. Add the chicken in batches and stirfry until the chicken turns white.*

2 *Return all the chicken to the wok and add the sherry, sugar and soy sauce. Stir a little then add the combined water and cornflour. Stir tossing until the sauce thickens.*

3 *Add the broccoli and fried almonds and toss to heat through. Serve immediately with boiled rice.*

Tip: *To blanch broccoli, place in a saucepan of boiling water for 30 seconds or until they turn bright green. Remove immediately and plunge into a bowl of iced water. When cold, drain in a colander.*

ingredients

**500g/1 lb chicken stirfry
3 teaspoons cornflour
½ teaspoon five spice powder
½ teaspoon salt
oil for frying
150g/5oz blanched almonds
1½ teaspoon finely
chopped fresh ginger
1 clove garlic, crushed
2 tablespoons dry sherry
1 teaspoon sugar
1 tablespoon soy sauce
2 teaspoons water
2 teaspoons cornflour
200g/7oz broccoli florets, blanched
boiled rice to serve**

portuguese
chicken

Method:

1 Heat 2 tablespoons oil in a frying pan over a medium heat, add chicken and cook for 2-3 minutes each side or until brown. Remove chicken from pan and set aside.

2 Heat remaining oil in pan, add onions and cook, stirring, for 5 minutes or until golden. Add garlic and cook for 1 minute longer.

3 Return chicken to pan, add tomatoes, mushrooms, stock and tomato paste (purée) and bring to the boil. Reduce heat, cover and simmer for 30 minutes or until chicken is cooked. Season to taste with black pepper and sprinkle with parsley.

Note: For a complete meal serve on a bed of boiled white or brown rice. The cooking time will vary according to the size of the chicken thighs.

Serves 4

ingredients

**4 tablespoons vegetable oil
8 chicken thighs, skinned and all
visible fat removed
2 onions, diced
3 cloves garlic, crushed
440g/14oz canned tomatoes,
drained and mashed
8 mushrooms, sliced
1/2 cup/125ml/4fl oz chicken stock
2 tablespoons tomato paste (purée)
freshly ground black pepper
2 tablespoons chopped fresh parsley**

vineyard chicken

spring
chicken

The freshness of spring arrives

and with it comes the availability of new season herbs, fruits and vegetables. Enjoy the temptations of Drumsticks in Dill Sauce, Chicken with Oregano and Lemon or Citrus and Spice Grilled Chicken.

vineyard
chicken

Photograph page 425

Method:
1 *Make a deep slit in the side of each chicken fillet to form a pocket.*
2 *To make filling, place ricotta cheese, basil and black pepper to taste in a bowl and mix to combine. Fill pockets with filling and secure with toothpicks.*
3 *Heat oil in a large frying pan, add onions and garlic and cook, stirring, for 3 minutes or until onions are soft. Add tomatoes, green capsicum (pepper) and wine to pan and cook, stirring, for 2 minutes.*
4 *Add chicken to pan, cover and simmer, turning chicken occasionally, for 30 minutes or until chicken is tender.*
Note: *To serve six, increase the ingredients by half. This recipe can be completed to the end of step 2 several hours in advance.*

Serves 4

ingredients

4 boneless chicken breast or thigh fillets
2 teaspoons vegetable oil
2 onions, sliced
2 cloves garlic, crushed
440g/14oz canned tomatoes, undrained and mashed
1 green capsicum (pepper), chopped
1 cup/250ml/4fl oz dry white wine

Ricotta filling
125g/4oz ricotta cheese, drained
2 tablespoons chopped fresh basil
freshly ground black pepper

chicken steaks
with herb sauce

Method:
1 *Pound thigh fillets on both sides with a meat mallet to flatten.*
2 *Heat enough butter to coat base of a large heavy-based frying pan. Place thigh fillets in and cook 3 minutes on each side over medium heat. Remove to a heated plate.*
3 *Add garlic and onions and fry over gentle heat until onions are soft. Add salt, pepper, lemon juice and parsley. Stir quickly to lift pan juices and pour over chicken steaks. Serve immediately with vegetable accompaniments.*
Serves 4

ingredients

500g/2lb chicken thigh fillets
1-2 tablespoons butter
1 clove garlic, finely chopped
1 medium onion, finely chopped
salt, pepper
1/4 cup/60ml/2fl oz lemon juice
1 tablespoon parsley, chopped

chicken
rissoles

Method:

1 Mix all rissole ingredients together and knead a little with one hand to distribute ingredients and make it fine in texture. Cover and rest in refrigerator for 20 minutes. With wet hands, form into small flat rissoles about 2¹/₂cm in diameter. Place on a flat tray until needed and refrigerate.

2 Prepare batter for flapjacks. Sift the flour, baking powder and salt into a bowl. Mix together the basil, garlic and milk, then beat in the egg. Make a well in the centre of the flour and pour in the milk mixture. Stir to form a smooth batter. Cover and set aside for 20 minutes.

3 Heat barbecue until hot and oil the grill bars and hotplate. Brush the rissoles with a little oil and place on grill bars. Grill for 2 minutes each side, cook the flapjacks at the same time, pour ¹/₄ cup of mixture onto the greased hotplate. Cook until bubbles appear over the surface and the bottom is golden. Flip over with an eggslice and cook until golden. Transfer to a clean towel and cover to keep hot.

4 Serve a flapjack on each plate and arrange 3 patties on top with a dollop of chilli yogurt sauce.

5 Serve with a side salad and the extra flapjacks.

Serves 6

ingredients

Rissoles
500g/1 lb ground chicken
¹/₂ teaspoon salt
¹/₄ teaspoon pepper
1 teaspoon crushed garlic
2 tablespoons freshly chopped chilli
2 tablespoons dried breadcrumbs
¹/₄ cup/60ml/2fl oz water

Flapjacks
1 cup/150g/5oz all purpose flour
1 teaspoon baking powder
¹/₄ teaspoon salt
2 tablespoons freshly blended basil and garlic
³/₄ cup/180ml/6fl oz milk
1 egg

Chilli Yogurt Sauce
200g/7 oz natural yogurt
1 tablespoon freshly chopped chilli
Mix yoghurt and chilli together

smoked
chicken salad

Method:

1 Arrange chicken, peppers, tomatoes and lettuce attractively in a salad bowl or on a serving platter.

2 To make dressing, place French dressing, mayonnaise, mustard and basil in a small bowl and mix to combine. Spoon dressing over salad and serve immediately.

Serving suggestion: Accompany with toasted rye or wholemeal bread.

Note: Smoked chicken is one of the more recent food products and is available from some supermarkets and delicatessens. It has been cured and smoked and has a pale pink flesh with a delicate flavour.

Serves 4

ingredients

1 ½kg/3 lb smoked chicken, skin removed and flesh shredded
2 red peppers, roasted and cut into thin strips
2 yellow peppers, roasted and cut into thin strips
2 green peppers, roasted and cut into thin strips
250g/8oz cherry tomatoes, halved
1 cos lettuce, leaves separated and torn into pieces

Basil dressing
3 tablespoons French dressing
½ cup/125 g/4 oz mayonnaise
1 tablespoon wholegrain mustard
2 tablespoons chopped fresh basil

southern-fried
chicken drumsticks

Method:

1 Rinse drumsticks and pat dry with paper towel. Smooth the skin over the drumstick if needed.

2 Mix flour, salt and pepper, place on paper-lined, flat plate. Beat eggs and milk well together in a deep plate.

3 Dip the drumsticks in the flour then into the egg, turning to coat both sides. Place again into the flour, lift end of paper to toss flour over drumstick and roll in flour until well covered. Place in single layer on a clean, flat tray.

4 Heat oil in a large frying pan. Add drumsticks and fry a few minutes on each side until just beginning to colour. Reduce heat, place a lid on the pan and cook slowly for 20 minutes, turning chicken after 10 minutes.

5 Remove lid and increase heat, continue cooking until golden brown and crisp, turning frequently. Remove from pan, drain on paper towels. Serve hot with vegetable accompaniments.

Serves 4

ingredients

1kg/2 lb chicken drumsticks
1 1/2 cups/180g/6fl oz flour
1 teaspoon salt and pepper
2 eggs
1/3 cup/80ml/3fl oz milk
1/2 cup/120ml/4fl oz canola oil

crunchy
drumsticks

Method:

1 Rinse drumsticks and pat dry. With fingers rub the curry paste well into the skin of the drumsticks.

2 Crush the corn chips or potato crisps and press onto drumsticks. Place on a rack over a shallow baking tray. Bake in a preheated oven 180°C/350°F for 35/40 minutes.

3 Serve hot with boiled rice and a portion of chutney on the side. They may also be served cold with salad.

Tip: A shallow dish is recommended as it aids the crisping process.

ingredients

1kg/2lb chicken drumsticks
2 tablespoons curry paste
2 cups/60g/2oz vinegar-flavored corn chips or potato crisps
Boiled rice or salad
mild chutney for serving

Oven temperature 180°C/350°F/Gas

rice

with chicken livers

Method:

1 Wash chicken livers, and remove any sinew. Chop livers into bite-size pieces.

2 Heat butter in a large saucepan and sauté the shallots for five minutes until tender. Add the chicken livers, and cook for a further few minutes until they change colour.

3 Add the rice and chicken stock to the saucepan, bring to the boil, then simmer with the lid on, stirring occasionally, for approximately 30 minutes, until the liquid has been absorbed and the rice is cooked. If the rice is not cooked and the mixture is looking a little dry, add a further cup of water, and cook for a further five minutes.

4 When rice is cooked, toss the chopped parsley, pinenuts and currants through the rice, and serve.

Serves 8

ingredients

1kg/2 lb chicken livers
75g/2¹/₂oz butter
12 shallots, chopped
375g/1¹/₂ cups short grain rice
2¹/₂cups/600ml/20fl oz chicken stock
1 bunch parsley, chopped
100g/3oz pine nuts
100g/3oz currants

chicken
with oregano and lemon

Method:

1 Season chicken with dried oregano, pepper and salt.
2 Heat oil in a large fry pan.
3 Add chicken, potatoes and onions, and brown quickly for 2-3 minutes.
4 Pour in stock, cover, and simmer for 10-15 minutes or until chicken is cooked.
5 Add lemon juice and fresh oregano. Season to taste. Cook for a further three minutes. Serve immediately.

ingredients

4 chicken breasts
2 teaspoons dried oregano
freshly ground pepper and salt
2 tablespoons olive oil
600g/20oz potatoes, sliced to 5mm/¹/₅in
1 bunch spring onions, trimmed and halved
125ml/4fl oz chicken stock
75ml/2¹/₂fl oz lemon juice
2 sprigs oregano, chopped
salt and pepper to taste

chicken

with ricotta, rocket & roasted red pepper

Method:

1 Preheat the oven to 200°C/400°F.
2 Combine ricotta, rocket, pinenuts, red pepper, and pepper & salt in a small bowl, and mix together until smooth.
3 Place 1-2 tablespoons of ricotta mixture under the skin of each chicken breast. Lightly grease a baking dish. Place the chicken breasts in the dish, sprinkle with pepper & salt, place 1 teaspoon butter on each breast, pour stock around the chicken, and bake for 20-25 minutes.
4 Serve chicken with pan-juices and a rocket salad.

Serves 4

ingredients

200g/7oz fresh ricotta
1 bunch rocket, roughly chopped
1/4 cup/30g/1oz pinenuts, toasted
1/2 red pepper, roasted
and finely chopped
freshly ground pepper & salt
4 chicken breasts with skin on;
each around 200g/7oz
1 tablespoon butter
250ml/8fl oz chicken stock

433

chicken
with basil cream sauce

Method:

1 *Combine the flour, pepper & salt in a bowl and coat the chicken evenly with the flour, shaking off the excess.*

2 *Heat oil and butter in a pan, add the chicken, and cook over medium heat for 5-6 minutes each side. Remove from the pan and keep warm.*

3 *Basil Cream Sauce: Wipe out the pan, heat the butter, add the garlic and cook for 2 minutes. Add chicken stock, cream and lemon juice, bring to boil and reduce a little.*

4 *Just before serving, add the basil season with pepper & salt, and serve the sauce with the chicken.*

Serves 4

ingredients

4 chicken breasts each 200g/7oz
3 tablespoons flour
freshly ground pepper & salt
1 tablespoon olive oil
1 tablespoon butter

Basil Cream Sauce
1 tablespoon butter
2 cloves garlic, crushed
1/2 cup/125ml/4fl oz chicken stock
1/2 cup/125ml/4fl oz cream
65ml/2oz cup lemon juice
2 tablespoons basil, finely chopped
freshly ground pepper
sea salt

citrus & spice
grilled chicken

Method:

1 Wash chicken inside and out and pat dry with paper towels. With a cleaver or large sharp knife, cut chicken through the breastbone and open out. Cut on each side of the backbone and discard. (May be used for stock).

2 Mix marinade ingredients together. Place chicken halves in a non-metal dish and smother with the marinade. Cover and refrigerate for 12 hours or overnight, turning occasionally.

3 Heat oven griller element or gas griller to medium. Place chicken halves in the base of the grill pan under the grill. Cook for 10 minutes on each side brushing frequently with marinade.

4 Lift chicken onto grilling rack so as to come closer to heat, cook 5 minutes on each side. Turn heat to high and cook about 2 minutes to brown and crisp. Remove chicken to a heated platter.

5 Skim the fat from the pan juices and pour juices over the chicken. Serve hot with vegetable accompaniments.

ingredients

1 kg/2lb whole chicken

For marinade
¹/₂ cup/120ml/4fl oz cider vinegar
¹/₂ cup/120ml/4fl oz orange juice
¹/₂ cup/120ml/4fl oz grapefruit juice
1 teaspoon cinnamon
¹/₂ teaspoon ground nutmeg
1 teaspoon sugar
¹/₂ teaspoon salt (optional)

Serves 2-3

435

oven baked
chicken schnitzels

Method:

1 *Place each chicken fillet between 2 pieces plastic wrap and flatten to even thinness with the side of a meat mallet or rolling pin. Place on a platter. Mix the salt, pepper, lemon juice and chilli sauce togethe and pour over the chicken. Cover and refrigerate for 20 minutes.*

2 *Spread flour onto a sheet of kitchen paper. Beat eggs with one tablespoon water and place in a shallow tray or dish. Spread breadcrumbs onto a sheet of kitchen paper. Coat each side of chicken fillets in flour, (shake off excess) then egg, and press into the breadcrumbs to coat both sides. Place on a flat surface in single layer. Lightly spray schnitzels with canola oil spray.*

3 *Place oiled side down on a rack over an oven tray (a cake-rack is suitable). Lightly spray top-side with canola oil spray. Place in a preheated oven (180°C/350°F) and cook for 8 minutes, turn with tongs and cook for a further 8 minutes.*

4 *Serve with vegetable accompaniments or a salad.*

ingredients

**1kg/2lb tray chicken breast
fillets (skin off)
salt, pepper
juice of 1 lemon
2 tablespoons sweet chilli sauce
³/₄ cup/90g/3oz flour
2 eggs
1¹/₂ cups/180g/6fl oz dried
breadcrumbs
canola oil spray**

436

Serves 5-6

chicken
and avocado focaccia

Method:

1 To make salsa, place avocado, coriander (cilantro), lime or lemon juice, mayonnaise and chilli in a bowl and mix gently to combine. Set aside.

2 Heat oil in a frying pan over a medium heat, add chicken, paprika and cumin and cook, stirring, for 5 minutes or until chicken is tender.

3 Top focaccia bases with chicken mixture, cheese and cucumber. Spoon over salsa and top with remaining focaccia halves. Serve immediately.

Note: A combination of chopped fresh chives and mint may be used instead of the coriander.

Serves 4

ingredients

2 teaspoons vegetable oil
2 boneless chicken breast fillets, sliced
1 teaspoon paprika
1 teaspoon ground cumin
4 x 12cm/5in focaccia squares, split
and toasted
4 slices Swiss cheese
¹/₂ cucumber, sliced

Avocado salsa
1 avocado, stoned, peeled and mashed
2 tablespoons chopped fresh coriander
(cilantro)
2 tablespoons lime or lemon juice
2 tablespoons mayonnaise
1 fresh red chilli, chopped

sizzling
summer

thigh steaks in fruity mint salsa

The tastes of summer....

a light and refreshing salad accompanied by the fragrant smell of perfectly barbecued chicken. Nothing else inspires us more than the combination of cooking, the great outdoors and friends.

thigh steaks
in fruity mint salsa

Photograph page 439

Method:

1 Pound thigh fillets on both sides with a meat mallet to flatten. Sprinkle with salt (if using), pepper and oregano.

2 Heat a non-stick frying pan and lightly spray with oil, place in the thigh steaks and cook for 3 minutes on each side. Remove to a heated plate and keep hot.

3 Add diced pear, banana, lemon juice, mint and chilli sauce to the pan. Scrape up pan juices and stir to heat fruit.

4 Pile hot fruit salsa on top of thigh steaks. Serve immediately with mashed potatoes or rice.

Serves 3-4

ingredients

500g/1 lb chicken thighs
canola oil spray
salt, pepper to taste (optional)
1/2 teaspoon dried oregano
1 pear, peeled and diced
1 banana, peeled and diced
2 tablespoons lemon juice
3 tablespoons finely chopped mint
2 teaspoons sweet chilli sauce

honey balsamic
barbequed drumsticks

Method:

1 Rinse and dry drumsticks with paper towel. Place in a single layer in a non-metal dish. Mix honey, vinegar, ginger, salt and pepper together and pour over drumsticks. Stand 1 hour or longer in refrigerator.

2 Heat barbecue or grill until hot. Place a wire cake rack over barbecue grill bars and lightly oil. Arrange drumsticks on rack and cook 20-25 minutes, turning frequently and brushing with honey mixture. For gas or electric grill place in base of grill tray.

3 Remove cake-rack from barbecue and transfer drumsticks directly onto grill bars, or elevate drumsticks onto the pan grilling rack under the grill. Cook approximately 5-10 minutes more until brown and crisp, turning occasionally. Serve hot with salads.

ingredients

1kg/2lb chicken drumsticks
1/2 cup/120g/4oz honey
3 tablespoons balsamic vinegar
2 teaspoons fresh ginger juice
or 1/2 teaspoon ground ginger
salt, pepper to taste

Tip: The drumsticks cook perfectly in an upright griller. Set griller to moderate for first 20 minutes then increase heat to high. Baste as directed but there is no need to turn.

Serves 4-5

southern
barbequed chicken

Method:

1 Prepare the Southern Barbecue Sauce in advance. Place all ingredients into a stainless steel saucepan, stir to combine. Bring to a simmer and continue to simmer over low heat for 15-20 minutes, stirring regularly to prevent from catching. Stand for 1 hour to cook and to allow flavours to blend. Store in jars or bottles in the refrigerator if not to be used immediately.

2 Cut chicken into pieces. As 2kg/4lb is a large bird, the breast may be cut into 3 or 4 pieces each side.

3 Heat barbecue to moderate and oil the grill plate. Lightly sear chicken pieces on all sides over direct heat about 4 minutes each side. Lift the chicken onto a plate.

4 Place 1 1/2 cups of the sauce into a bowl and place by the barbecue. Place a sheet of baking paper over the grill bars and prick at intervals between the runs to allow ventilation. Place the chicken onto the baking paper and brush well with the sauce.

5 Close the lid and cook for 10 minutes, then lift the lid, brush with sauce, turn chicken, brush underside with sauce, close lid and cook 10 minutes. Repeat this process every 10 minutes, a total of approximately 4-5 times or for 40-50 minutes until chicken is rich brown in colour and cooked through. If chicken is cooking too quickly, reduce heat by turning down gas or rake the coals to the sides. Heat extra sauce in a small saucepan on the barbecue.

6 Serve chicken with hot sauce and jacket potatoes cooked on the barbecue with the chicken. Accompany with a salad.

Note: This is best cooked on a charcoal or gas barbecue with a lid or hood.

Serves 6-8

ingredients

1 x 2kg/4lb chicken, cut into pieces
Southern Barbecue Sauce
350ml/12oz can tomato puree
1 cup/240ml/8fl oz cider vinegar
1/2 cup/120ml/4fl oz canola oil
1/3 cup/80ml/2 1/2oz Worcestershire sauce
1/2 cup/75g/2 1/2oz brown sugar
1/4 cup/60g/2oz golden syrup or molasses
2 tablespoons French-style mustard
2-3 cloves garlic, crushed
1/4 cup/60ml/2fl oz lemon juice
1 x 2kg/4lb chicken, cut into pieces

sizzling
summer

char-grilled
tarragon chicken

Method:

1 Place chicken in a single layer in a shallow glass or ceramic dish. Combine tarragon, wine, lemon rind and green peppercorns. Pour marinade over chicken. Turn to coat chicken with marinade and marinate at room temperature, turning once, for 20 minutes.

2 Remove chicken from marinade and cook on a preheated hot char grill or in a preheated grill pan for 5 minutes or until tender.

Note: Do not marinate chicken any longer than 20 minutes as the marinade will cause the chicken to break down. As an alternative to cooking the chicken on a char grill you can cook it under a preheated hot grill.

ingredients

6 boneless chicken breast fillets,
skin removed
3 tablespoons chopped fresh tarragon
or 2 teaspoons dried tarragon
1 cup/250ml/8fl oz dry white wine
2 tablespoons lemon rind strips
1 tablespoon green peppercorns in
brine, drained and crushed

442

Serves 6

spicy
mango chicken

Method:

1 *Preheat barbecue to a high heat. Place chicken between sheets of greaseproof paper and pound lightly with a meat mallet to flatten to 1 cm/¹/₂in thick.*

2 *Combine black pepper, cumin and paprika and sprinkle over chicken. Layer prosciutto or ham and mango slices on chicken, roll up and secure with wooden toothpicks or cocktail sticks. Place chicken on lightly oiled barbecue and cook for 3-5 minutes each side or until chicken is tender and cooked.*

3 *To make sauce, place mango, garlic, golden syrup and chilli sauce in a small saucepan and cook, stirring, over a low heat for 4-5 minutes or until sauce thickens slightly. Serve with chicken.*

Note: *Drained, canned mangoes can be used in place of fresh. You will need two 440g/14oz cans of mangoes. Use three-quarters of one can for the sauce and the remainder for the filling in the chicken.*

Serves 4

4 boneless chicken breast fillets
1 teaspoon freshly ground black pepper
1 teaspoon ground cumin
1 teaspoon paprika
4 slices prosciutto or ham, halved
2 mangoes, peeled and cut into 2cm/³/₄in thick slices

Mango sauce
1 mango, peeled and chopped
1 clove garlic, crushed
2 tablespoons golden syrup
1 tablespoon sweet chilli sauce

thai
lime spatchcocks

Method:

1 Cut spatchcocks (poussins) down middle of backs and flatten. Thread a skewer through wings and a skewer through legs of each spatchcock.

2 To make marinade, place lime juice, coriander, coconut milk, chilli, honey, and black pepper to taste in a large baking dish. Mix to combine. Place spatchcocks flesh side down in marinade. Cover and refrigerate for 4 hours or overnight.

3 Cook on a hot barbecue or under a hot grill, basting frequently with marinade. Cook 15 minutes each side, or until tender and cooked through.

ingredients

4 small spatchcocks (poussins)

Marinade
3 tablespoons lime juice
2 tablespoons chopped fresh coriander (cilanto)
1 cup/250ml/8fl oz coconut milk
1 red chilli, chopped
2 tablespoons honey
freshly ground black pepper

Serves 4

skewered
chicken livers with coriander

Method:

1 Place coriander pesto, crushed garlic, chopped ginger, oil and lemon juice in a bowl.
Cut chicken livers into 2 through centre membrane and carefully stir into the coriander marinade. Cover and refrigerate for 1 hour or more.

2 Cut each bacon strip into 3 approximately 10cm/4in strips. Wrap a strip of bacon around each halved liver and secure with a toothpick.

3 Heat the barbecue until hot. Place on overturned wire cake-rack over the grill bars. Arrange the skewered livers on the rack. Cook for 8-10 minutes, turning frequently and brushing with any remaining marinade. Serve as finger food.
Note: Cook on any flat-top barbecue or electric barbecue grill.

**Yields approximately
22 skewers**

ingredients

**2 tablespoons of coriander
with Feta cheese pesto
1 teaspoon crushed garlic
1 teaspoon chopped ginger
2 teaspoons oil
1 tablespoon lemon juice
250g/8oz chicken livers
6 rashers bacon
toothpicks**

chicken
and mushroom kebabs

Method:

1 Place lime or lemon juice, oil and chilli powder in a bowl and mix to combine. Add chicken and mushroom halves and toss to combine. Set aside to marinate for 30 minutes.

2 Preheat barbecue to a high heat. Drain chicken and mushrooms, reserving marinade. Thread a chicken cube and a mushroom half onto each bamboo skewer. Brush with reserved marinade and cook on lightly oiled barbecue, turning several times, for 4-5 minutes or until chicken is cooked.

ingredients

**1 tablespoon lime or lemon juice
1 tablespoon vegetable oil
1 pinch chilli powder
1 chicken breast fillet, skin removed,
cut into 10 cubes
5 button mushrooms, halved**

Serves 4

chicken
caesar salad

Method:

1 Trim the chicken fillets. Mix together the garlic, salt, pepper, oil and lemon juice. Cover and marinate the chicken for 30 minutes in the refrigerator.

2 Heat grill or chargrill until hot. Sear the fillets one minute on each side, then cook 3 minutes each side. Remove and rest for 5 minutes before cutting into $1/2$cm slices on the diagonal.

3 Separate the leaves of the cos lettuce, discard outer leaves and wash well. Drain and shake dry in a clean tea towel. Cut greener leaves into bite-sized pieces and leave the pale inner leaves whole. Cover and place in refrigerator until ready for use.

4 Place the anchovy in base of the salad bowl and mash with the back of a fork while the oil is being added. Gradually add the lemon juice while beating, and sprinkle in the salt and pepper. Break in the coddled egg, scraping the set white from inside the shell and lightly stir. Add the mustard and Worcestershire sauce.

5 Add the cos lettuce leaves; toss to coat lightly with dressing while sprinkling over the grated Parmesan cheese. Toss in the chicken and croutons. Rearrange the whole leaves to stand upright and garnish with shaved Parmesan cheese. Serve immediately.

Tip: To make croutons. Use unsliced day-old white bread. Cut slices $11/2$cm thick, remove crusts and cut into $11/2$cm cubes. Peel 2 cloves garlic and cut in half. Add enough oil to be $1/2$cm deep in the frying pan, add garlic and heat. Remove garlic when golden; add bread cubes, stir and toss as they fry to golden colour. Remove quickly from pan and drain on paper towels.

To coddle egg. Bring the egg to room temperature. Boil water in a small saucepan and when it reaches the boil, turn heat off and immediately lower in the egg.

2 chicken breast fillets
1 clove garlic, crushed
salt and pepper
2 teaspoons olive oil
1 tablespoon lemon juice
1 cos lettuce

Dressing
2 anchovy fillets
4 tablespoons olive oil
2$1/2$ tablespoons lemon juice
$1/2$ teaspoon salt
$1/4$ teaspoon pepper
1 coddled egg
pinch of dry mustard
1 teaspoon Worcestershire sauce
1 cup/60g/2oz garlic croutons
$1/4$ cup/30g/1oz grated Parmesan cheese
shaved Parmesan cheese for garnish

Stand for 1 minute in the water. If egg is cold from refrigerator allow $11/2$ minutes.

Tip: To joint a chicken: Remove leg and thigh at the joint. Separate the leg and thigh cutting through the joint. Remove wings at the joint. Cut the breast from the back bone along the fine rib bones an each side. Cut through the centre breast bone. Cut each breast into 2 pieces.

Serves 5

447

teriyaki
tenderloins

Method:

1 Place tenderloins in a non-metal container and stir in about ³/₄ cup Teriyaki marinade. Cover and marinate for 30 minutes at room temperature or several hours or overnight in the refrigerator.

2 Heat the barbecue until hot. Place a sheet of baking paper over the grill bars and make a few slits between the bars for ventilation, or place baking paper on the hot plate. Place the tenderloins on grill and cook for 2 minutes on each side until cooked through and golden. Brush with marinade as they cook. Serve immediately with extra Teriyaki marinade as a dipping sauce.

Serves 4

ingredients

500g/1 lb chicken tenderloins
375g/12¹/₂oz bottle Teriyaki marinade

Serving Suggestions:

1 Serve with steamed rice and vegetables.

2 Toss into salad greens to make a hot salad. Dress salad with 1 tablespoon Teriyaki marinade, 1 tablespoon vinegar and 3 tablespoons salad oil.

3 Stuff into heated pocket breads along with shredded lettuce, cucumber and onion rings and drizzle with an extra spoonful of Teriyaki marinade.

lemon barbecue
roasted chicken with vegetables

Method:

1 Wash chicken inside and out, drain then pat dry with paper towels.

2 Wash lemons then peel off the zest with a potato peeler. Dice the zest finely. Juice the lemons. Mix together half of the lemon zest, lemon juice, garlic, salt, pepper, oregano and oil.

3 Stand the chicken in a dish and spoon half of the lemon mixture over the chicken and in the cavity. Place remaining zest in the cavity.

4 Prepare fire for the kettle barbecue for indirect heat according to manufacturer's instructions or preheat gas barbecue. Place chicken directly onto oiled grill over direct heat and sear on all sides. Move to indirect heat over dripping pan.

5 Place potatoes and pumpkin in 2 foil trays; sprinkle with remaining lemon mixture, tossing around to coat all pieces. Place trays over direct heat. Cover barbecue with lid or hood and cook for 1 to 1½ hours, brushing chicken with lemon and herb mixture every 20 minutes. Turn vegetables.

6 Remove vegetables when cooked, cover to keep hot. Rest chicken for 5 minutes before carving. Serve hot with roasted vegetables and a side salad.

Serves 4

ingredients

1 x 1.8kg/4lb chicken
2 lemons
2 cloves garlic, crushed
salt, pepper
2 teaspoons chopped fresh oregano
2 tablespoons olive oil

<u>Vegetables</u>
4 medium-sized brown potatoes, peeled and quartered
500g/1 lb pumpkin cut into portions (skin on)

chicken
and fresh herb terrine

Photograph page 451

ingredients

1 bunch/500g/1 lb spinach or silverbeet
250g/8oz chicken livers, cleaned
1 tablespoon seasoned flour
15g/1oz butter
1 teaspoon olive oil
375g/12oz chicken meat, a mixture of
white and dark meat, ground
375g/12oz lean pork, ground
2 teaspoons finely chopped fresh
thyme or 1 teaspoon dried thyme
3 cloves garlic, crushed
2 onions, diced
1 tablespoon green peppercorns in
brine, drained
3 eggs
1/2 cup/125ml/4fl oz dry white wine
2 tablespoons port or sherry
3 tablespoons chopped fresh parsley
freshly ground black pepper

Method:

1 Pre-heat oven to 180°C/350°F.

2 Boil, steam or microwave spinach or silverbeet leaves to soften. Drain; refresh under cold running water and drain again. Line a lightly greased terrine dish or an 11 x 21cm/4 1/2 x 8 1/2 in loaf tin with overlapping spinach leaves. Allow leaves to overhang the sides.

3 Toss chicken livers in seasoned flour to coat. Heat butter and oil in a frying pan over a medium heat until foaming. Add chicken livers and cook, stirring, for 3-5 minutes or until they just change colour. Remove livers from pan and set aside to cool.

4 Chop chicken livers. Place chicken livers, chicken, pork, thyme, garlic, onions, green peppercorns, eggs, wine, port or sherry, parsley and black pepper to taste in a bowl and mix to combine.

5 Pack meat mixture into prepared terrine dish or loaf tin, fold overhanging spinach leaves over filling and cover with aluminium foil. Place terrine dish of loaf in a baking dish with enough boiling water to come halfway up the sides of the dish and bake for 2 hours. Drain off any juices, cover top of terrine with foil, then weight and set aside to cool. When cold refrigerate overnight. To serve, unmould and cut into slices.

Note: The terrine will improve if kept for 1-2 days before serving. Accompanied by a tossed salad of watercress of rocket, a bowl of gherkins and some French bread this makes a truly delicious starter or light meal.

Serves 10

marinated
chicken and pear salad

Method:

1 Remove the flesh from the chicken. Carve chicken and discard the bones. Place chicken in a flat, non-metal dish and place dried pears on top.
2 Mix marinade ingredients together, pour over chicken and pears and refrigerate for 2 hours.
3 Place salad greens on serving plate, arrange the chicken strips and pear halves on the salad.
4 Whisk the remaining marinade with a little extra oil and spoon over the salad.

Serves 6-8

ingredients

1 x 1.5kg/3lb chicken (oven barbecued)
200g/7oz packet dried pears

Marinade
¹/₂ cup/120ml/4fl oz olive oil
¹/₂ cup/120ml/4fl oz orange juice
2 tablespoons red wine vinegar
3 whole cloves
3 small bay leaves
2 tablespoons pine nuts
¹/₄ cup/45g/1¹/₄oz raisins
1 teaspoon sweet chilli sauce

Salad
500g/1 lb mixed salad greens, crisped
2 cucumbers, thinly sliced
1 small spanish onion

chicken kebabs
with yogurt and lemon sauce

Method:

1 Soak satay sticks in cold water for 30 minutes.
2 Place yogurt, garlic, paprika, cummin seeds, lemon juice, parsley, oregano and pepper in a bowl, and mix until combined.
3 Place chicken on satay sticks and brush-over with half the mixture. Leave to marinate in refrigerator for 2-3 hours.
4 Heat oil on barbecue (or chargrill pan), add chicken kebabs and cook 4-5 minutes each side.
5 Serve with remaining marinade mixture.

Serves 4

ingredients

6 chicken thigh fillets, cubed
300g/10oz plain yogurt
2 clove garlic, crushed
1½ teaspoon paprika, ground
1½ teaspoon cummin seeds
60ml/2oz lemon juice
2 tablespoons parsley, chopped
2 teaspoons oregano, chopped
freshly ground pepper
24 satay sticks

grilled
chicken salad

Method:
1. Place coriander, chilli, soy sauce and lime juice in a bowl and mix to combine. Add chicken, toss to coat and marinate at room temperature for 30 minutes.
2. Preheat barbecue to a medium heat. Arrange rocket or watercress, tomatoes, feta cheese and olives attractively on a serving platter. Set aside.
3. To make dressing, place oil, lime juice and black pepper to taste in a screwtop jar and shake well to combine. Set aside.
4. Drain chicken, place on lightly oiled barbecue grill and cook for 4-5 minutes each side or until cooked through. Slice chicken, arrange on salad, drizzle with dressing and serve immediately.

Note: The chicken will come to no harm if marinated for longer than 30 minutes, but if you think the marinating will exceed 1 hour it is safer to place it in the refrigerator. When entertaining, this recipe can be prepared to the end of step 3 several hours in advance, then cover and store in the refrigerator until required.

Serves 4

ingredients

2 tablespoons chopped fresh coriander (cilantro)
1 fresh red chilli, chopped
2 tablespoons soy sauce
2 tablespoons lime juice
4 boneless chicken breast fillets
1 bunch rocket or watercress
250g/8oz cherry tomatoes, halved
155g/5oz feta cheese, crumbled
90g/3oz marinated olives

Lime dressing
2 tablespoons olive oil
2 tablespoons lime juice
freshly ground black pepper

chicken
pesto burgers

Method:

1 Preheat barbecue to a medium heat. To make patties, place basil leaves, pine nuts, Parmesan cheese, garlic and oil in a food processor or blender and process until smooth. Transfer mixture to a bowl, add chicken, breadcrumbs, red capsicum (pepper), onion, egg white and black pepper to taste and mix well to combine.

2 Shape chicken mixture into four patties. Place patties on lightly oiled barbecue plate (griddle) and cook for 3 minutes each side or until cooked.

3 To serve, top bottom half of each roll with rocket or watercress, then with a pattie, tomato slices and top half of roll. Serve immediately.

Note: Peppers are easy to roast on the barbecue. Remove seeds cut into quarters and place skin side down on a preheated hot barbecue. Cook until skins are charred and blistered, then place in a plastic food bag or paper bag and set aside until cool enough to handle. Remove skin and use as desired.

ingredients

4 rolls, slit and toasted
125g/4oz rocket or watercress
1 tomato, sliced

Chicken pesto patties
¹/₂ bunch fresh basil
2 tablespoons pine nuts
1 tablespoon grated Parmesan cheese
1 clove garlic, crushed
2 tablespoons olive oil
500g/1 lb chicken ground
1 cup/60g/2oz breadcrumbs, made from stale bread
1 red pepper, roasted and diced
1 onion, diced
1 egg white
freshly ground black pepper

Serves 4

barbecued
spatchcocks

Method:
1 Preheat barbecue to a medium heat.
2 Place spatchcocks (poussins) on oiled barbecue grill and cook for 6-7 minutes each side or until tender and cooked through.
3 To make dressing, place olives, parsley, anchovies, garlic, vinegar, oil and black pepper to taste in a bowl and mix to combine. Spoon dressing over spatchcocks (poussins) and serve immediately.

Serves 6

ingredients

6 spatchcocks (poussins), halved and backbones removed

Green olive dressing
75g/2¹/₂oz green olives, pitted and finely chopped
4 tblspns chopped fresh flat-leaf parsley
2 canned anchovy fillets, chopped
I clove garlic, crushed
¹/₄ cup/60ml/2fl oz red wine vinegar
2 tablespoons olive oil
freshly ground pepper

spiced
chicken burgers

Method:

1. Preheat barbecue to a medium heat.
2. To make marinade, place yogurt, coriander, curry paste, chutney and lemon juice in a shallow dish and mix to combine. Add chicken breasts, turn to coat and marinate for 20 minutes.
3. To make raita, cut cucumber in half, lengthwise and scrape out seeds. Cut cucumber into fine slices and place in a bowl. Add yogurt, garlic and lemon juice and mix to combine. Cover and chill until ready to serve.
4. Drain chicken and cook on oiled barbecue grill for 4 minutes each side or until tender and cooked through. To serve, place chicken fillets on four pieces of bread, then top with tomatoes and raita and remaining pieces of bread.

Note: Turkish bread (pide) is a flat white leavened bread similar to Italian flatbread. It is usually baked in ovals measuring 30-40cm/12-16in. If Turkish bread is unavailable, country-style Italian bread, rye bread, sourdough, ciabatta or focaccia are all good alternatives for this recipe.

Makes 4 burgers

ingredients

4 boneless chicken breast fillets
4 pieces Turkish (pide) bread, halved
4 tomatoes, sliced

Spiced yogurt marinade
$^1\!/_2$ cup/100g/3$^1\!/_2$oz natural yogurt
4 tablespoons chopped fresh coriander
2 tablespoons mild red curry paste
2 tablespoons mango chutney
2 tablespoons lemon juice

Cucumber raita
1 cucumber
1 cup/200g/6$^1\!/_2$oz thick natural yogurt
1 clove garlic, crushed
1 tablespoon lemon juice

chicken
pineapple kebabs

Photograph page 459

Method:

1 Bring a medium saucepan of water to the boil, add the pumpkin and cook for 3 minutes, then drain.
2 Thread the chicken cubes, one pineapple cube and one pumpkin cube onto each skewer.
3 Brush chicken with the combined garlic, soy sauce, lemon juice and honey and grill under moderate heat or on a barbecue plate for about 3 minutes each side or until cooked through.

Serves 4

ingredients

4 chicken breast fillets, cut into 2cm/³/₄in cubes
200g/7oz pineapple, cut into 2cm/³/₄in cubes
200g/7oz pumpkin, cut into 2cm/³/₄in cubes
8 wooded skewers, soaked
2 cloves garlic, crushed
2 tablespoons soy sauce
4 tablespoons freshly squeezed lemon juice
1 tablespoon honey

sweet chicken
drumsticks with polenta crust

Photograph page 459

Method:

1 Brush each drumstick with the jam, then roll in the flour. Coat with the beaten eggs, then roll in the combined extra flour, salt and polenta, and coat well.
2 Deep-fry drumsticks until golden and cooked through (about 20 minutes).

Serves 4

ingredients

8 chicken drumsticks
¹/₄ cup/60g/2oz apricot jam (jelly)
1 cup/120g/4oz plain flour
2 eggs, beaten
¹/₂ cup/60g/2oz flour, extra
1 tablespoon salt
³/₄ cup/90g/3oz polenta (cornmeal)
oil for deep-frying

Chicken stock is the rich, flavorsome liquid obtained by slowly simmering chicken pieces, bones or a boiler chicken in water, with celery, carrot and onion added for extra flavour if desired. It is used as a base for soups, sauces, stews and casseroles and small quantities are used in stir-fry dishes. It is therefore handy to always have some in the freezer for the various cooking needs. A recipe for chicken stock is included in this section.

Helpful tips:

* Bags of chicken bones and carcasses may be bought for very little cost. Rinse well and break the carcasses so they will flatten. A combination of bones and a few chicken pieces, particularly wings and thigh pieces make a richer stock. Collect wing tips, chicken trimmings, bones and chicken neck, place in a plastic freezer bag and freeze. When enough is collected, proceed to make stock.

* Place the bones, trimming or pieces in a large saucepan and add enough cold water to cover the chicken by 5cm/2in. The amount will depend on the amount of bones and chicken pieces; too much water will result in a weaker stock, or extravagance of fuel until the excess water evaporates off. Bring stock slowly to simmering point over low heat to allow the extraction of the juices. Skim off the scum as it rises with a slotted spoon to remove impurities.

* Add salt, carrot, celery and onion cut into large pieces, as small pieces will pulp and cloud the stock. Avoid using starchy vegetables such as potato, peas, sweet potato, as they can also cloud the stock.

Also avoid strongly flavoured vegetables such as cabbage and cauliflower. Add bay leaf, sprig of thyme and parsley, or a bouquet garni sachet and peppercorns. Simmer uncovered for 45 minutes for small quantities or 1½-2 hours for large quantities or until the stock is rich in flavour.

* Strain the stock into a clean container. If it is to be used immediately, blot the surface with absorbent paper to remove the fat, otherwise refrigerate for 1 hour, then lift off the solidified fat from the surface. Place into covered containers and freeze. Freeze some stock in small lots to have ready for gravy, sauces and stir-fry.

* Fresh stock may be stored in the refrigerator for 4 days and in the freezer for 3-4 months.

Simple Soups and Sauces

Light Noodle Soup

Bring to a slow boil 1½ cups of chicken stock, crumble in 1 coil of egg noodles and cook for 10 minutes. A teaspoonful of tomato paste or a chopped fresh tomato may be added if desired.

Light Vegetable Soup

To 1½ cups of chicken stock add 1 cup of diced vegetables, e.g. pumpkin, sweet potato, carrot, leek, celery, in any combination, and a tablespoon of rolled oats or rice. Add ½ cup of water, simmer for 15-20 minutes.

Vegetable Cream Soup

Add puréed boiled pumpkin, carrot, sweet potato, broccoli, asparagus or spinach to chicken stock in equal ratio of stock to vegetables. Heat to boiling then simmer 2 minutes. Stir in a little cream and season to taste.

Create Your Own Sauce

After pan frying chicken, add ½ to ¾ cup chicken stock to the pan, stir over low heat and scrape up all the brown cooked-on juices. Add wine or fruit juice, herbs or spices, a dash of cream or a little flour thickening, simmer for a minute then pour over the cooked chicken. A crushed plain cookie or gingernut cookie makes a good thickener for sauces.

Handy Tips

Do not let your stock liquid boil continuously as it will turn cloudy. It is best to let it gently simmer.

White pepper is stronger than black pepper. It is ground from ripe pepper - use about half as much as black pepper.

Gravy and sauces may be thickened by adding 2 teaspoons of cornflour, blended with a little water, added slowly to the sauce or liquid.

461

great
ground meat
recipes

introduction

introduction

The wonderful recipes and ideas in this book for preparing and serving ground meat are sure to impress family and friends. Ground meat is a popular, economic and without doubt the most versatile form of meat. Just think of what you can do with it – roll or shape it, then poach, bake, pan cook, stir-fry or even roast it. Supermarkets and butchers, recognising the popularity of ground meat, plus the fact that many people are becoming increasing health-conscious, are now producing low-fat or slimmer's ground meat. This is a boom for the family slimmer and those who are generally concerned about what they and their families are eating. The recipes in this book use lean ground meat, however they are just as delicious made with standard ground meat.

Nutritive value of meat

Lean ground beef, chicken, lamb and pork are highly nutritious foods with unique features. Packed full of high quality protein and essential vitamins and minerals, meat is a valuable contributor to a healthy body.

One of meat's prime nutritional benefits is as a supplier of the mineral iron. Iron is indispensable to carrying oxygen around our bodies, via our bloodstream. If you do not eat enough iron, you may become tired, have poor stamina and even become anaemic.

Lean ground beef, chicken, lamb and pork are some of the highest iron foods and this so called "haem iron" is the most easily used by our bodies. The haem iron in meat also helps the body maximise the iron in poorer iron ("non haem") foods such as vegetables, nuts, legumes and grains.

An average serve of lean red meat not only boosts your iron status, it easily provides up to half your daily requirements of zinc. Zinc is another mineral essential for humans, being necessary for growth and reproduction, healing and a healthy immune system.

That serving of meat is also brimming with B vitamins. Valuable thiamin, riboflavin, niacin, vitamin B6 and vitamin B12 will all be supplied in significant quantities, helping to release energy from food and maintain a healthy body. High quality protein, essential for the building and repair of all body cells will also be provided. Meat protein is perfectly matched to your body's needs, as it contains all of the 8 essential amino acids, or protein "building blocks', needed each day.

Lean ground beef, chicken, lamb and pork are a unique combination of many essential nutrients in the one versatile, low fat package. They make a great tasting and nutritious contribution to any meal.

Purchasing of meat

Getting the best out of your meat buying relies on the correct choice, the correct purchasing and storage of the meat, and the correct cooking method for the meat selected.

- Only buy the amount of meat that can be stored correctly in the space available.
- Before setting out to purchase a fresh supply of meat, prepare the refrigerator and freezer to store the meat. Make the necessary space available, wash meat trays and defrost the refrigerator and freezer if necessary, so that the meat will be stored immediately on arriving home.
- Choose meat which is bright pink to red in colour with a fresh (not dry) appearance.
- Keep meat cold while carrying home to prevent the growth of food spoilage bacteria. This may be achieved by using an insulated chiller bag.
  For larger quantities, if transporting by car, place an Eskie with a cooling brick in the car and store the meat in it immediately it is purchased, particularly if departure for home is not immediate.
- If you are unsure about which cuts of meat to buy ask advice from your local butcher. Butchers are trained professionals with a wealth of useful information and are always willing to assist.

- If calculating the quantity of meat to buy for a meal is a problem, allow 125g/4oz to 150g/5oz of lean boneless meat per person.

Storage of meat

In the Meat Compartment:
- Remove from pre-package (plastic makes meat sweat which shortens storage life) and arrange in stacks no more than 2-3 layers high. Make sure there is some air space between each piece of meat . Cover top of meat loosely with foil to stop surface drying.

In the Refrigerator Cabinet:
- Place a stainless steel or plastic rack in a dish deep enough to catch any meat drip. Unwrap meat and store as for "Meat Compartment" in coldest part of refrigerator. In a "refrigerator only" unit this is at the bottom. In a combination refrigerator freezer, the coldest air is at the top of the refrigerator, because of closeness to freezer.
- If meat is to be used on day of purchase, it can be left in its original wrapping.
- Meat kept in the refrigerator for 2-3 days will be more tender than meat cooked on day of purchase. This is because natural enzymes soften the meat fibres.
- Ground meat and sausages refrigerate for 2 days

Freezer storage of meat
- Trim visible fat off meat completely or leave a small selvedge.
- Pack ground meat in meal size portions in a freezer storage bag. Press out as flat as possible, seal and label. Wide, thin packages will thaw quicker than narrow, thick packages.
- Use freezer storage bags, or plastic wrap. Wrap well to exclude air and prevent freezer burn. When placing in the freezer bag, press out as much air as possible then fold over and tape end down.

- Lable packages with name, the amount and date of freezing.
- Leave sausages in links and place meal size portions in freezer bags, seal and label.
- Rotate stocks - first in first out.
- Defrost meats in the refrigerator, never at room temperature or in water. Allow 2 days for a large roast, 1 day or less for smaller cuts, according to quantity. Do not remove from package when thawing. Meat may also be defrosted quickly in a microwave oven. Follow manufacturer's instructions.
- Do not refreeze thawed meat unless cooked first.
- Do not overstock freezer, as its effectiveness will diminish. Frozen meats must be stored at a constant temperature of - 15°C/0°F.
- Prolonged storage time in the freezer will result in loss of quality. The following guide will assist.
- Ground meat and sausages freeze for 2-3 months

Cooking ground meat

Ground meat meat has many cut surfaces and therefore more vulnerable to spoilage by microorganisms than any other meat. Extra care must be taken during transport home and storage. Transport home quickly, make meat the last item on your shopping list, or take an insulated bag to place it in.

To freeze ground meat place it in plastic freezer bags about 500g/1lb per bag. Press out flat into corners, expel air and tape down. Label and date, use within 2 months. Flat pack ground meat defrosts more quickly than a thick ball of ground meat. If all of the pack is not to be used, a thin pack can easily be cut in half, before thawing. Do not refreeze ground meat that has been thawed. If using ground chicken to make loaves, rissoles and patties you will need the addition of breadcrumbs to lighten the texture. About 1/2 cup of dried or fresh breadcrumbs to 500g/1lb of ground meat. More may be added if you wish to extend the ground meat. Moisture is also required, a little oil or water will suffice, and a whole egg added or just the egg white will bind the mixture.

Flavor is added with salt, pepper, fresh chopped onion and a little garlic. Other flavours may be achieved by adding curry powder or chopped dried fruits.

Remember to mix well, kneading by hand is the best method. To shape balls or rissoles, wet hands first so that the ground meat does not stick to the hands.

Cooking sausages

- When grilling, roasting, barbecuing or frying sausages, it is usual to prick the skins to prevent them from bursting.
- An alternative method is to moisten them with warm water first to make their skins stretch, which will prevent them from bursting.
- Always cook sausages over moderate heat, so that heat can penetrate to centre. Quick cooking over high heat will scorch the outside and leave the centre raw. They will also burst their skins even though they have been pricked.
- Grilled, barbecued and roasted thick sausages take 15 minutes to cook and need turning often. Fried sausages take 12 minutes. Thin sausages take 2 minutes less.
- Blanching sausages before grilling, barbecuing or frying prevents them bursting, removes some of the fat and makes them quicker to cook. This method is ideal when cooking large quantities for a gathering. Place them in hot water, bring them to a simmer and simmer for 5 minutes. Remove and dry on paper towels. Proceed to cook on grill or barbecue.

Photograph page 467 also appears on recipe page 488 (Meatball and Bean Salad)

ground beef

carpetburgers with caper mayonnaise

If a recipe requires ground meat,

to be browned, heat a little oil in a saucepan, add ground meat and stir continuously until ground meat changes from red to a light brown colour. Ground meat must all break up and not form into lumps. Break up lumps as they form with the back of spoon or fork. For diet cooking and particularly when using very low fat ground meat, just place the ground meat in a saucepan and add water to make it very moist. Place on the heat and stir until ground meat changes from pink to grey. Add flavorings and simmer. Ground meat needs to simmer for 25-30 minutes.

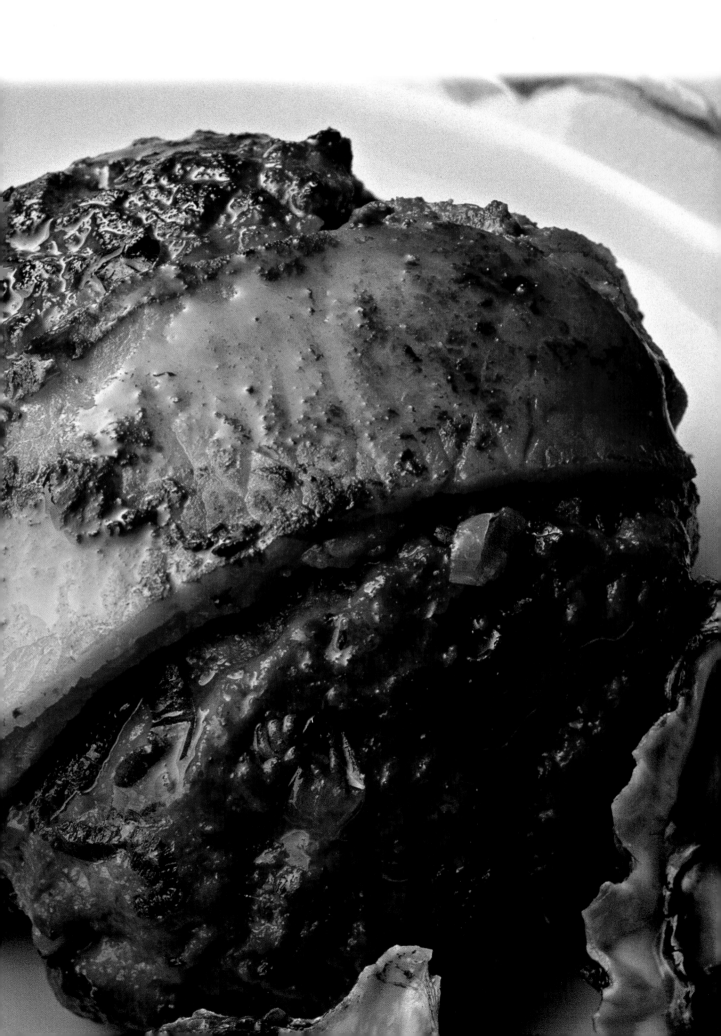

carpetburgers
with caper mayonnaise

Photograph page 469

ingredients

500g/1 lb lean ground beef
250g/8oz sausage meat
4 spring onions, finely chopped
2 cloves garlic, crushed
2 teaspoons finely grated lemon rind
1 teaspoon finely chopped fresh dill
18 bottled oysters
3 rashers bacon, cut in half lengthwise
and rind removed
2 tablespoons red wine
2 tablespoons olive oil

<u>Caper mayonnaise</u>
2 tablespoons mayonnaise
1/2 cup/125mL/4fl oz cream (heavy)
2 teaspoons chopped capers
1 teaspoon finely grated lemon rind
1 small gherkin, finely chopped

Method:

1 Place beef, sausage meat, spring onions, garlic, lemon rind and dill in a bowl and mix to combine. Shape mixture into twelve patties.

2 Top half the patties with 3 oysters each, then, with remaining patties, inch edges together to join and completely seal the filling. Wrap a piece of bacon around each pattie and secure with wooden toothpicks or cocktail sticks.

3 Place wine and oil in a large shallow glass or ceramic dish and mix to combine. Add patties and marinate for 10 minutes.

4 Drain patties and cook on a preheated medium barbecue for 5-7 minutes each side or until cooked.

5 To make mayonnaise, place mayonnaise, cream, capers, lemon rind and gherkin in a bowl and mix to combine. Serve with patties.
Note: A more economical, but just as tasty variation on that old favourite Carpetbag Steak. Prunes, dried apricots or sliced cheese can be used in place of the oysters.

Serves 6

Method:

1 Heat olive oil in a frying pan over a medium heat, add onion, garlic and green pepper and cook, stirring, for 3-4 minutes or until onion is soft. Stir in beef and cook for 5 minutes or until meat is brown.

2 Add paprika, chilli powder, cumin, chilli, tomato purée (passata), stock and wine to meat mixture, bring to simmering and simmer, stirring occasionally, for 25 minutes or until liquid is reduced by half. Stir in beans and black pepper to taste and cook for 10 minutes longer.

3 Heat vegetable oil in a large saucepan until a cube of bread dropped in browns in 50 seconds. Cook tortillas one at a time, pushing down with a small ladle, to make a basket shape, for 3-4 minutes or until golden. Drain on absorbent kitchen paper. Spoon meat mixture into tortilla baskets and top with sour cream.

Note: Another easy serving idea for this spicy meat mixture is to spoon it over hot baked potatoes. Cook four large potatoes in the oven at 200°C/400°F/Gas 6 for 1 hour or the microwave on HIGH (100%) for 15 minutes or until tender. Cut a cross in the top of the potatoes and using a clean cloth push up. Spoon meat mixture over potatoes and top with sour cream.

Serves 4

chilli
con carne

ingredients

**1 tablespoon olive oil
1 onion, finely chopped
2 cloves garlic, crushed
1 green pepper, chopped
500g/1 lb lean ground beef
2 teaspoons ground paprika
$^1/_2$ teaspoon chilli powder
$^1/_2$ teaspoon ground cumin
1 teaspoon ground red chilli
440g/14oz canned tomato
purée (passata)
$^1/_2$ cup/125mL/4fl oz beef stock
$^1/_2$ cup/125mL/4fl oz red wine
315g/10oz canned red kidney beans,
drained and rinsed
freshly ground black pepper
vegetable oil for deep-frying
4 tortillas
$^1/_2$ cup/125g/4oz sour cream**

Oven temperature 200°C, 400°F, Gas 6

nasi goreng

Photograph page 473

ingredients

Method:

1 *To make meatballs, place beef, onion, chilli, curry paste (vindaloo) and egg white in a bowl and mix to combine. Shape meat mixture into small balls.*

2 *Heat vegetable oil in a large saucepan until a cube of bread dropped in browns in 50 seconds. Cook meatballs a few at a time for 4-5 minutes or until golden and cooked through. Drain meatballs on absorbent kitchen paper, then thread onto short bamboo skewers, set aside and keep warm.*

3 *For rice, place eggs and 1 teaspoon soy sauce in a bowl and whisk to combine. Heat 1 tablespoon peanut (groundnut) oil in a heavy-based frying pan over a medium heat, add egg mixture and cook, without stirring, until set. Remove omelette from pan, cut half into small pieces and half into long strips. Set aside.*

4 *Heat remaining peanut (groundnut) oil in frying pan over a medium heat, add onions, garlic, red and green peppers and stir-fry for 3-4 minutes or until onion is soft. Add chilli, chicken and pork and stir-fry for 8-10 minutes longer or until meat is brown.*

5 *Add shrimp, bean sprouts and rice and stir-fry for 4-5 minutes or until mixture is heated through. Stir in coriander, chopped omelette and remaining soy sauce and stir-fry for 1-2 minutes longer.*

6 *To serve, spoon rice into the centre of a serving platter, top with omelette strips and surround with skewered meatballs.*

Note: *In this version of a traditional Indonesian dish ground chicken or pork are delicious alternatives for the meatballs.*

Serves 6

Chilli meatballs
**250g/8oz lean ground beef
1 onion, finely chopped
$^1/_2$ teaspoon ground red chilli
$^1/_2$ teaspoon curry paste (vindaloo)
1 egg white, lightly beaten
vegetable oil for deep-frying**

Nasi goreng rice
**2 eggs, lightly beaten
1 tablespoon soy sauce
$^1/_4$ cup/60mL/2fl oz peanut
(groundnut) oil
2 onions, thinly sliced
2 cloves garlic, crushed
$^1/_2$ red pepper, chopped
$^1/_2$ green pepper, chopped
1 teaspoon ground red chilli
1 boneless chicken breast fillet, chopped
1 x 375g/12oz fillet pork, chopped
250g/8oz uncooked shrimp,
shelled and deveined
125g/4oz bean sprouts
$2^1/_4$ cups/500g/1 lb long grain rice, cooked
1 tablespoon chopped fresh coriander**

nasi goreng

sausage
and roasted pepper salad

Method:

1 To make sausages, place beef, sausage meat, garlic, rosemary, basil, proscuitto or ham, olive oil and black pepper to taste in a bowl and mix to combine. Shape mixture into 10cm/4in long sausages. Cook sausages under a preheated medium grill, turning occasionally, for 10-15 minutes or until brown and cooked through. Set aside to cool slightly, then cut each sausage into diagonal slices.

2 To make dressing, place olive oil, vinegar, basil, oregano and black pepper to taste in a screwtop jar and shake well to combine.

3 Place sausage slices, penne, red peppers, yellow or green peppers, mushrooms and olives in bowl, spoon over dressing and toss to combine. Line a serving platter with spinach leaves, then top with sausage and vegetable mixture.

Note: To prevent pasta that is for use in a salad from sticking together, rinse it under cold running water immediately after draining. All this mouth-watering salad needs to make a complete meal is some crusty bread or wholemeal rolls.

Serves 4

ingredients

125g/4oz penne, cooked and cooled
2 red pepper, roasted
and cut into strips
2 yellow or green pepper, roasted
and cut into strips
125g/4oz button mushrooms, sliced
155g/5oz pitted black olives
5 spinach leaves, stalks removed
and leaves finely chopped

Herbed beef sausages
500g/1 lb lean ground beef
185g/6oz sausage meat
2 cloves garlic, crushed
1 teaspoon chopped fresh rosemary
1 tablespoon finely chopped fresh basil
2 slices proscuitto or lean ham,
finely chopped
1 tablespoon olive oil
freshly ground black pepper

Herb dressing
$^1/_2$ cup/125mL/4fl oz olive oil
$^1/_4$ cup/60mL/2fl oz balsamic or
red wine vinegar
2 teaspoons chopped fresh basil or
1 teaspoon dried basil
1 teaspoon chopped fresh oregano or
$^1/_2$ teaspoon dried oregano
freshly ground black pepper

sausage and roasted pepper salad

middle
eastern meatballs

Method:
1 Place beef, couscous, allspice, parsley and egg in a bowl and mix to combine. Shape into small balls, coat with flour and set aside.
2 Heat ghee or butter in a large saucepan and cook meatballs in batches, for 5 minutes or until brown on all sides. Return meatballs to pan, pour in stock, add cinnamon stick and bring to boil. Reduce heat and simmer for 10 minutes.
3 Stir honey, saffron, nutmeg, sultanas, apricots and chutney into pan, cover and simmer for 30 minutes. Stir in orange juice and simmer, uncovered, for 10 minutes longer or until liquid reduces and thickens slightly. Serve sprinkled with orange rind and almonds.

Note: These meatballs look great served on a bed of saffron rice or couscous. To make saffron rice, soak a few strands of saffron in 3 tablespoons warm water and add to water when cooking the rice. Instead of saffron you can use ¼ teaspoon ground turmeric, in which case there is no need to soak it; simply add to the water and rice.

Serves 4

ingredients

500g/1 lb lean ground beef
60g/2oz couscous, cooked
1 teaspoon ground allspice
2 tablespoons chopped fresh parsley
1 egg, lightly beaten
flour
60g/2oz ghee or butter
2 cups/500mL/16fl oz beef stock
1 cinnamon stick
2 tablespoons honey
¼ teaspoon saffron powder
½ teaspoon ground nutmeg
3 tablespoons sultanas (golden raisins)
3 tablespoons chopped dried apricots
2 tablespoons fruit chutney
¼ cup/60mL/2fl oz orange juice
2 teaspoons grated orange rind
30g/1oz blanched almonds, toasted

crunchy
cottage pie

Method:

1 Heat oil in a frying pan over a medium heat, add onion and cook, stirring, for 1 minute. Add garlic, mushrooms and bacon and cook, stirring constantly, for 2 minutes. Stir in beef and cook for 5 minutes or until meat is brown.

2 Stir tomato sauce, Worcestershire sauce, soy sauce, stock, thyme, parsley and black pepper to taste into pan. Bring to simmering and simmer, uncovered, for 25-30 minutes or until mixture reduces and thickens. Spoon meat mixture into an ovenproof pie dish.

3 To make topping, place potatoes, pumpkin or carrots, egg, sour cream and nutmeg in a bowl and mix to combine. Spoon vegetable mixture over meat mixture. Place pumpkin seeds (pepitas), breadcrumbs, Parmesan cheese and butter in a bowl and mix to combine. Sprinkle over vegetable mixture and bake for 45 minutes or until meat mixture is hot and bubbling and topping is golden.

Note: Any ground meat or combination of ground meats can be used to make this tasty cottage pie. The pie is almost a meal in itself, all you need for a complete meal are steamed green vegetables such as zucchini (courgettes), beans or cabbage.

Serves 4

ingredients

1 tablespoon olive oil
1 onion, finely chopped
1 clove garlic, crushed
125g/4oz mushrooms, sliced
2 rashers bacon, chopped
500g/1 lb lean ground beef
3 tablespoons tomato sauce
1 1/2 tablespoons Worcestershire sauce
1 teaspoon soy sauce
1 3/4 cup/440mL/14fl oz beef stock
1/4 teaspoon dried thyme
2 tablespoons chopped fresh parsley
freshly ground black pepper

Crunchy vegetable topping
3 large potatoes, chopped
250g/8oz pumpkin or carrots, chopped
1 egg, lightly beaten
1/4 cup/60g/2oz sour cream
1/4 teaspoon nutmeg
1/4 cup/30g/1oz chopped pumpkin seeds (pepitas)
1/4 cup/30g/1oz dried breadcrumbs
30g/1oz grated fresh Parmesan cheese
60g/2oz butter, melted

Oven temperature 180°C/350°F/Gas 4

crunchy cottage pie

devilled
corn muffins

Method:

1 To make filling, heat oil in a frying pan over a medium heat, add beef and cook, stirring, for 5 minutes or until meat is brown. Stir in curry powder and brown sugar and cook for 2 minutes longer. Mix in tomato sauce, Worcestershire sauce, soy sauce and lemon juice and bring to the boil. Reduce heat and simmer for 10 minutes or until mixture thickens. Set aside to cool.

2 Place flour, corn meal (polenta), sugar, cayenne pepper, pimiento or red pepper and cheese in a bowl and mix to combine. Stir in butter, milk and eggs and mix until just combined.

3 Half fill lightly greased muffin tins with corn meal (polenta) mixture, then top with a heaped teaspoonful of filling and enough corn meal (polenta) mixture to almost fill the tins. Bake for 20-25 minutes or until muffins are cooked when tested with a skewer.

Makes 12

ingredients

2 cups/250g/8oz self-rising flour, sifted
²/₃ cup/125g/4oz corn meal (polenta)
2 tablespoons sugar
pinch cayenne pepper
3 tablespoons chopped bottled pimiento
or roasted red pepper
90g/3oz tasty cheese
(mature cheddar), grated
125g/4oz butter, melted
³/₄ cup/185mL/6fl oz milk
2 eggs, lightly beaten

Devilled beef filling
1 tablespoon vegetable oil
250g/8oz lean ground beef
1 teaspoon curry powder
2 tablespoons brown sugar
2 tablespoons tomato sauce
2 teaspoons Worcestershire sauce
1 teaspoon soy sauce
2 teaspoons lemon juice

Oven temperature 200°C, 400°F, Gas 6

crispy
chilli turnovers

Method:

1 To make filling, melt ghee or butter in a large frying pan over a medium heat, add beef and cook, stirring, for 5 minutes. Stir in onion, ginger, garlic, chilli, turmeric, cumin, garam masala and black pepper to taste and cook until onion is soft.

2 Stir stock and chutney into meat mixture and bring to the boil. Reduce heat and simmer for 20 minutes or until most of the liquid evaporates. Remove pan from heat and set aside to cool.

3 Roll out pastry on a lightly floured surface to 5mm/^{1}/4in thick and using a 7^1/2cm/3in cutter cut out rounds.

4 Place a spoonful of the meat mixture in the centre of each pastry round. Brush edges lightly with water and fold pastry over filling. Press edges together, then pinch with your thumb and index finger. Fold pinched edges over and pinch again.

5 Heat oil in a large saucepan until a cube of bread dropped in browns in 50 seconds and cook a few turnovers at a time for 3-4 minutes or until filling is cooked and pastry golden.

Serves 6

ingredients

500g/1 lb prepared puff pastry
vegetable oil for deep-frying

Spicy beef filling
30g/1oz ghee or butter
500g/1 lb lean ground beef
1 onion, finely chopped
2 teaspoons finely grated fresh ginger
2 cloves garlic, crushed
1 small fresh green or red chilli, finely chopped
^{1}/2 teaspoon ground turmeric
^{1}/2 teaspoon ground cumin
^{1}/2 teaspoon garam masala
freshly ground black pepper
^{1}/2 cup/125mL/4fl oz beef stock
1 tablespoon lime or mango chutney

burritos
with avocado mayonnaise

Photograph page 481

ingredients

1 tablespoon vegetable oil
1 onion, finely chopped
500g/1 lb lean ground beef
30g/1oz packet chilli seasoning mix
**1/2 cup/125mL/4fl oz bottled
tomato salsa**
**440g/14oz canned tomatoes,
undrained and mashed**
1/2 cup/125mL/4fl oz beef stock
**315g/10oz canned red kidney beans,
drained and rinsed**
8 tortillas
90g/3oz butter, melted
1 red pepper, cut into strips

<u>Avocado mayonnaise</u>
1 large avocado, peeled and seeded
1/2 cup/125g/4oz sour cream
1/4 cup/60mL/2fl oz thickened (heavy) cream
2 teaspoons lemon juice
1 tablespoon mayonnaise
pinch chilli powder

Method:

1 *Heat oil in a frying pan over a medium heat, add onion and cook for 3-4 minutes or until soft. Add beef and cook, stirring, until meat is brown. Stir in seasoning mix, salsa, tomatoes, stock and beans and bring to the boil. Reduce heat and simmer for 20 minutes or until mixture thickens slightly. Remove pan from heat and set aside to cool.*

2 *Brush tortillas with butter and stack on a greased 30x60cm/12x24in piece of aluminium foil. Wrap tortillas tightly in foil and bake for 15 minutes.*

3 *Spoon meat mixture into the centre of each tortilla. Fold tortilla like an envelope to form a parcel and place seam side down in a* shallow ovenproof dish. Brush with butter and bake at 180°C/350°F/Gas 4 for 15 minutes or until heated through.

4 *To make mayonnaise, place avocado, sour cream, cream, lemon juice, mayonnaise and chilli powder in a food processor or blender and process until smooth.*

5 *To serve, spoon mayonnaise over hot burritos and top with red pepper strips.*

Serves 8

new spaghetti
and meatballs

new spaghetti and meatballs

ingredients

500g/1 lb lean ground beef
1 onion, finely chopped
1 clove garlic, crushed
1 tablespoon finely chopped fresh basil
or 1 teaspoon dried basil
4 slices Italian salami, finely chopped
2 teaspoons tomato paste (purée)
1 egg, lightly beaten
flour
2 tablespoons olive oil
250g/8oz spaghetti
60g/2oz grated fresh Parmesan cheese

Sun-dried tomato sauce
30g/1oz butter
1 clove garlic, crushed
4 slices proscuitto or ham, chopped
2 tablespoons chopped fresh rosemary
or 1 teaspoon dried rosemary
1/2 cup/125mL/4fl oz chicken stock
1/2 cup/125mL/4fl oz red wine
16 sun-dried tomatoes in olive oil,
drained and chopped
freshly ground black pepper
2 tablespoons chopped fresh basil

Method:

1 Place beef, onion, garlic, basil, salami, tomato paste (purée) and egg in a bowl and mix to combine. Shape mixture into small balls and roll in flour.

2 Heat oil in a large frying pan over a medium heat and cook meatballs in batches, for 5 minutes or until brown on all sides. Remove meatballs from pan and set aside.

3 To make sauce, wipe pan clean, add butter and melt over a medium heat. Add garlic, proscuitto or ham and rosemary and cook for 2 minutes. Stir in stock and wine and return meatballs to pan. Bring to the boil, then reduce heat and simmer for 15 minutes. Stir in sun-dried tomatoes and black pepper to taste and continue to cook until sauce reduces slightly. Remove pan from heat and stir in basil.

4 Cook pasta in boiling water in a large saucepan following packet directions. Drain well. To serve, spoon meatballs and sauce over hot spaghetti and sprinkle with Parmesan cheese.

Note: When shaping ground meat, dampen you hands and work on a lightly floured or dampened surface — this prevents the ground meat from sticking to your hands and the work surface. An egg added to ground meat mixtures binds them and makes them easier to shape.

Serves 4

beefy egg pies

Method:

1 *To make filling, heat oil in a frying pan over a medium heat, add onion and bacon and cook, stirring, for 3-4 minutes. Stir in beef and cook for 5 minutes or until meat is brown. Add flour and thyme and cook, stirring constantly, for 2 minutes. Stir in tomato sauce, Worcestershire sauce, stock, cornflour mixture and black pepper to taste and bring to the boil. Reduce heat and simmer for 5 minutes or until mixture thickens. Remove pan from heat and set aside to cool.*

2 *Line base and sides of eight greased small metal pie dishes with shortcrust pastry. Divide filling between pie dishes. Using the back of a spoon, make a depression in the centre of filling mixture and carefully slide an egg into each hollow. Sprinkle with cheese.*

3 *Cut rounds of puff pastry to fit tops of pies. Brush edges of shortcrust pastry with water, then top with puff pastry. Press edges together to seal. Brush with egg mixture, make two slits in the top of each pie and bake for 20-25 minutes or until golden.*

Note: *When you are making a pie with a cooked filling it is important that the filling is cold before you place it in the pie dish and top with the pastry lid. If the filling is hot or warm it will cause the pastry to go tough and soggy.*

Makes 8

ingredients

750g/1 ½ lb prepared shortcrust pastry
375g/12oz prepared puff pastry
1 egg, lightly beaten with
1 tablespoon water

Beef filling
1 tablespoon vegetable oil
1 onion, chopped
2 rashers bacon, chopped
375g/12oz lean ground beef
1 tablespoon flour
½ teaspoon dried thyme
¼ cup/60mL/2fl oz tomato sauce
1 tablespoon Worcestershire sauce
1 cup/250mL/8fl oz beef stock
2 teaspoons cornflour blended with
1 tablespoon water
freshly ground black pepper
8 eggs
125g/4oz grated tasty cheese
(mature cheddar)

Oven temperature 220°C, 425°F, Gas 7

483

Method:

1 Place beef, sausage meat, coriander, garlic, cumin and black pepper to taste in bowl and mix to combine. Set aside.

2 Toss hard-boiled eggs in flour. Divide meat mixture into eight portions. Using floured hands mould one portion of meat around each egg.

3 Place beaten egg and milk in a shallow dish and whisk to combine. Place breadcrumbs and sesame seeds in a separate shallow dish and mix to combine. Dip meat-coated eggs in egg mixture, then roll in breadcrumb mixture to coat. Place on a plate lined with plastic food wrap and refrigerate for 30 minutes.

4 Heat vegetable oil in a large saucepan until a cube of bread dropped in browns in 50 seconds. Cook prepared eggs a few at a time for 7-10 minutes or until golden and cooked through. Drain on absorbent kitchen paper and keep warm.

5 To make sauce, heat peanut (groundnut) oil in a saucepan over a medium heat, add onion, garlic and ginger and cook, stirring, for 2-3 minutes or until onion is soft. Stir in coconut milk, lime juice, peanut butter and chilli powder and cook, stirring constantly, until heated and well blended.

Serve with Spicy Egg Balls.

Note: This recipe is a variation on the old favourite Scotch Eggs. For something different use ground pork instead of beef. Just as good cold, these Spicy Egg Balls are great picnic food and leftovers are popular for packed lunches.

Serves 4

spicy
egg balls

Photograph page 485

ingredients

250g/8oz lean ground beef
250g/8oz sausage meat
2 tablespoons finely chopped
fresh coriander
2 cloves garlic, crushed
1 teaspoon ground cumin
freshly ground black pepper
8 hard-boiled eggs
flour
1 egg, lightly beaten
2 tablespoons milk
2 cups/250g/8oz dried breadcrumbs
2 tablespoons sesame seeds
vegetable oil for deep-frying

Peanut sauce

1 tablespoon peanut (groundnut) oil
1 small onion, finely chopped
1 clove garlic, crushed
$\frac{1}{2}$ teaspoon finely grated fresh ginger
1 cup/250mL/8fl oz coconut milk
1 tablespoon lime juice
4 tablespoons crunchy peanut butter
pinch of chilli powder

wellington
bread loaf

Photograph page 487

Method:

1 Cut base from bread loaf and reserve. Scoop bread from centre of loaf leaving a 1cm/½in shell. Make bread from centre into crumbs and set aside. Brush inside of bread shell with butter, spread with pâté, then press mushroom slices into pâté.

2 Place 1 cup/60g/2oz reserved breadcrumbs (keep remaining breadcrumbs for another use), beef, chives, black peppercorns, eggs, stock cube and tomato paste (purée) in a bowl and mix to combine.

3 Spoon beef mixture into bread shell, packing down well. Reposition base and wrap loaf in aluminium foil. Place loaf on a baking tray and bake for 1½ hours or until meat mixture is cooked.

4 To make sauce, melt butter in a saucepan over a medium heat, stir in flour and cook, stirring, for 1 minute. Remove pan from heat and gradually whisk in stock and wine. Return pan to heat and cook, stirring constantly, for 4-5 minutes or until sauce boils and thickens. Serve sauce with meatloaf.

Note: Breadcrumbs are easy to make, simply place the bread in a food processor and process to make crumbs, if you do not have a food processor rub the bread through a sieve. Breadcrumbs should be made with stale bread; for this recipe either use a loaf of bread that is a day or two old or scoop out the centre of the loaf as described in the recipe, then spread the bread out on a tray and leave for 2-3 hours to become stale, before making into crumbs.

Serves 8

ingredients

1 Vienna bread loaf
30g/1oz butter, melted
250g/8oz liver pâté
125g/4oz button mushrooms, sliced
750g/1½ lb lean ground beef
2 tablespoons snipped fresh chives
2 teaspoons crushed black peppercorns
2 eggs, lightly beaten
½ beef stock cube
1 tablespoon tomato paste (purée)

Red wine and thyme sauce
30g/1oz butter
2 tablespoons flour
½ cup/125mL/4fl oz beef stock
½ cup/125mL/4fl oz dry red wine
freshly ground black pepper

Oven temperature 180°C, 350°F, Gas 4

meatball
and bean salad

Photograph page 467 and below

Method:

1 Place onion, garlic, chilli powder, cumin, beef, tomato paste (purée), cheese, bread and egg white in a food processor and process to combine. Shape mixture into small balls.

2 Heat oil in a nonstick frying pan over a medium heat and cook meatballs in batches for 4-5 minutes or until brown and cooked through. Drain on absorbent kitchen paper.

3 To make dressing, place oil, vinegar, salsa, sugar, chilli and parsley in a screwtop jar and shake well to combine.

4 Place meatballs, beans and tomatoes in a large salad bowl. Spoon over dressing and toss to combine.

Note: Canola oil is the oil extracted from the rape plant, a member of the cabbage family. It differs from traditional rapeseed oil in that it does not contain the high levels of erucic acid. This has made rape a vaulable crop, as consumption of large quantities of eruric acid by humans has been shown to cause changes to heart muscles.

Serves 4

ingredients

I onion, chopped
I clove garlic, crushed
¹/₂ teaspoon chilli powder
2 teaspoons ground cumin
500g/I lb lean beef ground
2 tablespoons tomato paste (purée)
60g/2oz tasty cheese
(mature Cheddar), grated
I slice white bread, crusts removed
I egg white, lightly beaten
I tablespoon canola or olive oil
2x440g/I4oz canned three bean mix,
drain and rinsed
250g/8oz yellow teardrop or
cherry tomatoes

Chilli dressing
¹/₄ cup/60mL/2fl oz vegetable oil
I¹/₂ tablespoons red wine vinegar
¹/₄ cup/60mL/2fl oz bottled tomato salsa
¹/₂ teaspoon sugar
¹/₂ teaspoon bottled minced chilli
2 tablespoons chopped fresh parsley

classic
lasagne

Method:

1 **Meat Sauce:** *Brown beef in hot oil. Add remaining ingredients, cover and simmer for 20 minutes, stirring occasionally during cooking. Remove bay leaf.*

2 **Cheese Sauce:** *Melt butter, add flour and cook 1-2 minutes. Remove from heat, stir in milk and cheese. Bring to the boil stirring continuously. Season with salt, pepper and nutmeg.*

3 **To Assemble:**

a) *Spread ¹/₃ of the meat sauce over the base of a 20x30cm/8x12in ovenproof dish. Place a layer of lasagne pasta onto sauce.*

b) *Spread pasta with remaining meat sauce.*

c) *Top with another layer of lasagna sheets and spread with half the cheese sauce, sprinkle with mozzarella and parmesan cheese. Bake in a pre-heated oven at 190°C/370°F/Gas 5 for 30 minutes.*

d) *When cooked allow to stand for 5 minutes before cutting into squares to serve.*

Serves 4

ingredients

Meat Sauce
1 tablespoon olive oil
500g/1lb ground beef
1 onion, chopped
440g/14oz can peeled tomatoes
250g/8oz tomato paste
1 beef stock cube
1 teaspoon dried basil
1 teaspoon dried oregano
1 bay leaf
¹/₂ cup red wine

Cheese Sauce
3 tablespoons butter
3 tablespoons plain flour
2 cups milk
¹/₂ cup tasty cheese, grated
salt and pepper to taste
pinch of nutmeg

To Assemble
1 quantity of meat sauce
1 quantity of cheese sauce
250g/8oz packet of lasagne pasta
1 cup Mozzarella cheese
3 tablespoons grated
Parmesan cheese

Oven temperature 190°C, 370°F, Gas 5

clapshot
pie

Photograph page 491

Method:

1 *Heat the oil in a frying pan, then fry the onion, carrot and bacon for 10 minutes or until browned. Add the mince and fry for 10-15 minutes, breaking up any lumps with the back of a wooden spoon, until the meat has browned. Spoon off any excess fat, then stir in the stock, ketchup, Worcestershire sauce, thyme and seasoning. Simmer, partly covered, for 45 minutes, stirring occasionally, until thickened. Add a little water if the mixture becomes too dry.*

2 *Meanwhile, cook the potatoes and swede in boiling salted water for 15-20 minutes, until tender. Drain, then mash with 25g/1 oz butter and cream. Season with pepper and nutmeg.*

3 *Preheat the oven to 200°C/400°F/Gas Mark 6. Transfer the beef to a 1 1/2 litre/2 3/4 pint shallow ovenproof dish, then stir in the parsley. Smooth over the potato and swede mixture, then fluff up with a fork and dot with the remaining butter. Bake for 35-45 minutes, until browned. Garnish with parsley.*

Note: *Clapshot is the Scottish name for a mixture of mashed potato and swede, hence the name of this version of cottage pie.*

Serves 6

ingredients

1 tbsp olive or sunflower oil
1 large onion, chopped
1 large carrot, finely chopped
50g/2oz bacon, chopped
**750g/1 lb 11oz beef
steak mince**
300ml/1/2pint beef stock
2 tbsp tomato ketchup
1 tbsp Worcestershire sauce
1tsp chopped fresh thyme
Salt and black pepper
**2 tbsp chopped fresh parsley, plus
extra to garnish**

For the topping
450g/1 lb potatoes, chopped
450g/1 lb swede, chopped
50g/2oz butter
142ml carton single cream
Freshly grated nutmeg

chicken apricot roulade

Ground chicken is a combination

of white and dark chicken meat in equal proportions, which gives it tenderness and flavour. It can be made into all your old favourites; chicken meatloaf, rissoles, patties, chicken balls, burgers, chicken lasagne and chicken bolognese sauce. It is free of fat and therefore suitable for diet cooking where red ground meat may be too fatty.

chicken
apricot roulade

Photograph page 493 and below

Method:

1. In a large bowl mix all the ingredients for the chicken roulade together, knead well with hand. Set aside. Reserve 5 apricots for garnish, place remainder with water and sugar in small saucepan, cover and cook until apricots are soft. Uncover and allow most of the water to evaporate. Stir well to form a purée. Mix in remaining ingredients.

2. Place a 35cm/14in length of plastic wrap on work bench. Spread over the ground chicken mixture to form a rectangle approximately 28x23cm/11x9in. Spread the apricot filling over the ground mixture. Lift the plastic wrap in front of you, holding it towards the ends, and fold over the mixture 4cm. Pull the wrap towards the back, forming a roll as you pull. Place on greased oven slide. Press 5 apricots along top. Brush with glaze, place in a preheated oven 180°C/350°C/Gas 4 for 40 minutes, brushing with glaze every 10 minutes. Serve roulade hot with vegetable accompaniments, or cold with salad.

Serves 8

ingredients

Filling
1kg/2 lb ground chicken
120g/4oz dried apricots, chopped
1 cup/60g/2oz soft breadcrumbs
¾ cup/6fl oz water
1 small clove garlic, crushed
1 teaspoon sugar
1 teaspoon salt
1 small onion, finely chopped
¼ teaspoon pepper
1 stick celery, diced
2 tablespoons lemon juice
1 tablespoon water

Glaze
2 tablespoons chopped parsley
heat together
2 tablespoons apricot jam,
1 tablespoon water and
2 teaspoons Teriyaki sauce

Oven temperature 180°C, 350°F, Gas 4

Oven temperature 180°C, 350°F, Gas 4

chicken
cannelloni

Method:

1 Heat butter in a large pan, add onion and sauté 2 minutes, add ground chicken and bacon and stir until browned and cooked. Remove from heat. Add Parmesan cheese, salt and pepper to taste. Set aside.

2 Melt the 160g/5oz butter in a saucepan, add flour and stir 1 minute. Remove from heat, gradually add milk, stirring well. Return to heat, stir until sauce thickens and boils. Remove from heat, stir in seasonings, cheese and eggs. Fill cannelloni tubes with chicken mixture. Grease a large oven dish. Mix pasta sauce and water together and spread half over base of dish. Place cannelloni tubes in two rows in the dish then pour over remaining pasta sauce. Pour over the bechamel sauce, spread evenly and sprinkle with a little grated Parmesan cheese. Dot with 2 teaspoons butter and bake in preheated oven 180°C/350°F/Gas 4 for 30 to 35 minutes until golden brown. Serve hot with a tossed salad.

Serves 6

ingredients

2 tablespoons olive oil or butter
³/₄ cup/90g/3oz flour
1 onion, finely chopped
4 cups/1lt milk
500g/1lb ground chicken
salt, pepper
3 tablespoons grated Parmesan cheese
¹/₈ teaspoon nutmeg
2 eggs, beaten
cannelloni tubes
1 cup/250ml/8oz tomato pasta sauce
160g/5oz butter
¹/₂ cup/125ml/4fl oz water

curried
chicken rolls

Method:

1 Heat oil in a small pan, add onion and garlic and fry until onion is soft. Stir in curry paste and cook a little. Add lemon juice and stir to mix. Set aside. Combine the ground chicken, breadcrumbs, salt, pepper and coriander and add the onion/curry mixture. Mix well.

2 Place a thawed sheet of puff pastry on work surface and cut in half across the centre. Pile a ¼ of the ground chicken mixture in a thick 1½cm/½in wide strip along the centre of the strip. Brush the exposed pastry at the back with water, lift the front strip of pastry over the filling and roll to rest onto the back strip. Press lightly to seal. Cut the roll into 4 or 5 equal portions. Repeat with second half and then with second sheet. Glaze with milk and sprinkle with sesame seeds. Place onto a flat baking tray.

3 Cook in a preheated hot oven 220°C/440°F/Gas 7 for 10 minutes, reduce heat to 180°C/350°F/Gas 4 and continue cooking for 15 minutes until golden brown. Serve hot as finger food.

Tip: May be made in advance and reheated in a moderate oven. Yields 16-20

Serves 4

ingredients

2 teaspoons canola oil
1 medium onion, finely chopped
1 small clove garlic, crushed
2 teaspoons mild curry paste
1½ tablespoons lemon juice
500g/1 lb ground chicken
3 tablespoons dried breadcrumbs
½ teaspoon salt
½ teaspoon pepper
**2 tablespoons chopped
fresh coriander**
2 sheets frozen puff pastry with canola
1 tablespoon milk for glazing
1 tablespoon sesame seeds

chicken

cocktail balls in plum sauce

Method:

1 In a food processor place all chicken ball ingredients except frying oil and process together quickly. With wetted hands shape into small balls. Place on a flat tray in a single layer and refrigerate for 30 minutes.

2 Heat oil, at least 5cm deep in a frying pan, or half full in a deep fryer, to 180°C/350°F. Deep fry for about 3 to 4 minutes. Remove and drain on absorbent paper. Place a cocktail stick in each ball and arrange on platter. Place dipping sauce in a bowl and serve with the chicken balls.

Plum Sauce: Place all ingredients in a small saucepan and bring slowly to the boil while stirring. Simmer for 2 minutes. Remove from heat and cool. Pour into a small bowl.

Serves 4

ingredients

500g/1lb ground chicken
10 shallots, finely chopped
¼ teaspoon five spice powder
1½ tablespoons honey
1 teaspoon lemon zest
2 tablespoons lemon juice
1½ cups/90g/3oz fresh breadcrumbs
oil for frying

Plum Sauce
1 cup/250g/8oz plum jam
½ cup/125ml/4 fl oz white vinegar
¼ teaspoon ground ginger
¼ teaspoon ground allspice
⅛ teaspoon hot chilli powder

chicken
empanadas

Method:

1   Sift the flour and salt into a bowl, add butter and rub in with fingertips until fine like breadcrumbs. Mix egg and sour cream together, add to flour mixture and mix to a dough. Wrap in plastic wrap and refrigerate 30 minutes.

2   Heat butter in a pan, add onions and sauté a few minutes. Add ground chicken meat and stir while cooking until ground chicken changes colour to white and then to a slightly golden colour. Stir in chopped peach, salt and pepper. Allow to cool.

3   Roll out dough between 2 sheets of greaseproof paper. Remove top sheet. Cut rounds of pastry about 10 to 12 cm in diameter. Place heaped teaspoon of filling in the centre of each round, moisten edges with water and fold over. Pinch edges well together or press with prongs of a fork. Glaze with milk and bake in a preheated oven 200°C/400°F/Gas 6 for 10 to 15 minutes. Serve hot or cold as fingerfood, a snack, or a meal with vegetable accompaniments.

Makes 15-25

ingredients

Sour Cream Pastry
2¹/₂ cups/310g/10oz plain flour
pinch of salt
180g/6oz butter
1 egg
¹/₂ cup/125ml/4oz sour cream

Filling
1¹/₂ tablespoons butter or oil
1 onion, finely chopped
500g/1 lb ground chicken meat
1 cup/250g/8oz canned peach slices, finely chopped
salt, pepper

Oven temperature 200°C, 400°F, Gas

chicken
patties on basil flapjacks

Method:

1 Mix all patty ingredients together and knead a little with one hand to distribute ingredients and make it fine in texture. Cover and rest in refrigerator for 20 minutes. With wet hands, form into small flat patties about 2½cm/1in diameter. Place on a flat tray until needed and refrigerate.

2 Prepare batter for flapjacks. Sift the flour and salt into a bowl. Mix together the basil and garlic and the milk, then beat in the egg. Make a well in the centre of the flour and pour in the milk mixture. Stir to form a smooth batter. Cover and set aside for 20 minutes.

3 Heat barbecue until hot and oil the grill bars and hotplate. Brush the patties with a little oil and place on grill bars. Grill for 2 minutes each side, cook the flapjacks at the same time, pour ¼ cup/60ml/2fl oz of mixture onto the greased hotplate. Cook until bubbles appear over the surface and the bottom is golden. Flip over with an eggslice and cook until golden. Transfer to a clean towel and cover to keep hot.

4 Serve a flapjack on each plate and arrange 3 patties on top with a dollop of Chilli Yogurt Sauce.

5 Serve with a side salad and the extra flapjacks.

Serves 6

ingredients

Patties
500g/1 lb ground chicken meat
½ teaspoon salt
¼ teaspoon pepper
1 teaspoon crushed garlic
2 tablespoons freshly chopped chilli
2 tablespoons dried breadcrumbs
¼ cup/60ml/2fl oz water

Flapjacks
1 cup/150g/5oz self-raising flour
¼ teaspoon salt
1 tablespoons fresh basil, chopped
1 tablespoons fresh garlic, crushed
¾ cup/180ml/6fl oz milk
1 egg

Chilli Yogurt Sauce
200g/7oz natural yogurt
1 tablespoon freshly chopped chilli
mix yoghurt and chilli together

greek style
chicken rissoles in tomato sauce

Method:

1 *Place ground chicken in a bowl, grate onion into the ground chicken and add remaining ingredients. Mix well to combine, knead a little with hand. With wet hands roll into balls. Heat 1cm deep oil in a frying pan and sauté the rissoles until they change colour on both sides. Remove to a plate.*

2 *To the pan add the onion and garlic and sauté a little. Add remaining sauce ingredients and bring to the boil. Return the rissoles to the pan, reduce heat and simmer covered for 30 minutes. Serve over boiled spaghetti or other pasta.*

Serves 4-6

ingredients

Rissoles
500g/1 lb ground chicken
1 medium onion, grated
2 tablespoons finely chopped parsley
1/2 teaspoon salt
pepper
1 egg
1/2 cup/30g/1oz dried breadcrumbs
1 tablespoon water
oil for frying

Tomato Sauce
1 medium onion, finely chopped
1 clove garlic, crushed
1 tablespoon oil
440g/15oz can tomatoes
1 tablespoon tomato paste
1/2 cup water/125ml/4fl oz
1/2 teaspoon dried oregano
1 teaspoon sugar
salt, pepper
1 tablespoon chopped parsley

chicken
lemon balls

Method:

1 Place ground chicken meat in a bowl, grate onion into the ground chicken so as to catch juice also. Add egg, parsley, rice, salt and pepper to taste. Shape into balls the size of a walnut with wet hands. In a large saucepan heat butter and sauté onion until soft. Add water and stock cubes and bring to the boil. Drop the chicken balls into the boiling stock, reduce heat, cover and simmer for 40 minutes. Strain stock from chicken balls into a small saucepan keeping chicken balls covered and hot. Blend cornflour with 2 tablespoons cold water, add to the stock and stir until it boils and thickens, reduce heat and simmer.

2 Beat eggs and lemon juice together. Add spoonfuls of thickened stock to the egg mixture while beating the egg constantly. When half the stock is added return egg mixture to remaining sauce and stir for a little over very low heat.

Place chicken balls into serving dish and pour over the sauce. Garnish with parsley and lemon. Serve with crusty bread and a side salad.

Serves 4-6

ingredients

500g/1 lb ground chicken meat
1 onion, finely chopped
1 onion, finely grated
2 cups/500ml/16fl oz water
1 egg, beaten
2 chicken stock cubes
2 tablespoons chopped parsley
1 1/2 tablespoons cornflour
1/4 cup/55g/2oz raw rice
2 eggs
salt, pepper
3 tablespoons lemon juice
1 tablespoon butter

four
cheese calzone

Method:

1 Melt butter in a frying pan over a medium heat, add onion and cook for 3-4 minutes or until soft. Remove onion from pan and set aside. Add chicken to pan and cook for 3-4 minutes or until it changes colour.

2 Roll out pastry to 5mm/¹/₄in thick and cut out a 30cm/12in round. Spread ricotta cheese over pastry round, leaving a 2cm/³/₄in border around the edge. Top one half of pastry with mozzarella cheese, onion, chicken, salami, artichokes and black pepper to taste. Combine tasty cheese (mature cheddar) and Parmesan cheese and sprinkle three-quarters of the mixture over filling.

3 Brush border of pastry round with egg mixture, fold uncovered side over filling, rolling edges to seal, then crimp or flute to make a neat and decorative border.

4 Place calzone on a lightly greased baking tray, brush with egg mixture, sprinkle with remaining cheese mixture and bake for 20-25 minutes or until puffed and golden. Stand for 5-10 minutes before serving.

Note: A calzone is basically a pizza folded over to encase the filling. Because the filling is sealed in during baking it is much more succulent. This easy variation only needs a tossed green salad to make a complete meal.

Serves 4

ingredients

30g/1oz butter
1 onion, sliced
250g/8oz lean ground chicken
375g/12oz prepared puff pastry
125g/4oz ricotta cheese, drained
125g/4oz mozzarella cheese, sliced
4 slices Italian salami, chopped
3 canned artichokes, drained and sliced
freshly ground black pepper
60g/2oz tasty cheese (mature cheddar), grated
45g/1¹/₂oz grated fresh
Parmesan cheese
1 egg, lightly beaten with
1 tablespoon water

Oven temperature 220°C, 425°F, Gas 7

chicken
leek and potato pie

Method:

1 To make pastry, place cream cheese, tasty cheese (mature cheddar) and butter in a bowl and beat until soft and creamy. Mix in flour, sesame seeds and egg yolks to make a stiff dough. Turn dough onto a lightly floured surface and knead briefly. Wrap in plastic food wrap and refrigerate for 30 minutes.

2 To make filling, melt butter in a frying pan over a medium heat, add leeks and cook, stirring, for 3-4 minutes or until soft. Stir in chicken and cook for 4-5 minutes longer or until chicken changes colour. Stir in stock cube and black pepper to taste. Set aside to cool.

3 Roll out two-thirds of the pastry and use to line the base and sides of a 20cm/8in springform cake tin. Line with nonstick baking paper and fill with uncooked rice. Bake for 10 minutes, then remove rice and paper and bake for 10 minutes longer or until pastry is golden. Set aside to cool.

4 Spread half the chicken mixture over base of pastry shell, then top with half the potato slices. Repeat layers, finishing with a layer of potato. Combine cream, stock, egg and chives and pour over chicken.

5 Roll out remaining pastry large enough to cover pie. Brush rim of pastry shell with egg mixture and place pastry lid over filling, gently press edges together to seal then trim to neaten. Brush pie top with egg mixture. Make slits in top of pie using a small shape knife and bake for 15 minutes. Reduce temperature to 190°C/375°F/ Gas 5 and bake for 30 minutes.

Note: Great hot, warm or cold, this pie is a spectacular dish for a special picnic. When ground chicken is unavailable buy skinless, boneless chicken breast or thigh fillets and ground it yourself, alternatively you can use a whole chicken or chicken pieces, these will take a little more preparation as you will need to remove the skin and bones before grounding.

Serves 6

ingredients

1 egg, lightly beaten with
1 tablespoon water

Cheese pastry
60g/2oz cream cheese, softened
75g/2¹/₂oz tasty cheese (mature cheddar), grated
125g/4oz butter, softened
1¹/₂ cups/185g/6oz flour, sifted
3 tablespoons sesame seeds
2 egg yolks

Leek and chicken filling
60g/2oz butter
3 leeks, sliced
375g/12oz lean ground chicken meat
1 chicken stock cube
freshly ground black pepper
1 large potato, cooked and sliced
¹/₂ cup/125mL/4fl oz cream (heavy)
¹/₄ cup/60mL/2fl oz chicken stock
1 egg, lightly beaten
3 tablespoons snipped fresh chives

herbed
chicken loaf

Photograph page 505

Method:

1. Line a loaf pan with baking paper.
2. Combine all ingredients. Press into loaf pan, cover with foil. Place in a larger pan with sufficient water to come halfway up sides of chicken loaf pan. Bake in a moderate oven for 50 minutes. (Or use a microsafe loaf pan and cook on medium for 15-18 minutes.) Whichever cooking method is used, allow to stand for 10 minutes before turning out.
3. To make sauce, combine yogurt, herbs and lemon rind. Serve sliced with sauce, either hot or cold.

Serves 4-6

ingredients

750g/1¹/₂ lb ground chicken meat
100g/3oz lean ham, diced
¹/₂ cup/30g/1oz green shallots, sliced finely
2 tablespoons fresh chopped herbs
(tarragon, thyme, parsley,
sage or dill are suitable)
2 slices wholemeal bread,
made into breadcrumbs
2 eggs, beaten
1 teaspoon salt
freshly ground pepper
3 tablespoons whisky (or use apple juice)

For sauce

1 cup/250ml/8fl oz natural yogurt
1 tablespoon chopped herbs
1 teaspoon finely grated lemon rind

chicken
stuffed eggplant (aubergine)

Method:

1. Combine ground chicken meat, onion, parsley, spices and pine nuts.
2. Make 3 or 4 slashes in each eggplant (aubergine), taking care not to cut right through. Stuff chicken mixture into each slash. Place eggplants (aubergines) in a roaster pan, so that they fit snugly together. Pour tomato purée into dish. Sprinkle with salt and pepper. Drizzle over the olive oil and bake, uncovered, in a moderate oven for 40 minutes (or microwave on HIGH for 15-18 minutes). Serve hot, garnished with parsley, with salad and bread.

Serves 4

ingredients

500g/1lb ground chicken meat
1 medium onion, chopped finely
2 tablespoons chopped parsley
¹/₂ teaspoon allspice
¹/₂ teaspoon cinnamon
1 tablespoon pine nuts
4 eggplants (aubergine),
about 175-200g/6-7oz each
1 cup/250g/8fl oz tomato purée
¹/₂ teaspoon salt
¹/₂ teaspoon sugar
1 tablespoon olive oil

chicken
and rice balls

Method:

1 Cover rice with cold water and leave for 2 hours, drain well and place in a shallow dish.
2 Combine remaining ingredients and form into small balls.
3 Roll chicken balls in rice so that rice coats the entire surface.
4 Place rice balls in the top part of a bamboo or stainless steel steamer so that they are not touching each other. Steam with lid on for 15 minutes. Stand for 3-4 minutes. Serve with a small bowl of salt-reduced soy sauce for dipping. Not suitable to microwave.

Note: Batches of chicken and rice balls can be made in advance and stored in the refrigerator or freezer in plastic lock bags until required.

Makes 18

ingredients

1 cup/155g/5oz long grain rice
400g/13oz ground chicken meat
³/₄ cup/45g/1¹/₂oz finely chopped mushrooms
Small can water chestnuts, drained and chopped finely
3 shallots, sliced finely
1 teaspoon finely chopped ginger
1 tablespoon soy sauce
2 egg whites

chicken
patties

Method:

1 Place ground chicken meat in a bowl, add remaining ingredients except oil. Mix well to distribute ingredients.
2 With wet hands shape into 4 or 5 flat patties.
3 Heat grill on high, line with foil, brush foil with oil. Cook about 5 minutes on each side. For pan fry heat a little oil in a heavy based frying pan, cook about 3 minutes on each side. Patties may also be cooked on a barbecue plate.

Serve hot with vegetable accompaniments.

Serves 4-5

ingredients

500g/1 lb ground chicken meat
1/2 cup/60g/2 oz dried breadcrumbs
1 clove garlic, crushed
1 teaspoon salt
1/4 teaspoon pepper
2 tablespoons lemon juice
1 egg
1/4 cup/60ml/2 fl oz water
a little oil for frying

chicken
pie supreme

ingredients

3 rashers bacon, diced
2 large onions, finely chopped
125g/4oz mushrooms, sliced
½ red pepper, diced
500g/1 lb ground chicken
½ teaspoon mixed herbs
2 tablespoons lemon juice
salt, pepper to taste
1½ tablespoons flour
¾ cup/180ml/6fl oz milk
2 sheets frozen puff pastry

Method:

1 Heat a large wide based saucepan, add bacon and cook till fat runs. Add onion, mushrooms and pepper, stir well, turn down heat to low, cover and allow to sweat for 3 minutes. Stir occasionally. Add ground chicken, increase heat and stir until meat becomes white, then slightly brown. Add herbs, lemon juice and seasonings. Sprinkle in flour and mix well, then gradually stir in milk. Heat until mixture thickens. Set aside to cool.

2 Grease a large flat oven tray lightly. Cut off a 7½cm/3in strip of pastry from one sheet and place large portion onto baking tray. Pile chicken mixture in a neat rectangle 2½cm/1in in from each edge. Brush border with water and place over second sheet, moulding it down the sides of the chicken and pressing around the border to seal. Trim edges cutting through both layers then make cuts at 1cm/½in intervals around base to flute the edges. Brush all over with egg and milk glaze and decorate with lattice strips cut from trimmings. Glaze lattice. Cut 2 slits in top of pie. Bake in a preheated oven 220°C/440°F/Gas 7 for 10 minutes, reduce heat to 190°C/370°F/Gas 5 and cook 25 minutes more.

Serve hot with vegetable accompaniments.

Serves 4

chicken
ball soup

Method:

1 *Place ground chicken into a bowl, add chilli powder, salt, pepper, egg and breadcrumbs. Mix thoroughly to combine ingredients. Refrigerate for 20 minutes.*

2 *In a large saucepan heat butter, add shallots and sauté until soft. Add chicken stock or water and stock cubes and bring to the boil.*

3 *With wet hands roll ground chicken into small balls. Drop into the boiling stock, reduce heat and simmer 10 minutes. Stir in the creamed corn and simmer 2 minutes to heat well. Garnish with shallot curl, serve with crusty bread.*

Serves 2-4

ingredients

250g/8oz ground chicken
$^1/_4$ teaspoon Mexican style chilli powder
$^1/_2$ teaspoon salt
$^1/_4$ teaspoon pepper
I egg
2 tablespoons stale bread crumbs
I tablespoon butter
8 shallots, chopped
4 cups/32oz chicken stock or
4 cups/32oz water and 3 stock cubes
440g/I5oz can creamed style sweet corn

spicy lamb rolls

ground lamb

Lamb was the first meat to grace

the table of mankind. Its popularity still ranks amongst the first preference, for it is a fine to medium grained meat with a velvety texture and a delightful sweetish flavour. Ground lamb has a pleasant taste and is tender and moist. It is not uncommon for cooks to mix a little ground lamb with ground beef to add more flavours to meat loaves and patties.

spicy
lamb rolls

Photograph page 511

Method:

1 *Heat oil in a frying pan over a medium heat, add onion and cook for 2-3 minutes or until soft.*

2 *Add lamb, tomato paste (purée), honey, cinnamon, allspice, mint, lemon juice and lemon rind to pan and cook, stirring, for 5 minutes or until meat is brown. Remove pan from heat and set to cool. Stir in pine nuts.*

3 *Layer 4 sheets of pastry, brushing each with melted butter. Cut pastry in half, lengthways, then cut each half into quarters. Place a spoonful of meat mixture on one edge of each pastry piece and roll up, tucking in sides to make a thin roll. Repeat with remaining pastry and filling.*

4 *Place rolls on a baking tray, brush with remaining butter and bake for 10-15 minutes or until pastry is golden and filling cooked.*

Note: *If you do not have a food processor, mix the ground meat and other ingredients together in a bowl. The texture will not be as fine but the result and taste will be just as good. For a finer texture purchase fine ground lamb or grind it again yourself before preparing the rolls.*

Serves 4

ingredients

1 tablespoon olive oil
1 onion, finely chopped
315g/10oz lean ground lamb
1 tablespoon tomato paste (purée)
2 teaspoons honey
¼ teaspoon ground cinnamon
½ teaspoon ground allspice
2 teaspoons finely chopped fresh mint
2 teaspoons lemon juice
½ teaspoon finely grated lemon rind
1 tablespoon pine nuts
16 sheets filo pastry
125g/4oz butter, melted

greek
lamb kebabs

Method:

1 *Combine lemon juice, olive, oil, garlic, lemon thyme and salt and pepper in a bowl, and marinate the lamb for at least 1-2 hours, or overnight (if time permits).*

2 *Combine all salad ingredients in a bowl and set aside.*

3 *Mix all the ingredients for the yoghurt sauce together in a bowl, and set aside.*

4 *Chargrill the lamb pieces for a few minutes each side until lamb is cooked (but still slightly pink). Fill each pita bread with the lamb, salad and yogurt sauce, and serve warm.*

Serves 4-6

ingredients

1/2 cup/60ml/2fl oz lemon juice
1/3 cup/80ml/3fl oz olive oil
1 clove garlic (crushed)
1 teaspoon lemon thyme (chopped)
salt/pepper
350g/12oz trim lamb (cubed)
4 pieces of small pita bread

Salad
1 Lebanese cucumber (cubed)
2 Roma tomatoes (quartered)
1 Spanish onion (sliced)
50g/2oz feta cheese (crumbled)
2 tablespoons olive oil
1 tablespoon vinegar
salt and pepper

Yogurt Sauce
200g/7oz natural yogurt
1 clove garlic (crushed)
100g/3oz cucumber (grated)
1 teaspoon mint (chopped)
salt and pepper to taste

moussaka
filled shells

Photograph page 515

Method:

1 *Cut eggplant (aubergines) in half, lengthwise. Scoop out flesh leaving a 5mm/¹/₄in shell. Chop flesh and reserve to make the purée. Sprinkle eggplant (aubergine) shells with salt, turn upside down and set aside to stand for 20 minutes. Rinse shells under cold running water and pat dry. Brush eggplant (aubergine) shells inside and out with olive oil and place on a baking tray.*

2 *To make meat sauce, heat 1 tablespoon olive oil in a nonstick frying pan over a medium heat, add onion and garlic and cook, stirring, for 2-3 minutes or until onion is soft. Stir in lamb and cook until meat is brown. Add tomato supreme, wine, stock, basil, parsley and black pepper to taste to pan, or until mixture reduces and thickens.*

3 *To make cheese sauce, melt butter in a saucepan over a medium heat. Add flour and nutmeg and cook, stirring, for 3 minutes. Remove pan from heat and whisk in milk and sour cream. Return pan to heat and cook, stirring, for 3-4 minutes or until sauce boils and thickens. Remove pan from heat and stir in cheese.*

4 *Divide meat sauce between eggplant (aubergine) shells, top with cheese sauce, sprinkle with Parmesan cheese and dot with butter. Bake for 20-25 minutes or until filling is hot and bubbling and top is golden.*

5 *To make purée, place reserved eggplant (aubergine) flesh, ¹/₄ cup/60 mL/2 fl oz olive oil, garlic and onion in a nonstick frying pan and cook over a medium heat, stirring, for 4-5 minutes or until eggplant (aubergine) is soft. Place eggplant (aubergine) mixture, parsley, lemon juice and black pepper to taste in a food processor or blender and process until smooth. Serve with Moussaka-filled Shells.*

Note: *The tomato supreme used in this recipe consists of tomatoes, celery, peppers and various spices, if it is unavailable use canned tomatoes instead.*

Serves 4

ingredients

2 large eggplant (aubergines)
salt
olive oil
45g/1¹/₂oz grated Parmesan cheese
30g/1oz butter

Meat sauce
1 onion, finely chopped
1 clove garlic, crushed
500g/1 lb lean lamb ground meat
315g/10oz canned tomato supreme
¹/₂ cup/125mL/4fl oz dry white wine
¹/₂ cup/125mL/4fl oz chicken stock
2 tablespoons finely chopped fresh basil
1 tablespoon finely chopped fresh parsley
freshly ground black pepper

Cheese sauce
60g/2oz butter
¹/₄ cup/30g/1oz flour
¹/₄ teaspoon ground nutmeg
1 cup/250mL/8fl oz milk
¹/₂ cup/125g/4oz sour cream
125g/4oz tasty cheese (mature cheddar), grated

Eggplant (Aubergine) purée
reserved eggplant (aubergine) flesh
1 clove garlic, crushed
1 small onion, grated
3 tablespoons chopped fresh parsley
2 tablespoons lemon juice

515

mint glazed
lamb loaves

Method:

1 Place lamb, cooked burghul (cracked wheat), mint, egg, stock cube and black pepper to taste in a food processor and process to combine. Divide mixture into four portions and press into rectangles each measuring 10x15cm/4x6in.

2 To make filling, place burghul (cracked wheat) in a bowl cover with boiling water and set aside to stand for 15 minutes. Drain and rinse under cold water. Squeeze burghul (cracked wheat) to remove excess water and place in a bowl. Add breadcrumbs, parsley, mint, lemon rind, pine nuts, mint jelly, apple, butter and black pepper to taste and mix to combine.

3 Divide filling between meat rectangles and spread to cover surface, leaving a 2cm/³/₄in border. Roll up meat like a Swiss roll and pinch ends together to seal. Place rolls, seam side down in a lightly greased baking dish.

4 To make glaze, place mint jelly in a saucepan and heat for 3-4 minutes or until jelly melts. Stir in orange juice and maple syrup or honey and cook for 1-2 minutes longer. Brush rolls with glaze and bake, brushing with glaze several times, for 35-40 minutes or until cooked.

Note: For easy rolling up of meatloaves such as this one, shape the meat rectangles on pieces of plastic food wrap or aluminium foil, then use it to help roll the meat.

Serves 4

ingredients

500g/1 lb lean lamb ground meat
¹/₄ cup/45g/1¹/₂oz burghul (cracked wheat), cooked and drained
1 tablespoon chopped fresh mint
1 egg, lightly beaten
¹/₂ chicken stock cube
freshly ground black pepper

Wheat and mint filling
¹/₃ cup/60g/2oz burghul (cracked wheat)
¹/₂ cup/30g/1oz fresh breadcrumbs
3 tablespoons finely chopped fresh parsley
1 tablespoon finely chopped fresh mint
1 teaspoon finely grated lemon rind
1 tablespoon pine nuts, toasted
2 teaspoons mint jelly
1 apple, cored, peeled and grated
15g/¹/₂oz butter, melted

Mint glaze
3 tablespoons mint jelly
2 tablespoons orange juice
1 tablespoon maple syrup or honey

mint glazed lamb loaves

lamb sausages
in pitta pockets

Method:

1 *Place lamb, sausage meat, onion, chopped garlic, mint, parsley, lemon rind, egg white and black pepper to taste in a bowl and mix to combine. Shape mixture into six thick sausages.*

2 *Cook sausages, turning frequently, on a lightly oiled preheated medium barbecue for 15-20 minutes or until cooked. Place cucumbers, crushed garlic, yoghurt, mint and black pepper to taste in a bowl and mix to combine.*

3 *Top each pitta bread oval with a sausage, then with a spoonful of yogurt mixture. Serve immediately.*

Note: *When shaping ground meat, dampen your hands and work on a lightly floured or dampened surface – this will prevent the ground meat from sticking to your hands and the surface.*

Serves 6

ingredients

250g/8oz lean lamb ground meat
250g/8oz sausage meat
1 onion, finely chopped
2 cloves garlic, finely chopped
2 tablespoons finely chopped fresh mint
2 tablespoons finely chopped fresh parsley
2 teaspoons finely grated lemon rind
1 egg white, lightly beaten
freshly ground black pepper
2 small cucumbers, chopped
1 clove garlic, crushed
250g/8oz natural yogurt
1 tablespoon finely chopped fresh mint
6 pitta bread ovals

lamb
ragout with vegetables

Photograph page 519

Method:

1 *To make ragoût, place lamb, breadcrumbs, garlic, spring onion, parsley and egg in a bowl and mix to combine. Shape mixture into small meatballs. Heat 1 tablespoon oil in a large saucepan and cook meatballs in batches for 3-4 minutes or until brown.*

2 *Heat remaining oil in same pan, add celery and onion and cook for 3-4 minutes or until onion is soft. Stir in flour and cook, stirring, for 1-2 minutes or until flour is brown. Remove pan from heat and gradually whisk in wine, stock and tomato purée. Return pan to heat and bring to the boil. Reduce heat, add lemon rind, thyme, beans and meatballs and simmer, uncovered, for 30 minutes.*

3 *Place couscous in a bowl, pour over 2 cups/500mL/16fl oz boiling water and toss with a fork until couscous absorbs almost all the liquid.*

4 *Boil, steam or microwave turnip, carrot, potato, cauliflower, parsnip, zucchini (courgette) and sweet potato until tender. To serve, arrange couscous around the edge of a large serving platter, pile vegetables in the centre, then top with ragoût.*

Note: *Often thought of as a type of grain couscous is actually a pasta made from durum wheat, however cook and use it in the same way as a grain. The name couscous refers to both the raw product and the cooked dish. It is an excellent source of thiamin and iron as well as being a good source of protein and niacin. Considered to be the national dish of Morocco, couscous is also used widely in the cuisines of Algeria and Tunisia.*

Serves 4

ingredients

**1 cup/185g/6oz couscous
1 turnip, quartered
1 large carrot, quartered
1 large potato, quartered
1/2 head cauliflower, broken into large florets
1 large parsnip, quartered
1 large zucchini (courgette), quartered
1 sweet potato, quartered**

Lamb ragout
**500 g/1 lb lean ground lamb
3/4 cup/45g/11/2oz breadcrumbs, made from stale bread
3 cloves garlic, crushed
1 spring onion, finely chopped
2 tablespoons finely chopped fresh parsley
1 egg, lightly beaten
2 tablespoons olive oil
1 stalk celery, chopped
1 onion, chopped
1 tablespoon flour
3/4 cup/185mL/6fl oz dry white wine
1 cup/250mL/8 fl oz chicken stock
1/2 cup/125mL/4 fl oz tomato purée
2 teaspoons finely grated lemon rind
1 tablespoon finely chopped fresh thyme or 1 teaspoon dried thyme
315g/10oz canned butter beans, drained and rinsed**

lamb
and kidney loaf

Photograph page 521

Method:

1 Soak kidneys in a bowl of salted water for 10 minutes. Drain, then pat dry with absorbent kitchen paper. Cut into slices, discarding core and set aside.

2 Arrange bay leaves in the base of a greased 11x21cm/4¹/₂x8¹/₂in loaf tin and line tin with 4 bacon rashers.

3 Melt butter in a frying pan over a medium heat, add onion and cook for 2-3 minutes or until soft. Add kidneys and cook for 2-3 minutes or until they just change colour. Stir in brandy, thyme and green peppercorns and cook, stirring, for 5 minutes or until brandy reduces by half. Set aside to cool.

4 Place lamb, breadcrumbs, stock cube, tomato paste (purée), egg and kidney mixture in a bowl and mix to combine. Spoon lamb mixture into prepared loaf tin, lay remaining bacon rashers on top and cover with aluminium foil. Place tin in a baking dish with enough boiling water to come halfway up the sides of the tin and bake for 45 minutes. Remove foil, drain off juices and bake for 45 minutes longer or until meatloaf is cooked.

5 To make sauce, place sugar and butter in a frying pan and cook over a medium heat, stirring, for 3-4 minutes or until sugar dissolves. Stir in wine, brandy, chicken stock and green peppercorns, bring to simmering and simmer for 5 minutes or until sauce reduces and thickens. Whisk in cream, bring back to simmering and simmer for 2-3 minutes longer. Serve with meatloaf.

Note: Meatloaves are great when feeding a crowd and most are just as good cold as they are hot. Next time you are having a party why not serve a selection of cold meatloaves. Make them the day before and chill overnight; prior to serving cut the meatloaves into slices and arrange on beds of lettuce on large serving platters. Accompany with a selection of salads, mustards, chutneys and relishes and some crusty bread for a meal that is sure to appeal to all age groups.

Serves 8

ingredients

**3 lamb kidneys,
trimmed of all visible fat
3 bay leaves
6 rashers bacon, rind removed
30g/1oz butter
1 onion, finely chopped
¹/₄ cup/60 mL/2fl oz brandy
1 tablespoon finely chopped fresh
thyme or 1 teaspoon dried thyme
1 tablespoon green peppercorns in
brine, drained
750g/1¹/₂ lb lean ground lamb
³/₄ cup/45g/1¹/₂oz breadcrumbs, made
from stale bread
¹/₂ chicken stock cube
1 tablespoon tomato paste (purée)
1 egg, lightly beaten**

**<u>Green peppercorn sauce</u>
2 tablespoons brown sugar
30g/1oz butter
¹/₄ cup/60mL/2fl oz red wine
2 tablespoons brandy
1 cup/250mL/8fl oz chicken stock
2 teaspoons green peppercorns
in brine, drained
¹/₂ cup/125mL/4fl oz cream (heavy)**

lamb and kidney loaf

spring roll baskets

ground pork

Lean ground pork is 85% fat free,

made from the shoulder or forequarter which is trimmed of fat before mincing. Ground pork is the foundation of many patés and terines; it is used in forcemeat stuffings, fillings for pies, wantons, made into patties, meat loaves and meatballs. Ground pork is available from your local butcher or supermarket. It is best when used fresh, within a few days.

spring
roll baskets

Photograph page 523

Method:

1 Heat vegetable oil in a large saucepan until a cube of bread dropped in browns in 50 seconds. Place 2 spring roll or wonton wrappers, diagonally, one on top of the other, so that the corners are not matching. Shape wrappers around the base of a small ladle, lower into hot oil and cook for 3-4 minutes. During cooking keep wrappers submerged in oil by pushing down with the ladle to form a basket shape. Drain on absorbent kitchen paper. Repeat with remaining wrappers to make four baskets.

2 To make filling, heat peanut (groundnut) oil in a frying pan, add ginger, chilli and spring onions and stir-fry for 1 minute. Add pork and stir-fry for 5 minutes or until meat is brown. Add shrimp, soy sauce, fish sauce, honey, lemon juice, bean sprouts, carrot and coriander and stir-fry for 4-5 minutes longer or until shrimp change color.

3 To serve, spoon filling into baskets and sprinkle with cashews.

Note: Wonton or spring roll wrappers are available frozen from Asian food shops and some supermarkets.

Serves 4

ingredients

vegetable oil for deep-frying
8 spring roll or wonton wrappers, each 12¹/₂cm/5in square
2 tablespoons unsalted cashews, toasted and chopped

<u>Pork and prawn filling</u>
1 tablespoon peanut (groundnut) oil
2 teaspoons finely grated fresh ginger
1 small fresh red chilli, finely chopped
4 spring onions, finely chopped
250g/8oz lean ground pork
125g/4oz uncooked shrimp shelled and deveined
1 tablespoon soy sauce
2 teaspoons fish sauce
2 teaspoons honey
2 teaspoons lemon juice
30g/1oz bean sprouts
1 small carrot, cut into thin strips
1 tablespoon finely chopped fresh coriander

spiced apricot
pork balls

Method:

1 Soak the diced apricots in the brandy for 1 hour.

2 In a large bowl, combine the ground meat with the remaining ingredients except the oil. Knead well by hand for 2 minutes to distribute ingredients evenly, making a fine-textured mixture. Cover and refrigerate for 1 hour to allow the flavours to blend.

3 Take a heaped teaspoon of mixture and roll into a ball with wet hands. Flatten slightly and press the centre with your thumb to form a deep depression. Place ¼ teaspoon of soaked apricots in the depression and remould into a ball, covering the apricot dice. Place on a flat tray and continue to roll the remainder. Cover with plastic wrap and refrigerate for 30 minutes (or more) before frying.

4 Heat enough oil to be 1cm deep in a large, heavy-based frying pan or an electric fry pan set at 180°C/350°F. Fry the meat balls in 2 or 3 batches, rolling them around the pan to cook all over and keep their shape. Drain on kitchen paper. Place on a heated serving platter with dipping sauce in the centre and toothpicks for serving.

Apricot Dipping Sauce: Place diced apricots and water in a saucepan with any remaining brandy-soaked apricots. Bring to the boil, turn down heat and simmer for 15 minutes or until very soft. Stir in sugar, vinegar and teriyaki sauce, and simmer for 2 minutes. Purée in a blender or pass through a sieve. Stir in the fresh ginger juice, serve with the apricot meat balls.

Makes 20-25

ingredients

³/₄ cup/120g/4oz dried apricots
2 tablespoons brandy
500g/1 lb prime ground pork
1 medium onion, very finely chopped
1 slice white bread, crusts removed and soaked in ¼ cup/60mL/2fl oz water
½ teaspoon ground cinnamon
Pinch of ground nutmeg
1 teaspoon salt
½ teaspoon pepper
1 egg
oil for frying

apricot dipping sauce
½ cup/95g/3oz diced dried apricots
1 cup/250ml/8fl oz water
2 teaspoons sugar
2 teaspoons balsamic vinegar
1 teaspoon teriyaki sauce
1 teaspoon fresh ginger juice

ham roulade
with mustard sour cream sauce

Method:

1 Lightly oil roulade or Swiss roll pan. Line with non-stick baking paper, edges extending 12cm/5in at each end

2 In a large bowl combine ham, egg yolks, flour, butter, herbs, seasoning and Madeira. Beat egg whites until stiff and fold into ham mixture. Spread mixture into pan, bake in oven, preheated to 190°C/370°F/ Gas 5 for 20 minutes.

3 Turn out onto two overlapping sheets of non-stick baking paper, peel off lining paper. Use the non-stick paper to help roll up into a roulade. Place in serving dish.

4 Mix the sour cream with Dijon mustard, tarragon and chopped dill. Serve roulade sliced, with sauce. Serve with fresh garden salad.

Serves 4-6

ingredients

500g/1lb ham, finely ground
1 tablespoon olive oil
6 eggs, separated
4 tablespoons plain flour
4 tablespoons butter, melted and cooled
1/2 teaspoon ground pepper
2 tablespoons chopped parsley
2 tablespoons dried tarragon leaves
4 tablespoons Madeira wine

Sauce
1 cup/250ml/8fl oz sour cream
1 tablespoon Dijon mustard
1 tablespoon dried tarragon leaves
1 tablespoon chopped dill

Oven temperature 190°C, 370°F, Gas 5

sweet potato
and pork crumble

Method:

1 Melt butter in a frying pan over a medium heat, stir in orange juice, honey, brown sugar and ginger and cook for 2-3 minutes or until mixture is syrupy. Add sweet potatoes and toss to coat. Set aside.

2 Heat oil in a clean frying pan over a medium heat, add garlic and cinnamon and cook for 1 minute. Add pork and cook, stirring, for 5 minutes. Stir in tomato purée and port or wine, bring to the boil, then reduce heat and cook for 8 minutes or until most of the liquid evaporates. Place half the sweet potatoes in the base of a greased shallow ovenproof dish, top with pork mixture, then remaining sweet potatoes.

3 To make crumble, combine breadcrumbs, rolled oats, brown sugar and cinnamon in a bowl. Rub in butter and stir in pecans. Sprinkle over meat mixture and bake for 40 minutes.

Note: For something different make this recipe using pumpkin instead of sweet potatoes. You will need 750g-1kg/1 1/2-2 lb pumpkin.

ingredients

30g/1oz butter
1/4 cup/60mL/2fl oz orange juice
1 tablespoon honey
1 tablespoon brown sugar
1 teaspoon finely grated fresh ginger
2 sweet potatoes, cooked and sliced
1 tablespoon vegetable oil
1 clove garlic, crushed
1 teaspoon ground cinnamon
250g/8oz lean ground pork
1/4 cup/60mL/2fl oz tomato purée
1 tablespoon port or red wine

Pecan crumble
1 cup/60g/2oz wholemeal breadcrumbs, made from stale bread
1/2 cup/45g/1 1/2oz rolled oats
1/2 cup/90g/3oz brown sugar
1 teaspoon ground cinnamon
60g/2oz butter
60g/2oz chopped pecans

Oven temperature 180°C, 350°F, Gas 4

527

hungarian
pork slice

Photograph page 529

Method:

1 Boil or microwave cabbage leaves until tender. Drain, refresh under cold water and drain again. Line a greased, shallow ovenproof dish with some of the cabbage leaves. Set remaining leaves aside.

2 Heat oil in a frying pan, add onion and garlic and cook until onion is soft. Cool. Combine pork, rice, breadcrumbs, milk, marjoram, caraway seeds, paprika, eggs, black pepper to taste and onion mixture.

3 Spoon half the pork mixture into cabbage-lined dish, top with a layer of cabbage leaves and the remaining pork. Arrange bacon over top, cover and bake for 1 hour or until cooked. Drain off cooking juices and reserve.

4 To make sauce, melt butter in a saucepan over a low heat, add flour and cook, stirring, for 2-3 minutes. Remove pan from heat and whisk in stock and reserved cooking juices. Return pan to heat and cook, stirring constantly, for 3-4 minutes or until sauce boils and thickens. Remove pan from heat and whisk in sour cream and black pepper to taste. To serve, invert slice onto a serving plate, cut into wedges and accompany with sauce.

Note: This slice is delicious served hot, warm or cold. Cold it is perfect in packed lunches or as part of a picnic feast. If serving it cold you may prefer to accompany the slice with a tasty tomato sauce.

Serves 4

ingredients

¹/₂ **large cabbage, leaves separated**
1 **tablespoon vegetable oil**
1 **onion, chopped**
2 **cloves garlic, crushed**
500 g/1 lb **lean ground pork**
¹/₃ **cup/75g/2¹/₂oz short grain rice, cooked**
³/₄ **cup/45g/1¹/₂oz breadcrumbs,
made from stale bread**
¹/₂ **cup/125mL/4fl oz milk**
¹/₂ **teaspoon dried marjoram**
¹/₄ **teaspoon caraway seeds**
1 **tablespoon ground paprika**
2 **eggs, lightly beaten**
freshly ground black pepper
4 **rashers bacon, rind removed**

Sour cream sauce
30g/1oz **butter**
1 **tablespoon flour**
¹/₂ **cup/125mL/4fl oz chicken stock**
¹/₂ **cup/125g/4oz sour cream**

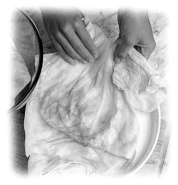

chilli meat

pattie casserole

Photograph page 531

chilli meat pattie casserole

ingredients

500g/1 lb lean ground pork
2 tablespoons taco seasoning mix
1 egg
³/₄ cup/45g/1¹/₂oz breadcrumbs,
made from stale bread
250g/8oz tasty cheese (mature
cheddar), grated
vegetable oil
1 onion, finely chopped
1 small fresh red chilli, finely chopped
2 cloves garlic, crushed
440g/14oz canned tomatoes,
undrained and mashed
¹/₂ cup/125mL/4fl oz bottled
tomato salsa
1¹/₂ tablespoons tomato paste (purée)

<u>Hash brown topping</u>
2 large potatoes, scrubbed
2 eggs, lightly beaten
155g/5oz packet corn chips, crushed

Method:

1 *Place pork, taco seasoning mix, egg, breadcrumbs and half the cheese in a bowl and mix to combine. Shape meat mixture into eight patties.*

2 *Heat 2 tablespoons oil in a nonstick frying pan over a medium heat, add patties and cook for 3-4 minutes each side or until brown. Place patties in a shallow ovenproof dish and set aside.*

3 *Heat 1 tablespoon oil in pan over a medium heat, add onion, chilli and garlic and cook, stirring, for 3-4 minutes or until onion is soft. Stir in tomatoes, salsa and tomato paste (purée) and bring to the boil. Reduce heat and simmer for 5 minutes. Pour sauce over meat patties.*

4 *To make topping, boil, steam or microwave potatoes until just tender. Drain and refresh under cold running water. Peel potatoes and grate coarsely. Place potatoes, eggs and corn chips in a bowl and mix to combine.*

5 *Heat 2 tablespoons oil a large frying pan over a medium heat and cook spoonfuls of potato mixture for 3-4 minutes each side or until golden. Remove from pan, drain on absorbent kitchen paper and place slightly overlapping, on top of patties, sprinkle with remaining cheese and bake for 40 minutes.*

Serves 4

meatball
and noodle soup

Photograph page 533

meatball and noodle soup

ingredients

220g/7oz lean ground pork
125g/4oz lean ground chicken
I egg white, lightly beaten
4 tablespoons chopped fresh coriander
I teaspoon chilli paste (sambal oelek)
125g/4oz rice noodles
2 teaspoons vegetable oil
8 oyster mushrooms, stems removed
3 cups/750mL/1½pt chicken stock
I tablespoon lime juice
2 tablespoons fish sauce
I tablespoon brown sugar
I carrot, cut into thin strips
3 spring onions, cut into thin strips

<u>Oriental Dressing</u>
I teaspoon sesame oil
I teaspoon grated fresh ginger
2 teaspoons soy sauce
I tablespoon water
I teaspoon vinegar
¼ teaspoon crushed garlic

Method:

1 Place pork, chicken, egg white, 2 tablespoons fresh coriander and chilli paste (sambal oelek) in a food processor and process to combine. Shape mixture into small balls and steam or microwave until cooked. Set aside.

2 Place noodles in a bowl, pour over boiling water to cover and set aside to stand for 8 minutes. Drain well. Heat oil in a large saucepan, add mushrooms and cook for 2 minutes. Stir in stock, lime juice, fish sauce and sugar, bring to the boil and boil for 5 minutes. Stir in carrot and spring onions and cook for I minute. Divide meatballs and noodles between soup bowls, ladle over hot soup and sprinkle with remaining coriander.

Note: A tasty oriental-style soup that is a meal in itself. For a more substantial meal start or finish with naan bread and a salad of shredded chinese cabbage, chopped spring onions, chopped fresh basil and coriander tossed with oriental dressing. To make oriental dressing place ingredients in a screwtop jar and shake well to combine.

Serves 4

pork
and apple cabbage rolls

Photograph page 535

Method:

1 *Heat oil in a frying pan over a medium heat, add onion and bacon and cook, stirring, for 3-4 minutes or until onion is soft. Stir in apple and caraway seeds and cook for 2 minutes longer. Remove pan from heat and set aside to cool.*

2 *Place pork, rice, egg, black pepper to taste and onion mixture in a bowl and mix to combine.*

3 *Boil, steam or microwave cabbage leaves until soft. Refresh under cold running water, pat dry with absorbent kitchen paper and trim stalks.*

4 *Divide meat mixture between cabbage leaves and roll up, tucking in sides. Secure with wooden toothpicks or cocktail sticks.*

5 *Melt 30g/1oz butter in a frying pan, add rolls and cook, turning several times, until lightly browned. Transfer rolls to a shallow ovenproof dish.*

6 *Melt remaining butter in pan over a medium heat, stir in paprika and flour and cook for 2 minutes. Stir in tomato paste (purée), wine and stock and bring to the boil. Reduce heat and simmer, stirring, for 5 minutes. Remove pan from heat and whisk in sour cream. Pour sauce over rolls, cover and bake for 1 hour.*

Note: *These rolls are delicious if made using ground lamb instead of the pork. This recipe is a good way to use up leftover cooked rice and spinach or silverbeet leaves can be used instead of cabbage.*

Serves 4

ingredients

2 tablespoons vegetable oil
1 onion, finely grated
2 rashers bacon, chopped
1 green apple, peeled, cored and grated
1 teaspoon caraway seeds
500g/1 lb lean ground pork
125g/4oz brown rice, cooked
1 egg, lightly beaten
freshly ground black pepper
8 large cabbage leaves
60g/2oz butter
1¹/₂ tablespoons paprika
1¹/₂ tablespoons flour
1 tablespoon tomato paste (purée)
¹/₂ cup/125mL/4fl oz red wine
1¹/₂ cups/375mL/12fl oz chicken stock
¹/₂ cup/125g/4oz sour cream

sweet
pork buns

Photograph page 537

Method:

1 *To make dough, place yeast and water in a bowl and whisk with a fork until yeast dissolves. Set aside in a warm draught-free place for 5 minutes or until foamy. Place butter and milk in a saucepan and cook over a medium heat, stirring constantly, until butter melts. Remove pan from heat and set aside until lukewarm. Pour milk mixture into yeast mixture, then stir in sugar, eggs and salt and beat to combine. Stir in flour and beat vigorously until mixture is smooth and satiny. Cover bowl with plastic food wrap and set aside in a warm draught-free place for 40 minutes or until doubled in volume.*

2 *To make filling, heat oil in a frying pan over a medium heat, add pork, garlic and ginger and cook, stirring, for 5 minutes or until meat is brown. Stir in hoisin sauce, oyster sauce, soy sauce, sesame oil and cornflour mixture and bring to the boil. Reduce heat and simmer for 5 minutes or until mixture thickens. Remove pan from heat, add spring onions and set aside to cool.*

3 *Turn dough onto a floured surface and knead for 10 minutes or until dough is smooth and no longer sticky. Roll dough out to 1cm/1/2in thick and using a 5cm/2in cutter, cut out twelve rounds.*

4 *Using your index finger make an indent in centre of half the dough rounds. Place a spoonful of filling in each indent. Brush remaining dough rounds with egg mixture and place over rounds with filling. Pinch edges together firmly and place buns on a greased baking tray, cover and set aside in a warm draught-free place for 30 minutes or until almost doubled in size. Bake for 10 minutes, then reduce temperature to 200°C/400°F/Gas 6 and bake for 5 minutes longer or until buns are golden.*

5 *To make glaze, place sugar and water in a saucepan and cook over a medium heat, stirring constantly, without boiling until sugar dissolves. Bring to boil, then boil rapidly until mixture becomes syrupy. Set aside to cool slightly. Brush warm buns with glaze.*

ingredients

30g/1oz fresh yeast, crumbled or
1 3/4 teaspoons active dry yeast
1/4 cup/60mL/2fl oz lukewarm water
60g/2oz butter
1 cup/250mL/8fl oz milk
1/4 cup/60g/2oz sugar
2 eggs, lightly beaten
1 teaspoon salt
3 3/4 cups/470g/15oz flour, sifted

Pork filling
2 teaspoons peanut (groundnut) oil
250g/8oz lean ground pork
1 clove garlic, crushed
1/2 teaspoon finely grated fresh ginger
1 tablespoon hoisin sauce
1 tablespoon oyster sauce
2 tablespoons soy sauce
1/2 teaspoon sesame oil
3 teaspoons cornflour blended with
1/2 cup/125mL/4fl oz chicken stock
3 spring onions, finely chopped
1 egg, lightly beaten with
1 tablespoon water

Glaze
1/4 cup/60g/2oz sugar
1/3 cup/90mL/3fl oz water

Note: *There are two types of yeast commonly used in baking – fresh and dried. Dried yeast works as well as fresh but takes longer to activate. It is twice as concentrated as fresh yeast, so you will require half as much. You will find that 15g/1/2oz dried yeast has the same rising power as 30g/1oz fresh yeast. Fresh yeast is also known as baker's or compressed yeast.*

Makes 6

marvellous
meat

introduction

introduction

Lean beef, lamb, pork and veal all play an important part in a balanced diet. In recent years there has been some concern about the amount of fat and cholesterol that meat contains. However, more recent studies show that as long as the meat chosen is lean and the portion size is around 125g/4oz then meat plays a valuable part in our diets. This book presents you with a range of recipes suitable for family meals and special occasions, all of which make the most of meat.

Lean beef, veal and Trim Lamb are highly nutritious foods with unique features. Low in fat, yet packed full of high quality protein and essential vitamins and minerals, lean red meat is a valuable contributor to a healthy body.

One of meat's prime nutritional benefits is as a supplier of the mineral iron. Iron is indispensable to carrying oxygen around our bodies, via our bloodstream. If you do not eat enough iron, you may become tired, have poor stamina and even become anaemic.

Lean beef, veal and Trim Lamb are some of the highest iron foods and this so called "haem iron" is the most easily used by our bodies. The haem iron in meat also helps the body maximise the iron in poorer iron ("non haem") foods such as vegetables, nuts, legumes and grains.

An average serve of lean red meat not only boosts your iron status, it easily provides up to half your daily requirements of zinc. Zinc is another mineral essential for humans, being necessary for growth and reproduction, healing and a healthy immune system.

That serving of meat is also brimming with B vitamins. Valuable thiamin, riboflavin, niacin, vitamin B6 and vitamin B12 will all be supplied in significant quantities, helping to release energy from food and maintain a healthy body.

High quality protein, essential for the building and repair of all body cells will also be provided. Meat protein is perfectly matched to your body's needs, as it contains all of the 8 essential amino acids, or protein "building blocks', needed each day.

Lean beef, veal and Trim Lamb are a unique combination of many essential nutrients in the one versatile, low fat package. They make a great tasting and nutritious contribution to any meal.

meat
purhasing guide

When purchasing meat, these tips will ensure that you purchase the best quality.

Allow 125 g/4 oz lean boneless meat per serve.

Lamb and beef should be bright red in colour with a fresh appearance. Pork should be pale-fleshed with a sweet smell, not slimy or bloody. Select lean meat. If there is any fat it should be pale cream in colour.

In hot climates, take an insulated shopping bag with you to ensure meat remains cold until you get it home and refrigerate it.

Meat storage guide

The following tips will ensure that the meat you purchase stays at its best for the longest possible time.

Fresh meat should be kept as dry as possible and should not sit in its own 'drip' during storage. Store meat in the coldest part of the refrigerator. This will be the bottom shelf if your refrigerator does not have a special meat compartment.

The more cutting and preparation meat has had, the shorter the storage time - for example, mince has a shorter storage time than chops or steaks.

When storing meat in the refrigerator, place a stainless steel or plastic rack in a dish deep enough to catch any drip from the meat. Unwrap the meat and place on a rack in stacks of not more than three layers. Cover loosely with aluminium foil or waxed paper.

If your refrigerator has a special meat storage compartment, unwrap the meat, arrange in stacks of not more than three layers and cover meat loosely with aluminium foil or waxed paper.

If meat is to be used within two days of purchase, it can be left in its original wrapping. Store the package in the special meat compartment or the coldest part of the refrigerator.

Meat that has been kept in the refrigerator for two to three days will be more tender than meat cooked on the day of purchase, because the natural enzymes soften the muscle fibres.

Always store raw meat away from cooked meat or other cooked food. If your refrigerator does not have a special meat compartment, store the raw meat at the bottom of the refrigerator and the cooked meat at the top. Storing meat in this way prevents the raw meat from dripping onto the cooked meat and so lessens the likelihood of cross-contamination.

Raw and cooked meats both store well in the freezer, but as with any food to be frozen, it should be in good condition before freezing. To prepare raw meat for freezing, cut into portions required for a single occasion, such as a family meal. It is easier and more economical to take two packs out of the freezer for extra people than to cook too much through over-packing. If the meat is packed when you purchase it, remove it from the wrapping and repackage in freezer bags or suitable freezing containers.

Storage guide

Mince and sausages	2 days
Cubed beef, lamb and pork	3 days
Steaks, chops and cutlets	4 days
Roasting joints (with bone in)	3-5 days
Roasting joints (boned and rolled)	2-3 days
Corned beef and pickled pork	7 days

cooking
techniques

Cooking techniques can be divided into two groups: dry heat and moist heat methods. The moist heat methods are pot roasting, casseroling, braising, stewing and simmering. The dry heat methods are pan-frying, stir-frying, crumb-frying, grilling, barbecuing and oven roasting. The following guide will help you choose the correct cut of meat for the cooking technique you wish to use.

Pot roast

Beef: blade, brisket, chuck, round, fresh silverside, skirt, topside
Lamb: forequarter (shoulder), shank
Veal: shoulder/forequarter

Casserole

Beef: blade, brisket, chuck, round, spareribs, shin, fresh silverside,
skirt, topside
Lamb: best neck, forequarter (shoulder), neck chop, shank, shoulder chop
Veal: shoulder/forequarter chop and steak, neck chop, knuckle
Pork: diced pork, leg steak

Braise

Beef: blade, brisket, chuck, round, spare-ribs, shin, fresh silverside, skirt, topside
Lamb: best neck, forequarter (shoulder), neck chop, shank, shoulder chop
Veal: shoulder/forequarter chop and steak, neck chop, knuckle
Pork: leg steak

Stew

Beef: blade, brisket, chuck, round, spareribs, shin, fresh silverside,
skirt, topside
Lamb: best neck, forequarter/shoulder

and neck chop, shank
Veal: forequarter/shoulder chop and steak, neck chop, knuckle
Pork: diced pork

Simmer

Beef: corned (salted) silverside, corned (salted) brisket
Pork: pickled pork

Pan-fry or Pan-cook

Beef: blade, fillet, round (minute), rump, rib eye, spareribs, sirloin/T-bone
Lamb: best neck chop and cutlet, chump, leg and mid loin chop, loin chop and cutlet
Veal: cutlet, leg steak, loin chop, schnitzel (escalope)
Pork: butterfly (valentine) steak, cutlet, fillet, forequarter (sparerib) chop and steak, leg steak, loin chop and medallion steak, schnitzel (escalope)

Stir-fry

Beef: fillet, round, rump, rib eye, topside, sirloin steak
Lamb: boneless leg, boneless shoulder, boneless mid loin, fillet
Pork: diced pork, schnitzel (escalope)

Crumb-fry

Beef: round (minute), topside steak
Lamb: best neck chop, rib loin cutlet
Veal: leg steak, schnitzel (escalope), loin chop, cutlet
Pork: schnitzel (escalope)

Grill

Beef: fillet, rump, rib eye, spareribs, sirloin/T-bone
Lamb: best neck chop and cutlet, chump,

forequarter, leg and mid loin chop, rib loin chop and cutlet, shoulder chop

Veal: leg steak, loin chop and cutlet

Pork: butterfly (valentine) steak, cutlet, fillet, forequarter (sparerib) chop and steak, leg steak, loin chop and medallion steak, schnitzel (escalope), spareribs

Barbecue

Beef: fillet, rump, rib eye, spareribs, sirloin/T-bone steak

Lamb: chump, forequarter, leg, shoulder and mid loin chop, rib loin chop and cutlet

Veal: leg steak, loin chop and cutlet

Pork: boneless loin, butterfly (valentine) steak, cutlet, fillet, loin, forequarter (sparerib) chops and steak, leg steak, loin medallion steak, spareribs

Oven roast

Beef: fillet, rump, rib roast, spareribs, sirloin, fresh silverside, topside

Lamb: breast, forequarter (shoulder), leg, mid loin, rib loin, rack, crown roast, shank

Veal: leg, loin, rack, shoulder/forequarter

Pork: fillet, loin, leg, boneless loin, schnitzel (escalope), shoulder (hand or spring), spareribs

Keeping it safe

The casual style of barbecuing can sometimes lead to casual handling of food which in turn can lead to unwelcome health problems. Follow these easy rules for safe entertaining.

Preparation

- Do not handle cooked and uncooked meat at the same time, as this encourages the transfer of bacteria from the raw to the cooked meat.
- Wash thoroughly in hot soapy water all utensils and boards that have been used for cutting raw meat, before using them to cut cooked meat.
- Remember to thoroughly wash your hands after preparing raw meat and frequently during all food preparation.
- To thaw frozen food, remove food from wrappings and place on a rack in a shallow dish. Cover loosely with plastic food wrap and place in the refrigerator to thaw. Food should be completely defrosted before cooking, this is particularly important for foods which are intended for barbecuing and for those which only have a short cooking time.
- Thawing food at room temperature, especially during the warmer months can create the ideal conditions for bacteria to multiply. If the food is then not cooked long enough or a high enough internal temperature is not reached to kill the bacteria, there is the potential for food poisoning to occur.
- Cook food as soon as possible after thawing.

healthy meat

pork and orange kebabs

Eating the right foods is essential

to your total health. It influences your vitality, your weight and your ability to fight off infections and serious illnesses. This chapter brings together which can help you and your family towards a better way of eating.

pork
and orange kebabs

Photograph page 545

Method:

1 To make marinade, place orange juice, lemon juice, garlic, tomato purée, onion, oil and honey in a bowl and mix to combine.
2 Add pork, toss to coat and set aside to marinate for 1 hour.
3 Preheat barbecue to a medium heat.
4 Thread pork, orange and red pepper (capsicum) cubes, alternately, onto lightly oiled bamboo skewers and cook on lightly oiled barbecue grill, basting frequently with marinade for 5-6 minutes each side or until pork is cooked.

Serves 4

ingredients

**500g/1 lb pork fillet, cut into
2¹/₂cm/1in cubes
2 oranges, rind and pith removed, cut
into 2¹/₂cm/1in cubes
1 red pepper (capsicum), cut into
2¹/₂cm/1in cubes**

Orange marinade
**¹/₄ cup/60mL/2fl oz orange juice
2 tablespoons lemon juice
2 cloves garlic, crushed
3 tablespoons tomato purée
1 onion, grated
1 tablespoon olive oil
2 tablespoons honey**

OSSO
bucco

ingredients

**1 tablespoon olive oil
2 red peppers (capicum), cut into strips
2 onions, chopped
4 thick slices shin veal on the bone
¹/₂ cup/60g/2oz flour
30g/1oz butter
¹/₂ cup/125mL/4fl oz dry white wine
¹/₂ cup/125mL/4fl oz chicken stock
440g/14oz canned tomatoes,
undrained and mashed
freshly ground black pepper
1 tablespoon chopped fresh parsley**

Method:

1 Heat oil in a large frying pan and cook red peppers (capsicum) and onions over a medium heat for 10 minutes or until onions are transparent. Using a slotted spoon, remove onion mixture and set aside. Toss veal in flour and shake off excess. Add butter to frying pan and cook until butter foams. Add veal and cook for 4-5 minutes each side or until browned.
2 Stir in wine and stock and bring to the boil, stirring to lift sediment from base of pan. Boil until liquid is reduced by half. Add tomatoes and return onion mixture to pan, cover and simmer for 1 hour or until meat falls away from the bone. Season to taste with black pepper and sprinkle with parsley.

Serves 4

curried
lamb soup

Method:

1 Place split peas in a bowl, cover with water and set aside to soak for 10 minutes.

2 Heat oil in a large saucepan and cook lamb shanks for 5-6 minutes or until browned on all sides. Add garlic, onion and curry powder and cook, stirring, for 5 minutes longer. Drain peas and add peas and boiling water to pan. Bring soup to the boil, skimming off any scum from the surface, then reduce heat and simmer for 1 hour.

3 Remove shanks from soup and set aside to cool. Remove meat from bones and cut into even-sized pieces. Remove peas from soup and place in a food processor or blender and process until smooth. Return pea purée and meat to pan, then stir in mint and carrots and cook for 5 minutes. Add celery, coconut milk, lemon juice and black pepper to taste and cook over a medium heat without boiling for 3-5 minutes.

Serves 4

ingredients

185g/6oz yellow split peas, washed
2 tablespoons vegetable oil
375g/12oz lamb shanks, cut in half
3 cloves garlic, crushed
1 onion, finely chopped
2 tablespoons curry powder
5 cups/1¼ litres/2pt boiling water
2 tablespoons chopped fresh mint
2 carrots, diced
2 stalks celery, sliced
½ cup/125mL/4fl oz coconut milk
1 tablespoon lemon juice
freshly ground black pepper

basil
meatball soup
Photograph page 549

ingredients

1 tablespoon olive oil
2 carrots, cut into thin strips
4 cups/1 litre/1³/₄pt beef stock
125g/4oz vermicelli
freshly ground black pepper

Basil meatballs
250g/8oz lean ground beef
1 egg, lightly beaten
3 tablespoons dried breadcrumbs
2 tablespoons grated Parmesan cheese
1 tablespoon finely chopped fresh basil
or 1 teaspoon dried basil
1 tablespoon tomato sauce
3 cloves garlic, crushed
1 onion, finely chopped

Method:

1 To make meatballs, place ground beef, egg, breadcrumbs, Parmesan cheese, basil, tomato sauce, garlic and onion in a bowl and mix to combine. Using wet hands, roll mixture into small balls. Place meatballs on a plate lined with plastic food wrap and refrigerate for 30 minutes.

2 Heat oil in a large frying pan and cook meatballs for 10 minutes or until cooked through and browned on all sides. Add carrots and cook for 3 minutes longer.

3 Place stock in a large saucepan and bring to the boil. Add vermicelli and cook for 4-5 minutes or until vermicelli is tender. Add carrots and meatballs, season to taste with black pepper and cook for 4-5 minutes longer.

Note: The meatballs for this soup are also delicious made with thyme, rosemary or parsley. Or you might like to try a mixture of herbs for something different.

Serves 4

pea
and ham soup
Photograph page 549

ingredients

15g/¹/₂oz butter
1 tablespoon olive oil
2 cloves garlic, crushed
1 onion, finely chopped
125g/4oz button mushrooms, sliced
4 cups/1 litre/1³/₄pt chicken stock
¹/₂ teaspoon paprika
3 stalks celery, chopped
10 large lettuce leaves, shredded
250g/8oz fresh or frozen peas
125g/4oz diced ham
¹/₄ red pepper (capsicum), finely chopped
2 tablespoons chopped fresh parsley
freshly ground black pepper

Method:

1 Heat butter and oil in a large saucepan and cook garlic, onion and mushrooms for 3 minutes. Stir in stock and paprika and bring to the boil, then reduce heat and simmer for 10 minutes.

2 Add celery, lettuce and peas and cook for 5 minutes longer or until peas are tender. Stir in ham, red pepper (capsicum), parsley and black pepper to taste and cook for 3-4 minutes.

Serves 4

beef
in beer

Method:

1 Heat oil in a large nonstick frying pan and cook beef over a high heat until browned on all sides. Transfer beef to a large casserole dish.

2 Reduce heat to medium and cook onions and carrots for 4-5 minutes or until onions start to soften. Stir in flour and cook for 1 minute, stirring continuously, then add beer and $^1/_2$ cup/125 mL/4 fl oz stock and cook for 3-4 minutes, stirring to lift any sediment from base of pan. Stir in remaining stock, garlic, ginger, honey, orange rind and black pepper to taste.

3 Pour stock mixture over meat, cover and cook for $1^3/_4$-2 hours or until meat is tender.

Serves 4

ingredients

2 tablespoons vegetable oil
750g/1$^1/_2$lb lean topside beef, cut into 2$^1/_2$cm/1in cubes
2 onions, chopped
2 carrots, cut into 1cm/$^1/_2$in slices
2 tablespoons flour
$^1/_2$ cup/125mL/4fl oz beer
2 cups/500 mL/16 fl oz beef stock
2 cloves garlic, crushed
1 tablespoon grated fresh ginger
2 tablespoons honey
1 tablespoon finely grated orange rind
freshly ground black pepper

Oven temperature 210°C/420°F/Gas 7

steak
and kidney pie

Method:

1 Place steak, kidneys and flour in a plastic food bag and shake to coat meat with flour. Shake off excess flour and set aside. Heat oil in a large frying pan and cook meat over a high heat, stirring, until brown on all sides. Reduce heat to medium, add garlic and onions and cook for 3 minutes longer. Stir in mustard, parsley, Worcestershire sauce, stock and tomato paste (purée), bring to simmering, cover and simmer, stirring occasionally, for 2½ hours or until meat is tender. Remove pan from heat and set aside to cool completely.

2 Place cooled filling in a 4 cup/1 litre/1¾pt capacity pie dish. On a lightly floured surface, roll out pastry to 5cm/2in larger than pie dish. Cut off a 1cm/½in strip from pastry edge. Brush rim of dish with water and press pastry strip onto rim. Brush pastry strip with water. Lift pastry top over filling and press gently to seal edges. Trim and knock back edges to make a decorative edge. Brush with milk and bake for 30 minutes or until pastry is golden and crisp.

Serves 6

ingredients

1 kg/2 lb lean topside steak, cut into
2½cm/1in cubes
6 lamb's kidneys or 1 ox kidney,
cored and roughly chopped
4 tablespoons flour
1 tablespoon vegetable oil
2 cloves garlic, crushed
2 onions, chopped
½ teaspoon dry mustard
2 tablespoons chopped fresh parsley
2 tablespoons Worcestershire sauce
1½ cups/375mL/12fl oz beef stock
2 teaspoons tomato paste (purée)
375g/12oz prepared puff pastry
2 tablespoons milk

beef
fillet wrapped in pastry

Photograph page 553

Method:

1 Melt half the butter in a large frying pan. When sizzling, add fillet and cook over a medium heat for 10 minutes, turning to brown and seal all sides. Remove meat from pan and set aside to cool completely.

2 Melt remaining butter in frying pan and cook onion for 5 minutes or until soft. Add mushrooms and cook, stirring, for 15 minutes or until mushrooms give up all their juices and these have evaporated. Season to taste with black pepper and nutmeg, stir in parsley and set aside to cool completely.

3 Roll out pastry to a length 10cm/4in longer than meat and wide enough to wrap around fillet. Spread half the mushroom mixture down centre of pastry and place fillet on top. Spread remaining mushroom mixture on top of fillet. Cut out corners of pastry. Brush pastry edges with egg. Wrap pastry around fillet like a parcel, tucking in ends. Place pastry-wrapped fillet seam side down on a lightly greased baking sheet and freeze for 10 minutes.

4 Roll out remaining pastry to 10x30cm/4x12 in length and cut into strips 1cm/¹/₂in wide. Remove fillet from freezer and brush pastry all over with egg. Arrange 5 pastry strips diagonally over pastry parcel, then arrange remaining strips diagonally in opposite direction. Brush top of strips only with egg and bake for 30 minutes for medium-rare beef. Place on a warmed serving platter and set aside to rest in a warm place for 10 minutes.

5 To make sauce, place wine in a small saucepan and cook over a medium heat until reduced by half. Add thyme, parsley and black pepper to taste. Remove pan from heat and quickly whisk in one piece of butter at a time, ensuring that each piece is completely whisked in and melted before adding the next. Whisk in cornflour mixture and cook over a medium heat, stirring until sauce thickens. Serve with sliced beef.

Serves 6

ingredients

60g/2oz butter
1 kg/2 lb fillet steak, in one piece,
trimmed of all visible fat
1 onion, chopped
375g/12oz button mushrooms,
finely chopped
freshly ground black pepper
pinch ground nutmeg
1 tablespoon chopped fresh parsley
500g/1 lb prepared puff pastry
1 egg, lightly beaten

Red wine sauce
1 cup/250mL/8fl oz red wine
1 teaspoon finely chopped fresh thyme or
¹/₄ teaspoon dried thyme
1 teaspoon finely chopped fresh parsley
100g/3¹/₂oz butter,
cut into small pieces
2 teaspoons cornflour blended with
1 tablespoon water

lamb
with satay sauce

Method:

1 Preheat barbecue to a medium heat.

2 Place lamb, parsley, oregano, cumin, tomato paste (purée), onions, bread crumbs and egg whites in a large bowl and mix to combine. Divide mixture into eight portions and shape each portion into a sausage shape. Thread each sausage onto a lightly oiled bamboo skewer.

3 Cook lamb kebabs on lightly oiled barbecue grill or plate (griddle), turning frequently, for 10 minutes or until cooked through.

4 To make sauce, heat oil in a saucepan and cook garlic and onion over a medium heat for 1 minute. Stir in peanut butter, tomato paste (purée), chutney, sherry, lemon juice, coconut milk, coriander and chilli paste (sambal oelek) and cook, stirring constantly, over a low heat for 10 minutes or until sauce thickens slightly. Serve with kebabs.

Makes 8 kebabs

ingredients

750g/1½ lb lean ground lamb
3 tablespoons chopped fresh parsley
1 teaspoon dried oregano
2 teaspoons ground cumin
2 tablespoons tomato paste (purée)
2 onions, grated
¾ cup/90g/3oz dried bread crumbs
2 egg whites, lightly beaten

Satay sauce
1 tablespoon peanut (groundnut) oil
2 cloves garlic, crushed
1 onion, finely chopped
4 tablespoons crunchy peanut butter
1 teaspoon tomato paste (purée)
2 tablespoons sweet fruit chutney
2 tablespoons dry sherry
1 tablespoon lemon juice
4 tablespoons coconut milk
2 teaspoons ground coriander
1 teaspoon chilli paste (sambal oelek)

veal
and apricot skewers

Method:

1 To make marinade, place yogurt, onion, garlic, chilli paste (sambal oelek), lime juice, cumin and coriander in a food processor or blender and process to combine. Transfer to large bowl, add veal and apricots and toss to combine. Cover and marinate for 2 hours.

2 Preheat barbecue to a medium heat. Drain veal and apricots and reserve marinade. Thread veal and apricots, alternately, onto lightly oiled bamboo skewers and cook on lightly oiled barbecue grill, turning and basting with reserved marinade, for 10 minutes or until cooked.

Serves 4

ingredients

375g/12oz topside veal, cut into
2 cm/³/₄in cubes
125 g/4 oz dried apricots

<u>Chilli yogurt marinade</u>
1¹/₂ cups/300g/9¹/₂oz natural yogurt
1 onion, grated
2 cloves garlic, crushed
2 teaspoons chilli paste (sambal oelek)
1 tablespoon lime juice
1 teaspoon ground cumin
1 tablespoon chopped fresh coriander

sausage
and pancetta risotto

Method:

1 Heat oil in a large frying pan, add pancetta or bacon, carrot and onion and fry for 10 minutes, stirring occasionally. Stir in tomatoes, lower heat and simmer for 15 minutes. Stir in stock and beans, remove pan from heat and set aside.

2 In a saucepan, melt butter and fry sausages with sage, rosemary and garlic for 7 minutes, stirring frequently until sausage is crumbly.

3 Add rice and wine. Stir mixture until liquid has evaporated, then add 250ml/8fl oz of bean/stock mixture. Cook until liquid has evaporated.

4 Continue adding bean/stock mixture in this fashion until all liquid has been absorbed and rice is tender, about 20 minutes. Stir in chopped pepper (capsicum) and Parmesan.

Serves 4

ingredients

2 tablespoons olive oil
90g/3oz pancetta or rindless back bacon, chopped
1 small carrot, sliced
1 onion, thinly sliced
2 x 410g/13oz cans chopped tomatoes
600ml/1pt chicken stock
185g/6oz drained canned kidney beans
30g/1oz butter
4 Italian sausages, casings removed
¹/₂ teaspoon dried sage
¹/₂ teaspoon dried rosemary
2 cloves garlic, crushed
185g/6oz Arborio rice
125ml/4fl oz red wine
¹/₂ red or yellow pepper (capsicum), roughly chopped
90g/3oz grated Parmesan cheese

apple
pork casserole

Method:

1 Heat butter in a large frying pan and cook onions and pork over a medium heat for 5 minutes. Add apples, herbs, stock and black pepper to taste, bring to the boil, then reduce heat and simmer for 1 hour or until pork is tender. Using a slotted spoon remove pork and set aside.

2 Push liquid and solids through a sieve and return to pan with pork.

3 To make sauce, melt butter in a frying pan and cook apple over a medium heat for 2 minutes. Stir in chives and tomatoes and bring to the boil, reduce heat and simmer for 5 minutes. Pour into pan with pork and cook over a medium heat for 5 minutes longer. Just prior to serving, sprinkle with cracked black peppercorns.

Serves 4

ingredients

30g/1oz butter
2 onions, chopped
500g/1 lb lean diced pork
3 large apples, peeled, cored and chopped
1 tablespoon dried mixed herbs
3 cups/750mL/1¼pt chicken stock
freshly ground black pepper

Apple sauce
30g/1oz butter
2 apples, peeled, cored and chopped
2 tablespoons snipped fresh chives
440g/14oz canned tomatoes, undrained and mashed
1 teaspoon cracked black peppercorns

moroccan
stew

Method:

1 Heat oil in a heavy-based saucepan and cook meat over a high heat for 4-5 minutes or until browned on all sides. Stir in stock and cinnamon, bring to the boil, then reduce heat and simmer for 10 minutes, stirring to lift any sediment from base of pan.

2 Add honey, turmeric, nutmeg, raisins and apricots to pan, cover and simmer for 30 minutes.

3 Stir in onions, orange juice and almonds and simmer, uncovered, for 30 minutes longer or until meat is tender. Season to taste with black pepper.

Serves 4

ingredients

1 tablespoon vegetable oil
500g/1 lb chuck steak, cut into 2¹/₂cm/1in cubes
2 cups/500mL/16fl oz beef stock
2 teaspoons ground cinnamon
2 tablespoons honey
¹/₂ teaspoon ground turmeric
¹/₂ teaspoon ground nutmeg
60g/2oz raisins
60g/2oz dried apricots, chopped
8 baby onions
2 tablespoons orange juice
60g/2oz blanched almonds
freshly ground black pepper

shepherd's
pie

Method:

1 Heat oil in a frying pan over a medium heat, add onion and cook, stirring, for 2-3 minutes or until onion is tender. Stir in meat. Blend flour with a little of the stock or water to form a smooth paste. Stir flour mixture, remaining stock or water and tomatoes into pan and, stirring constantly, bring to the boil. Add peas, tomato paste (purée) and Worcestershire sauce and simmer, stirring frequently, for 5 minutes or until mixture thickens. Spoon mixture into a deep ovenproof dish or individual ramekins.

2 To make topping, place potatoes in saucepan, cover with cold water and bring to the boil. Reduce heat, cover and simmer for 15-20 minutes or until potatoes are tender. Drain well, add milk or cream and black pepper to taste and mash. Top meat mixture with potatoes, sprinkle with cheese and breadcrumbs and bake for 15-20 minutes or until top is golden.

Serves 4

ingredients

1 tablespoon olive oil
1 onion, chopped
500g/1 lb chopped cooked beef, lamb, pork or chicken
1 tablespoon flour
½ cup/125mL/4fl oz beef stock or water
440g/14oz canned tomatoes, undrained and mashed
60g/2oz frozen peas
2 tablespoons tomato paste (purée)
1 tablespoon Worcestershire sauce

Cheesy potato topping
3 potatoes, chopped
¼ cup/60mL/2fl oz milk or cream (heavy)
freshly ground black pepper
60g/2oz grated tasty cheese (mature cheddar)
¼ cup/30g/1oz dried breadcrumbs

fruity
pork roulade

Method:

1 To make filling, place pine nuts, prunes, apricots, ginger, sage, chutney, bacon, brandy and black pepper to taste in a food processor and process until finely chopped.

2 Open out steaks and pound to about 5mm/¼in thick. Spread filling over steaks and roll up tightly. Secure each roll with string.

3 Place stock, celery and onions in a large saucepan and bring to the boil. Add pork rolls, cover and simmer for 20 minutes or until pork is cooked. Transfer pork rolls to a plate, set aside to cool, then cover and refrigerate for 2-3 hours. To serve, cut each roll into slices.

Serves 6

ingredients

4 lean butterfly pork steaks
2 cups/500mL/16fl oz beef stock
4 stalks celery, chopped
2 onions, chopped

Fruit filling
60g/2oz pine nuts
100g/3½oz pitted prunes
60g/2oz dried apricots
1 tablespoon grated fresh ginger
1 teaspoon chopped fresh sage
3 tablespoons fruit chutney
4 rashers bacon, chopped
3 tablespoons brandy
freshly ground black pepper

carpaccio
with mustard mayonnaise

Method:

1 Trim meat of all visible fat and cut into wafer-thin slices. Arrange beef slices, lettuce leaves and watercress attractively on four serving plates. Sprinkle with Parmesan cheese.

2 To make mayonnaise, place egg, lemon juice, garlic and mustard in a food processor or blender and process to combine. With machine running, slowly add oil and continue processing until mayonnaise thickens. Season to taste with black pepper. Spoon a little mayonnaise over salad and serve immediately.

Note: To achieve very thin slices of beef, wrap the fillet in plastic food wrap and place in the freezer for 15 minutes or until firm, then slice using a very sharp knife.

Serves 4

ingredients

500g/1 lb eye fillet beef, in one piece
1 lettuce, leaves separated and washed
1 bunch/250g/8oz watercress
90g/3oz Parmesan cheese, grated

Mustard mayonnaise
1 egg
1 tablespoon lemon juice
2 cloves garlic, crushed
2 teaspoons Dijon mustard
½ cup/125mL/4fl oz olive oil
freshly ground black pepper

lamb
and spinach strudel

Method:

1 Heat 2 tablespoons oil in a large frying pan and cook onion and lamb over a high heat for 4-5 minutes or until lamb is browned. Add mushrooms and cook for 2 minutes longer. Transfer lamb mixture to a large bowl and stir in mustard, spinach, red pepper (capsicum), parsley and bread crumbs.

2 Fold filo sheets in half, brush each sheet with remaining oil and layer sheets one on top of the other. Spoon filling along the short side of pastry, leaving a 3cm/1 1/4in border of pastry. Shape filling into a sausage, tuck in long sides of pastry and roll up.

3 Place strudel, seam side down, on a lightly greased baking tray, brush with oil and sprinkle with sesame seeds. Bake for 40 minutes or until pastry is golden.

Serves 4

ingredients

3 tablespoons vegetable oil
1 onion, finely chopped
375g/12oz lean boneless lamb, finely chopped
185g/6oz mushrooms, finely chopped
2 tablespoons German mustard
200g/6 1/2oz frozen spinach, excess liquid squeezed out, and chopped
1 red pepper (capsicum), finely chopped
2 tablespoons chopped fresh parsley
1/2 cup/30g/1oz bread crumbs, made from stale bread
6 sheets filo pastry
1 tablespoon sesame seeds

oriental
spareribs

Method:

1 To make marinade, place hoisin sauce, tomato sauce, soy sauce, honey, garlic, ginger, chilli sauce and five spice powder in a bowl and mix to combine. Add ribs and toss to coat. Cover and refrigerate for 8 hours or overnight.

2 Remove ribs from marinade and reserve marinade. Place ribs in a single layer on a rack set over a baking dish. Bake, basting occasionally with reserved marinade, for 40 minutes or until ribs are tender.

Serves 8

ingredients

I kg/2 lb pork spareribs, trimmed of all visible fat and cut in 15cm/6in lengths

Oriental marinade
¹/₄ cup/60mL/2 fl oz hoisin sauce
¹/₄ cup/60 mL/2 fl oz tomato sauce
2 tablespoons soy sauce
¹/₄ cup/90g/3oz honey
2 cloves garlic, crushed
2 teaspoons grated fresh ginger
I teaspoon chilli sauce
I teaspoon Chinese five spice powder

boiled beef dinner

country kitchen

In recipes from a Country Kitchen,

the cook will discover just how easy it is to make flaky pies and pastries, nourishing soups and slowly cooked meals to warm the heart and feed hungry families.

pork
with sauerkraut

Method:

1 Melt butter in a large saucepan and cook pork slices over a medium heat for 3-4 minutes each side, or until meat just changes colour. Remove from pan and set aside.

2 Add onions and apples to pan and cook for 4-5 minutes or until onions soften. Stir in paprika and caraway seeds and cook over a medium heat for 1 minute. Season to taste with black pepper.

3 Combine stock, wine and tomato paste. Pour into pan and cook over a medium heat, stirring constantly to lift sediment from base of pan. Bring to the boil, then reduce heat and simmer for 10 minutes.

4 Return meat to pan, stir in sauerkraut and cook for 2-3 minutes. Remove pan from heat, stir in sour cream and serve immediately.

Serves 6

ingredients

30g/1oz butter
750g/1 1/2lb pork fillets, sliced
2 onions, sliced
2 green apples, cored, peeled and sliced
2 teaspoons ground paprika
1 teaspoon caraway seeds
freshly ground black pepper
3/4 cup/185mL chicken stock
3 tablespoons dry white wine
2 tablespoons tomato paste
440g/14oz canned or bottled sauerkraut, drained
1/2 cup/125g sour cream

boiled
beef dinner

Photograph page 565

Method:

1 Place meat in a large heavy-based saucepan. Add brown sugar, vinegar, mint, onion, peppercorns and enough water to cover meat. Bring to the boil, then reduce heat and simmer for 1 1/4-1 1/2 hours.

2 Add carrots, onions and parsnips to pan and cook over a low heat for 40 minutes longer or until vegetables are tender.

3 To make glaze, place redcurrant jelly, orange juice and Grand Marnier in a small saucepan and cook over a low heat, stirring occasionally, until well blended. Transfer meat to a serving plate and brush with redcurrant mixture. Slice meat and serve with vegetables and any remaining redcurrant mixture.

Cook's tip: To make horseradish cream, whip 1/2 cup/125mL cream until soft peaks form then fold through 3 tablespoons horseradish relish.

Note: Simple and satisfying, this Boiled Beef Dinner is served with creamy mashed potatoes and horseradish cream. There are sure to be requests for second helpings.

Serves 6

ingredients

1 1/2kg/3lb corned beef silverside
2 tablespoons brown sugar
1 tablespoon cider vinegar
2 sprigs fresh mint
1 onion, peeled and studded with 4 whole cloves
6 peppercorns
6 small carrots, peeled
6 small onions, peeled
3 parsnips, peeled and halved

Redcurrant glaze
1/2 cup/155g redcurrant jelly
2 tablespoons orange juice
1 tablespoon Grand Marnier Liqueur

potato
bacon chowder

Method:

1. Place bacon in a large, heavy-based saucepan and cook over a medium heat for 5 minutes or until golden and crisp. Remove from pan and drain on absorbent kitchen paper.

2. Melt butter in pan and cook onions, celery and thyme over a low heat for 4-5 minutes or until onion is soft.

3. Return bacon to pan, then stir in flour and cook for 1 minute. Remove pan from heat and gradually blend in stock. Bring to the boil, then reduce heat. Add potatoes and cook for 10 minutes or until potatoes are tender.

4. Remove pan from heat and stir in sour cream and parsley. Return to heat and cook without boiling, stirring constantly, for 1-2 minutes. Ladle soup into bowls, sprinkle with chives and serve immediately.

Serves 6

ingredients

250g/8oz bacon, chopped
30g/1oz butter
2 large onions, chopped
4 stalks celery, chopped
2 teaspoons dried thyme
2 tablespoons plain flour
6 cups/1 ½ litres chicken stock
2 large potatoes, peeled and cubed
300g/10oz sour cream
3 tablespoons chopped fresh parsley
2 tablespoons snipped fresh chives

old
english pork pie

Method:

1 To make pastry, place flour and salt in a large mixing bowl and make a well in the centre.

2 Place shortening and water in a saucepan and cook over a medium heat until lard melts and mixture boils. Pour boiling liquid into flour and mix to form a firm dough. Turn pastry onto a floured surface and knead lightly until smooth. Cover and set aside to stand for 10 minutes.

3 Lightly knead two-thirds of pastry. Roll out to line base and sides of a greased deep 20cm /8in springform pan and bake for 15 minutes. Remove from oven and set aside to cool.

4 To make filling, combine pork, sage and black pepper to taste. Pack mixture firmly into pastry case and brush edges with a little of the egg yolk mixture.

5 Knead remaining pastry, then roll out to a circle large enough to cover pie. Place pastry over filling, trim pastry and press top to pastry case. Cut a 2¹/₂cm/1in circle from centre of pastry. Brush pastry with remaining egg yolk mixture and bake for 30 minutes. Reduce temperature to 160°C/325°F/Gas 3 and bake for 1¹/₂ hours. Using a spoon, remove any juices that appear in the hole during cooking. Remove from oven and set aside to cool in pan for 2 hours. Place chicken consomme in a saucepan and cook over a low heat until melted. Set aside to cool slightly, then gradually pour into pie through hole in the top. Allow to cool. Refrigerate pie overnight.

Note: Probably the most famous English pie, the pork pie dates back to the fourteenth century when it included raisins and currants. This pie is sure to be popular and is delicious as a picnic food.

Serves 8

ingredients

Pastry
3 cups/375g plain flour, sifted
1 teaspoon salt
125g/4oz shortening
1 cup/250mL water
1 egg yolk, lightly beaten with
1 tablespoon water

Filling
1¹/₂ kg/3lb lean boneless pork,
cut into 5mm/2in cubes
¹/₂ teaspoon ground sage
freshly ground black pepper
2 cups/500mL chicken consomme

pea
and salami soup

Method:

1 Place split peas and water in a large, heavy-based saucepan and set aside to stand overnight.

2 Add bacon bones to pan with peas. Bring to the boil, then reduce heat and simmer for 2 hours or until soup thickens.

3 Stir in onion, celery leaves and celery and cook over a low heat for 20 minutes longer.

4 Remove bacon bones from soup and discard. Add salami and cook until heated through. Season to taste with black pepper.

5 Ladle soup into serving bowls.

Note: Variations of this soup have been around since the Middle Ages. This one with salami is perfect for a fireside supper.

Serves 6

ingredients

3 cups/750g dried split peas, rinsed
16 cups/4 litres water
500g/1lb bacon bones
4 onions, finely chopped
4 tablespoons chopped celery leaves
4 stalks celery, chopped
250g/8oz salami, cut into 1cm/½ in cubes
freshly ground black pepper

beef
and mushroom pie

Photograph page 571

ingredients

Puff pastry
90g/3oz butter, softened
90g/3oz shortening, softened
2 cups/250g plain flour
¹/₂ cup/125mL cold water

Beef and mushroom filling
I kg/2lb lean beef, cut into 2¹/₂cm/Iin cubes
¹/₂ cup/60g seasoned flour
60g/3oz butter
3 tablespoons olive oil
2 onions, chopped
2 cloves garlic, crushed
250g/8oz button mushrooms, sliced
¹/₂ cup/125mL red wine
¹/₂ cup/125mL beef stock
I bay leaf
2 tablespoons finely chopped fresh parsley
I tablespoon Worcestershire sauce
freshly ground black pepper
I tablespoon cornflour blended with
2 tablespoons water
I egg, lightly beaten

Method:

1 To make filling, toss meat in flour to coat. Shake off excess flour. Melt butter and oil in a large heavy-based saucepan and cook meat in batches for 3-4 minutes or until browned on all sides. Remove meat from pan and set aside.

2 Add onions and garlic to pan and cook over a medium heat for 3-4 minutes or until onion softens. Stir in mushrooms and cook for 2 minutes longer. Combine wine and stock, pour into pan and cook for 4-5 minutes, stirring constantly to lift sediment from base of pan. Bring to the boil, then reduce heat. Return meat to pan with bay leaf, parsley, Worcestershire sauce and black pepper to taste. Cover and simmer for 1¹/₂ hours or until meat is tender. Stir in cornflour mixture and cook, stirring, until mixture thickens. Remove pan from heat and set aside to cool.

3 To make pastry, place butter and shortening in a bowl and mix until well combined. Cover and refrigerate until firm. Place flour in a large mixing bowl. Cut one-quarter of butter mixture into small pieces and rub into flour using fingertips until mixture resembles coarse bread crumbs. Mix in enough water to form a firm dough.

4 Turn pastry onto a floured surface and knead lightly. Roll pastry out to a 15x25cm/6x10in rectangle. Cut another one-quarter of butter mixture into small pieces and place over top two-thirds of pastry. Fold the bottom third of pastry up and top third of pastry down to give three even layers. Half turn pastry to have open end facing you and roll out to a rectangle as before. Repeat folding and rolling twice. Cover pastry and refrigerate for 1 hour.

5 Place cooled filling in a 4 cup/1 litre oval pie dish. On a lightly floured surface, roll out pastry 4cm/1¹/₂in larger than pie dish. Cut off a 1cm/¹/₂in strip from pastry edge. Brush rim of dish with water and press pastry strip onto rim. Brush pastry strip with water. Lift pastry top over filling and press gently to seal edges. Trim and knock back edges to make a decorative edge. Brush with egg and bake for 30 minutes or until pastry is golden and crisp.

Note: *Homemade puff pastry takes a little time to make but the result is well worth it.*

Serves 4

cornish
pasties

Method:

1 To make pastry, place butter and shortening in a bowl and mix well to combine. Refrigerate until firm. Place flour in a large mixing bowl. Chop butter mixture into small pieces and rub in flour using fingertips until mixture resembles coarse bread crumbs. Mix in enough water to form a soft dough. Turn pastry onto a floured surface and knead lightly. Cover and refrigerate for 30 minutes.

2 To make filling, place meat, onion, potato, turnip, parsley, Worcestershire sauce and black pepper to taste in a bowl and mix well to combine.

3 Roll out pastry on a lightly floured surface and using an upturned saucer as a guide cut out six 15cm rounds. Divide filling between pastry rounds. Brush edges with water and fold the pastry rounds in half upwards to enclose filling.

4 Press edges together well to seal, then flute between finger and thumb. Place pasties on a well greased oven tray. Brush with egg and bake for 15 minutes. Reduce temperature to 160°C/330°F/Gas 3 and bake for 20 minutes or until golden.

Note: Originally the portable lunch of the Cornish working man, these pasties are great eaten hot, warm or cold and are ideal for a picnic or lunch box.

Makes 6

ingredients

Pastry
60g/2oz butter, softened
60g/2oz shortening, softened
2 cups/250g plain flour, sifted
4 tablespoons cold water
I egg, lightly beaten

Filling
250g/8oz lean ground beef
I small onion, grated
I potato, peeled and grated
½ small turnip, peeled and grated
2 tablespoons finely chopped fresh parsley
I tablespoon Worcestershire sauce
freshly ground black pepper

lamb roast
with vegetables

Method:

1 Melt 30g/1oz butter in a large heavy-based saucepan and cook meat on all sides until well browned.

2 Combine tomatoes, red wine, tomato paste, Worcestershire sauce, herbs, sugar and black pepper to taste. Pour over meat, bring to the boil, then reduce heat, cover, and simmer for 1 1/2 hours or until meat is tender.

3 About 30 minutes before meat finishes cooking, heat oil and remaining butter in a large heavy-based frypan. Add carrots, turnips, onions and potatoes and cook until vegetables are lightly browned. Reduce heat to low and cook gently for 15-20 minutes or until vegetables are tender.

4 Remove meat from pan, place on a serving platter and set aside to keep warm. Bring sauce that remains in pan to the boil and cook for 10 minutes or until sauce reduces and thickens slightly. Serve sauce with meat and vegetables.

Cook's tip: A nut of veal, a whole chicken or a piece of topside beef are also delicious cooked in this way.

Note: Pot roasting dates back to prehistoric times when clay pots were filled with game, whole cuts of meat or poultry and vegetables then hung over a fire to simmer. Lean meats that need long slow cooking, are ideal for pot roasting.

Serves 6

ingredients

90g/3oz butter
1.5-2kg/3-4lb leg of lamb
440g/14oz canned tomatoes, mashed and undrained
1/2 cup/125mL red wine
2 tablespoons tomato paste
1 tablespoon Worcestershire sauce
1/4 teaspoon mixed dried herbs
1 teaspoon sugar
freshly ground black pepper
olive oil
3 carrots, peeled and halved lengthwise
3 turnips, peeled and halved lengthwise
6 small onions, peeled
3 large potatoes, peeled and halved

lamb
and vegetable hotpot

Method:

1 *Toss meat in flour. Heat butter and 1 tablespoon oil in a large heavy-based saucepan and cook meat in batches until brown on all sides. Remove from pan and set aside.*

2 *Heat remaining oil in pan and cook onions and potatoes until brown on all sides. Remove from pan and set aside. Add garlic, celery, red pepper (capsicum) and bacon and cook for 4-5 minutes. Return meat, onions and potatoes to pan. Mix in carrot, stock, wine, tomato paste and rosemary, bring to the boil, then reduce heat and simmer, covered, for 1 hour or until meat is tender. Stir in beans and cornflour mixture, season to taste with black pepper and cook for 10 minutes longer.*

Serves 6

ingredients

750g/1¹/₂lb leg lamb, cut in 2¹/₂cm/1in cubes
2 tablespoons seasoned flour
15g/1¹/₂oz butter
2 tablespoons oil
6 baby onions, peeled and bases left intact
6 baby new potatoes, scrubbed
2 cloves garlic, crushed
3 stalks celery, sliced
1 red pepper (capsicum), sliced
2 rashers bacon, chopped
1 carrot, sliced
1¹/₂ cups/375mL beef stock
¹/₂ cup/125mL red wine
1 tablespoon tomato paste
2 tablespoons finely chopped fresh rosemary
250g/8oz green beans, trimmed and cut into 2¹/₂cm/1in lengths
freshly ground black pepper
1 tablespoon cornflour blended with
2 tablespoons water

individual
meat pies

Method:

1 To make filling, heat a nonstick frypan and cook meat over a medium heat, stirring constantly, for 6-8 minutes or until meat browns. Drain pan of any juices and add stock. Season to taste with black pepper.

2 Bring mixture to the boil, then reduce heat, cover and simmer, stirring occasionally, for 20 minutes. Stir in cornflour mixture, Worcestershire and soy sauces and cook, stirring constantly, until mixture boils and thickens. Set aside to cool.

3 Line base and sides of eight greased small metal pie dishes with shortcrust

Note: An individual homemade pie served with mashed potatoes and peas was once the traditional working man's lunch and is still a great favourite. The secret to a really good pie is a generous filling with plenty of flavour.

Makes 8 individual pies

ingredients

750g/1¹/₂lb prepared or ready-rolled
shortcrust pastry, thawed
375g/12oz prepared or ready-rolled
puff pastry, thawed
1 egg, lightly beaten

Beef filling
750g/1¹/₂lb lean ground beef
2 cups/500mL beef stock
freshly ground black pepper
2 tablespoons cornflour blended with
¹/₂ cup/125mL water
1 tablespoon Worcestershire sauce
1 teaspoon soy sauce

Oven temperature 220°C, 440°F, Gas 7

575

cooking on a budget

almond lamb pilau

It is the challenge of every home

cook to produce tasty and economical meals for the family. In this chapter you will find a collection of old favourites as well as some great new ideas that will fit the bill perfectly. Ideal for entertaining family and friends or for special family celebrations, you will never worry again about being able to afford to celebrate a special occasion.

veal
piccata

ingredients

30g/1oz flour
8 medium veal escalopes, tenderized
60g/2oz butter
125ml/4fl oz lemon juice
125ml/4fl oz dry white wine
1 lemon, thinly sliced, for garnish

Method:

1 *Lightly flour the veal escalopes on both sides. Shake off excess.*

2 *Melt the butter in a medium frying pan over moderate heat. When the butter bubbles, add the veal escalopes and saute for about 2 minutes on each side. When the veal is almost cooked, sprinkle on the lemon juice. Using tongs or a fish slice, transfer the escalopes to a serving dish; keep hot.*

3 *Add the wine to the frying pan and boil over high heat, stirring constantly until the liquid is reduced to about 125ml/4fl oz. Pour the sauce over the veal.*

4 *Cut the lemon into paper thin slices and place 3 slices on each escalope. Serve immediately.*

Serves 4

almond
lamb pilau

Photograph page 577

ingredients

2 tablespoons olive oil
1 onion, chopped
1 clove garlic, crushed
500g/1lb diced lamb
2 teaspoons curry powder
2 teaspoons ground coriander
1 teaspoon ground cumin
1 teaspoon ground ginger
1/2 teaspoon ground turmeric
2 1/2 cups/600mL/1 pt chicken stock
1 tomato, chopped
freshly ground black pepper
2 cups/440g/14oz rice
90g/3oz almonds, toasted
90g/3oz raisins

Method:

1 *Heat oil in a frying pan over a medium heat, add onion and garlic and cook, stirring, for 5 minutes or until onion is tender. Add lamb and cook, stirring occasionally, for 5 minutes or until lamb is brown on all sides.*

2 *Add curry powder, coriander, cumin, ginger and turmeric to pan and cook, stirring constantly, for 2 minutes or until fragrant. Add 1/2cup/125mL/4fl oz stock, tomato and black pepper to taste and bring to the boil. Reduce heat, cover and simmer, stirring occasionally, for 20 minutes or until lamb is tender.*

3 *Add remaining stock to pan and bring to the boil. Stir in rice, reduce heat, cover and simmer for 15 minutes or until rice is cooked. Add almonds and raisins and using a fork toss to combine.*

Serves 6

sweet
meat curry

Method:

1 Heat oil in a large saucepan over a medium heat, add onion and garlic and cook, stirring, for 3-4 minutes or until onion is tender. Add curry powder, ginger and chilli, if using, and cook, for 1 minute or until fragrant.

2 Add carrots, celery, apple, banana, sultanas, vinegar, chutney and sugar and cook for 2-3 minutes. Stir in water and black pepper to taste and bring to the boil. Reduce heat, cover and simmer for 15-20 minutes or until vegetables are tender.

3 Stir flour mixture into curry and cook, stirring constantly, for 5 minutes or until mixture boils and thickens. Stir in meat and simmer for 5-10 minutes or until heated through.

Note: Serve curry with rice and traditional Indian accompaniments such as pappadums, chutney and sambals, or boiled potatoes and steamed vegetables.

Serves 6

ingredients

2 tablespoons olive oil
1 onion, chopped
1 clove garlic, crushed
1 tablespoon curry powder
1 teaspoon ground ginger
1 teaspoon chopped fresh red chilli
(optional)
2 carrots, chopped
2 stalks celery, chopped
1 apple, chopped
1 banana, sliced
2 tablespoons sultanas (golden raisins)
2 tablespoons malt vinegar
1 tablespoon fruit chutney
2 teaspoons brown sugar
2¹/₂ cups/600mL/1pt water
freshly ground black pepper
¹/₄ cup/30g/1oz flour blended with
¹/₃ cup/90mL/3fl oz water
500g/1 lb chopped cooked beef,
lamb, pork or chicken

veal
goulash

Method:

1 Trim meat of all visible fat and cut into 2cm/³/₄in cubes. Place paprika, flour and black pepper to taste in a plastic food bag, add meat and shake to coat meat evenly. Shake off excess flour.

2 Heat oil in a large saucepan and cook onion and garlic over a medium heat for 3-4 minutes or until onion softens. Combine tomato paste (purée), wine and stock. Stir stock mixture and meat into onion mixture. Bring to the boil, then reduce heat and simmer, covered, for 25-30 minutes or until meat is tender.

3 Remove from heat and stir one-third of the sour cream or yogurt into one serving of goulash. Serve immediately.

Serving suggestion: Serve with fettuccine and boiled, steamed or microwaved vegetables of your choice.

Freeze it: Omitting sour cream or yogurt, freeze remaining goulash in serving portions in airtight freezerproof containers or sealed freezer bags. Defrost, covered, in the refrigerator overnight. Reheat in a saucepan over a medium heat, stirring, until hot. To reheat in microwave, place in a microwave-safe dish and cook on HIGH (100%), stirring occasionally, for 2-3 minutes or until sauce boils. Add sour cream or yogurt just prior to serving.

Makes 4 servings

ingredients

4x125g/4oz lean veal steaks,
cut 1cm/¹/₂in thick
1¹/₂ tablespoons paprika
2 tablespoons flour
freshly ground black pepper
1 tablespoon vegetable oil
2 onions, chopped
1 clove garlic, crushed
1 tablespoon tomato paste (purée)
3 tablespoons red wine
¹/₂ cup/125mL/4fl oz beef stock
¹/₄ cup/60g/2oz sour cream
or natural yogurt

veal chops
with sun-dried tomatoes

Method:

1 Coat chops with flour. Melt butter in a frypan and cook garlic, prosciutto and rosemary over a high heat for 2 minutes. Add chops and brown on both sides.

2 Stir in wine. Bring to the boil, reduce heat and simmer for 30 minutes or until veal is cooked.

3 Remove chops and prosciutto from pan and set aside to keep warm. Increase heat, stir in tomatoes and cook until sauce is reduced by half. Stir in basil and spoon sauce over chops and top with prosciutto.

Note: Sun-dried tomatoes are becoming increasingly popular and are available from most delicatessens.

Serves 4

ingredients

8 veal chops, trimmed of all visible fat
seasoned flour
60g/2oz butter
1 clove garlic, crushed
6 slices prosciutto, chopped
2 tablespoons chopped fresh rosemary
250 mL/8fl oz dry white wine
16 sun-dried tomatoes, chopped
4 tablespoons chopped fresh basil

veal
escalopes

Method:

1 Place veal slices between plastic food wrap and flatten using a mallet, until very thin. Coat veal in flour, dip in egg then coat with breadcrumbs.

2 Melt butter in a frypan until foaming. Add veal and cook for 2 minutes each side or until golden. Wrap each veal steak in a slice of prosciutto, place in a shallow baking dish and sprinkle with mozzarella and Parmesan cheeses. Spoon cream over and cook under a preheated grill for 3-4 minutes, or until cheese melts and is golden.

Note: Serve this easy veal dish with a fresh green salad.

Serves 4

ingredients

8 small, thin veal steaks
seasoned flour
1 egg, lightly beaten
185g/6oz breadcrumbs, made from
stale bread
60g/2oz butter
8 slices prosciutto
125g/4oz grated mozzarella cheese
3 tablespoons grated fresh Parmesan
cheese
125mL/4fl oz thickened cream (heavy)

Oven temperature 210°C/420°F/Gas 7

crunchy
family meatloaf

Method:

1 *Place beef, potato, carrot, onion, breadcrumbs, egg, tomato sauce or chutney, herbs and black pepper to taste in a bowl and mix well to combine.*

2 *Press mixture into a lightly greased 11x21cm/ 4¹/₂x8¹/₂in loaf tin and bake for 1 hour at 210°C/420°F/Gas 7 or until cooked.*

3 *Drain off excess juices and turn meatloaf onto a lightly greased baking tray. Brush with tomato sauce mixture. Combine breadcrumbs and butter, sprinkle over meatloaf and bake for 15-20 minutes longer or until topping is crisp and golden. Serve hot or cold.*

Serves 6

ingredients

**750g/1¹/₂ lb ground lean beef
1 potato, grated
1 carrot, grated
1 onion, finely chopped
¹/₂ cup/30g/1oz breadcrumbs, made
from stale bread
1 egg, beaten
2 tablespoons tomato sauce or
fruit chutney
1 teaspoon dried mixed herbs
freshly ground black pepper**

Crunchy topping
**¹/₄ cup/60mL/2fl oz tomato sauce mixed
with 2 tablespoons Worcestershire
¹/₂ cup/30g/1oz breadcrumbs, made
from stale bread
60g/2oz butter, melted**

daube
of beef

Method:

1 Toss beef in flour. Shake off excess and set aside. Heat half the oil in a large frying pan over a medium heat and cook beef in batches for 3-4 minutes or until brown. Place in a casserole dish.

2 Heat remaining oil in same pan, add onion and garlic and cook over a medium heat, stirring, for 4-5 minutes. Add leek and cook for 2-3 minutes longer. Add vegetables to casserole dish.

3 Add stock, wine, herbs and black pepper to taste to pan and stirring, bring to the boil. Reduce heat and simmer until liquid reduces by half. Add stock mixture, bay leaf and orange rind, if using, to casserole dish and bake for 1½-2 hours at 210°C/420°F/Gas7 or until beef is tender.

4 Add zucchini (courgettes), sweet potato and parsnip and bake for extra 30 minutes or until vegetables are tender.

Serves 4

ingredients

1 kg/2 lb chuck or blade steak, trimmed of all visible fat and cubed
½ cup/60g/2oz seasoned flour
¼ cup/60mL/2fl oz olive oil
1 onion, chopped
1 clove garlic, crushed
1 leek, sliced
2 cups/500 mL/16fl oz beef stock
1 cup/250mL/8fl oz red wine
1 teaspoon dried mixed herbs
freshly ground black pepper
1 bay leaf
few thin strips orange rind (optional)
2 zucchini (courgettes), sliced
1 large sweet potato, chopped
1 parsnip, sliced

Oven temperature 210°C/420°F/Gas

584

Oven temperature 210°C/420°F/Gas 7

family
roast

Method:

1 Place beef on a wire rack set in a flameproof roasting dish or tin. Brush beef with 1 tablespoon oil and sprinkle with black pepper to taste. Bake for 1-1¼ hours for medium rare or until cooked to your liking.

2 For vegetables, place potatoes, pumpkin or parsnips and onions in a large saucepan, cover with water and bring to the boil. Reduce heat and simmer for 3 minutes, then drain. Arrange vegetables in a baking dish and brush with ¼ cup/60mL/2fl oz oil. Bake at 210°C/420°F/Gas 7, turning once during cooking, for 45 minutes or until vegetables are tender and browned.

3 To make gravy, transfer roast to a serving platter, cover with foil and rest for 15 minutes. Stir wine or stock, mushrooms, tarragon and black pepper to taste into meat juices in roasting dish or tin and place over a medium heat. Bring to the boil, stirring to loosen sediment, then reduce heat and simmer until sauce reduces and thickens. Slice beef and serve with vegetables and gravy.

Serves 6-8

ingredients

**1½ kg/3 lb piece fresh round beef
1 tablespoon olive oil
freshly ground black pepper**

**Roast vegetables
6 large potatoes, halved
6 pieces pumpkin or 3 parsnips, halved
6 onions, peeled
¼ cup/60mL/2fl oz olive oil**

**Mushroom gravy
1 cup/250mL/8fl oz red wine
or beef stock
60g/2oz button mushrooms, sliced
½ teaspoon dried tarragon**

family
paella

Method:

1 Heat oil in a large frying pan over a medium heat, add chicken and pork and cook, stirring, for 3 minutes. Using a slotted spoon, remove from pan and set aside.

2 Add onions, red or green pepper and salami to pan and cook, stirring, for 5 minutes or until onions are tender. Add rice and cook, stirring, for 1 minute or until rice is coated with oil.

3 Stir stock or water, turmeric and black pepper to taste into pan and bring to the boil. Reduce heat and simmer for 5 minutes. Add mussels and peas, cover and simmer for 5 minutes or until mussels open. Discard any mussels that do not open after 5 minutes cooking.

4 Return chicken and pork to pan and simmer, uncovered, for 5-10 minutes or until all the liquid is absorbed and rice is tender. Serve immediately.

Serves 6

ingredients

^{1}/$_4$ **cup/60mL/2fl oz olive oil**
4 chicken thigh fillets or 2 boneless chicken breast fillets, sliced
250g/8oz diced lean pork
2 onions, chopped
1 small red or green pepper, sliced
60g/2oz hot Spanish salami, sliced
3 cups/660g/1 lb 5oz rice
3 cups/750mL/1^1/$_4$pt chicken stock or water
^{1}/$_2$ teaspoon ground turmeric
freshly ground black pepper
500g/1 lb mussels, scrubbed, beards removed
60g/2oz frozen peas

spinach
burghul salad

Method:

1 Place bread on a baking tray and bake for 10 minutes or until crisp and golden. Set aside to cool, then store in an airtight container until needed.

2 Place cracked wheat (burghul) in a bowl, add water and lemon juice and mix to combine. Set aside to soak for 15 minutes or until all the liquid is absorbed.

3 Place spinach leaves in a salad bowl, add cracked wheat (burghul), tomatoes, onion, bacon, oil, vinegar and basil and toss to combine. Just prior to serving, scatter with croûtons.

Serves 6

ingredients

2 slices bread, crusts removed, cubed
¹/₄ cup/45g/1¹/₂oz cracked wheat (burghul)
¹/₄ cup/60mL/2fl oz water
2 tablespoons lemon juice
1 bunch/500g/1 lb spinach
2 tomatoes, chopped
1 onion, sliced
3 rashers bacon, grilled and chopped
2 tablespoons olive oil
1 tablespoon cider vinegar
¹/₂ teaspoon dried basil leaves

glazed pork spare ribs

barbecue meals

Whether it's a special celebration

or just a few friends around for a bite to eat and a chat, barbecuing is a wonderful way to entertain. A barbecue can be as formal or as casual as the host chooses and the food as simple or as sophisticated as is required.

best
barbecue sausages

Method:

An enticingly wide range of sausages is available in packages or loose from butchers, food stores and delicatessens. They may be thick, thin or chipolata (cocktail sausages). Sausages require careful cooking so the outside is crispy brown and the centre cooked through, but not dry. Blanching the sausages first plumps up the meal or filler, releases some of the fat and ensures that thick sausages will be cooked through. Separate sausages by cutting between the links with a sharp knife. Place in a saucepan, cover with cold water, bring to the boil and simmer gently for 5 minutes. Drain, then pierce sausages all over with a skewer. Place sausages, in 1 layer, on an oiled rack over moderately hot coals and cook, turning constantly, for 10-15 minutes for thick sausages, 5-8 minutes for thin ones, or until cooked through and browned.

Method:

1. *Place spare ribs on a large sheet of heavy-duty foil and cover both sides generously with marinade. Wrap into a double-folded parcel, making sure all joins are well-sealed to prevent leakage. Stand for at least half an hour before cooking. Place in refrigerator if not to be cooked immediately.*

2. *Prepare the barbecue for direct-heat cooking. Place a wire cake-rack on the grill bars to stand 2¹/₂cm/1in above the bars. Place ribs in the foil parcel on the rack and cook for 10 minutes each side.*

3. *Remove to a plate, remove ribs and discard foil, then return ribs to rack. Continue cooking brushing with fresh sauce or marinade and turning each minute until ribs are well browned and crisp (about 10 minutes). Total cooking time is approximately 30/35 minutes.*

Note: *Ribs may be cooked by indirect heat in a hooded barbecue. There is no need to wrap in foil. Place over indirect heat after marinating. Brush and turn frequently with lid down for 1 hour or more. Cooking in the foil over direct heat cuts cooking time in half.*

Serves 4

glazed
pork spare ribs

Photograph page 589

ingredients

1kg/2lb pork spare ribs (American-Style)

Soy and honey marinade
¹/₄ cup/60ml/2fl oz soy sauce
2 tablespoons honey
1 tablespoon sherry
2 cloves garlic, crushed
1 teaspoon grated fresh ginger

kettle
roasted honey beef

Method:
1 To make marinade, place mustard seeds and wine in a bowl and soak for 30 minutes. Add black peppercorns, tarragon leaves, sage leaves and honey and mix to combine.
2 Place beef in a shallow dish and pour over marinade. Cover and marinate, turning occasionally, for at least 1 hour.
3 Preheat a covered barbecue to a high heat.
4 Drain beef and reserve marinade. Place beef on barbecue grill and cook, turning frequently, until brown on all sides. Remove beef from barbecue and reduce heat to medium. Line a barbecue roasting rack with bay branches and place beef on top. Strain reserved marinade and spread mustard seeds and herbs over beef. Pour marinating liquid into a roasting tin. Place rack in roasting tin, cover barbecue with lid and cook, turning occasionally for 35-55 minutes or until beef is cooked to your liking.

Serves 8

ingredients

1 ¹/₂ kg/3 lb piece sirloin, trimmed of excess fat
6-8 branches bay tree

Mustard wine marinade
4 tablespoons mustard seeds
1 ¹/₂ cups/375mL/12fl oz red wine
1 tablespoon coarsely crushed black peppercorns
1 tablespoon fresh tarragon leaves
1 tablespoon fresh sage leaves
2 tablespoons honey

sweet
rosemary cutlets

Method:

1 Make 2 slits in the thin outer fat covering of each cutlet and insert a rosemary sprig into each one. Place prepared cutlets in a shallow dish.

2 To make marinade, place wine, honey, mustard and black peppercorns to taste in a bowl and mix to combine. Pour marinade over cutlets, turn to coat and marinate for 40 minutes.

3 Preheat barbecue to a high heat. Drain cutlets, place on oiled barbecue grill and cook for 4-5 minutes each side or until cooked to your liking.

Serves 6

ingredients

**12 small double lamb cutlets
(allow 2 double cutlets per serve)
24 small sprigs rosemary**

Honey and wine marinade
1 cup/250mL/8fl oz red wine
¹/₃ cup/90mL/3fl oz honey
**2 tablespoons wholegrain mustard
crushed black peppercorns**

italian
hamburgers

Method:

1 To make patties, place beef, sun-dried tomatoes, parsley, basil, garlic and Worcestershire sauce in a bowl and mix to combine. Shape mixture into 8 mini patties, place on a plate lined with plastic food wrap and chill until required.

2 Preheat barbecue to a high heat. Brush eggplant (aubergine) slices and pepper (capsicum) quarters with oil and cook on barbecue grill for 2 minutes each side or until tender. Place in a bowl, add vinegar and toss to combine.

3 Reduce barbecue heat to medium, then cook patties for 4 minutes each side or until cooked to your liking. To assemble, spread base of rolls with pesto, then top with some rocket leaves, a patty, some slices of eggplant (aubergine) and a piece of red pepper (capsicum) and cover with top of roll. Serve immediately.

Makes 8 mini hamburgers

ingredients

2 small eggplant (aubergines), thinly sliced
2 red peppers (capsicum), quartered
2 tablespoons olive oil
⅓ cup/90mL/3fl oz balsamic vinegar
8 mini rosetta rolls, split
3 tablespoons ready-made pesto
125g/4oz rocket leaves

Beef patties
500g/1 lb lean ground beef
3 tablespoons finely chopped sun-dried tomatoes
2 tablespoons chopped fresh parsley
1 tablespoon chopped fresh basil
2 cloves garlic, crushed
1 tablespoon Worcestershire sauce

barbecued
port-glazed lamb

Method:

1 *Preheat covered barbecue to a medium heat.*
2 *To make glaze, place mustard, orange rind, nutmeg, port, honey and vinegar in a saucepan, bring to simmering over a low heat and simmer until mixture thickens and reduces slightly.*
3 *Place lamb on a wire rack set in a roasting tin and brush with glaze. Pour port wine and water into roasting tin, cover barbecue with lid and cook for 2 hours, brushing with glaze at 15-minute intervals, or until cooked to your liking.*

Serves 8

ingredients

2¹/₂kg/5 lb leg of lamb
1 cup/250mL/8fl oz port
1¹/₂ cups/375mL/12fl oz water

Port glaze
4 tablespoons Dijon mustard
2 teaspoons finely grated orange rind
¹/₂ teaspoon grated nutmeg
1¹/₂ cups/375mL/12fl oz port wine
¹/₂ cup/125mL/4fl oz honey
2 tablespoons balsamic vinegar

slow-roasted
leg of lamb

Method:
1 To make marinade, place rosemary, mint, vinegar, oil and black pepper to taste in a bowl and mix to combine.
2 Cut several deep slits in the surface of the lamb. Fill each slit with a slice of garlic. Place lamb in a glass or ceramic dish, pour over marinade, turn to coat, cover and marinate in the refrigerator for 4 hours.
3 Preheat covered barbecue to a medium heat. Place lamb on a wire rack set in a roasting tin and pour over marinade. Place roasting tin on rack in barbecue, cover barbecue with lid and cook, basting occasionally, for 1¹/₂-2 hours or until lamb is tender. Cover and stand for 15 minutes before carving.

Serves 6

ingredients

1¹/₂kg/3 lb leg of lamb
3 cloves garlic, thinly sliced

Fresh herb marinade
4 tablespoons chopped fresh rosemary
4 tablespoons chopped fresh mint
¹/₂ cup/125mL/4fl oz white wine vinegar
¹/₄ cup/60mL/2fl oz olive oil
freshly ground black pepper

herbed
and spiced pork loin

Method:

1 To make marinade, place onion, pink peppercorns, green peppercorns, coriander, black pepper, cumin, garam masala, mixed spice, turmeric, paprika, salt, peanut oil, sesame oil and vinegar into a food processor or blender and process to make a paste.

2 Rub marinade over pork, place in a glass or ceramic dish, cover and marinate in the refrigerator overnight.

3 Place pork on a wire rack set in a baking dish and bake for 1 hour. Preheat barbecue to a medium heat. Transfer pork to lightly oiled barbecue grill and cook, turning frequently, for 1¹/₂ hours or until pork is tender and cooked through. Stand for 10 minutes before carving and serving.

Note: This recipe can be cooked in a covered barbecue, in which case it is not necessary to precook the pork in the oven. If cooking in a covered barbecue preheat the barbecue to a medium heat and cook for 2-2¹/₂ hours. When scoring the rind take care not to cut through into the flesh.

Serves 8

ingredients

2 kg/4 lb boneless pork loin, rolled and rind scored at 2cm/³/₄in intervals

Herb and spice marinade
1 onion, chopped
2 tablespoons crushed pink peppercorns
2 tablespoons crushed green peppercorns
2 tablespoons ground coriander
1 tablespoon freshly ground black pepper
1 tablespoon ground cumin
1 teaspoon garam masala
1 teaspoon ground mixed spice
1 teaspoon turmeric
1 teaspoon paprika
1 teaspoon sea salt
2 tablespoons peanut oil
2 tablespoons sesame oil
1 tablespoon white vinegar

californian
pork kebabs

Method:

1 To make marinade, place onion, garlic, chillies, thyme, oregano, cumin, black pepper, lemon juice, pineapple juice and oil into a food processor or blender and process until smooth.

2 Place pork in a glass or ceramic bowl, pour over marinade and toss to combine. Cover and marinate at room temperature for 2 hours or in the refrigerator overnight.

3 Preheat barbecue to a medium heat. Drain pork well. Thread pork and pineapple, alternately, onto lightly oiled skewers. Place skewers on lightly oiled barbecue grill and cook, turning several times, for 5-8 minutes or until pork is tender and cooked through.

Serves 6

ingredients

500g/1 lb pork fillets, cut
into 2cm/³/₄in cubes
1 small pineapple, cut into
2cm/³/₄in cubes

<u>Pineapple marinade</u>
1 onion, chopped
3 cloves garlic, chopped
2 dried red chillies
2 tablespoons chopped fresh thyme
2 tablespoons chopped fresh oregano
2 teaspoons ground cumin
2 teaspoons freshly ground black pepper
¹/₃ cup/90mL/3fl oz lemon juice
¹/₃ cup/90mL/3fl oz pineapple juice
2 tablespoons olive oil

drunken
sirloin steaks

Method:

1 *To make marinade, place beer, garlic, Worcestershire sauce and tomato sauce in a large shallow glass or ceramic dish and mix to combine.*

2 *Add steaks to marinade, turn to coat, cover and set aside to marinate at room temperature for at least 3 hours or in the refrigerator overnight. Turn occasionally during marinating.*

3 *Preheat barbecue to hot. Drain steaks and reserve marinade. Cook steaks on lightly oiled barbecue, brushing with reserved marinade, for 3-5 minutes each side or until cooked to your liking. Serve immediately.*

Note: *When testing to see if a steak is cooked to your liking, press it with a pair of blunt tongs. Do not cut the meat, as this causes the juices to escape. Rare steaks will feel springy, medium slightly springy and well-done will feel firm.*

Serves 8

ingredients

8 sirloin steaks, trimmed of all visible fat

Drunken marinade
³/₄ cup/185mL/6fl oz beer
2 cloves garlic, crushed
¹/₄ cup/60mL/2fl oz Worcestershire sauce
¹/₄ cup/60mL/2fl oz tomato sauce

pork
skewers with salsa

Method:

1 Place pork, breadcrumbs, onion, garlic, oregano, cumin, chilli powder and egg in a bowl and mix to combine.

2 Shape tablespoons of pork mixture into balls, place on a plate lined with plastic food wrap, cover and refrigerate for 30 minutes.

3 Preheat barbecue to a medium heat. Thread four balls onto a lightly oiled skewer. Repeat with remaining balls. Place skewers on lightly oiled barbecue grill and cook, turning frequently, for 8 minutes or until cooked through.

4 To make salsa, heat oil in a frying pan over a medium heat, add onion and cook, stirring, for 3 minutes or until onion is golden. Add artichokes, tomatoes, tomato paste (purée) and oregano and cook, stirring, for 3-4 minutes longer or until heated through. Serve with skewers.

Serves 4

ingredients

500g/1lb lean ground pork
1 cup/60g/2oz breadcrumbs, made from stale bread
1 onion, chopped
2 cloves garlic, crushed
1 tablespoon chopped oregano
1 teaspoon ground cumin
1/2 teaspoon chilli powder
1 egg, lightly beaten

Artichoke salsa
1 tablespoon olive oil
1 onion, chopped
185g/6oz marinated artichoke hearts, chopped
4 tomatoes, seeded and chopped
2 tablespoons tomato paste (purée)
1 tablespoon chopped fresh oregano

Thai fried noodles

exotic tastes

Sensational Eastern food, based on

traditional recipes and cooking techniques which reflect
a style of cuisine that appeals to the modern cook.

warm
lamb salad

ingredients

250g/8oz assorted lettuce leaves
1 cucumber, sliced lengthwise
into thin strips
2 teaspoons vegetable oil
500g/1 lb lamb fillets, trimmed of all
visible fat, thinly sliced

Coriander and chilli dressing
2 tablespoons chopped fresh coriander
1 tablespoon brown sugar
1/4 cup/60mL/2fl oz soy sauce
2 tablespoons sweet chilli sauce
2 tablespoons lime juice
2 teaspoons fish sauce

Method:
1 *To make dressing, place coriander, sugar, soy and chilli sauces, lime juice and fish sauce in a bowl and mix to combine. Set aside.*
2 *Arrange lettuce leaves and cucumber on a serving platter and set aside.*
3 *Heat oil in a wok over a high heat, add lamb and stir-fry for 2 minutes or until brown. Place lamb on top of lettuce leaves, drizzle with dressing and serve immediately.*
Serves 4

thai
fried noodles

Photograph page 601

ingredients

vegetable oil for deep-frying
250g/8oz rice vermicelli noodles
2 teaspoons sesame oil
2 onions, chopped
2 cloves garlic, crushed
185g/6oz pork fillets, chopped
185g/6oz boneless chicken
breast fillets, chopped
1 teaspoon dried chilli flakes
125g/4oz bean sprouts
2 tablespoons Thai fish sauce (nam pla)
1 tablespoon lemon juice
2 teaspoons tamarind concentrate

Method:
1 *Heat vegetable oil in a wok or large saucepan over a high heat until very hot. Deep-fry noodles, a few at a time, for 1-2 minutes or until lightly golden and puffed. Remove and set aside.*
2 *Heat sesame oil in a wok or frying pan over a meduim heat, add onions and garlic and stir-fry for 4 minutes or until soft and golden. Add pork, chicken and chilli flakes and stir-fry for 4 minutes or until pork and chicken are brown and cooked.*
3 *Add bean sprouts, fish sauce, lemon juice, tamarind and noodles and stir-fry for 2 minutes or until heated through. Serve immediately.*
Serves 4

spiced
grilled beef

Method:

1 Place onion, garlic, coriander roots, peppercorns, soy sauce, lime juice and fish sauce in a food processor and process to make a paste. Coat beef with spice mixture and cook over a medium charcoal or gas barbecue, turning occasionally, for 15 minutes or until beef is cooked to medium doneness. Alternatively, bake beef in oven for 30-45 minutes or until cooked to medium doneness.

2 Arrange lettuce, tomatoes and cucumber on a serving plate. Slice beef thinly and arrange over lettuce. Serve with lime wedges.

Serves 4

ingredients

1 red onion, chopped
4 cloves garlic, crushed
2 fresh coriander roots
1 teaspoon crushed black peppercorns
2 tablespoons light soy sauce
2 teaspoons lime juice
2 teaspoons Thai fish sauce (nam pla)
500g/1 lb rib-eye (scotch fillet)
of beef, in one piece
6 lettuce leaves
185g/6oz cherry tomatoes, halved
1 cucumber, cut into strips
lime wedges

pork
spring rolls

Photograph page 605

ingredients

**24 spring roll wrappers, each
12½cm/5in square
vegetable oil for deep-frying
sweet chilli sauce**

Pork and coriander filling
**2 teaspoons peanut oil
3 red or golden shallots, chopped
2 teaspoons finely grated fresh ginger
1 fresh red chilli, seeded and chopped
500g/1 lb ground pork meat
2 tablespoons chopped fresh
coriander leaves
2 tablespoons kechap manis**

Method:

1 To make filling, heat peanut oil in a frying pan over a high heat, add shallots, ginger and chilli and stir-fry for 2 minutes. Add pork and stir-fry for 4-5 minutes or until pork is brown. Stir in coriander and kechap manis and cook for 2 minutes longer. Remove pan from heat and set aside to cool.

2 To assemble, place 2 tablespoons of filling in the centre of each wrapper, fold one corner over filling, then tuck in sides, roll up and seal with a little water.

3 Heat vegetable oil in a wok or large saucepan until a cube of bread dropped in browns in 50 seconds and cook spring rolls, a few at a time, for 3-4 minutes or until crisp and golden. Drain on absorbent kitchen paper and serve with chilli sauce for dipping.
Note: When working with spring roll and wonton wrappers place them under a damp teatowel to prevent them from drying out.
Kechap manis is a thick sweet seasoning sauce. It is made from soy sauce, sugar and spices. If unavailable soy sauce or a mixture of soy sauce and dark corn syrup can be used in its place.
Makes 24

beef
curry puffs

Photograph page 605

ingredients

**625g/1¼ lb prepared puff pastry
vegetable oil for deep-frying
sweet chilli sauce**

Spicy beef filling
**2 teaspoons vegetable oil
4 red or golden shallots, chopped
1 tablespoon mild curry paste
2 teaspoons ground cumin
500g/1 lb lean ground beef
2 tablespoons chopped fresh coriander leaves**

Method:

1 To make filling, heat oil in a frying pan over a high heat, add shallots, curry paste and cumin and stir-fry for 2 minutes. Add beef and stir-fry for 5 minutes or until brown. Remove pan from heat and stir in coriander. Set aside to cool.

2 Roll out pastry to 3mm/⅛in thick and cut into 10cm/4in squares. With one point of the pastry square facing you, place 2-3 tablespoons of filling in the centre and lightly brush edges with water, then fold over point to meet the one opposite. Press together and roll edges to form a crescent-shaped parcel. Repeat with remaining pastry and filling.

3 Heat vegetable oil in a large saucepan until a cube of bread dropped in browns in 50 seconds and cook puffs, a few at a time, for 2 minutes or until puffed and golden. Drain on absorbent kitchen paper and serve with chilli sauce for dipping.
Makes 24

thai
fried rice

ingredients

2 tablespoons oil
4 cloves garlic, crushed
400g/13oz lean pork, chopped
2 red or green peppers, chopped
4 spring onions, chopped
4 tablespoons fish sauce
4 tablespoons tomato sauce
375g/12oz cooked shrimp, peeled
8 cups/1 ½kg/3lb cooked long-grain rice
2 eggs, lightly beaten

Method:

1 Heat oil in a large frying pan. Add garlic and pork and fry until pork is golden brown.
2 Add pepper, spring onions, fish sauce, tomato sauce, shrimp and rice, cook over a moderate heat for 3 minutes.
3 Stir in beaten eggs and mix lightly through. Cover with a lid and cook for 2-3 minutes, stirring once or twice
Note: This fried rice is great when entertaining a crowd. It serves 8 as a main meal or 10-12 with other dishes at a party. The recipe is easily doubled or halved.
Serves 8

minted
pork and mango salad

Photograph page 607

ingredients

1 tablespoon vegetable oil
500g/1 lb lean ground pork meat
60g/2oz canned water chestnuts, chopped
2 stalks fresh lemon grass, finely chopped
or 1 teaspoon dried lemon grass, soaked
in hot water until soft
2 tablespoons lime juice
1 tablespoon fish sauce
60g/2oz bean sprouts
3 spring onions, chopped
4 tablespoons chopped fresh mint
2 tablespoons chopped fresh coriander
freshly ground black pepper
250g/8oz assorted lettuce leaves
2 mangoes, peeled and sliced
60g/2oz hazelnuts, roasted and chopped

Method:

1 Heat oil in a wok over a medium heat, add pork, water chestnuts and lemon grass and stir-fry for 5 minutes or until pork is brown. Remove from wok and set aside to cool.
2 Place pork mixture, lime juice and fish sauce in a bowl and mix to combine. Add bean sprouts, spring onions, mint, coriander and black pepper to taste and toss gently.
3 Line a serving platter with lettuce leaves, then top with mangoes and pork mixture. Scatter with hazelnuts.
Note: This salad can be prepared to the end of step 2 several hours in advance. Cover and keep at room temperature.
If preparing more than 2 hours in advance store in the refrigerator and remove 30 minutes before you are ready to assemble and serve it.
Serves 4

chilli
beef

Method:

1 Place beef, garlic, ginger and curry paste in a bowl and mix to combine.

2 Heat sesame and vegetable oils together in a wok over a high heat, add beef mixture and stir-fry for 5 minutes or until beef is brown. Remove beef mixture from pan and set aside.

3 Add onion to pan and stir-fry over a medium heat for 3 minutes or until golden. Add green pepper, red pepper, sweet corn and bamboo shoots and stir-fry for 5 minutes longer or until vegetables are tender.

4 Return beef to pan, stir in fish sauce, sugar and stock and bring to simmering. Simmer, stirring occasionally, for 10 minutes or until beef is tender.

Note: When handling fresh chillies, do not put your hands near your eyes or allow them to touch your lips. To avoid discomfort and burning, you might like to wear gloves. Chillies are also available minced in jars from supermarkets.

Serves 6

ingredients

750g/1 ¹/₂lb rump steak, cut into strips
2 cloves garlic, crushed
1 tablespoon finely grated fresh ginger
1 tablespoon Thai Red Curry Paste
1 tablespoon sesame oil
1 tablespoon vegetable oil
1 onion, cut into wedges
1 green pepper, chopped
1 red pepper, chopped
440g/14oz canned baby sweet corn, drained
220g/7oz canned bamboo shoots, drained
1 tablespoon Thai fish sauce (nam pla)
1 tablespoon brown sugar
¹/₂ cup/125ml/4fl oz beef stock

pork
and pineapple with basil

Method:

1 *Place shallots, chillies, galangal or ginger, lime leaves, lemon grass, tamarind, 1 tablespoon lime juice, water, shrimp paste and dried shrimps in a food processor and process to make a thick paste, adding a little more water if necessary.*

2 *Place pork in a bowl, add spice paste and toss to coat pork well.*

3 *Heat oil in a wok or large saucepan over a medium heat, add pork and stir-fry for 5 minutes or until fragrant and pork is just cooked.*

4 *Stir in sugar, coconut cream and milk and fish sauce and simmer, uncovered, for 8-10 minutes or until pork is tender.*

5 *Add pineapple and remaining lime juice and simmer for 3 minutes or until pineapple is heated. Stir in basil.*

Serves 4

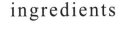

ingredients

4 red or golden shallots, chopped
2 fresh red chillies, finely chopped
3 cm/1¼in piece fresh galangal or ginger, finely chopped, or 5 slices bottled galangal, chopped
4 kaffir lime leaves
1 stalk fresh lemon grass, tender white part only, finely sliced, or
½ teaspoon dried lemon grass, soaked in hot water until soft
1 tablespoon tamarind concentrate
2 tablespoons lime juice
1 tablespoon water
2 teaspoons shrimp paste
1 tablespoon dried shrimps
350g/11oz pork fillets, cut into 3cm/1¼in cubes
1 tablespoon vegetable oil
1 teaspoon palm or brown sugar
1½ cups/375mL/12fl oz coconut cream
½ cup/125mL/4fl oz coconut milk
2 tablespoons Thai fish sauce (nam pla)
½ small (about 200g/6½oz) fresh pineapple, cut into 2cm/¾in wide strips
60g/2oz fresh basil leaves

beef
and bean stirfry

Method:

1 *Heat oil and garlic together in a wok over a medium heat, increase heat to high, add beef and stir-fry for 3 minutes or until beef changes colour.*

2 *Add beans, lime leaves, sugar and soy and fish sauces and stir-fry for 2 minutes or until beans change colour. Stir in coriander and serve immediately.*

Note: *Kaffir limes are a popular Thai ingredient. Both the fruit and the leaves have a distinctive flavor and perfume and are used in cooking. The leaves are available dried, fresh frozen or fresh from Oriental food shops and some greengrocers. If kaffir lime leaves are unavailable a little finely grated lime rind can be used instead.*

Serves 4

ingredients

2 teaspoons vegetable oil
2 cloves garlic, crushed
**500g/1 lb topside or round steak,
cut into thin strips**
**185g/6oz green beans, cut into
10cm/4in lengths**
2 kaffir lime leaves, shredded
2 teaspoons brown sugar
2 tablespoons light soy sauce
1 tablespoon Thai fish sauce (nam pla)
2 tablespoons coriander leaves

lamb
in mint

Method:

1 Cut eggplant (aubergine) into bite-sized chunks, place in a colander ad sprinkle with salt, mix well and leave to drain for 20 minutes. Rinse under cold water and drain well.

2 Heat oil in a wok or large frying pan. Add lamb and garlic and fry until well browned (you may need to do this in batches). Add eggplant (aubergine) and chilli and stirfry over a moderate heat for 5 minutes.

3 Stir in fish sauce, brown sugar, water and mint leaves and fry for a further 1 minute or until eggplant (aubergine) is softened. If sauce becomes too thick, add a little extra water. Serve with steamed long-grain rice.

Serves 4

ingredients

1 medium eggplant (aubergine)
1 tablespoon salt
2 tablespoons oil
500g/1lb lean lamb, thinly sliced
2 cloves garlic, chopped
1 red chilli, seeded and chopped
2 tablespoons brown sugar, well packed
$^1/_3$ cup 80ml/2$^1/_2$fl oz water
20 fresh mint leaves

muslin
beef curry

1 Place curry paste, shrimp paste, coconut milk, fish sauce, sugar, beef, peanuts, cinnamon and cardamom into a large saucepan and mix to combine. Bring to simmering over a medium heat, then simmer, stirring occasionally, uncovered, for 40 minutes or until beef is tender.

2 Stir in tamarind mixture and cook for 5 minutes longer. Remove cinnamon sticks and cardamom pods before serving.

Serves 4

ingredients

2 tablespoons Mussaman Curry Paste
$^1/_2$ teaspoon shrimp paste
2 cups/500mL/16fl oz coconut milk
1 tablespoon Thai fish sauce (nam pla)
1 tablespoon sugar
500g/1 lb rump steak, cut into
2cm/$^3/_4$in cubes
155g/5oz peanuts, roasted
2 cinnamon sticks
5 cardamom pods
2 teaspoons tamarind concentrate,
dissolved in 2 tablespoons hot water

coconut
beef curry

Method:

1 Heat oil in a wok over a medium heat, add curry paste and stir-fry for 3 minutes or until fragrant. Add beef to pan and stir-fry for 5 minutes longer or until beef is brown.

2 Stir coconut milk into pan and bring to the boil. Reduce heat and simmer, stirring occasionally, for 15 minutes. Add zucchini (courgettes), red pepper (capsicum), tomatoes and spring onions and cook for 10 minutes longer or until beef is tender. Stir in basil leaves and serve.

Serves 4

ingredients

1 tablespoon vegetable oil
1 tablespoon Thai Red Curry
500 g/1 lb rump steak, thinly sliced
1¹/₂ cups/375mL/12fl oz coconut milk
2 zucchini (courgettes), sliced
1 red pepper (capsicum), chopped
125g/4oz cherry tomatoes
4 spring onions, sliced diagonally
12 fresh basil leaves

brilliant
barbecues

introduction

introduction

Which barbecue?

There are many different barbecues available. The one you choose will depend on your budget, how many people you regularly feed and whether barbecuing is usually a planned or an impromptu affair.

Gas barbecues:

These barbecues contain lava rocks which are heated by gas burners. The lava rocks evenly distribute the heat and if you have a barbecue with multiple burners it is possible to have the rocks hot on one side and a medium heat on the other. The rack on which you cook the food is set above the rocks. Gas barbecues also require a gas bottle, which needs to be refilled on a regular basis – this is relatively inexpensive. When lighting a gas barbecue it is important to follow the manufacturer's instructions. If the barbecue does not ignite immediately, turn it off, wait for any build up of gas to disperse, then try again.

Wood or coal barbecues:

The key to using these types of barbecues is patience and planning. These barbecues take up to an hour to heat, so you need to remember to light the barbecue well in advance.

Electric barbecues:

These are ideal for people who want to barbecue indoors and, like gas barbecues, they produce almost instant heat.

How hot?

The recipes in this book were cooked on a gas barbecue. Gas barbecues heat up very quickly and the heat is relatively easy to control, however if your barbecue uses coal, wood or barbecue fuel, you need to allow 30-45 minutes for coals to heat and 45 minutes to 1 hour for wood. The following is a guide for assessing the heat of these barbecues.

Hot fire:

There will be a red glow showing through the thin layer of white ash and when you hold your hand 15 cm/6 in above the coals you will only be able to leave it there for 3 seconds. This fire is ideal for searing and quick cooking.

Medium fire:

The red glow will be almost gone and the ash thicker and more grey in colour. When you hold your hand 15 cm/6 in above the coals you will be able to leave it there for 5-7 seconds. Most barbecuing is done on this heat.

which
barbecue

Low fire:

The red glow will have disappeared and there will be a thick coating of grey ash. This heat is ideal for slow cooking of foods.

The amount of heat reaching the food on these barbecues can also be controlled by moving the rack closer to or further away from the fire.

If you have a wood barbecue, interesting flavors can be imparted to the food by using different types of wood. It is well to be aware that there are some plants that are poisonous and wood from those plants or chemically treated timber, is not suitable for barbecuing. Depending on where you live some of the following may be available: fruit woods, such as cherry and apple, which give a mild sweet flavor that is delicious when cooking pork, poultry and fish; grapevine cuttings – these give a delicate sweet flavor that is excellent for fish and poultry. Herbs such as rosemary and thyme also give interesting flavors when burned on the barbecue.

which
barbecue

Play it safe

As with any type of cooking, basic safety rules should always be observed. However with barbecuing there are a few extra that you need to remember.

- If you have a gas barbecue, before lighting it check that all the gas fittings and hose connections are tight.
- If your gas barbecue does not light first time, turn it off, wait 20 seconds and try again. This will ensure that there is no gas build-up.
- Always turn a gas barbecue off at the gas bottle as well as at the controls.
- Check the barbecue area before lighting the barbecue. Do not have the barbecue too close to the house and sweep up any dry leaves or anything that might catch fire if hit by a spark.
- Watch a lighted barbecue at all times. Keep children and pets away from hot barbecues and equipment.
- Do not barbecue in enclosed areas. If wet weather has forced you to move your barbecue undercover, ensure there is plenty of ventilation.
- Remember always to check the manufacturer's safety instructions that come with your barbecue.

Equipment check

Use this checklist to ensure that you have the basic equipment for successful barbecuing.

oven mitt or cloth – important for handling hot skewers, racks and frying pans.

tongs – these should be long-handled so that you can turn food without burning your hands. Use tongs for turning food, testing to see if steak is done and moving coals and hot racks.

basting brushes – these are used to brush food with marinades, oil, butter or sauce during cooking.

spatulas – essential for turning delicate foods, such as fish, so that they do not fall apart. The best type has a long, wide blade and a long handle.

selection of sharp knives – use for preparation and carving cooked food.

hinged grills, wire baskets – these come in many shapes and sizes for cooking whole fish and other foods that are difficult to turn. Always oil the grill or basket before using so that the food does not stick.

skewers – bamboo or wooden skewers are good for quick cooking of foods. Before use, soak them in water to prevent them from burning during cooking. Before threading food onto bamboo or wooden skewers, lightly oil them so that the cooked food will slip off easily. Metal skewers are better for heavier foods.

marinating pans and bowls – remember that most marinades contain an acid ingredient so the best choice of dish for marinating is glass, ceramic, stainless steel or enamel. Deep-sided disposable aluminium dishes are also good for marinating.

Middle Eastern dip

appetizer

Whilst the barbecue is warming up

and to put your guests into a casual mood, serve a selection of off-barbecue appetizers with drinks. These tasty morsels will really get things going.

middle
eastern dip

Photograph page 621

ingredients

1 large eggplant (aubergine)
1 onion, unpeeled
2 cloves garlic, crushed
olive oil
2 tablespoons lemon juice
2 tablespoons chopped fresh parsley
1/4 cup/60g/2oz sour cream
4 pieces lavash bread, cut into triangles

Method:

1 *Preheat barbecue to a high heat. Place eggplant (aubergine) and onion on lightly oiled barbecue grill and cook, turning occasionally, for 20-30 minutes or until skins of eggplant (aubergine) and onion are charred and flesh is soft. Cool slightly, peel and chop roughly.*

2 *Place eggplant (aubergine), onion, garlic, 1/4 cup/60mL/2fl oz oil and lemon juice in a food processor or blender and process until smooth. Add parsley and sour cream and mix to combine.*

3 *Brush bread lightly with oil and cook on barbecue for 1-2 minutes each side or until crisp. Serve immediately with dip.*
Lavash bread is a yeast-free Middle Eastern bread available from Middle Eastern food shops and some supermarkets. If unavailable use pitta bread instead.

Serves 6

spicy
barbecued nuts

ingredients

250g/8oz honey roasted peanuts
185g/6oz pecans
125g/4 oz macadamia nuts
125g/4oz cashews
1 tablespoon sweet paprika
1 tablespoon ground cumin
2 teaspoons garam masala
1 teaspoon ground coriander
1 teaspoon ground nutmeg
1/4 teaspoon cayenne pepper or according to taste
1 tablespoon olive oil

Method:

1 *Preheat barbecue to a medium heat. Place peanuts, pecans, macadamia nuts and cashews in a bowl and mix to combine. Add paprika, cumin, garam masala, coriander, nutmeg and cayenne pepper and toss to coat.*

2 *Heat oil on barbecue plate (griddle), add nut mixture and cook, turning frequently, for 5 minutes or until nuts are golden. Cool slightly before serving.*
Warning: *the nuts are very hot when first removed from the barbecue and they retain their heat for quite a long time - so caution your guests when you serve these delicious nibbles.*

Serves 6

Oven temperature 180°C, 350°F, Gas 4

smoked
salmon and watercress roulade

Method:

1 Place watercress leaves, parsley, egg yolks, flour and pepper to taste in a food processor and process until mixture is smooth. Transfer watercress mixture to a bowl. Place egg whites in a bowl and beat until stiff peaks form. Fold egg white mixture into watercress mixture.

2 Spoon roulade mixture into a greased and lined 26x32cm/10½x12¾ in Swiss roll tin and bake for 5 minutes or until just cooked. Turn roulade onto a damp teatowel and roll up from short side. Set aside to cool.

3 To make filling, place cream cheese, sour cream, smoked salmon and lemon juice in a food processor and process until mixture is smooth. Stir gelatine mixture into smoked salmon mixture.

4 Unroll cold roulade, spread with filling and reroll. Cover and chill. Cut into slices to serve.

Serves 10

ingredients

1 bunch/90g/3oz watercress
1 teaspoon finely chopped fresh parsley
2 eggs, separated
2 tablespoons flour
freshly ground black pepper

Smoked salmon filling
60g/2oz cream cheese
2 tablespoons sour cream
90g/3oz smoked salmon
1 teaspoon lemon juice
1½ teaspoons gelatine dissolved in
1½ tablespoons hot water, cooled

fruit
and cheese platter

Photograph page 625

Method:

1 *Place lemon juice in a small bowl, add red and green apple wedges and toss to coat. This will help prevent the apple wedges from going brown.*
2 *Arrange red and green apple wedges, kiwifruit slices, orange segments, Camembert, Stilton and tasty (mature cheddar) cheeses attractively with biscuits and dip on a large platter.*
Note: *Choose fruit in season and arrange with your favorite cheeses on a large platter.*
Serves 10

ingredients

**3 tablespoons fresh lemon juice
2 red-skinned apples, cored and cut into wedges
2 green-skinned apples, cored and cut into wedges
4 kiwifruit, peeled and cut into slices
2 oranges, peeled, segmented and white pith removed
100g/4oz Camembert cheese
100g/4oz Stilton cheese
100g/4oz tasty cheese (mature cheddar), choose your favourite brand
cheese biscuits, purchased or homemade**

passion fruit
yogurt dip

Photograph page 625

Method:

1 *Place yogurt, honey and passion fruit pulp in a bowl and mix to combine.*
The perfect accompaniment to any fresh fruit.
Makes 2 cups/400g/12¹/₂oz

ingredients

**2 cups/400 g/12¹/₂oz unsweetened natural yogurt
2 tablespoons honey
3 tablespoons passion fruit pulp or pulp 4-5 passion fruit**

guacamole
with tortillas

Photograph page 627

Method:

1 *To make Chilli Butter, place butter, lemon rind, chilli sauce and cumin in a bowl and mix to combine.*
2 *To make Guacamole, place avocado in a bowl and mash with a fork. Stir in tomato, lemon juice and coriander or parsley.*
3 *Place tortillas in a single layer on a baking tray and heat on barbecue for 3-5 minutes or until warm.*
  To serve: *Place Chilli Butter, Guacamole and tortillas on a platter so that each person can spread a tortilla with Chilli Butter, top with Guacamole, then roll up and eat.*

Serves 6

ingredients

6 corn tortillas

Chilli butter
90g/3oz butter
2 teaspoons finely grated lemon rind
2 teaspoons sweet chilli sauce
1 teaspoon ground cumin

Guacamole
1 avocado, halved, stoned and peeled
1 tomato, peeled and finely chopped
2 tablespoons lemon juice
1 tablespoon finely chopped fresh coriander or parsley

cheese
and bacon nachos

Photograph page 627

Method:

1 *Cook bacon, spring onions and chillies in a nonstick frying pan over a medium heat for 4-5 minutes or until crisp. Remove from pan and drain on absorbent kitchen paper.*
2 *Place corn chips in a shallow oven-proof dish and sprinkle with bacon mixture and cheese. Bake for 5-8 minutes or until heated through and cheese is melted. Serve immediately, accompanied with sour cream for dipping.*
  Jalapeño chillies: *These are the medium-to-dark green chillies that taper to a blunt end and are 5-7 1/2 cm/2-3 in long and 2-2 1/2 cm/ 3/4-1 in wide. They are medium-to-hot in taste and are also available canned or bottled.*

Serves 6

ingredients

6 rashers bacon, finely chopped
6 spring onions, finely chopped
4 jalapeño chillies, finely chopped
200g/6 1/2 oz packet corn chips
125g/4oz grated tasty cheese (mature cheddar)
1 cup/250g/8oz sour cream

grilled cod and potatoes

sizzling seafood

With their cooking times fish and

seafood are perfect for barbecuing. This imaginative selection of dishes will have you serving these water creatures from the barbecue regularly.

whole fish
in banana leaves

Method:

1 *Preheat barbecue to a medium heat. Blanch banana leaf in boiling water for 1 minute, drain, pat dry and set aside.*

2 *To make stuffing, place rice, pistachio nuts, sun-dried peppers or tomatoes, spring onions, dill, lemon rind and garlic in a bowl and mix to combine. Spoon stuffing into cavity of fish and secure opening with wooden toothpicks or cocktail sticks.*

3 *Place fish in centre of banana leaf, top with lime slices and dill and fold banana leaf around fish to completely enclose. Secure with wooden toothpicks or cocktail sticks. Alternately wrap fish in lightly oiled aluminium foil.*

4 *Place fish on barbecue grill and cook for 7-10 minutes, turn and cook for 7-10 minutes longer or until flesh flakes when tested with a fork.*

Serves 4

ingredients

1 large banana leaf
1 large whole fish such as sea bass or snapper, cleaned and skin scored at 3cm/1¼in intervals
1 lime, thinly sliced
4 sprigs fresh dill

<u>Nutty rice stuffing</u>
1 cup/220g/7oz wild rice blend, cooked
90g/3oz pistachio nuts, chopped
3 tablespoons finely chopped sun-dried peppers or tomatoes
3 spring onions, chopped
1 tablespoon chopped fresh dill
1 teaspoon finely grated lemon rind
1 clove garlic, chopped

grilled
cod and potatoes

Photograph page 629

Method:

1 *Preheat barbecue to a medium heat. Place 1 tablespoon oil, lime juice and black peppercorns in a bowl and mix to combine. Brush oil mixture over fish and marinate at room temperature for 10 minutes.*

2 *Brush potatoes with oil and sprinkle with salt. Place potatoes on lightly oiled barbecue grill and cook for 5 minutes each side or until tender and golden. Move potatoes to side of barbecue to keep warm.*

3 *Place fish on lightly oiled barbecue grill and cook for 3-5 minutes each side or until flesh flakes when tested with a fork. To serve, arrange potatoes attractively on serving plates and top with fish.*

Serves

ingredients

3 tablespoons olive oil
2 tablespoons lime juice
1 teaspoon crushed black peppercorns
4 cod cutlets
6 potatoes, very thinly sliced
sea salt

hot
chilli shrimp

Method:

1 To make marinade, place black pepper, chilli sauce, soy sauce, garlic and lemon juice in a bowl and mix to combine. Add shrimp, toss to coat, cover and set aside to marinate for 1 hour. Toss several times during marinating.

2 To make Mango Cream, place mango flesh and coconut milk in a food processor or blender and process until smooth.

3 Preheat barbecue to a medium heat. Drain shrimp and cook on lightly oiled barbecue for 3-4 minutes or until prawns change colour. Serve immediately with Mango Cream.

Coconut milk: *This can be purchased in a number of forms: canned, as a long-life product in cartons, or as a powder to which you add water. Once opened it has a short life and should be used within a day or so. It is available from Asian food stores and some supermarkets, however if you have trouble finding it you can easily make your own. To make coconut milk, place 500 g/1 lb desiccated coconut in a bowl and add 3 cups/750mL/1¼pt of boiling water. Set aside to stand for 30 minutes, then strain, squeezing the coconut to extract as much liquid as possible. This will make a thick coconut milk. The coconut can be used again to make a weaker coconut milk.*

Serves 6

ingredients

1½kg/3 lb uncooked large shrimp, peeled and deveined with tails left intact

Chilli marinade
2 teaspoons cracked black pepper
2 tablespoons sweet chilli sauce
1 tablespoon soy sauce
1 clove garlic, crushed
¼ cup/60 mL/2 fl oz lemon juice

Mango cream
1 mango, peeled, stoned and roughly chopped
3 tablespoons coconut milk

salmon
cutlets with pineapple salsa

Method:

1 *Preheat barbecue to a medium heat. Cook salmon cutlets on lightly oiled barbecue for 3-5 minutes each side or until flesh flakes when tested with a fork.*

2 *To make salsa, place pineapple, spring onions, chilli, lemon juice and mint in a food processor or blender and process to combine. Serve at room temperature with salmon cutlets.*

Cook's tip: *If fresh pineapple is unavailable use a can of drained crushed pineapple in natural juice in its place.*

Note: *This salsa is delicious served with any fish or barbecued chicken.*

Serves 4

ingredients

4 salmon cutlets, cut 2¹/₂cm/I in thick

Pineapple salsa
250g/8oz roughly chopped fresh pineapple
2 spring onions, finely chopped
I fresh red chilli, seeded and finely chopped
I tablespoon lemon juice
2 tablespoons finely chopped fresh mint

squid
and scallop salad

Method:

1 To make dressing, place ginger, rosemary, garlic, oil, lime juice and vinegar in a screwtop jar and shake well to combine. Set aside.

2 Preheat barbecue to a high heat. Place red and yellow or green pepper halves, skin side down on lightly oiled barbecue grill and cook for 5-10 minutes or until skins are blistered and charred. Place peppers in a plastic food bag or paper bag and set aside until cool enough to handle. Remove skins from peppers and cut flesh into thin strips.

3 Cut squid (calamari) tubes lengthwise and open out flat. Using a sharp knife cut parallel lines down the length of the squid (calamari), taking care not to cut through the flesh. Make more cuts in the opposite direction to form a diamond pattern. Cut into 5cm/2in squares.

4 Place squid (calamari) and scallops on lightly oiled barbecue plate (griddle) and cook, turning several times, for 3 minutes or until tender. Set aside to cool slightly.

5 Combine red and yellow or green peppers, asparagus, onion and coriander. Line a large serving platter with rocket or watercress, top with vegetables, squid (calamari) and scallops. Drizzle with dressing and serve immediately.

Serves 4

ingredients

I red pepper, seeded and halved
I yellow or green pepper, seeded and halved
2 squid (calamari) tubes
250g/8oz scallops, roe (coral) removed
250g/8oz asparagus, cut into 5cm/2in pieces, blanched
I red onion, sliced
3 tablespoons fresh coriander leaves
I bunch rocket or watercress

Herb and balsamic dressing
I tablespoon finely grated fresh ginger
I tablespoon chopped fresh rosemary
I clove garlic, crushed
$^1/_4$ cup/60mL/2fl oz olive oil
2 tablespoons lime juice
I tablespoon balsamic or red wine vinegar

home
smoked trout

Method:

1 Place smoking chips and wine in a non-reactive metal dish and stand for 1 hour.

2 Preheat covered barbecue to a low heat. Place dish, with smoking chips in, in barbecue over hot coals, cover barbecue with lid and heat for 5-10 minutes or until liquid is hot.

3 Place trout on a wire rack set in a roasting tin. Brush trout lightly with oil, then top with onions, lemon and dill. Position roasting tin containing trout on rack in barbecue, cover barbecue with lid and smoke for 15-20 minutes or until trout flakes when tested with fork.

Note: This recipe is also suitable for a smoke box.

Serves 4

ingredients

1 cup/125g/4oz smoking chips
¹/₂ cup/125mL/4fl oz white wine
4 small rainbow trout, cleaned, with head and tail intact
1 tablespoon vegetable oil
3 red onions, thinly sliced
1 lemon, thinly sliced
8 sprigs dill

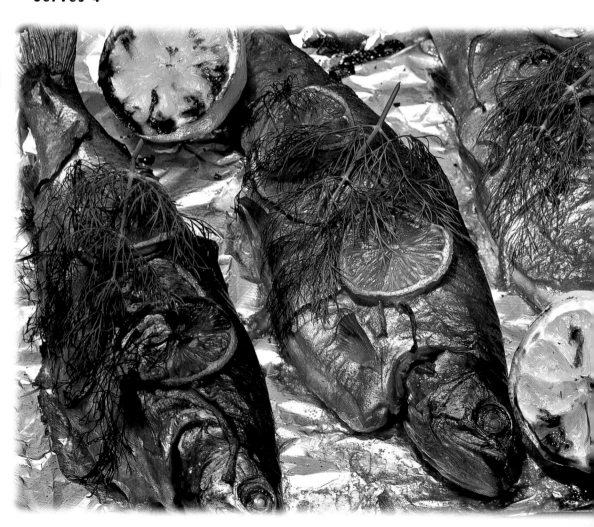

salmon
skewers

Method:

1 Preheat barbecue to a medium heat. Thread salmon and snow peas (mangetout), alternately, onto lightly oiled skewers.

2 Place mustard, thyme, cumin, lemon juice and honey in a bowl and mix to combine. Brush mustard mixture over salmon and cook on lightly oiled barbecue grill for 2-3 minutes each side or until salmon is just cooked.

Note: Watch a lit barbecue at all times and keep children and pets away from hot barbecues and equipment.

Serves 4

ingredients

500g/1 lb salmon fillet, cut into
2¹/₂cm/1 in squares
250g/8oz snow peas (mangetout), trimmed
1 tablespoon wholegrain mustard
2 teaspoons chopped fresh
lemon thyme or thyme
¹/₂ teaspoon ground cumin
2 tablespoons lemon juice
2 teaspoons honey

sesame shrimp
cakes

Photograph page 637

Method:

1 Preheat barbecue to a medium heat. Place shrimp, crab meat, spring onions, basil, chilli, cumin, paprika and egg white into a food processor and process until well combined. Take 4 tablespoons of mixture, shape into a pattie and roll in sesame seeds to coat. Repeat with remaining mixture to make six patties.

2 Heat oil on barbecue plate (griddle) for 2-3 minutes or until hot, add patties and cook for 10 minutes each side or until patties are golden and cooked.

Note: If fresh crab meat is unavailable drained canned crab can be used instead. These fish cakes are delicious served with a sweet chilli sauce for dipping. Sweet chilli sauce is available from Oriental food shops and some supermarkets.

Serves 6

ingredients

315g/10oz uncooked, shelled and deveined shrimp
250g/8oz fresh crab meat
3 spring onions, chopped
2 tablespoons finely chopped fresh basil
1 fresh red chilli, finely chopped
1 teaspoon ground cumin
1 teaspoon paprika
1 egg white
155g/5oz sesame seeds
1 tablespoon vegetable oil

lemon grass
shrimp

Photograph page 637

Method:

1 Wash shrimp, leaving shells and heads intact and place in a shallow glass or ceramic dish.

2 Place lemon grass, spring onions, chillies, garlic, ginger and shrimp paste in a food processor or blender and process until smooth. Add sugar and coconut milk and process to combine. Spoon mixture over prawns, toss to combine, cover and marinate in the refrigerator for 3-4 hours.

3 Preheat barbecue to a high heat. Drain shrimp, place on barbecue and cook, turning several times, for 5 minutes or until shrimp change color. Serve immediately.

Note: Fresh lemon grass and shrimp paste are available from Oriental food shops and some supermarkets. Lemon grass can also be purchased dried; if using dried lemon grass, soak it in hot water for 20 minutes or until soft before using.

Serves 4

ingredients

1 kg/2 lb uncooked medium shrimp
3 stalks fresh lemon grass, finely chopped
2 spring onions, chopped
2 small fresh red chillies, finely chopped
2 cloves garlic, crushed
2 tablespoons finely grated fresh ginger
1 teaspoon shrimp paste
1 tablespoon brown sugar
1/2 cup/125mL/4fl oz coconut milk

blackened
tuna steaks

Method:

1 *Preheat barbecue to a high heat. To make salsa, place tomatoes, fennel, onion, capers, mint, garlic, lemon juice and orange juice in a bowl and toss to combine. Set aside until ready to serve.*

2 *To make spice mix, place paprika, ground garlic, onion powder, black peppercorns, herbs and cayenne pepper in a bowl and mix to combine. Add tuna, toss to coat and shake off excess.*

3 *Heat oil on barbecue plate (griddle) for 2-3 minutes or until hot, add tuna and cook for 3-4 minutes each side or until blackened and cooked to your liking. Serve immediately with salsa.*

Note: *If tuna is unavailable swordfish or salmon are delicious alternatives. Dried ground garlic is available in the spice section of supermarkets. It has a pungent taste and smell and should be used with care.*

Serves 4

ingredients

**4 thick tuna steaks
2 tablespoons olive oil**

Cajun spice mix
**2 tablespoons sweet paprika
1 tablespoon dried ground garlic
1 tablespoon onion powder
2 teaspoons crushed black peppercorns
2 teaspoons dried mixed herbs
1 teaspoon cayenne pepper**

Fennel tomato salsa
**4 plum (egg or Italian tomatoes), chopped
1 bulb fennel, finely chopped
1 red onion, finely chopped
2 tablespoons capers
1 tablespoon chopped fresh mint
1 clove garlic, crushed
1 tablespoon lemon juice
1 tablespoon orange juice**

oysters
and mussels in shells

Method:

1 Preheat barbecue to a high heat. Place mussels and oysters on barbecue grill and cook for 3-5 minutes or until mussel shells open and oysters are warm. Discard any mussels that do not open after 5 minutes cooking.

2 Place butter, parsley, lemon juice, orange juice and wine in a heavy-based saucepan, place on barbecue and cook, stirring, for 2 minutes or until mixture is bubbling. Place mussels and oysters on a serving platter, drizzle with butter mixture and serve immediately.

Note: Mussels will live out of water for up to 7 days if treated correctly. To keep mussels alive, place them in a bucket, cover with a wet towel and top with ice. Store in a cool place and as the ice melts, drain off the water and replace ice. It is important that the mussels do not sit in the water or they will drown.

Serves 6

ingredients

500g/1 lb mussels, scrubbed and beards removed
24 oysters in half shells
60g/2oz butter, softened
1 tablespoon chopped fresh parsley
2 tablespoons lemon juice
1 tablespoon orange juice
1 tablespoon white wine

cranberry chicken skewers

perfect poultry

This exciting selection of recipes

for chicken, duck and quail are sure to become
barbecue favourites. Included are such tempting
dishes as Cranberry Chicken Skewers, Plum Duck Salad
and Festive Smoked Turkey.

cranberry
chicken skewers

Photograph page 641

Method:

1 *Place ground chicken meat, breadcrumbs, onion, garlic, sage, mixed spice, egg and Tabasco sauce in a bowl and mix to combine.*

2 *Shape chicken mixture around lightly oiled skewers to form 7¹/₂cm/3in sausage shapes. Place skewers on a plate, cover and refrigerate for 2 hours.*

3 *Preheat barbecue to a medium heat. Place skewers on lightly oiled barbecue grill and cook, turning several times, for 5-10 minutes or until skewers are cooked. Drizzle with cranberry sauce and serve immediately.*

Note: *Remember always check the barbecue area before lighting the barbecue. Do not have the barbecue too close to the house and sweep up any dry leaves or anything that might catch fire if hit by a spark.*

Serves 6

ingredients

750g/1¹/₂ lb ground chicken meat
¹/₂ cup/30g/1oz breadcrumbs, made from stale bread
1 onion, diced
2 cloves garlic, crushed
2 tablespoons chopped fresh sage or
1 teaspoon dried sage
1 teaspoon ground mixed spice
1 egg, lightly beaten
¹/₄ teaspoon Tabasco sauce or according to taste
¹/₂ cup/125mL/4fl oz cranberry sauce, warmed

oriental
chicken livers

Method:

1 *To make marinade, place sugar and water in a bowl and mix to dissolve sugar. Add soy sauce, oyster sauce, five spice powder and garlic and mix to combine. Add chicken livers, cover and marinate in the refrigerator for 3 hours.*

2 *Preheat barbecue to a high heat. Drain livers well. Place a piece of liver and water chestnut on each piece of bacon and wrap to enclose. Secure with a wooden toothpick or cocktail stick. Place on lightly oiled barbecue grill and cook, turning several times, for 6-8 minutes or until bacon is crisp and livers are just cooked.*

Note: *Heat the barbecue plate (griddle) or grill and brush lightly with oil before adding the food. This will prevent the food sticking to the barbecue. Remember when brushing with oil to use a brush that can withstand heat - if you use one with nylon bristles they will melt.*

Makes 16

ingredients

125g/4oz chicken livers, trimmed, cleaned and cut into sixteen pieces
8 water chestnuts, halved
8 rashers bacon, rind removed and cut in half

Oriental marinade
1 teaspoon brown sugar
1 tablespoon hot water
2 tablespoons soy sauce
1 tablespoon oyster sauce
¹/₂ teaspoon five spice powder
2 cloves garlic, crushed

chilli
honey drumsticks

Method:

1 To make marinade, place lemon juice, honey, garlic and chilli powder in a bowl and mix to combine.

2 Place drumsticks in a shallow glass or ceramic dish, pour marinade over and toss to coat. Cover and marinate in the refrigerator for at least 2 hours, or overnight, turning several times during marinating.

3 Preheat barbecue to a medium heat. Drain drumsticks and reserve marinade. Cook drumsticks on lightly oiled barbecue, brushing frequently with marinade for 10-15 minutes, or until chicken is tender.

Serves 10

ingredients

10 chicken drumsticks

Chilli honey marinade
¹/₂ **cup/125 mL/4fl oz lemon juice**
¹/₂ **cup/170g/5¹/₂oz honey**
1 clove garlic, crushed
pinch chilli powder

caribbean
spatchcock

Method:

1 To make marinade, place rum, lime rind, lime juice, honey, garlic and ginger in a bowl and mix to combine. Place spatchcock (poussin) halves in a shallow glass or ceramic dish and rub marinade into spatchcocks (poussins). Cover and set aside to marinate for 1 hour.

2 Preheat barbecue to a medium heat. Thread a skewer through wings and legs of each spatchcock (poussin) half and brush with any remaining marinade. Combine black pepper and coriander and press onto skin of birds. Cook on lightly oiled barbecue grill, turning frequently for 15-20 minutes or until birds are cooked through.

Cook's tip: This is also a delicious way to prepare and cook chicken pieces. Instead of using spatchcocks, simply use chicken pieces and prepare and marinate as in this recipe - the cooking time for the chicken pieces will be about the same as for the spatchcocks. You should cook them until the juices run clear.

Serves 6

ingredients

**3 spatchcocks (poussins), halved
2 tablespoons cracked black pepper
1 teaspoon ground coriander**

**Lime marinade
3 tablespoons white rum
2 teaspoons finely grated lime rind
1 tablespoon lime juice
2 tablespoons honey
2 cloves garlic, crushed
1 teaspoon grated fresh ginger**

cajun
chicken with lime sauce

Method:

1. *Preheat barbecue to a high heat.*
2. *To make spice mix, place garlic, paprika, oregano, thyme, salt and black pepper in a bowl and mix to combine. Add chicken and toss to coat. Shake off excess spice mix and cook, turning frequently, on lightly oiled barbecue plate (griddle) for 5-7 minutes or until chicken is tender.*
3. *To make sauce, place yogurt, lime juice, lime rind and cordial in a bowl and mix to combine. Serve with chicken.*

   Note: *For an attractive presentation, place a bowl of dipping sauce in the centre of a serving platter, surround with chicken and garnish with lime wedges.*

Serves 6

ingredients

4 boneless chicken breast fillets, cut into 2cm/³/₄in wide strips

Cajun spice mix
5 cloves garlic, crushed
4 tablespoons paprika
2 tablespoons dried oregano
2 tablespoons dried thyme
2 teaspoons salt
2 teaspoons freshly ground black pepper

Lime dipping
1¹/₂ cups/315g/10oz low-fat natural yogurt
2 tablespoons fresh lime juice
1 tablespoon finely grated lime rind
1 teaspoon lime juice cordial

chilli
lime legs

Photograph page 647

ingredients

¹/₄ cup/60mL/2fl oz lime juice
¹/₄ cup/60mL/2fl oz buttermilk
2 tablespoons sweet chilli sauce
2 tablespoons reduced-salt soy sauce
12 chicken drumsticks, skinned

Method:

1 *Place lime juice, buttermilk, chilli sauce and soy sauce in a shallow glass or ceramic dish and mix to combine. Score each drumstick in several places, add to lime juice mixture, turn to coat, cover and marinate in the refrigerator for 3 hours.*

2 *Preheat barbecue to a medium heat. Drain chicken well and reserve marinade. Place chicken on lightly oiled barbecue grill and cook, basting frequently with reserved marinade and turning occasionally, for 25 minutes or until chicken is cooked.*

Note: *Buttermilk, which has a similar nutritional value to skim milk, is mildly acidic with a creamy taste and a thick consistency. A mixture of 2 tablespoons low-fat natural yogurt and 1 tablespoon reduced-fat milk can be used instead.*

Serves 6

buffalo
chilli chicken

Photograph page 647

ingredients

1 kg/2 lb chicken pieces, skinned
3 spring onions, chopped
2 cloves garlic, crushed
1 cup/250 mL/8 fl oz tomato sauce
¹/₄ cup/60mL/2fl oz beer
1 tablespoon cider vinegar
1 tablespoon honey
1 tablespoon Tabasco sauce or according to taste

Method:

1 *Score larger pieces of chicken at 2cm/³/₄in intervals and set aside.*

2 *Place spring onions, garlic, tomato sauce, beer, vinegar, honey and Tabasco sauce in a shallow glass or ceramic dish and mix to combine. Add chicken, toss to coat, cover and marinate in the refrigerator for 3-4 hours.*

3 *Preheat barbecue to a medium heat. Drain chicken and reserve marinade. Place chicken on lightly oiled barbecue grill and cook, basting frequently with reserved marinade and turning several times, for 10-15 minutes or until chicken is tender and cooked through.*

Note: *The cooking times for the chicken will vary according to the size of the pieces. If you have a variety of sizes, place the larger, longer cooking pieces such as drumsticks and thighs on the barbecue first and cook for 5 minutes, before adding the smaller quicker cooking pieces such as wings and breasts.*

Serves 4

chicken
with creamy pesto stuffing

Method:

1 *To make stuffing, place basil leaves, pine nuts and Parmesan cheese in a food processor and process to finely chopped. Stir basil mixture into cream cheese.*

2 *Cut through backbone of each chicken. Remove both halves of backbone, then turn chicken over and press to flatten.*

3 *Using your fingers or the handle of a wooden spoon, loosen skin over breasts, thighs and legs of chicken. Push stuffing under loosened skin, then thread skewers through wings and legs of chickens.*

4 *Preheat barbecue to a medium heat. Cook chicken on lightly oiled barbecue for 15-20 minutes each side or until chicken is cooked through.*

When is the chicken cooked?

To test your chicken for doneness pierce the thickest part of the chicken at the thigh joint and when the juices run clear the bird is cooked.

Serves 10

ingredients

3 x 1 ½ kg/3 lb chickens

<u>**Creaming pesto stuffing**</u>
90g/3oz basil leaves
60g/2oz pine nuts
½ cup/60g/2oz finely grated
Parmesan cheese
250g/8oz cream cheese, softened

undercover
chicken

Method:

1 *Preheat covered barbecue to a medium heat. Wash chicken inside and out and pat dry with absorbent kitchen paper.*

2 *Place butter, garlic, chives and parsley in a bowl and mix to combine. Using your fingers, loosen skin on breast of chicken. Push butter mixture under skin and smooth out evenly. Place chicken on a wire rack set in a roasting tin and brush with oil. Place prosciutto or ham over chicken breast in a criss-cross pattern and secure in place with wooden toothpicks or cocktail sticks. Pour wine over chicken.*

3 *Place roasting tin on rack in barbecue, cover barbecue with lid and cook for 1½ hours or until chicken is tender. Cover and stand for 10 minutes before carving.*

Note: *Do not handle cooked and uncooked meat and poultry at the same time. This encourages the transfer of bacteria from raw food to cooked food. Always make sure that you have a clean tray or dish to place barbecued food on - do not place it on the same dish as was used for holding it raw - unless it has been thoroughly washed in hot soapy water.*

Serves 6

ingredients

1½ kg/3 lb chicken, cleaned
125 g/4 oz butter, softened
I clove garlic, crushed
2 tablespoons snipped fresh chives
2 tablespoons chopped fresh parsley
I tablespoon olive oil
8 slices prosciutto or lean ham
I cup/250mL/8fl oz white wine

tikka
skewers

Method:

1 Pierce fish strips several times with a fork and place in a shallow glass or ceramic dish.

2 To make marinade, place onion, garlic, ginger, cumin, garam masala, cardamom, turmeric, chilli powder, coriander and tomato paste (purée) in a food processor or blender and process until smooth. Add yogurt and mix to combine. Spoon marinade over fish, toss to combine, cover and marinate in the refrigerator for 3 hours.

3 Preheat barbecue to a medium heat. Drain fish and thread onto lightly oiled skewers. Place skewers on lightly oiled barbecue grill and cook, turning several times, for 5-6 minutes or until fish is cooked.

4 To make raitha, place cucumber, mint and yogurt in a bowl and mix to combine. Serve skewers with lemon wedges and raitha.

Note: When buying fish fillets look for those that are shiny and firm with a pleasant sea smell. Avoid those that are dull, soft, discoloured or oozing water when touched.

Serves 6

ingredients

750g/1¹/₂ lb firm white fish fillets, cut into 2cm/³/₄in wide strips
1 lemon, cut into wedges

Spicy yogurt marinade
1 onion, chopped
4 cloves garlic, crushed
2 teaspoons finely grated fresh ginger
1 tablespoon ground cumin
1 tablespoon garam masala
3 cardamom pods, crushed
1 teaspoon ground turmeric
2 teaspoons chilli powder
2 teaspoons ground coriander
1 tablespoon tomato paste (purée)
1³/₄ cups/350g/11oz natural yogurt

Cucumber raitha
1 cucumber, finely chopped
1 tablespoon chopped fresh mint
1 cup/200g/6¹/₂oz natural yogurt

fragrant
orange quail

Method:

1 To make marinade, place herbs, mustard, orange rind, garlic, cider, orange juice, brandy and oil in a shallow glass or ceramic dish and mix to combine. Add quail, turn to coat, cover and marinate in the refrigerator for 2 hours.

2 Preheat barbecue to a medium heat. Drain quail, place skin side up, on lightly oiled barbecue grill and cook, turning occasionally, for 10 minutes or until quail is tender.

3 For couscous, place couscous in a bowl, pour over boiling water, cover and set aside to stand for 10 minutes or until water is absorbed. Toss with a fork, add sultanas, hazelnuts, spring onions and lemon juice and toss to combine. To serve, line a large serving platter with couscous then arrange quail attractively on top.

Note: Often thought of as a type of grain couscous is actually a pasta made from durum wheat, however cook and use it in the same way as a grain. The name couscous refers to both the raw product and the cooked dish. It is an excellent source of thiamin and iron as well as being a good source of protein and niacin.

Serves 4

ingredients

6 quail, halved

Brandy orange marinade
6 tablespoons chopped fresh mixed herbs
2 tablespoons Dijon mustard
1 tablespoon finely grated orange rind
2 cloves garlic, crushed
¹/₂ cup/125mL/4fl oz cider
¹/₂ cup/125mL/4fl oz orange juice
¹/₄ cup/60mL/2fl oz brandy
1 tablespoon macadamia or walnut oil

Nutty couscous
1 cup/185g/6oz couscous
2 cups/500mL/16fl oz boiling water
90g/3oz sultanas (golden raisins)
60g/2oz hazelnuts, toasted and chopped
2 spring onions, chopped
1 tablespoon lemon juice

chicken
in coals

Photograph page 653

ingredients

**1 ¹/₂ kg/3 lb chicken
60g/2oz butter, melted
2 tablespoons soy sauce
1 tablespoon honey
2 star anise
1 cinnamon stick**

Method:

1 Heat barbecue until flames die down and coals are glowing. The barbecue is ready when you can hold your hand about 10cm/4in from the coals for 4-5 seconds.

2 Cut chicken down back bone and press to flatten. Place butter, soy sauce and honey in a bowl and mix to combine. Brush butter mixture over chicken and place on a sheet of nonstick baking paper large enough to completely enclose chicken. Top chicken with star anise and cinnamon stick and wrap in baking paper. Then wrap paper parcel in a double thickness of aluminium foil.

3 Place chicken in coals and cook, turning several times, for 45-60 minutes or until chicken is cooked and tender.

Note: For this recipe the chicken is actually cooked in the coals of the barbecue so it is important that the fire is not too hot. If using wood the fire should burn down to red hot glowing embers. When using charcoal or heat beads the coals should be glowing and partially covered by grey ash. Charcoal takes 15-20 minutes to reach this stage, heat beads 30-40 minutes and wood an hour or more, depending on the variety used.

Serves 4

indian
yogurt kebabs

Photograph page 653

ingredients

6 chicken thigh fillets, halved

Yogurt marinade
**1 tablespoon chopped fresh coriander
2 teaspoons finely grated fresh ginger
1 clove garlic, crushed
2 teaspoons paprika
1 teaspoon ground cumin
¹/₂ teaspoon ground turmeric
¹/₂ teaspoon chilli powder
¹/₂ teaspoon ground cinnamon
1 cup/200g/6¹/₂oz natural yogurt
2 tablespoons lemon juice**

Method:

1 To make marinade, place coriander, ginger, garlic, paprika, cumin, turmeric, chilli powder, cinnamon, yogurt and lemon juice in a shallow glass or ceramic dish and mix well to combine. Add chicken, toss to coat and marinate at room temperature for 30 minutes.

2 Preheat barbecue to a medium heat. Drain chicken and thread three pieces onto a lightly oiled skewer. Repeat with remaining chicken to make four kebabs. Place kebabs on lightly oiled barbecue grill and cook for 4-5 minutes each side or until chicken is cooked and tender.

Note: If chicken thigh fillets are unavailable chicken breast fillets can be used instead. You will need 3 boneless chicken breast fillets, each cut into four pieces.

Serves 4

festive
smoked turkey

Method:

1 Soak smoking chips in brandy in a non-reactive metal dish for 1 hour.

2 To make stuffing, melt butter in a frying pan over a medium heat, add leek and spring onions and cook, stirring, for 3 minutes. Add bacon and cook for 5 minutes longer. Add breadcrumbs, pecans and sage and cook, stirring, for 5 minutes or until breadcrumbs are crisp. Remove from heat, add rice and mix to combine.

3 Preheat covered barbecue to a medium heat. Place dish, with smoking chips in, in barbecue over hot coals, cover barbecue with lid and heat for 5-10 minutes or until liquid is hot.

4 Spoon stuffing into body cavity of turkey. Secure openings with metal or bamboo skewers. Tuck wings under body and tie legs together. Place turkey on a wire rack set in a roasting tin. Combine stock and oil and brush over turkey.

5 Position roasting tin containing turkey on rack in barbecue, cover barbecue with lid and smoke, basting frequently, for 2¹/₂-3 hours or until turkey is cooked.

Note: Disposable aluminium foil trays available from supermarkets are ideal for putting the smoking chips in. The quantity of smoking chips used will determine the final flavor of the smoked food. For a guide follow the manufacturer's instructions, but don't be afraid to experiment.

Serves 8

ingredients

1 cup/125g/4oz smoking chips
¹/₂ cup/125mL/4fl oz brandy
3 kg/6 lb turkey, neck and giblets removed, trimmed of excess fat
¹/₂ cup/125mL/4fl oz chicken stock
2 tablespoons vegetable oil

Sage and rice stuffing
60g/2oz butter
1 leek, thinly sliced
4 spring onions chopped
3 rashers bacon, chopped
1 cup/60g/2oz breadcrumbs, made from stale bread
60g/2oz pecans, chopped
2 tablespoons chopped fresh sage or
1 teaspoon dried sage
1¹/₂ cups/280g/9oz rice, cooked

plum
duck salad

Method:

1 To make marinade, place ginger, mustard, garlic, plum sauce, vinegar and oil in a shallow glass or ceramic dish and mix to combine. Add duck and onions, turn to coat, cover and marinate in the refrigerator for 4 hours.

2 Preheat barbecue to a medium heat. Drain duck and onions well and reserve marinade. Place duck and onions on lightly oiled barbecue plate (griddle) and cook, basting frequently with reserved marinade and turning occasionally, for 10 minutes or until duck is tender. Set aside to cool slightly, then cut duck into thin slices.

3 Line a serving platter with lettuce and snow peas (mangetout), top with duck, onions, Camembert cheese, raspberries and almonds and toss gently to combine.

4 To make dressing, place orange juice, oil, vinegar and mustard in a bowl and whisk to combine. Drizzle dressing over salad and serve immediately.

Note: Mizuna lettuce has a long thin jagged leaf and makes a pretty base for this salad. If it is unavailable any soft leaf lettuce of your choice is a suitable alternative.

Serves 6

ingredients

3 duck breasts, skinned
2 onions, thinly sliced
1 mizuna lettuce, leaves separated
185g/6oz snow peas (mangetout),
cut into thin strips
185g/6oz Camembert cheese, sliced
185g/6oz raspberries
60g/2oz raw almonds, roasted

Mustard marinade
1 tablespoon grated fresh ginger
1 tablespoon wholegrain mustard
1 clove garlic, crushed
1/4 cup/60mL/2fl oz plum sauce
1 tablespoon raspberry or
white wine vinegar
1 tablespoon vegetable oil

Orange dressing
1/4 cup/60mL/2fl oz orange juice
2 tablespoons vegetable oil
1 tablespoon raspberry vinegar
1 tablespoon Dijon mustard

thai lamb noodle salad

make
mine
meat

Here you will find new ways to

make the most of your favourite cuts of meat. Why not try a Marinated Leg of Lamb or Mixed Satays at your next barbecue.

thai lamb
and noodle salad

Photograph page 657

Method:

1 *Combine lemon grass, garlic, lime juice, oil, chilli sauce and fish sauce in a glass or ceramic dish and mix to combine. Add lamb, turn to coat, cover and marinate in the refrigerator for 3 hours.*

2 *Preheat barbecue to a medium heat. To make salad, prepare noodles according to packet directions. Drain and place in a bowl. Add spring onions, red pepper, bean sprouts and coriander and toss to combine. Set aside.*

3 *To make dressing, place lime juice, fish sauce, honey and chilli powder in a screwtop jar and shake well to combine. Set aside.*

4 *Drain lamb and cook on lightly oiled barbecue, turning several times, for 5-10 minutes or until cooked to your liking. Slice lamb diagonally into 2cm/³⁄₄in thick slices.*

5 *To serve, place salad on a large serving platter, arrange lamb attractively on top and drizzle with dressing. Serve immediately.*

Note: Rice noodles, also called rice vermicelli or rice sticks, vary in size from a narrow vermicelli style to a ribbon noodle about 5 mm/1/4 in wide. Made from rice flour, the noodles should be soaked before using; the narrow noodles require about 10 minutes soaking, while the wider ones will need about 30 minutes.

Serves 6

ingredients

**1 stalk fresh lemon grass, chopped or
¹⁄₂ teaspoon dried lemon grass, soaked
in hot water until soft
2 cloves garlic, crushed
¹⁄₄ cup/60mL/2fl oz lime juice
2 tablespoons vegetable oil
2 tablespoons sweet chilli sauce
1 tablespoon fish sauce
750g/1¹⁄₂ lb lamb fillets, trimmed of
excess fat and sinew**

**<u>Rice noodle salad</u>
155g/5oz rice noodles
6 spring onions, chopped
1 red pepper, chopped
60g/2oz bean sprouts
3 tablespoons fresh coriander leaves**

**<u>Lime and chilli dressing</u>
¹⁄₄ cup/60mL/2fl oz lime juice
1 tablespoon fish sauce
1 tablespoon honey
pinch chilli powder or
according to taste**

lamb
with honeyed onions

Method:

1 To make marinade, place mint, garlic, yogurt, mustard and mint sauce in a shallow glass or ceramic dish and mix to combine. Add lamb, turn to coat, cover and marinate in the refrigerator for 3 hours.

2 Preheat barbecue to a medium heat. For Honeyed Onions, heat oil on barbecue plate (griddle), add onions and cook, stirring constantly, for 10 minutes. Add honey and vinegar and cook, stirring, for 5 minutes longer or until onions are very soft and golden.

3 Drain lamb, place on lightly oiled barbecue and cook for 2-3 minutes each side or until cooked to your liking. Serve with onions.

Note: Before lighting a gas barbecue check that all the gas fittings and hose connections are tight and fitting correctly.

Serves 6

ingredients

12 lamb cutlets, trimmed of excess fat

Yogurt marinade
1 tablespoon chopped fresh mint
1 clove garlic, crushed
1 cup/200 g/61/2 oz low-fat natural yogurt
2 tablespoons wholegrain mustard
1 tablespoon prepared mint sauce

Honeyed onions
2 tablespoons olive oil
2 red onions, sliced
1 tablespoon honey
2 tablespoons red wine vinegar

mixed
satays

Method:

1 Weave chicken, beef and pork strips onto skewers and place in a shallow glass or ceramic dish.
2 To make marinade, place soy sauce, lime or lemon juice, garlic, ginger, chilli and coriander in a small bowl and mix to combine. Pour marinade over skewers in dish, cover and set aside to marinate for at least 1 hour.
3 Preheat barbecue to a medium heat. Cook kebabs on lightly oiled barbecue, turning frequently for 5-6 minutes, or until meats are cooked.
4 To make sauce, place peanut butter, onion, hoisin sauce, garlic and coconut milk in a food processor or blender and process until smooth. Stir in coriander. Serve with skewers for dipping.

Makes 12 skewers

ingredients

250g/8oz chicken breast fillets, skin removed and sliced into thin strips, lengthwise
250g/8oz beef fillet, sliced into thin strips, lengthwise
250g/8oz pork fillet, sliced into thin strips, lengthwise
12 skewers, lightly oiled

Chilli marinade
¹/₄ cup/60mL/2fl oz soy sauce
2 tablespoons lime or lemon juice
2 cloves garlic, crushed
2 teaspoons finely grated fresh ginger
1 fresh red chilli, finely chopped
1 tablespoon finely chopped fresh coriander

Peanut sauce
¹/₂ cup/125g/4oz crunchy peanut butter
1 onion, finely chopped
2 tablespoons hoisin sauce
2 cloves garlic, crushed
¹/₂ cup/125mL/4fl oz coconut milk
2 tablespoons finely chopped fresh coriander

barbecued
steak sandwiches

Method:

1 To make marinade, place wine, oil, garlic and ginger in a bowl and mix to combine. Place steaks in a shallow glass or ceramic dish. Pour marinade over, cover, and marinate at room temperature for 2-3 hours or overnight in the refrigerator.

2 Cook onions on lightly oiled barbecue plate (griddle) or in a lightly oiled frying pan on barbecue for 10-15 minutes or until golden. Preheat barbecue to a medium heat. Drain steaks and cook on lightly oiled barbecue for 3-5 minutes each side or until cooked to your liking.

3 Lightly brush bread slices with oil and cook on barbecue grill for 1-2 minutes each side or until lightly toasted. To assemble sandwiches, top 6 toasted bread slices with steak, onions and remaining bread slices.

Cook's tip: You may like to add some salad ingredients to your sandwiches. Mustard or relish is also a tasty addition.

Marinated steak, barbecued and placed between slices of grilled bread makes the best steak sandwiches you will ever taste.

Serves 6

ingredients

6 lean rump steaks, cut 1cm/¹/₂in thick
3 onions, finely sliced
12 thick slices wholemeal or grain bread
olive oil

Ginger wine marinade
1 cup/250mL/8fl oz red wine
¹/₂ cup/125mL/4fl oz olive oil
1 clove garlic, crushed
2 teaspoons grated fresh ginger

lamb
cutlets with honey butter

Method:

1 To make Honey Butter, place butter, mint, honey and black pepper to taste in a small bowl and mix to combine. Place mixture on plastic food wrap and roll into a cylindrical shape. Refrigerate until hard.

2 Preheat barbecue to a medium heat. Place oil and garlic in a small bowl and mix to combine. Wrap ends of cutlet bones in aluminium foil to prevent burning during cooking. Brush cutlets with oil mixture and cook on barbecue plate (griddle) for 3 minutes each side or until lamb is tender.

3 Cut butter into small rounds and serve with cutlets.

Cook's tip: Interesting butter shapes can be made by using small cookie cutter shapes.

Serves 4

ingredients

1 tablespoon vegetable oil
1 clove garlic, crushed
8 lamb cutlets

Honey butter
90g/3oz butter, softened
2 tablespoons chopped fresh mint
1 tablespoon honey
freshly ground black pepper

pork steaks
with apple stuffing

Method:

1 Place butterfly steaks on a board and, using a meat mallet, flatten slightly.

2 To make stuffing, melt butter in a frying pan and cook onion and bacon for 4-5 minutes or until bacon is crisp. Add apple and cook until apple is soft. Place apple mixture in a bowl, add bread crumbs, egg, mozzarella cheese and parsley and mix to combine. Season to taste with black pepper.

3 Preheat barbecue to a medium heat. Place spoonfuls of stuffing on one side of each butterfly steak, then fold over and secure with toothpicks. Cook on lightly oiled barbecue for 5-6 minutes each side or until steaks are cooked.

Serves 6

ingredients

6 pork butterfly steaks

Apple stuffing
30g/1oz butter
1 onion, finely chopped
2 rashers bacon, finely chopped
1 apple, cored and finely chopped
1¹/₂ cups/90g/3oz bread crumbs, made from stale bread
1 egg, lightly beaten
155g/5oz mozzarella cheese, cut into small cubes
2 tablespoons chopped fresh parsley
freshly ground black pepper

fruity
barbecued lamb

Photograph page 665

Method:

1 *Score the thickest part of each lamb shank (knuckle) to allow for even cooking.*

2 *Place chutney, crushed garlic, ginger, apple juice, wine and oil in a shallow ovenproof glass, ceramic or enamel dish and mix to combine. Add lamb, turn to coat, cover and marinate in the refrigerator for 2 hours. Remove lamb from refrigerator and bake in oven for 1 hour.*

3 *Preheat barbecue to a medium heat. Remove lamb from baking dish and place on lightly oiled barbecue, add garlic bulbs and cook, turning occasionally, for 30 minutes or until lamb and garlic are tender.*

Note: *Use fresh young garlic for this recipe, its flavor is milder than more mature garlic and when cooked develops a delicious nutty taste. Lamb chops are also delicious cooked in this way, however no precooking is required and the cooking time on the barbecue will only be 3-5 minutes each side.*

Serves 4

ingredients

4 lamb shanks (knuckles)
2 tablespoons mango chutney
2 cloves garlic, crushed
1 tablespoon finely grated fresh ginger
1/4 cup/60mL/2fl oz apple juice
1/4 cup/60ml/2fl oz white wine
2 tablespoons olive oil
**4 bulbs young garlic,
cut in half horizontally**

Oven temperature 180°C, 350°F, Gas 4

rosemary
and thyme chops

Photograph page 665

Method:

1 *To make marinade, place rosemary, thyme, garlic, oil, vinegar and lime juice in a shallow glass or ceramic dish and mix to combine. Add lamb, turn to coat, cover and marinate at room temperature for 1 hour.*

2 *Preheat barbecue to a high heat. Drain lamb, place on lightly oiled barbecue and cook for 3-5 minutes each side or until chops are cooked to your liking.*

Note: *Long-handled tongs are a must for turning food without burning your hands.*

Serves 6

ingredients

**12 lamb neck chops, trimmed
of excess fat**

Fresh herb marinade
2 tablespoons chopped fresh rosemary
2 tablespoons chopped fresh thyme
2 cloves garlic, crushed
1/4 cup/60mL/2fl oz olive oil
**1/4 cup/60mL/2fl oz balsamic or
red wine vinegar**
2 tablespoons lime juice

marinated
leg of lamb

Method:

1 Lay lamb out flat and season well with black pepper. Place in a shallow glass or ceramic dish.

2 To make marinade, place garlic, oil, lemon juice, marjoram and thyme in a small bowl and mix to combine. Pour marinade over lamb, cover and allow to marinate at room temperature for 3-4 hours, or overnight in the refrigerator.

3 Preheat barbecue to a medium heat. Remove lamb from marinade and reserve marinade. Cook lamb on lightly oiled barbecue grill, turning several times during cooking and basting with reserved marinade, for 15-25 minutes or until cooked to your liking.

Cook's tip: Try lemon thyme instead of ordinary thyme in this recipe. Your butcher will butterfly the leg in minutes for you, or you can do it yourself.

Serves 6

ingredients

1 ¹/₂-2 kg/3-4 lb leg of lamb, butterflied
freshly ground black pepper

Lemon herb marinade
2 cloves garlic, crushed
¹/₄ cup/60mL/2fl oz olive oil
¹/₄ cup/60mL/2fl oz lemon juice
1 tablespoon finely chopped fresh
marjoram or 1 teaspoon dried marjoram
1 tablespoon finely chopped fresh thyme
or 1 teaspoon dried thyme

hot chilli
pork spareribs

Method:

1 Season ribs with black pepper and place in a shallow glass or ceramic dish. Combine apple juice, lime juice and Tabasco sauce, pour over ribs and toss to coat. Cover and refrigerate for 1-2 hours.

2 To make glaze, heat oil in a saucepan and cook onions, garlic and chilli over a medium heat for 10 minutes or until onions are soft. Stir in apple purée, jelly and juice, bring to simmering and simmer, stirring frequently, for 15 minutes or until mixture thickens. Stir in lime juice and season to taste with black pepper and cook for 15 minutes longer or until mixture thickens.

3 Preheat barbecue to a medium heat. Drain ribs and sear on lightly oiled barbecue for 5 minutes each side, brushing with reserved apple juice mixture frequently. Brush ribs with warm glaze and cook, turning, for 5 minutes longer. Serve ribs with remaining glaze.

Note: Apple, pork and chilli combine for the tastiest spareribs ever.

Serves 6

ingredients

6 small pork back rib racks
freshly ground black pepper
¹/₂ cup/125mL/4fl oz apple juice
¹/₄ cup/60mL/2fl oz lime juice
dash Tabasco sauce

Apple chilli glaze
1 tablespoons vegetable oil
2 onions, finely chopped
2 cloves garlic, crushed
1 fresh red chilli, seeded
and finely chopped
125g/4oz canned apple purée
1 cup/315g/10oz apple jelly
¹/₂ cup/125mL/4fl oz apple juice
2 tablespoons lime juice
freshly ground black pepper

steaks
with blue butter

Method:

1 *To make Blue Butter, place butter, blue cheese, parsley and paprika in a bowl and beat to combine. Place butter on a piece of plastic food wrap and roll into a log shape. Refrigerate for I hour or until firm.*

2 *Preheat barbecue to a high heat.*

3 *Place black pepper and oil in a bowl and mix to combine. Brush steaks lightly with oil mixture. Place steaks on lightly oiled barbecue grill and cook for 3-5 minutes each side or until steaks are cooked to your liking.*

4 *Cut butter into 2cm/³⁄₄in thick slices and top each steak with I or 2 slices. Serve immediately.*
   Note: *Any leftover Blue Butter can be stored in the freezer to use at a later date. It is also delicious served with grilled lamb chops or cutlets and grilled vegetables such as eggplant (aubergine), red and green peppers and zucchini (courgettes).*
   Serves 6

ingredients

I tablespoon freshly ground
black pepper
2 tablespoons olive oil
6 fillet steaks, trimmed of excess fat

<u>Blue butter</u>
125g/4oz butter, softened
60g/2oz blue cheese
I tablespoon chopped fresh parsley
I teaspoon paprika

beef
and bacon burgers

Method:
1 Preheat barbecue to a medium heat. Place beef, spring onions, chives, egg, tomato sauce, Worcestershire sauce and chilli sauce in a bowl and mix to combine. Shape mixture into twelve patties. Top six patties with mozzarella cheese, then with remaining patties and pinch edges together to seal. Wrap a piece of bacon around each pattie and secure with a wooden toothpick or cocktail stick. Place on a plate and refrigerate for 2 hours or until patties are firm.

2 Place patties in a lightly oiled hinged wire barbecue frame and cook on barbecue grill for 10-15 minutes or until patties are cooked to your liking and cheese melts.

Note: A hinged wire frame is a useful barbecue accessory. It is ideal for cooking fragile and delicate foods such as fish - whole, fillets and cutlets - and burgers which can fall apart when turning.

Serves 6

ingredients

750g/1 ¹/₂ lb lean ground beef
3 spring onions, chopped
2 tablespoons snipped fresh chives
1 egg, lightly beaten
2 tablespoons tomato sauce
1 tablespoon Worcestershire sauce
1 tablespoon chilli sauce
125g/4oz grated mozzarella cheese
6 rashers bacon, rind removed

cajun
spiced steaks

Method:

1 Preheat barbecue to a high heat. To make salsa, place pineapple, spring onions, coriander, chilli, sugar and vinegar in a bowl and toss to combine. Set aside.

2 To make spice mixture, combine paprika, black peppercorns, thyme, oregano and chilli powder. Rub spice mixture over steaks. Place steaks on lightly oiled barbecue and cook for 3-5 minutes each side or until cooked to your liking. Serve with salsa.

Note: When testing to see if a steak is cooked to your liking, press it with a pair of blunt tongs. Do not cut the meat, as this causes the juices to escape. Rare steaks will feel springy, medium steaks slightly springy and well-done steaks will feel firm. As a guide a 2.5 cm/1 in thick steak cooked to rare takes about 3 minutes each side, a medium steak 4 minutes and a well-done steak 5 minutes.

Serves 4

ingredients

**4 sirloin or fillet steaks, trimmed
of excess fat**

Cajun spice mixture
1 tablespoon sweet paprika
1 teaspoon crushed black peppercorns
1 teaspoon ground thyme
1 teaspoon ground oregano
¼ teaspoon chilli powder

Pineapple chilli salsa
½ pineapple, peeled and chopped
2 spring onions, chopped
1 tablespoon chopped fresh coriander
1 fresh red chilli, chopped
1 tablespoon brown sugar
1 tablespoon white vinegar

korean
bulgogi

Method:

1 Place garlic, ginger, soy sauce, honey and chilli sauce in a bowl and mix to combine. Add beef, toss to coat, cover and marinate in the refrigerator for 4 hours.

2 Preheat barbecue to a high heat. Heat 1 tablespoon oil on barbecue plate (griddle), add beef and stir-fry for 1-2 minutes or until beef just changes colour. Push beef to side of barbecue to keep warm.

3 Heat remaining oil on barbecue plate (griddle), add onions and bean sprouts and stir-fry for 4-5 minutes or until onions are golden. Add beef to onion mixture and stir-fry for 1-2 minutes longer. Sprinkle with sesame seeds and serve immediately.

Note: Serve with steamed white or brown rice and a tossed green salad.

Serves 6

ingredients

4 cloves garlic, crushed
2 teaspoons finely grated fresh ginger
1/4 cup/60mL/2fl oz soy sauce
3 tablespoons honey
1 tablespoon sweet chilli sauce
**750g/1 1/2 lb rump steak, trimmed of
visible fat and thinly sliced**
2 tablespoons vegetable oil
2 onions, sliced
125g/4oz bean sprouts
2 tablespoons sesame seeds

barbecued pumpkin pizza

vegetarian variety

Given the number of people who now

choose to be vegetarians or semi-vegetarians it is a good idea to serve a vegetarian alternative - these recipes fit the bill and are sure to be popular with everyone.

vegetarian
variety

basic
pizza dough

ingredients

1 teaspoon active dry yeast
pinch sugar
$^2/_3$ cup/170mL/5$^1/_2$fl oz warm water
2 cups/250g/8oz flour
$^1/_2$ teaspoon salt
$^1/_4$ cup/60mL/2fl oz olive oil

Method:

1 *Place yeast, sugar and water in a bowl and mix to dissolve. Set aside in a warm, draught-free place for 5 minutes or until mixture is foamy.*

2 *Place flour and salt in a food processor and pulse once or twice to sift. With machine running, slowly pour in yeast mixture and oil and process to form a rough dough. Turn dough onto a lightly floured surface and knead for 5 minutes or until soft and shiny. Add more flour if necessary.*

3 *Place dough in a lightly oiled large bowl, roll dough around bowl to cover surface with oil. Cover bowl with plastic food wrap and place in a warm draught-free place for 1-1/1$_2$ hours or until doubled in size. Knock down, knead lightly and use as desired.*

Note: *There are two types of yeast commonly used in bread-making - fresh and dry. Dry yeast is twice as concentrated as fresh yeast. You will find that 15g/$^1/_2$oz dry yeast has the same raising power as 30g/1oz fresh yeast.*

Makes enough dough for 4 individual pizzas or 1 large pizza

barbecued
pumpkin pizza

Photograph page 673

ingredients

1 quantity Basic Pizza Dough (as above)

Pumpkin feta topping
1 tablespoon olive oil
8 large slices pumpkin, peeled and seeds removed
1 onion, sliced
315g/10oz feta cheese, crumbled
1 tablespoon chopped fresh thyme
freshly ground black pepper

Method:

1 *Preheat barbecue to a high heat. To make topping, heat oil on barbecue plate (griddle) for 2-3 minutes or until hot, add pumpkin and onion and cook for 5 minutes each side or until soft and golden. Set aside.*

2 *Divide dough into four portions and roll into rounds 3mm/$^1/_8$in thick. Place dough rounds on lightly oiled barbecue and cook for 3-5 minutes or until brown and crisp. Turn over, top with pumpkin, onion, feta cheese, thyme and black pepper to taste and cook for 4-6 minutes longer or until pizza crust is crisp, golden and cooked through. Serve immediately.*

Note: *Orange sweet potatoes make a delicious alternative to the pumpkin in this recipe.*

Serves 4

char-grilled
mushrooms and toast

Method:

1 *Preheat barbecue to a medium heat. Brush mushrooms with oil and cook on lightly oiled barbecue for 4-5 minutes or until cooked. Brush both sides of the bread with remaining oil and cook for 2-3 minutes each side or until golden.*

2 *Rub one side of each bread slice with cut side of garlic clove. Top each slice of bread with mushrooms, sprinkle with parsley, chives and basil. Season to taste with black pepper and serve immediately.*

Note: *This delicious first course takes only minutes to cook.*

Serves 2

ingredients

6 flat mushrooms
¹/₄ cup/60mL/2fl oz olive oil
2 thick slices of bread
I clove garlic, cut in half
2 teaspoons finely chopped fresh parsley
2 teaspoons snipped fresh chives
I teaspoon finely chopped fresh basil
freshly ground black pepper

vegetable
burgers

Method:

1 To make patties, boil, steam or microwave broccoli, zucchini (courgettes) and carrots until tender. Drain, rinse under cold running water and pat dry.

2 Place broccoli, zucchini (courgettes), carrots, onions, garlic and parsley in a food processor and process until puréed. Transfer vegetable mixture to a mixing bowl, add bread crumbs and flour, season with black pepper and mix to combine. Cover and refrigerate for 30 minutes.

3 Shape mixture into ten patties. Place on a tray lined with nonstick baking paper, cover and refrigerate until required.

4 To make sauce, heat oil in a saucepan and cook onion, garlic, chilli and green pepper for 5 minutes or until onion and green pepper are soft. Add tomatoes, bring mixture to the boil, then reduce heat and simmer for 15-20 minutes or until sauce thickens. Season to taste with black pepper.

5 Preheat barbecue to a medium heat. Cook patties on lightly oiled barbecue plate (griddle) or in a lightly oiled frying pan on barbecue for 3-4 minutes each side. Toast rolls on barbecue. Place a lettuce leaf, a pattie, and a spoonful of sauce on the bottom half of each roll, top with remaining roll half and serve immediately.

Makes 10 burgers

ingredients

10 wholemeal rolls, split
10 lettuce leaves

Mixed vegetable patties
500g/1 lb broccoli, chopped
500g/1 lb zucchini (courgettes), chopped
250g/8oz carrots, chopped
2 onions, finely chopped
2 cloves garlic, crushed
3 tablespoons chopped parsley
3 cups/185g/6oz dried bread crumbs
1/2 cup/60g/2oz flour, sifted
freshly ground black pepper

Spicy tomato sauce
1 tablespoon olive oil
1 onion, finely chopped
1 clove garlic, crushed
1 fresh red chilli, seeded and finely chopped
1 green pepper, finely chopped
440g/14oz canned tomatoes,
undrained and mashed
freshly ground black pepper

char-grilled
vegetable slices

Method:

1 *Preheat barbecue to a medium heat. Place oil and garlic in a small bowl and whisk to combine. Brush eggplant (aubergine) slices, zucchini (courgette) slices, red pepper slices and tomato slices with oil mixture.*

2 *Cook eggplant (aubergine), zucchini (courgette) and red pepper slices on lightly oiled barbecue, turning frequently, for 4-5 minutes or until almost cooked. Add tomato slices to barbecue and cook all vegetables for 2-3 minutes longer.*

Serves 6

ingredients

¹/₂ cup/125mL/4fl oz olive oil
1 clove garlic, crushed
1 large eggplant (aubergine), cut lengthwise into thick slices
3 large zucchini (courgettes), cut lengthwise into thick slices
2 red peppers, cut into quarters, seeds removed
3 large firm tomatoes, cut into thick slices
freshly ground black pepper

mushroom
risotto cakes

Method:

1 Melt butter and oil together in saucepan over a medium heat, add garlic and bacon and cook, stirring, for 3 minutes or until bacon is crisp. Add leek and cook for 3 minutes or until leek is golden. Add rice and mushrooms to pan and cook, stirring, for 3 minutes longer.

2 Stir in ³/₄ cup/185mL/6fl oz hot stock and ¹/₄ cup/60mL/2fl oz wine and cook, stirring constantly, over a medium heat until liquid is absorbed. Continue adding stock and wine in this way, stirring constantly and allowing liquid to be absorbed before adding more.

3 Remove pan from heat, add Parmesan cheese and black pepper to taste and mix to combine. Set aside to cool, then refrigerate for at least 3 hours.

4 Preheat barbecue to a medium heat. Shape tablespoons of rice mixture into patties. Toss in flour to coat and shake off excess. Dip patties in eggs and roll in breadcrumbs to coat. Cook patties on lightly oiled barbecue plate (griddle) for 5 minutes each side or until golden and heated through.

Note: These bite-sized morsels are sure to be a hit with drinks before any barbecue. They can also be cooked in a frying pan over a medium heat on the cooker top.

For a vegetarian version of this recipe omit the bacon and use vegetable stock.

ingredients

30g/1oz butter
1 tablespoon olive oil
2 cloves garlic, crushed
3 rashers bacon, chopped
1 leek, thinly sliced
1¹/₄ cups/280g/9oz Arborio or risotto rice
125g/4oz button mushrooms, sliced
3 cups/750mL/1¹/₄pt hot chicken or vegetable stock
1 cup/250mL/8fl oz dry white wine
60g/2oz grated Parmesan cheese
freshly ground black pepper
¹/₄ cup/30g/1oz flour
2 eggs, lightly beaten
1¹/₂ cups/90g/3oz wholemeal breadcrumbs, made from stale bread

Serves 6

wild
rice and bean patties

Method:
1 *Preheat barbecue to a medium heat. Place soya beans, fresh coriander, spring onions, ginger, cumin, ground coriander and turmeric into a food processor and process for 30 seconds or until mixture resembles coarse breadcrumbs. Transfer mixture to a bowl, add rice, flour and egg and mix to combine. Shape mixture into patties.*

2 *Heat oil on barbecue plate (griddle) for 2-3 minutes or until hot, add patties and cook for 5 minutes each side or until golden and heated through.*

3 *To make chilli yogurt, place yogurt, chilli sauce and lime juice in a bowl and mix to combine. Serve with patties.*

Serves 6

ingredients

440g/14oz canned soya beans, drained and rinsed
6 tablespoons chopped fresh coriander
3 spring onions, chopped
1 tablespoon finely grated fresh ginger
1 tablespoon ground cumin
1 tablespoon ground coriander
¹/₂ teaspoon ground turmeric
¹/₂ cup/100g/3¹/₂oz wild rice blend, cooked
¹/₂ cup/75g/2¹/₂oz wholemeal flour
1 egg, lightly beaten
2 tablespoons vegetable oil

<u>Sweet chilli yogurt</u>
1 cup/200g/6¹/₂oz low-fat natural yogurt
2 tablespoons sweet chilli sauce
1 tablespoon lime juice

nutty
crusted ricotta salad

Method:

1 *Place ricotta cheese in a colander lined with muslin and drain for 1 hour.*

2 *Preheat barbecue to a medium heat. Place Parmesan cheese, pine nuts, paprika, oregano and 2 tablespoons oil in a bowl and mix to combine. Press nut mixture over surface of ricotta cheese to coat.*

3 *Heat remaining oil on barbecue plate (griddle) until hot, then cook ricotta cheese, turning occasionally, for 10 minutes or until golden. Stand for 10 minutes, then cut into slices.*

4 *Line a large serving platter with salad leaves, then arrange snow pea (mangetout) sprouts or watercress, teardrop or cherry tomatoes, avocado, sun-dried tomatoes and ricotta cheese slices attractively on top.*

5 *To make dressing, place garlic, cumin, coriander, chilli flakes, oil, vinegar and honey in a bowl and whisk to combine. Drizzle over salad and serve.*

Note: *If a gas barbecue does not light first time, turn if off, wait 20 seconds and try again. This will ensure that there is no gas build-up.*

Serves 4

ingredients

315g/10oz ricotta cheese in one piece
90g/3oz grated Parmesan cheese
60g/2oz pine nuts, toasted and finely chopped
1 tablespoon sweet paprika
1 tablespoon dried oregano
4 tablespoons olive oil
315g/10oz assorted salad leaves
90g/3oz snow pea (mangetout) sprouts or watercress
185g/6oz yellow teardrop or cherry tomatoes
1 avocado, stoned, peeled and chopped
30g/1oz sun-dried tomatoes, sliced

Spiced honey dressing
2 cloves garlic, crushed
1 teaspoon ground cumin
1 teaspoon ground coriander
pinch red chilli flakes
$^1/_4$ cup/60mL/2fl oz olive oil
1 tablespoon cider vinegar
1 teaspoon honey

couscous
filled mushrooms

Method:

1 *Preheat barbecue to a high heat. Place couscous in a bowl, pour over boiling water, cover and set aside to stand for 5 minutes or until water is absorbed. Add butter and toss gently with a fork.*

2 *Heat oil in a frying pan over a medium heat, add onion and garlic and cook, stirring, for 3 minutes or until onion is soft. Add garam masala and cayenne pepper and cook for 1 minute longer. Add onion mixture to couscous and toss to combine.*

3 *Fill mushrooms with couscous mixture, top with feta cheese and cook on lightly oiled barbecue grill for 5 minutes or until mushrooms are tender and cheese melts.*

Note: *If your barbecue only has a grill, use a large long-handled frying pan when a recipe calls for food to be cooked on the barbecue plate (griddle).*

Serves 4

ingredients

²/₃ cup/125g/4oz couscous
²/₃ cup/170mL/5¹/₂fl oz boiling water
15g/¹/₂oz butter
2 teaspoons olive oil
1 onion, chopped
2 cloves garlic, crushed
1 teaspoon garam masala
pinch cayenne pepper
12 large mushrooms, stalks removed
200g/6¹/₂oz feta cheese, crumbled

warm
vegetable salad

Photograph page 683

ingredients

**6 zucchini (courgettes),
cut lengthwise into quarters
2 red onions, sliced
155g/5oz snow pea (mangetout) sprouts
or watercress
1 yellow or red pepper, chopped
1 avocado, stoned, peeled and chopped**

**<u>Orange dressing</u>
2 tablespoons snipped fresh chives
¼ cup/60mL/2fl oz orange juice
1 tablespoon white wine vinegar
2 teaspoons French mustard**

Method:

1 Preheat barbecue to a medium heat. Place zucchini (courgettes) and onions on lightly oiled barbecue and cook for 2-3 minutes each side or until golden and tender.

2 Arrange snow pea (mangetout) sprouts or watercress, yellow or red pepper and avocado attractively on a serving platter. Top with zucchini (courgettes) and onions.

3 To make dressing, place chives, orange juice, vinegar and mustard in a screwtop jar and shake well to combine. Drizzle over salad and serve immediately.

Note: This salad is delicious served with toasted olive bread.

Serves 4

kebabs
with herb sauce

Photograph page 683

ingredients

**1 green pepper, seeded and cut into
2cm/¾in squares
2 zucchini (courgettes), cut into 2cm/¾in pieces
1 red onion, cut into 2cm/¾in cubes
1 eggplant (aubergine), cut into 2cm/¾in cubes
16 cherry tomatoes
2 tablespoons olive oil
2 tablespoons lemon juice
1 tablespoon chopped fresh oregano or
1 teaspoon dried oregano**

**<u>Herb sauce</u>
1 tablespoon chopped fresh dill
2 tablespoons snipped fresh chives
1 cup/250g/8oz sour cream
2 tablespoons lemon juice**

Method:

1 Preheat barbecue to a medium heat. Thread a piece of green pepper, zucchini (courgette), onion, eggplant (aubergine) and a tomato onto a lightly oiled skewer. Repeat with remaining vegetables to use all ingredients.

2 Combine oil, lemon juice and oregano and brush over kebabs. Place kebabs on lightly oiled barbecue grill and cook, turning several times, for 5-10 minutes or until vegetables are tender.

3 To make sauce, place dill, chives, sour cream and lemon juice in a bowl and mix to combine. Serve with kebabs.

Note: Always keep water close at hand when barbecuing. If a hose or tap is not close by, then have a bucket of water next to the barbecue. A fire extinguisher or fire blanket is also a sensible safety precaution.

Serves 4

grilled
pepper polenta

Method:

1 Place water in a saucepan and bring to the boil. Reduce heat to simmering, then gradually whisk in corn meal (polenta) and cook, stirring, for 20 minutes or until mixture is thick and leaves the sides of the pan.

2 Stir in butter, black peppercorns and grated Parmesan cheese. Spread mixture evenly into a greased 18x28cm/7x11in shallow cake tin and refrigerate until set. Cut polenta in triangles.

3 Brush polenta and vegetables with oil, then cook under a preheated hot grill or on a barbecue grill for 3-5 minutes each side or until polenta is golden and vegetables are brown and tender.

4 To serve, top polenta triangles with rocket, grilled vegetables, pesto and Parmesan cheese shavings.

Note: When grilling or barbecuing polenta as in this recipe it is important that the polenta is placed on the preheated surface and left alone until a crust forms. Once the crust forms completely the polenta can easily be turned. Do not be tempted to try turning it too soon or the delicious crust will be left on the grill.

ingredients

8 cups/2 litres/3 ¹/₂ pt water
2 cups/350g/11oz corn meal (polenta)
125g/4oz butter, chopped
1 tablespoon crushed black peppercorns
125g/4oz grated Parmesan cheese
2 tablespoons olive oil
2 zucchini (courgettes), cut into strips
1 red pepper, cut into thin strips
1 eggplant (aubergine), cut into strips
125g/4oz rocket leaves
¹/₂ cup/125g/4oz ready-made pesto
fresh Parmesan cheese shavings

Serves 8

vegetable
skewers with tahini

Method:

1 Thread zucchini (courgettes), red and yellow or green peppers, squash and feta cheese onto lightly oiled skewers. Brush skewers with oil and cook on a preheated hot barbecue or under a hot grill for 2 minutes each side or until brown and vegetables are tender crisp.

2 To make dip, place tahini, yogurt, lime juice, chilli sauce, tomato paste (purée) and black pepper to taste in a bowl and mix to combine. Serve with kebabs.

Note: When threading the vegetables onto the skewers make sure that the vegetables have a flat outside surface – this will make them easier to grill.

Tahini is a thick oily paste made from crushed toasted sesame seeds. On standing the oil tends to separate out and before using it is necessary to beat it back into the paste. It is available from Middle Eastern food and health food stores and most supermarkets.

Serves 4

ingredients

3 zucchini (courgettes), cut into 2cm/³/₄in cubes
2 red peppers, cut into 2cm/³/₄in cubes
2 yellow or green peppers, cut into 2cm/³/₄in cubes
8 patty pan squash, halved
185 g/6 oz feta cheese, cut into 2cm/³/₄in cubes
2 tablespoons chilli oil

Tahini dip
¹/₂ cup/125g/4oz tahini
3 tablespoons thick natural yogurt
2 tablespoons lime juice
1 tablespoon sweet chilli sauce
1 tablespoon tomato paste (purée)
freshly ground black pepper

No barbecue book would be complete without a section on the extras that seem to make everyone else's barbecue a raging success. In this chapter you will find many secrets for perfect barbecuing.

Savory Butters

Savory butters are a great way to add taste after cooking – place a piece on a steak or in a baked potato. Garlic butter is probably the best known, but you can make a variety of tasty butters.

To make a parsley butter, place 125 g/4 oz softened butter, a dash of lemon juice, 1 tablespoon finely chopped fresh parsley and pepper to taste in a food processor or blender and process to combine. Shape butter into a log, wrap in plastic food wrap and refrigerate until firm.

This is the basic recipe for a savory butter and the parsley can be replaced with any flavoring of your choice. Any fresh herbs can be used in place of the parsley – you might like to try chives, rosemary, thyme or basil. Combining different herbs can create an interesting flavor. Other delicious flavors are horseradish, anchovy, roasted red or green pepper, curry paste, mustard, onion, spring onions, capers, finely grated lemon or lime rind.

Barbecue sauce

1 tablespoon vegetable oil
1 onion, chopped
1 clove garlic, crushed
1 teaspoon mustard powder
1 tablespoon Worcestershire sauce
1 tablespoon brown sugar
3 tablespoons tomato sauce
1 teaspoon chilli sauce
3/4 cup/185mL/6fl oz beef stock
freshly ground black pepper

Heat oil in a saucepan and cook onion and garlic for 3-4 minutes or until soft. Stir in mustard powder, Worcestershire sauce, sugar, tomato sauce, chilli sauce and stock. Bring to the boil, then reduce heat and simmer for 8-10 minutes or until sauce reduces and thickens slightly. Season to taste with black pepper.

Makes 1 cup/250 mL/8 fl oz

Mexican chilli sauce

Wonderful with steak, chops or sausages, this sauce will spice up any meal.

2 tablespoons vegetable oil
2 small fresh red chillies, seeded and finely chopped
3 small fresh green chillies, seeded and finely chopped
3 cloves garlic, crushed
2 onions, finely chopped
1 tablespoon finely chopped fresh coriander
440g/14oz canned tomatoes, undrained and mashed
1 teaspoon brown sugar

½ **teaspoon ground cinnamon**
¼ **teaspoon ground cloves**
¼ **teaspoon ground ginger**
2 **tablespoons lemon juice**
3 **tablespoons water**

Heat oil in a frying pan and cook red and green chillies, garlic, onions and coriander for 2-3 minutes. Stir in tomatoes, sugar, cinnamon, cloves, ginger, lemon juice and water. Bring to the boil, then reduce heat and simmer for 15-20 minutes or until sauce reduces and thickens.

Makes 2 cups/500 mL/16 fl oz

Sweet and sour barbecue sauce

A sweet and sour sauce is always a popular accompaniment for chicken and pork, but is also delicious served with sausages and fish.

1 **tablespoon vegetable oil**
1 **small onion, chopped**
1 **red pepper, chopped**
1 **tablespoon soy sauce**
2 **tablespoons honey**
1 **tablespoon tomato paste (purée)**
2 **tablespoons cornflour**
½ **cup/125mL/4fl oz cider vinegar**
½ **cup/125mL/4fl oz chicken stock or water**
440g/14oz **canned pineapple pieces, drained**

1 Heat oil in a saucepan and cook onion and red pepper for 4-5 minutes or until soft. Place soy sauce, honey, tomato paste (purée), cornflour and vinegar in a bowl and mix to combine.

2 Stir cornflour mixture into vegetables, then stir in stock or water. Cook, stirring, over a medium heat for 2-3 minutes or until sauce boils and thickens. Stir in pineapple pieces and cook for 2-3 minutes longer.

Makes 2 cups/500 mL/16 fl oz

Apple and horseradish sauce

Delicious served with beef and sausages, this condiment also makes an interesting accompaniment for barbecued fish.

½ **cup/125mL/4fl oz cream (double)**
1 **green apple, cored and grated**
3 **tablespoons horseradish relish**
freshly ground black pepper

Place cream in a bowl and whip until soft peaks form. Fold in apple and horseradish relish and season to taste with black pepper.

Makes 1 cup/250 mL/8 fl oz

barbecue
secrets

What's in a marinade
A marinade tenderises the tough, moistens the dry and flavors the bland. It can be that secret ingredient that turns an otherwise ordinary piece of meat, fish, poultry or game into a taste sensation.

A marinade consists of an acid ingredient, an oil and flavorings – each ingredient playing an important role in the marinating process.

The acid ingredient:
This can be lemon or lime juice, vinegar, wine, soy sauce, yogurt or tomatoes. The acid in a marinade tenderises foods such as beef, lamb, pork, poultry and seafood.

The oil:
The moisturiser in the marinade. Olive and vegetable oils are the most popular but nut, herb or seed oils can also add an interesting flavor. A rule of thumb is that a marinade for barbecuing or grilling should contain at least 25 per cent oil, so each 1 cup/250mL/8fl oz of marinade, should include ¼ cup/60mL/2fl oz oil.

The flavorings:
Most commonly these are fresh or dried herbs and spices, garlic, ginger or onions.

How to marinate:
As marinades contain acid ingredients, the food and marinade should be placed in stainless steel, enamel, glass or ceramic dishes. The marinade should come up around the sides of the food, but need not completely cover it. Turn the food several times during marinating. Food can also be marinated in a plastic food bag. This is particularly good for marinating large pieces of meat such as roasts. Place the food and marinade in the bag, squeeze out as much air as possible and seal with a rubber band or tie with a piece of string. Turn the bag several times during marinating.

How long to marinate:
Marinating times can be anywhere between 15 minutes and 2 days. As a general rule, the longer you marinate the more tender and flavorsome the food will be. Food marinates faster at room temperature than in the refrigerator. But remember, in hot weather it is usually better to allow a longer marinating time in the refrigerator to ensure that the food stays safe to eat. Fish and seafood should not be marinated for longer than 30 minutes, as the acid ingredient in the marinade will 'cook' the fish. If marinating in the refrigerator, allow the food to stand at room temperature for 30 minutes before cooking to ensure even cooking of the marinated food.

Cooking marinated food:
Drain the food well before cooking, especially when cooking in a frying pan or on a barbecue plate (griddle). Wet food will stew rather than brown. The remaining marinade can be brushed over the food several times during cooking.

Coffee honey marinade
This delicious no-salt-added marinade is excellent for beef and lamb.

1 tablespoon honey
1 tablespoon instant coffee powder
¼ cup/60 mL/2 fl oz lemon juice
2 cloves garlic, crushed

1 Place honey, coffee powder, lemon juice and garlic in a small bowl and mix to combine.
2 Pour marinade over meat, cover and set aside to marinate.

White wine and herb marinade

This tasty marinade is ideal for fish and poultry. Choose the herbs that you like or that are in season.

¾ cup/185 mL/6fl oz white wine
¼ cup/60 mL/2 fl oz olive oil
2 spring onions, finely chopped
1 tablespoon chopped fresh herbs, or
1 teaspoon dried herbs

1 *Place wine, oil, spring onions and herbs in a bowl and mix to combine.*
2 *Pour marinade over poultry or fish, cover and set aside to marinate.*

Red wine marinade

An excellent marinade for any type of red meat or game. For lighter meat, such as lamb, choose a lighter red wine – for example a Pinot Noir – while for game you can use a heavier red wine such as a Hermitage.

1½ cups/375mL/12fl oz red wine
½ cup/125mL/4fl oz olive oil
1 small onion, diced
1 bay leaf, torn into pieces
1 teaspoon black peppercorns, cracked
1 clove garlic, crushed
3 teaspoons finely chopped fresh
thyme or 1 teaspoon dried thyme

1 *Place wine, oil, onion, bay leaf, peppercorns, garlic and thyme in a small bowl and mix to combine.*
2 *Pour marinade over meat, cover and set aside to marinate.*

Lemon herb marinade

½ cup/125 mL/4fl oz olive oil
¼ cup/60 mL/2fl oz lemon juice
¼ cup/60 mL/2fl oz white wine vinegar
1 clove garlic, crushed
1 teaspoon finely grated lemon rind
2 teaspoons finely chopped fresh parsley
2 teaspoons snipped fresh chives

3 teaspoons finely chopped fresh
rosemary or 1 teaspoon finely chopped
dried rosemary

1 *Place oil, lemon juice, vinegar, garlic, lemon rind, parsley, chives and rosemary in a small bowl and mix to combine.*
2 *Pour marinade over meat or poultry, cover and set aside to marinate.*

Hot chilli marinade

¼ cup/60 mL/2fl oz soy sauce
¼ cup/60 mL/2fl oz hoisin sauce
½ cup/125 mL/4fl oz dry sherry
1 clove garlic, crushed
1 teaspoon grated fresh ginger
2 spring onions, finely chopped
1 teaspoon hot chilli sauce

1 *Place soy sauce, hoisin sauce, sherry, garlic, ginger, spring onions and chilli sauce in a small bowl and mix to combine.*
2 *Pour marinade over meat or poultry, cover and set aside to marinate. Use the marinade as a baste when barbecuing.*

casseroles

& slow cooking

introduction

Casserole meals are popular for three main reasons: they can be prepared ahead of time; they cook without constant attention; and they are quick, tasty and easy to serve.

Casseroles are based on a blending of the flavors of the ingredients, and most casseroles improve by being prepared in advance. Many can be fixed long before needed and frozen until used. Others lend themselves to being cooked a day in advance and refrigerated until reheated to serve. Casseroles are also excellent for last-minute meals: many can be prepared from ingredients generally in the cupboard, and can be extended to feed almost any number.

The slow cooking required for many casseroles means that they are an excellent way to utilise less expensive (and less tender) cuts of meat, which will become as tender and tasty as the most expensive steak when cooked slowly for a long time. Casseroles are an ideal way of using leftovers; combined with other ingredients they can present a "new" meal.

Many casseroles contain all the necessary ingredients for a balanced meal - meat, vegetables and sauce - and can be served with a simple salad or crusty bread, thus relieving the cook of last-minute attention to other chores, such as cooking vegetables or preparing a salad. Casseroles should be served in the containers in which they were cooked; with the large number of attractive ovenproof dishes now available, it should be easy to find one with the right colour, shape and size for your personal preferences.

The best part of a casserole, of course, is that it cooks itself. Once all the ingredients are combined (which may be well in advance of cooking), all you have to do is relax and let it cook in the oven or on the stove while you enjoy your guests or family.

Photograph and recipe page 763 (spanish chicken with chorizo)

lamb shank in root vegetables

luscious lamb

Braising and casseroling lamb opens

up a plethora of tantalising tastes to enjoy, from Mediterranean style stews to oriental curries and fruity casseroles.

lamb
shanks with root vegetables

Photograph on page 695 and below

ingredients

**500g/1lb lean diced lamb
2 onions, chopped
1 teaspoon ground cinnamon
½ teaspoon ground cloves
1 teaspoon garam masala
440g/14oz canned tomatoes,
undrained and mashed
2 cups/500mL/16fl oz beef stock
250g/8oz canned chickpeas,
drained and rinsed
3 potatoes, chopped
2 carrots, chopped
45g/1½oz sultanas (golden raisins)
2 teaspoons finely grated orange rind
3 teaspoons cornflour, blended with
one tablespoon water
couscous for serving**

Method:

1 Heat a non-stick frying pan over a medium heat. Add lamb and cook, stirring, for 5 minutes or until lamb is brown. Remove lamb from pan and place in casserole.

2 Add onions, cinnamon, cloves and garam masala to pan and cook, stirring, for 3 minutes or until onions are soft.

3 Add onion mixture, tomatoes, stock, chickpeas, potatoes, carrots, sultanas and orange rind to casserole dish and bake for 75-90 minutes or until lamb is tender.

4 Stir cornflour mixture into lamb mixture, return to oven and cook for 5-10 minutes longer or until tangine thickens slightly. Serve with couscous.

Serves 4

Oven temperature 150°C/300°F/Gas 2

spicy lamb
tagine

Method:

1 Heat a non-stick frying pan over a medium heat. Add lamb and cook, stirring, for 5 minutes or until lamb is brown. Remove lamb from pan and place in casserole.
2 Add onions, cinnamon, cloves and garam masala to pan and cook, stirring, for 3 minutes or until onions are soft.
3 Add onion mixture, tomatoes, stock, chickpeas, potatoes, carrots, sultanas and orange rind to casserole dish and bake for 75-90 minutes or until lamb is tender.
4 Stir cornflour mixture into lamb mixture, return to oven and cook for 5-10 minutes longer or until tangine thickens slightly. Serve with couscous.

Serves 4

ingredients

500g/1lb lean diced lamb
2 onions, chopped
1 teaspoon ground cinnamon
$^{1}/_{2}$ teaspoon ground cloves
1 teaspoon garam masala
440g/14oz canned tomatoes,
undrained and mashed
2 cups/500mL/16fl oz beef stock
250g/8oz canned chickpeas,
drained and rinsed
3 potatoes, chopped
2 carrots, chopped
45g/1$^{1}/_{2}$oz sultanas (golden raisins)
2 teaspoons finely grated orange rind
3 teaspoons cornflour, blended with
one tablespoon water
couscous for serving

Oven temperature 150°C/300°F/Gas 2

athenian
lamb hotpot

Method:

1 *Trim meat of all visible fat. Heat 2 tablespoons of oil in a large saucepan. Cook the meat in batches until well browned on all sides. Transfer to a plate and set aside.*

2 *Heat remaining oil and cook onion and pepper for 2-3 minutes or until onion softens. Stir in tomato paste and stock. Stir well to lift pan sediment.*

3 *Add cardamom, cinnamon and pepper. Bring to the boil, reduce heat and simmer for 5 minutes. Return meat to the pan with coriander. Cover and simmer for 1 1/2 hours or until meat is tender and sauce thickens.*

Serves 6

ingredients

I kg/2 lb boneless lamb, cubed
3 tablespoons olive oil
2 onions, finely chopped
I green pepper, seeded and chopped
250mL/8 fl oz tomato paste
185mL/6 fl oz chicken stock
1/2 teaspoon ground cardamom
I large cinnamon stick
freshly ground black pepper
2 tablespoons chopped
fresh coriander

garlicky
lamb pot roast

Method:

1. Combine garlic, garam masala, breadcrumbs, pine nuts, currants and rind in a glass bowl. Spoon mixture into lamb cavity and secure with string. Combine nutmeg, cinnamon and pepper, rub over all surfaces of lamb.

2. Heat oil in large saucepan. Add meat and cook over high heat until browned. Add stock, cover and simmer over low heat for 25 minutes, turning occasionally. Mix in lemon juice, cover and simmer for 25 minutes longer. Add kumera and simmer for 5 minutes more. Remove lamb from pan and set aside and keep warm. Add beans and cook until tender. Season to taste. To serve, slice lamb and accompany with vegetables.

Serves 8

ingredients

3 cloves garlic, crushed
1 teaspoon garam masala
125g/4 oz fresh breadcrumbs
2 tablespoons pine nuts
1 tablespoon currants
1 teaspoon grated lemon rind
1 1/2 kg/3 lb leg lamb, tunnel boned
1/2 teaspoon ground nutmeg
1/2 teaspoon ground cinnamon
1/2 teaspoon ground black pepper
2 tablespoons olive oil
2 cups chicken stock
2 tablespoons lemon juice
250g/8oz kumera (orange sweet potato),
peeled, cut into julienne
250g/8oz green beans, topped and tailed

baked
eggplant with lamb

Method:

1 Remove stems from eggplants (aubergines). Cut almost through eggplants (aubergines) crosswise at 2cm/³/₄in intervals, taking care not to cut right through. Sprinkle salt liberally onto cut surfaces and set aside for 30 minutes. Rinse in cold water and pat dry on absorbent paper.

2 Combine lamb, onion, garlic, red pepper, basil, oregano and chilli powder. Stuff some meat mixture in each cut of the eggplants (aubergines), filling generously. Place filled eggplants (aubergines) in a baking pan.

3 Blend tomato puree and stock together and pour over eggplants (aubergines). Top with cheese and dot with butter. Bake at 180°C/350°F/Gas 4, for 45 minutes, basting with pan juices during cooking.

Serves 8

ingredients

8 eggplants (aubergines), each 125g/4oz
salt
500g/1 lb lean ground lamb
1 onion, finely chopped
1 clove garlic, crushed
freshly ground black pepper
1 small red pepper,
seeded and chopped
2 tablespoons finely chopped fresh basil
¹/₂ teaspoon dried oregano
¹/₄ teaspoon chilli powder
125mL/4 fl oz tomato puree
125mL/4 fl oz chicken stock
4 tablespoons grated Parmesan cheese
2 tablespoons butter

Oven temperature 180°C/350°F/Gas 4

Oven temperature 180°C/350°F/Gas 4

lamb
pot roast

Method:

1 Cut slits in the surface of the lamb with a sharp knife. Insert garlic slivers and rosemary sprigs. Dust with pepper and place in a roasting pan. Bake at 180°C/350°F/Gas 4 for 1 hour. Remove pan from oven and drain off pan juices.

2 Cut potato halves part way down through rounded side. Brush with lemon juice and arrange around lamb. Top with tomatoes and onions. Combine stock and vermouth and pour over lamb and vegetables. Add the lemon peel and cinnamon stick. Dot with butter and bake at 180°C/350°F/Gas 4 for 1¹/₂ hours longer.

3 Remove lamb from roasting pan. Wrap in aluminium foil and stand for 15 minutes before carving. Skim any excess fat from pan contents. To serve, slice meat and accompany with potatoes and tomato and onion sauce.

Note: An adaptation of a Middle Eastern recipe that traditionally would have been prepared at home and then taken to the local baker's oven for cooking.

Serves 6

ingredients

2 kg/4 lb leg lamb
2 cloves garlic, crushed
6 small sprigs fresh rosemary
freshly ground black pepper
6 potatoes, peeled and halved lengthways
2 tablespoons lemon juice
4 tomatoes, peeled and chopped
2 onions, chopped
125mL/4fl oz chicken stock
3 tablespoons dry vermouth
1 cm/¹/₂in piece lemon peel
small piece cinnamon stick
2 tablespoons butter

Oven temperature 150°C/300°F/Gas 2

tomato
and thyme shanks

Method:

1 Place shanks, shallots and red pepper in a large casserole dish. Combine tomato sauce, vinegar, water, garlic and thyme and pour over shanks.

2 Cover and bake at 150°C/300°F/Gas2 for 2½ hours or until meat is very tender. Season to taste with pepper. Serve immediately or allow to cool and serve at room temperature.
Note: Served either hot or cold, these lamb shanks are a delicious and filling family meal. When cooked, the meat should be very tender and almost falling off the bone.

Serves 4

ingredients

**4 lamb shanks
2 shallots, chopped
1 red pepper, chopped
250mL/8fl oz tomato sauce
125mL/4fl oz cider vinegar
250mL/8fl oz water
1 clove garlic, crushed
1 teaspoon finely chopped fresh thyme
freshly ground black pepper**

lamb shanks
with broad beans, olives and risoni

Method:

1 *Heat oil in a large saucepan, add garlic, lamb shanks and onion, and cook for five minutes (or until shanks are lightly browned).*

2 *Add the beef stock, sprigs of oregano, tomato paste and half the water, bring to the boil, reduce heat, and leave to simmer (with lid on) for 40 minutes.*

3 *Remove shanks, slice meat off bone, and set aside.*

4 *Add the risoni and water, cook for a further five minutes, then add broad beans, olives, meat, oregano and salt and pepper, cook for five minutes more, and serve.*

Note: *If broad beans are large, peel off outer skin.*

Serves 4-6

ingredients

2 tablespoons olive oil
2 cloves garlic, crushed
4 lamb shanks
1 onion, chopped
500mL/16fl oz beef stock
4 sprigs oregano
2 tablespoons tomato paste
500mL/16fl oz water
1 cup risoni (rice)
1 cup broad beans*
½ cup olives
2 teaspoons fresh oregano (chopped)
salt and freshly ground pepper

lamb casserole
with cous cous & gremolata

Method:

1 Pre-heat the oven to 180°C/350°F/Gas 4. Season the flour and place on a large plate, toss the meat until coated. Heat the oil in a large frying pan and cook the meat, over a medium heat, for 2-3 minutes each side, until browned (you will need to do this in two batches). Transfer the browned meat to a casserole dish, using a slotted spoon.

2 Add the peppers (capsicum) to the frying pan and cook for 2 minutes. Add the tomatoes and bring to the boil. Add these to the lamb and cook in the oven for 40 minutes or until the meat is tender. Meanwhile, mix all the ingredients for the gremolata together.

3 Prepare the couscous according to packet instructions, then fluff up with a fork. Heat the oil in a small frying pan and cook the onion over a medium heat for 10 minutes until golden brown. Add to the couscous and mix well. Sprinkle the gremolata over the lamb casserole and serve with the couscous.

Note: Gremolata is a mixture of finely chopped herbs, garlic and citrus rind. Adding this to the casserole, just before serving, lends a fresh new dimension of flavor.

Serves 4

ingredients

sea salt and freshly ground
black pepper
2 tablespoons plain white flour
800g/25oz diced lamb,
trimmed of any excess fat
2-3 tablespoons extra virgin olive oil
1 yellow and 1 green pepper
(capsicum), deseeded and chopped
420g/14oz can chopped tomatoes

For the gremolata
1 garlic clove, very finely chopped
3 tablespoons finely chopped
fresh parsley
grated rind of 1 lemon

For the couscous
250g/9oz couscous
1 tablespoon extra virgin olive oil
1 large onion, finely sliced

Oven temperature 180°C/350°F/Gas 4

Oven temperature 160°C/325°F/Gas 3

lamb
and apricot casserole

Method:

1 *Preheat the oven to 160°C/325°F/Gas 3. Heat the oil in a flameproof and ovenproof casserole dish on the hob. Add the lamb and cook for about 5 minutes or until browned. Remove and keep warm.*

2 *Add the onion and garlic to the juices in the dish and cook for 5 minutes or until softened. Return the lamb to the dish with the flour, coriander and cumin and cook for 1 minute, stirring. Slowly add the stock and wine and bring to the boil, stirring. Stir in the mushrooms, tomato purée, bouquet garni and black pepper. Cover and cook in the oven for 1 hour.*

3 *Stir in the apricots and cook for a further 30 minutes or until the lamb is tender. Remove and discard the bouquet garni, stir in the chopped coriander, then garnish with more fresh coriander.*

Note: *The leg is the leanest cut of lamb and is also considerably lower in calories than other cuts. Dried apricots are a good source of soluble and insoluble fibre and beta carotene.*

Serves 4

ingredients

1 tablespoon sunflower oil
450g/1lb lean boneless lamb leg or fillet, cut into 2½cm/1in cubes
1 large onion, chopped
1 clove garlic, finely chopped
2 tablespoons plain flour
1 teaspoon ground coriander
1 teaspoon ground cumin
350mL/12fl oz vegetable stock
150mL/5fl oz red wine
225g/8oz baby button mushrooms
1 tablespoon tomato purée
1 bouquet garni
black pepper
175g/6oz ready-to-eat dried apricots
2 tablespoons chopped, fresh coriander, plus extra leaves to garnish

lamb
and spinach curry

Method:

1 Heat the oil in a flameproof casserole dish or a large, heavy-based saucepan. Fry the onions, garlic, ginger, cinnamon, cloves and cardamom for 5 minutes to soften the onions and garlic, and to release the flavors of the spices.

2 Add the lamb and fry for 5 minutes, turning, until it begins to color. Mix in the cumin and coriander, then add the yogurt, 1 tablespoon at a time, stirring well each time.

3 Mix together the tomato purée and the stock and add to the lamb. Season to taste. Bring to the boil, then reduce the heat, cover and simmer for 30 minutes or until the lamb is tender.

4 Stir in the spinach, cover and simmer for another 15 minutes or until the mixture has reduced. Remove the cinnamon stick and the cardamom pods and mix in the almonds.

Note: There's plenty of flavor but no chilli in this dish, so it will be a hit even with those who don't like hot curries. You can serve it with pilau or plain rice.

Serves 4

ingredients

2 tablespoons vegetable oil
2 onions, chopped
2 cloves garlic, chopped
2¹/₂cm/1in piece fresh root ginger, finely chopped
1 cinnamon stick
¹/₄ teaspoon ground cloves
3 cardamom pods
600g/1lb 5oz diced lamb
1 tablespoon ground cumin
1 tablespoon ground coriander
4 tablespoons natural yogurt
2 tablespoons tomato purée
200mL/7fl oz beef stock
salt and black pepper
500g/16oz fresh spinach, finely chopped
2 tablespoons roasted flaked almonds

lamb
osso bucco

Method:

1 Preheat the oven to 160°C/325°F/Gas 3. Mix together the flour, salt and pepper on a plate. Dip the lamb pieces into the mixture to coat well. Heat 1 tablespoon of the oil in a large heavy-based frying pan until hot but not smoking. Add the coated lamb and cook over a medium to high heat for 5-8 minutes, turning frequently, until browned on all sides. Transfer to a deep ovenproof dish.

2 Heat the remaining oil in the pan, add the onion, carrot and celery and cook over a low heat for 4-5 minutes, until softened. Add the tomatoes, tomato purée, wine and stock and bring to the boil, stirring occasionally. Pour over the lamb, cover with foil and bake for 1³/₄-2 hours, until the meat is tender, turning it over halfway through. Season to taste.

3 To make the garnish, mix together the parsley, mint, lemon rind and garlic. Sprinkle the garnish over the lamb and serve.

Note: The lamb is cooked very slowly in this Italian recipe, leaving it meltingly tender, and there should be enough to satisfy the biggest of appetites. Serve with pasta ribbons.

Serves 4

ingredients

2 tablespoons plain flour
salt and black pepper
4 lamb leg shanks, trimmed of excess fat
2 tablespoons olive oil
1 onion, finely chopped
1 carrot, finely chopped
1 stick celery, finely chopped
410g/13oz can chopped tomatoes with garlic and herbs
1 tablespoon sun-dried tomato purée
150mL/5 fl oz dry white wine
500mL/16 fl oz lamb stock

For the garnish
1 tablespoon chopped fresh parsley
1 tablespoon chopped fresh mint
finely grated rind of 1 lemon
1 clove garlic, finely chopped

Oven temperature 160°C/325°F/Gas 3

lamb hotpot
cooked in cider

Method:

1 Preheat the oven to 180°C/350°F/Gas 4. Heat 1 tablespoon of the oil in a large heavy based frying pan. Add the chops and cook for 1-2 minutes each side, until browned. Remove from the pan, then add the kidneys and cook for 30 seconds on each side or until lightly browned.

2 Arrange half the onion and potatoes in the base of a casserole dish. Top with the chops, add half the carrots, leek and celery, then the kidneys. Add the rest of the carrots, leek and celery, seasoning each layer well. Finish with a layer of onions and potatoes, then tuck in the majoram or oregano sprigs. Pour over the cider and brush the top with the remaining oil.

3 Cover and cook for 1½-2 hours, until the meat is tender. Remove the lid, place near the top of the oven and cook for 20-30 minutes, until brown.

Note: This slow-cooked hotpot produces meltingly tender meat. It's an ideal weekend lunch - once it's in the oven you can forget about it for a couple of hours.

Serves 4

ingredients

2 tablespoons olive oil
4 lamb loin chops
6 lamb's kidneys, halved and skins and cores removed
1 onion, sliced
750g/1½lb potatoes, sliced
2 carrots, sliced
1 large leek, sliced
2 sticks celery, sliced
salt and black pepper
3 sprigs fresh marjoram or oregano
300mL/10fl oz dry cider

Oven temperature 180°C/350°F/Gas 4

Oven temperature 200°C/400°F/Gas 6

lancashire
hotpot

Method:

1 Preheat the oven to 200°C/400°F/Gas 6. Heat 25g/1oz of the butter or dripping in a frying pan and cook the chops or cutlets for 5 minutes on each side to brown. Arrange half the potatoes in a large casserole dish, and top with half the onions, then half the carrots, seasoning each layer lightly. Add the chops or cutlets and a final layer each of onions, carrots and potatoes, again seasoning each layer. Pour over the stock, then dot with the remaining butter or dripping.

2 Cover the casserole and cook for 30 minutes. Reduce the oven temperature to 150°C/300°F/ Gas 2 and cook for a further hour. Increase the oven temperature to 200°C/400°F/ Gas 6, then uncover the dish and cook for 30-40 minutes, until the potatoes have browned.

Note: Layers of potato, onions and carrots sandwich tender loin chops in this traditional hotpot. It's a meal in itself - all it needs is a glass of ale or cider to wash it down.

Serves 4

ingredients

40g/1½oz butter or dripping
4 large lamb loin chops or
8 lamb cutlets, trimmed
750g/1½lb potatoes, thinly sliced
2 large onions, sliced
3 large carrots, sliced
salt and black pepper
400mL/14fl oz lamb stock

lychee
lamb

Method:
1 *Preheat oven to 170°C/340°F/Gas 3. Trim lamb fillets of any fat, remove silver skin. Butterfly lamb fillets and pound lightly to flatten. Drain lychees, reserve juice. Insert a pecan between 2 lychees, place onto 1 lamb fillet, roll up and secure with toothpicks. Repeat.*

2 *Brown lamb in non-stick frypan. Transfer to large casserole dish. Heat butter in frypan, fry onion. Add cornflour blended with 1/4 cup reserved juice, stock and wine, bring to boil. Season to taste. Pour sauce over lamb, cover. Place vegetables in separate casserole dish with a little water, cover.*

3 *Cook lamb and vegetables in oven 30 minutes. Cook noodles according to packet directions. Remove toothpicks from lamb, serve with vegetables and noodles. Garnish with extra lychees and pecans.*

Serves 4-6

ingredients

12 trim lamb fillets
565g/17oz can lychees
50g/1²/₃oz pecans
2 teaspoons butter
1 onion, sliced
1/4 cup cornflour
1 cup chicken stock
1 cup white wine
400g/13oz yellow baby squash
**300g/9¹/₂oz green beans,
topped and tailed**
2 cups shell or spiral noodles

Oven temperature 170°C/340°F/Gas 4

sweet
lamb chop curry

Method:

1 Trim excess fat from the chops. Wipe over with kitchen paper. Heat oil in a large, heavy-based saucepan or lidded skillet. Add onion and garlic and fry until golden over moderate heat. Remove onion with a slotted spoon, set aside.

2 Increase heat, and brown chops quickly on both sides. Do only 2 or 3 at a time. Remove to plate and drain almost all fat from the pan. Add the curry powder and ginger to the hot saucepan and stir over heat to roast until aroma rises. Stir in the water, lifting the pan juices as you stir. Season with salt and pepper.

3 Return lamb and onion, cover and simmer for 1 hour. Add dried fruit, brown sugar and cinnamon stick and simmer for approximately 1 hour, until lamb is very soft and tender. Add more water during cooking if necessary.

4 Remove chops to a hot serving platter. Stir yogurt into the sauce (if desired) and pour sauce over the chops. Serve with boiled rice.

Serves 4-6

ingredients

6 forequarter lamb chops (850g/28oz)
1 tablespoon oil
1 large onion, finely chopped
1 clove garlic, crushed
1½ tablespoons Madras-style curry powder
½ teaspoon ground ginger
2 cups water
salt and pepper
¾ cup dried fruit mix
1 teaspoon brown sugar
½ cinnamon stick
½ cup plain yogurt (optional)

lamb
korma

Method:

1 *Cut the lamb from the bone into 4cm/1³/₄in cubes. Season with salt and pepper.*

2 *Heat ghee in a large, heavy-based saucepan, add ¹/₃ of the lamb and brown well on all sides. Remove and brown the remainder in 2 batches.*

3 *Add the onion and garlic and sauté until transparent. Stir in the curry paste, spices and flour and cook 1 minute. Add the chicken stock, sultanas and lamb. Cover with a lid and simmer gently for 1 hour or until the lamb is very tender. Stir occasionally during cooking.*

4 *Stir in the yogurt and lemon juice. Serve with boiled rice and sambals.*

Serves 4-6

ingredients

1 ½ kg/3 ¹/₃lb shoulder of lamb
salt and freshly ground black pepper
2 tablespoons ghee
1 Spanish onion, finely chopped
1 clove garlic, finely chopped
1 tablespoon curry paste
¼ teaspoon ground ginger
¼ teaspoon turmeric
⅛ teaspoon cayenne pepper
2 tablespoons flour
1 ¼ cups chicken stock
¾ cup/150g dried sultanas
(golden raisins)
150mL/5fl oz yogurt
1 tablespoons lemon juice

ruaraka
lamb and apricot stew

Method:

1 Cut peeled tomatoes in half crosswise (through 'equator'), gently squeeze out seeds and chop the tomato.

2 Heat half the oil in a heavy-based, lidded frying pan or saucepan, add tomato, capsicum (pepper), onion and mint, and sauté 5 minutes. Remove from pan.

3 Heat remaining oil, add lamb pieces, stir quickly to brown on all sides. Return vegetables to the pan, add the apricots and enough water to almost cover the meat. Bring to the boil, turn down heat and simmer 1 hour.

4 After the hour season with salt and pepper. Check liquid content and add more if needed. Simmer one hour more, until lamb is very tender. Serve with boiled rice.

Serves 6

ingredients

**4 ripe tomatoes, blanched and peeled
2 tablespoons oil
1 green capsicum (pepper), seeded
and finely chopped
1 large onion, chopped
2 tablespoons fresh mint, chopped
1kg/2lb lamb cubes, cut from
the leg or shoulder
125g/4oz dried apricots
salt and freshly ground black pepper**

seafood casserole

simmer with seafood

While certain seafood's, such as

octopus and calamari, will benefit from extended cooking times, most of them require limited time in the pot to ensure a flavorsome, fresh and moist eating experience.

baby octopus
in red wine

Method:

1 Remove tentacles, intestines and ink sac from octopus. Cut out the eyes and beak. Remove skin and rinse well.

2 Place octopus in a large saucepan, cover and simmer for 15 minutes. Drain off any juices and set aside to cool slightly.

3 Heat oil in a saucepan and cook shallots for 2-3 minutes. Add garlic and octopus and cook for 4-5 minutes. Pour wine into pan and cook over medium heat, until almost all the wine has evaporated.

4 Combine stock, tomatoes, lemon rind, pepper and coriander. Cover and simmer gently for 1 1/2 hours until octopus is tender.

Serves 6

ingredients

1 kg/2 lb baby octopus
3 tablespoons polyunsaturated oil
6 shallots, chopped
2 cloves garlic, crushed
125mL/4fl oz dry red wine
125mL/4fl oz chicken stock
440g/14oz canned tomatoes,
undrained and mashed
1 teaspoon grated lemon rind
freshly ground black pepper
2 tablespoons finely chopped coriander

seafood
casserole

Photograph on page 715

ingredients

1 tablespoon olive oil
1 medium onion, roughly chopped
1 leek, finely chopped
2 cloves garlic, crushed
400g/13oz can tomatoes
2 bay leaves
60mL/2fl oz dry white wine
salt and freshly ground black pepper
1kg/2lb assorted fish and seafood*
1 tablespoon parsley, chopped
2 teaspoons oregano, chopped

Method:

1 Heat the oil in a flame-proof casserole dish. Sauté the onion, leek and garlic until softened and slightly golden. Add the tomatoes, bay leaves, parsley, wine, salt and freshly ground black pepper. Bring to the boil, cover, and simmer gently for 20 minutes.

2 Stir in any firm-fleshed fish and simmer for five minutes. Stir in the remaining soft-fleshed fish placing shell fish on the top.

3 Cover with a lid and continue cooking for 5-7 minutes (until the fish is tender) and the shell fish have opened (discarding any that remain closed).

4 Serve garnished with a fresh bay leaf.
*Suitable fish and seafood include red mullet, monk fish, sea bream, cod, calamari, mussels, shelled shrimps and clams.

Serves 4-6

bouillabaisse

Method:

1 Combine fish, 3 tablespoons oil, garlic and juice in medium bowl. Cover and set aside for 20 minutes.

2 Heat remaining oil in large saucepan. Stir in onions and leeks and cook over low heat for 10 minutes or until soft. Stir in tomatoes, bouquet garni, saffron and pepper. Bring to boil, reduce heat and simmer, covered, for 10 minutes.

3 Stir stock into vegetable sauce. Bring to the boil, reduce heat and simmer, uncovered, for 10 minutes. Add fish and marinade to pan. Stir in crab and lobster, bring to the boil, reduce heat and simmer, uncovered, for 8 minutes. Add mussels to pan and cook until mussels open. Stir in parsley and serve immediately.

Note: A tasty medley of all fishy favourites. Serve this one-pot meal with crusty garlic or herbed bread for an informal lunch.

Serves 8

ingredients

500g/1 lb firm boneless fish fillets, cubed
3 tablespoons olive oil
4 cloves garlic, crushed
3 tablespoons lemon juice
4 tablespoons olive oil, extra
2 onions, peeled and chopped
2 large leeks, chopped
410g/13oz canned tomatoes, crushed
bouquet garni
pinch saffron threads
$1/2$ teaspoon ground black pepper
600mL/1 pt rich fish stock
2 large uncooked crabs,
chopped into pieces (shell on)
1 green lobster tail,
chopped into pieces (shell on)
16 mussels, uncooked
3 tablespoons finely chopped parsley

fish stew
with lemongrass and coconut milk

Method:

1 Peel the outer covering from the lemon grass stalks. Finely chop the lower white bulbous parts and discard the fibrous tops. Heat the oil in a large, heavy-based saucepan, then add the chillies and lemon grass and fry for 1 minute.

2 Add the garlic and carrots and fry for 3-4 minutes, until the garlic starts to turn golden. Stir in the stock and coconut milk and bring to the boil, then reduce the heat and simmer, uncovered, for 15 minutes or until reduced slightly.

3 Meanwhile, slit open the back of each shrimp and scrape out any black vein with a small knife. Add the monkfish to the coconut milk mixture, then cover and simmer for 4-5 minutes, until the fish has started to turn opaque. Add the spring onions, scallops and shrimp and cook for 3-4 minutes, until the prawns have turned pink and the scallops are tender and cooked through. Stir in the lime rind and juice, then sprinkle with chives.

Note: This fish stew with its lemon fragrance draws its inspiration from Thailand. Monkfish has a delicate flavor and texture that works well here, but you can use any white fish.

ingredients

3 stalks lemon grass
2 tablespoons groundnut or sesame oil
2 green chillies, deseeded and sliced
4 cloves garlic, thinly sliced
200g/7oz carrots, thinly sliced
315mL/10fl oz fish stock
410mL/13oz can coconut milk
500g/1lb 2oz raw peeled tiger shrimp
410g/13oz monkfish, cut into bite-size pieces
bunch of spring onions, shredded
200g/7oz scallops
grated rind and juice of 1 lime
fresh snipped chives to garnish

Serves 6

mediterranean
fish stew with rouille

Method:

1 First make the rouille. Crush together the garlic, chilli and coriander with a pinch of salt in a pestle and mortar. Stir in the mayonnaise and oil, mix well and season to taste. Refrigerate until needed.

2 Skin the fish, if necessary, and cut into 5cm /2in chunks. Shell the shrimp, then slit open the back of each one and scrape out any black vein. Rinse well. Cut the squid into 5cm/2in rings. Shell the mussels, reserving a few with shells on to garnish.

3 Heat the oil in a large heavy-based saucepan and fry the onion for 4 minutes to soften. Add the fennel seeds and fry for another minute, then add the wine, tomatoes and seasoning. Bring to the boil, then simmer, uncovered, for 5 minutes, until slightly thickened. Add the fish, squid and shrimp and simmer, covered, for a further 5-6 minutes, stirring occasionally, until the shrimp are pink and everything is cooked. Add all the mussels and heat through. Season and serve with the rouille.

Note: This recipe from the south of France is one of the best examples of a rich Mediterranean fish stew. You can stir in as much of the spicy, garlicky mayonnaise as you want.

Serves 4

ingredients

1kg/2lb mixed fish and shellfish, such as cod, red mullet or mackerel fillet, raw shell-on tiger shrimp and prepared squid
500g/1lb Irish cooked mussels in garlic butter sauce
2 tablespoons olive oil
1 onion, finely chopped
1 teaspoon fennel seeds
200mL/7fl oz dry white wine
400g/13oz can chopped tomatoes

For the rouille
2 cloves garlic, chopped
1 small red chilli, deseeded and chopped
3 tablespoons chopped fresh coriander
salt and black pepper
3 tablespoons mayonnaise
1 tablespoon olive oil

steak and kidney puffs

beef & veal

Braising, casseroling and stewing

beef are all moist methods of cookery and will tenderise less tender cuts of beef. Veal, on the other hand, is already a very tender meat which is made even more tender, moist and flavorsome by moist heat and slow cookery.

steak
& kidney puffs

Photograph on page 721 and below

Method:

1 *Preheat the oven to 160°C/325°F/Gas 3. Heat half the oil in a large flameproof casserole dish, add the onion and cook for 5 minutes. Add half the steak and kidney and fry over a high heat, stirring, for 6 minutes or until browned. Keep warm. Fry the remaining meat, adding more oil if necessary.*

2 *Return all the meat to the dish, add the flour and stir for 2 minutes. Add the tomato purée, Worcestershire sauce, stock, lemon rind, herbs and salt and pepper. Bring to the boil, stirring, then cover.*

3 *Transfer to the oven. After 1½ hours, stir in the mushrooms and a little water, if needed. Cook for 35 minutes more. Meanwhile, unroll the pastry and cut into 4x12cm/4½in circles. Put on a baking sheet.*

4 *Take the casserole out of the oven. Increase the oven temperature to 200°C/400°F/Gas Mark 6. Meanwhile, place the casserole over a very low heat. Keep covered but stir occasionally. Bake the pastry for 20 minutes or until golden brown. Top each pastry circle with the steak and kidney. Garnish with herbs.*

Note: *These puffs have all the flavor of a steak and kidney pie but they're much lighter and very easy to prepare.*

Serves 4

ingredients

4 tablespoons groundnut oil
1 onion, finely chopped
500g/1lb braising steak, trimmed of excess fat and cubed
350g/12oz pig's kidney, halved, cores removed, then cut into 1cm/½in pieces
3 tablespoons plain flour
1 tablespoon tomato purée
2 teaspoon Worcestershire sauce
420mL/14fl oz beef stock
finely grated rind of 1 lemon
2 tablespoons finely chopped fresh parsley, plus extra to garnish
1 teaspoon dried mixed herbs
salt and black pepper
150g/5oz baby button mushrooms
375g/12oz pack ready-rolled puff pastry
fresh rosemary to garnish

Oven temperature 160°C/325°F/Gas 3

veal
couscous casserole

Method:

1 Place couscous in heatproof bowl and cover with boiling water. Set aside for 1 hour or until all liquid is absorbed.

2 Heat oil in medium saucepan. Add onions, seeds, cinnamon stick and curry leaves, cook stirring until onions soften and seeds begin to pop. Add veal and cook over high heat, until veal is well browned. Mix in tomato paste, tomatoes and stock. Bring to the boil and simmer, uncovered for 5 minutes.

3 Add green pepper, corn and couscous to saucepan, mix well to combine. Cover and simmer for 10 minutes.

Note: A tasty casserole reminiscent of Morocco is just as good made with lamb.

Serves 6

ingredients

125g/4oz couscous
2 tablespoons oil
2 onions, peeled, sliced
¹/₂ teaspoon cardamom seeds
2 teaspoons brown mustard seeds
2 cinnamon sticks
4 dried curry leaves
500g/1 lb ground veal
1 tablespoon tomato paste
410g/13oz canned tomatoes, crushed
250mL/8fl oz chicken stock
1 green pepper, chopped
125g/4 oz canned corn kernels, drained

beef
provençal

Method:

1 Brown small quantities of diced lean beef in hot oil in a large deep pan. Add onions, pepper and mushrooms. Cook until onions are well browned.

2 Stir in tomatoes, wine, olives, fresh herbs, bay leaves and pepper to taste. Cover and simmer on a low heat for 1½-2 hours or until the meat is tender.

3 Stir occasionally. Blend cornflour in a little cold water. Stir into casserole until thickened. Adjust seasonings to taste.

4 Serve with new potatoes and steamed greens.

Serves 8

ingredients

1½kg/3lb diced lean beef
1 tablespoon oil
2 onions, sliced
1 red pepper
1 green pepper
250g/8oz buttoned mushrooms
2 x 410g/13oz cans tomatoes
½ cup red wine
½ cup black olives, pitted
2 tablespoons chopped fresh herbs
(basil, oregano, majoram and sage)
2 bay leaves
freshly cracked pepper
¼ cup cornflour
salt to taste

burmese
beef curry

Method:

1 Cut meat into 2½ squares, place in a bowl with soy sauce, tumeric, vinegar, stir to mix. Cover and marinate at room temperature 4 hours, or overnight in refridgerator.

2 Grate onion on fine grater over a bowl to catch juices. Add garlic, ginger and chilli.

3 Heat oil in a pan, add onion mixture and fry until brown, stirring constantly. Add beef and stir to brown all over. Add bay leaves, cinnamon stick and enough water to half cover beef. Cover and simmer over low heat for 45 minutes or until meat is tender. Add a little water during cooking if necessary.

4 Adjust seasoning and place in a dish. Garnish with fried onion rings, serve with boiled rice or coconut rice.

Note: Burmese curries are dry curries, cooked with little liquid. Marinate beef overnight for best results. Onion, garlic, ginger and chilli form base of Burmese curries and are pounded together.

Serves 4

ingredients

1kg/2lb chuck or skirt steak
1 tablespoon soy sauce
½ teaspoon ground turmeric
1 tablespoon malt vinegar
2 medium onions, grated
4 teaspoons freshly crushed garlic
2 teaspoons fresh ginger
1 teaspoon chilli powder
4 tablespoons vegetable oil
3 bay leaves
1 cinnamon stick
water
fried onion rings for garnish

beef
with pumpkin
& lemon grass

Method:

1 Heat oil in large heavy based saucepan. Cook onions over medium heat until golden. Stir in allspice, cinnamon, ginger and peppers.

2 Add meat to pan, cook over high heat until browned. Stir in lemon grass and chicken stock. Bring to the boil, reduce heat and simmer, covered, for 45 minutes.

3 Stir in pumpkin, cover and simmer for 45 minutes or until beef is tender. Remove from heat and stir in garlic. Season to taste.

Note: Serve this unusual and flavorsome dish accompanied by bowls of unflavored yogurt and topped with freshly chopped coriander.

Serves 4

ingredients

2 tablespoons oil
2 onions, chopped
1 teaspoon whole allspice
1 cinnamon stick
1 teaspoon grated fresh ginger
2 green peppers, sliced
750g/1½ lb chuck steak,
cut into 5cm/2in cubes
2 tablespoons chopped fresh lemon grass
500mL/16fl oz chicken stock
500g/1 lb pumpkin, peeled,
cut into 4cm/1½in cubes
2 cloves garlic, crushed

paprika
beef

Method:
1. To make marinade, combine turmeric, paprika, chilli powder, yogurt and rind in bowl. Add steak and toss to coat. Cover and refrigerate for 2-4 hours or overnight.
2. Heat oil in large saucepan. Add onions and cook over medium heat for about 5 minutes or until onions soften. Add steak and marinade and cook over high heat for about 10 minutes or until steak is well browned.
3. Stir in wine and water. Bring to the boil, cover and simmer for about 1 1/2 hours or until steak is tender. Stir in olives and parsley, cook over medium heat for 3 minutes longer. Season to taste.

Note: Chunks of beef are marinated and then cooked in a flavorsome liquid. Remember, the longer your meat is in the marinade, the more tasty and tender it will be.

Serves 8

ingredients

1 kg/2 lb chuck steak,
cut into 2 1/2cm/1in squares
4 tablespoons oil
2 onions, peeled, sliced
125mL/4fl oz dry white wine
250mL/8fl oz water
185g/6 oz stuffed Spanish olives
4 tablespoons chopped fresh
flat- leafed parsley

Marinade
1 teaspoon ground turmeric
1 1/2 tablespoons mild paprika
1/2 teaspoon chilli powder
220g/7oz plain natural yogurt
2 teaspoons grated lemon rind

seasoned
sausage ragout

Method:

1 Combine ground veal, parsley, basil, nuts, oil, garlic, pepper, breadcrumbs and cheese in large bowl, mix until well combined. Shape into 12 sausages, 10cm/4in long. Roll in seasoned flour.

2 Heat oil in deep frypan. Cook sausages a few at a time until browned but not cooked through. Remove sausages and drain on absorbent kitchen paper. Repeat with remaining sausages.

3 Arrange sausages, potatoes and onions in deep saucepan. Combine soy sauce, juice, stock, wine and basil in bowl, pour into saucepan. Bring to the boil, reduce heat and simmer, covered, for 20 minutes or until potatoes are tender. Thicken sauce in pan, if desired.

Note: For a complete meal, serve this tasty ragout with a chilled tomato salad and crusty French bread.

Serves 6

ingredients

500g/1 lb ground veal
60g/2oz finely chopped fresh parsley
60g/2oz finely chopped fresh basil
3 tablespoons pine nuts
1 tablespoon olive oil
2 cloves garlic, crushed
1 teaspoon cracked black pepper
185g/6oz fresh breadcrumbs
60g/2oz grated fresh Parmesan cheese
seasoned flour
oil for deep frying
3 tablespoons soy sauce
125mL/4fl oz lemon juice
250mL/8fl oz chicken stock
250mL/8fl oz dry white wine
12 whole baby potatoes, scrubbed
12 whole baby onions, peeled
3 tablespoons chopped fresh basil

Oven temperature 180°C/350°F/Gas 4

beef
with artichokes, olives and oregano

Method:

1 *Pre-heat oven to 180°C/350°F/Gas 4.*

2 *In a large heavy based oven-proof dish heat one table spoon olive oil, add meat and sear quickly on all sides. Take out and set aside.*

3 *Heat extra olive oil, add garlic and onions, and cook for 2-3 minutes. Add white wine, cook for one minute, then add beef stock, tomato paste, oregano, and salt and pepper. Bring to boil, return meat to dish, add arti chokes, cover, and bake for 30-40 minutes.*

4 *Add olives in the last five minutes of cooking time.*

5 *Slice the meat and arrange with vegetables; pour the sauce over meat and vegetables. *Trim artichokes of outer leaves and stems. Place in a bowl of water with lemon juice. This stops the artichokes from going brown.*

Serves 4

ingredients

2 tablespoons olive oil
750g/2lb fillet steak
1 clove garlic (crushed)
1 bunch spring onions (trimmed and halved)
125mL/4fl oz white wine
250mL/8fl oz beef stock
1 tablespoon tomato paste
2 teaspoons oregano (chopped)
salt and freshly ground pepper
2 globe artichokes (trimmed, and cut into quarters*)
⅓ cup olives (pitted)

Oven temperature 200°C/400°F/Gas 6

tasty veal
and potato bake

Method:

1 Heat butter in large frypan. Add meat and cook until browned on all sides. Remove from pan and arrange in a shallow ovenproof dish, cover and keep warm.

2 Add onion, cloves, cardamom, cumin, coriander, peppercorns and garlic to pan and cook over low heat for 5 minutes or until onion is soft. Stir in tomato puree, stock and sauce, bring to the boil and simmer, uncovered, for about 20 minutes or until sauce has thickened slightly, stirring occasionally. Strain sauce through fine sieve and pour over veal.

3 Slice potatoes thinly, arrange over veal. Drizzle with butter and bake, uncovered, at 200°C/400°F/Gas 6 for 25-30 minutes or until veal is tender and potatoes are golden.

Serves 6

ingredients

3 tablespoons butter
12 veal loin chops, boned and rolled
1 onion, finely chopped
3 whole cloves
1 cardamom pod, bruised
$^1/_2$ teaspoon cumin seeds
$^1/_2$ teaspoon coriander seeds
1 teaspoon black peppercorns
2 cloves garlic, chopped
410g/13oz canned tomato puree
500mL/16fl oz beef stock
2 tablespoons tomato sauce
2 potatoes, peeled and parboiled
2 tablespoons butter, melted

mediterranean
beef & olive casserole

Method:

1 Fill a large non-metallic bowl with cold water and add the lemon juice. Rinse the meat in the lemon water then drain well. Mix together all the ingredients for the marinade, then add the meat and coat. Cover and refrigerate for 4 hours, or overnight.

2 Preheat the oven to 160°C/325°F/Gas 3. Lift the meat out of the bowl, reserving the marinade, and drain well. Coat a large, flameproof and ovenproof casserole dish with 1 tablespoon of oil. Add half the meat and fry for 6-7 minutes, until browned, turning once. Set aside, then fry the remaining meat. Stir in the marinade and the pitted olives and mix well.

3 Cover the dish with a double layer of foil, then a lid. Cook for 2 hours. Remove the lid and foil, press the meat down with the back of a wooden spoon and top with the tomatoes. Season lightly and drizzle over the remaining oil. Cover the dish with the foil and lid again and cook for 1 hour or until the beef is tender.

4 Skim off any surface fat. Season if necessary, then sprinkle over the lemon rind, the parsley and the whole olives. Serve from the dish.

Note: Long, slow cooking makes this beef steak gloriously tender. Black olives and fresh fennel lend their distinctive flavors to the rich wine and tomato sauce.

ingredients

grated rind and juice of 1 lemon
1½kg/3lb lean braising steak,
cut into 5cm/2in chunks
2 tablespoons olive oil
3 tablespoons drained pitted black olives,
plus 15 unpitted to serve
4 tomatoes, quartered and deseeded
salt and black pepper
chopped fresh parsley to garnish

For the marinade
375g/13oz onions, chopped
2 cloves garlic, crushed
3 bay leaves
2 teaspoons dried thyme
1 teaspoon dried oregano
2 tablespoons chopped fresh parsley
1 small bulb fennel, chopped
2 carrots, sliced
8 black peppercorns
2 tablespoons olive oil
750 mL/26oz bottle dry white wine

Oven temperature 160°C/325°F/Gas 3

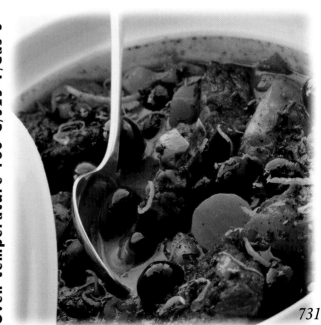

731

Oven temperature 160°C/325°F/Gas 3

beef
carbonade

Method:

1 *Preheat the oven to 160°C/325°F/Gas 3. Heat 2 tablespoons of the oil in a flameproof casserole dish. Add a third of the beef and fry over a high heat for 6-7 minutes, turning until browned on all sides. Remove from the pan while you cook the remaining batches, adding more oil if necessary. Set the beef aside.*

2 *Lower the heat, add the onion and cook for 5 minutes, stirring. Sprinkle in the flour and sugar and stir for 1-2 minutes, then pour in the stout and beef stock and bring to the boil, stirring. Return the beef to the dish and add the tomato purée and bouquet garni. Season and stir well, then cover.*

3 *Transfer the dish to the oven and cook for 1½-2 hours, until the beef is tender and cooked through. Stir 2-3 times during cooking, adding a little water if necessary. Discard the bouquet garni and season again if necessary. Garnish with parsley.*

Note: *Almost everyone loves a good old-fashioned stew and you can't beat a beef one. Serve it with plenty of creamy mashed potatoes to soak up the rich gravy.*

ingredients

**2-3 tablespoons vegetable oil
1kg/2lb braising or stewing steak, cut
into 2½cm/1in cubes
1 large onion, thinly sliced
1 tablespoon plain flour
2 tablespoon soft dark or light
brown sugar
275mL/8fl oz can stout
500mL/18fl oz beef stock
1 tablespoon tomato purée
1 bouquet garni
salt and black pepper
fresh parsley to garnish**

Serves 4

rich beef
stew with shallots

Method:

1 *Preheat the oven to 240°C/475°F/Gas Mark 9. Place the shallots, garlic, carrots and celery in a roasting tin, pour over 2 tablespoons of oil, then mix well. Cook for 15 minutes, turning frequently, or until the vegetables are browned.*

2 *Heat the remaining oil in a large, heavy-based saucepan, add one-third of the meat and fry for 5-8 minutes, until browned all over. Remove from the pan and set aside while you cook the remaining meat in two more batches. Return all the meat to the dish. Add the vegetables, herb bundle, wine, stock, pearl barley and peppercorns. Season and bring to the boil.*

3 *Reduce the heat and simmer, partly covered, for 2-2½ hours, until the meat is tender. Check from time to time and add a little more stock or water if the stew starts to dry out. Remove the herb bundle before serving.*
Note: *There are times when all you want is a warming stew, especially if the weather is bad. Serve with comforting mashed potato with chopped fresh parsley stirred in.*

Serves 6

ingredients

6 shallots, quartered
6 large cloves garlic, quartered
3 large carrots, sliced
4 sticks celery, sliced
4 tablespoons olive oil
1kg/2lb lean stewing beef, cut into 5cm/2in cubes
few thyme sprigs, 1 bay leaf, 1 rosemary sprig and 1 strip of lemon rind, tied with string
500mL/18fl oz claret or other full-bodied red wine
300mL/10fl oz beef stock
3 tablespoons pearl barley
10 black peppercorns, crushed
salt and black pepper

Oven temperature 240°C/475°F/Gas 9

slowly
simmered indonesian
beef curry

Method:

1 Peel the outer layers from the lemon grass stalks, then finely chop the lower white bulbous parts discarding the fibrous tops. Heat a large saucepan and dry-fry the coconut for 5 minutes or until golden, stirring frequently. Finely grind the coconut in a food processor or use a pestle and mortar.

2 Blend or grind the lemon grass, onions, garlic, ginger and chilli to a paste. Heat the oil in the pan and fry the paste for 5 minutes to release the flavors, stirring often. Add the beef, stir to coat and fry for 3-4 minutes, until sealed.

3 Add the ground coconut, turmeric, coconut milk, sugar and salt to taste and mix well. Bring to the boil, stirring, then reduce the heat. Simmer, uncovered, for 3 hours, stirring from time to time, until the sauce reduces to a rich gravy. Garnish with the sliced chilli.

Note: Rendang, a classic Indonesian dish, can also be made with lamb or venison. Slow cooking in the rich coconut sauce results in meltingly tender meat. Serve with rice.

Serves 4

ingredients

2 stalks lemon grass
4 tablespoons desiccated coconut
2 onions, chopped
2 cloves garlic, chopped
5cm/2in piece fresh root ginger, chopped
1 red chilli, deseeded and chopped, plus 1 red chilli, deseeded and sliced, to garnish
2 tablespoons vegetable oil
750g/1½ lb topside beef, cut into 2½cm/1in cubes
1 teaspoon turmeric
420ml/14fl oz can coconut milk
1 teaspoon sugar
Salt

Oven temperature 180°C/350°F/Gas 4

beef
braised in red wine

Method:

1 *Preheat the oven to 180°C/350°F/Gas 4. Heat the oil in a flameproof casserole dish or large saucepan and fry the meat over a high heat, stirring, for 5-10 minutes, until browned. Remove from the pan, then add the shallots, garlic and celery. Cook, stirring, for 3-4 minutes, until lightly browned.*

2 *Add the mushrooms and cook for 1 minute or until softened. Stir in the allspice, wine, passata, 1 sprig of thyme and season. Return the meat to the dish or pan and bring the mixture to a simmer.*

3 *Cover and cook in the oven or over a low heat on the hob for 1½-2 hours, until the beef is tender. Season again if necessary, then serve garnished with the remaining thyme.*

Note: *This Spanish casserole is perfect on a cold day, served with garlic mash. You can use any type of mushroom, but ceps or chestnut ones are especially good.*

Serves 4

ingredients

**3 tablespoons olive oil
750g/1½ lb stewing beef,
trimmed of fat and cut into
6cm/2½in chunks
6 shallots, finely chopped
2 garlic cloves, crushed
2 sticks celery, thickly sliced
300g/10oz mushrooms, thickly sliced
½ teaspoon ground allspice
½ bottle Rioja or other
full-bodied red wine
250mL/9fl oz passata
2 sprigs fresh thyme
salt and black pepper**

Oven temperature 150°C/300°F/Gas 2

mexican
style beef olives

Method:

1 Preheat the oven to 150°C/300°F/Gas 2. Place the beef between sheets of cling film and flatten slightly with a rolling pin, remove film. Put the bacon into a large frying pan and fry gently for 2-3 minutes, until cooked. Remove from the heat and stir in the parsley, marjoram and breadcrumbs.

2 Mix together the flour, salt and pepper in a shallow dish. Divide the bacon mixture between the slices of beef, then roll up each slice from the short end, turn in the seasoned flour and secure with a wetted cocktail stick.

3 Heat the oil in a flameproof casserole dish, add the beef and cook for 2 minutes, turning until browned all over. Remove from the dish and set aside. Add the chilli powder, onion, garlic and red pepper to the dish and cook for 3 minutes to soften. Return the meat to the dish, pour in the stock, then bring to the boil. Cover the dish, then bake for 45 minutes. Add the kidney beans and cook for another 45 minutes. Remove the cocktail sticks and serve.

Note: A little beef goes a long way in this twist on chilli con carne. Serve it with bread or mashed potatoes.

ingredients

4 thin cut beef steaks
4 rashers rindless bacon, finely chopped
1 tablespoon chopped fresh parsley
$\frac{1}{2}$ teaspoon dried marjoram
75g/2$\frac{1}{2}$oz fresh breadcrumbs
45g/1$\frac{1}{2}$oz plain flour
salt and black pepper
1 tablespoon vegetable oil
1-2 teaspoon hot chilli powder
1 onion, chopped
2 cloves garlic, finely chopped
1 red pepper,
deseeded and chopped
200mL/7fl oz beef stock
410g/13oz can red kidney beans,
drained and rinsed

Serves 4

Oven temperature 150°C/300°F/Gas 2

venison
casserole with chilli beans

Method:

1 Preheat the oven to 150°C/300°F/Gas 2. Mix together the flour, salt and pepper on a plate. Dip the venison into the mixture to coat. Heat the oil in a large flameproof casserole dish and fry the venison in batches over a medium to high heat for 5 minutes or until browned on all sides. Remove from the pan and set aside.

2 Lower the heat and add the onion to the dish with a little more oil, if necessary. Stir for 5 minutes or until lightly browned, then add the garlic, chillies and chilli powder and stir for 1 minute.

3 Add the tomatoes, beef stock, tomato purée and sugar. Bring to the boil, stirring. Add the venison, stir well and cover tightly with the lid. Transfer the dish to the oven and cook for 2 hours or until the venison is tender, stirring twice and adding the kidney beans for the last 30 minutes of cooking.

Note: Tender chunks of slow-cooked venison are set off by a spicy mixture of beans and tomatoes in this casserole. Serve with rice or crusty bread and a large salad.

Serves 4

ingredients

2 tablespoons plain flour
salt and black pepper
690g/22oz diced shoulder of venison
2 tablespoons groundnut oil
1 Spanish onion, finely chopped
2 cloves garlic, crushed
2 fresh green chillies,
deseeded and finely chopped
1 tablespoon chilli powder
410g/13oz can chopped tomatoes
410mL/13fl oz beef stock
2 tablespoons tomato purée
2 teaspoons soft light or
dark brown sugar
410g/13oz can red kidney beans,
drained and rinsed

steak pie
with guinness

Method:

1 Preheat the oven to 180°C/350°F/Gas 4. Combine the flour, mustard and pepper, then coat the beef in the mixture. Heat 2 tablespoons of oil in a heavy-based frying pan. Fry a third of the beef for 3-4 minutes, until browned. Transfer to an ovenproof dish and fry the rest of the beef in 2 more batches.

2 Add another tablespoon of oil to the pan, then fry the onions for 5 minutes. Add the garlic and cook for 2 minutes. Stir in the Guinness, Worcestershire sauce, herbs and sugar and simmer for 2-3 minutes. Pour over the beef, then cover and cook in the oven for 2 hours. Remove the beef and increase the oven temperature to 190°C/375°F/ Gas 5. Fry the mushrooms in the rest of the oil. Stir into the beef, then transfer to a 15x20cm/6x8in pie dish.

3 Sift together the flour and i teaspoon of salt, then add the thyme and pepper. Stir in the suet and bind with 10-12 tablespoons of water to form a soft dough. Roll it out, dampen the edges of the dish and cover with the pastry. Trim, then make a small slit in the centre. Cook for 30-40 minutes, until golden.

Note: Guinness adds its creamy richness to this slow-cooked steak pie. Serve it with mash and peas or cabbage.

Serves 6

ingredients

3 tablespoons plain flour
1 teaspoon English mustard powder
salt and black pepper
750g/1 ½ lb stewing beef, trimmed and cut into cubes
4 tablespoons vegetable oil
2 onions, sliced
2 cloves garlic, finely chopped
500mL/16fl oz bottle Guinness stout
2 tablespoons Worcestershire sauce
2 bay leaves
1 tablespoon chopped fresh thyme
1 teaspoon soft dark brown sugar
250g/9oz chestnut mushrooms, halved if large

For the pastry crust
250g/9oz self-rising flour
2 teaspoon chopped fresh thyme
125g/4oz shredded suet or shortening

Oven temperature 180°C/350°F/Gas 4

spicy beef
with lime pickle

Method:

1 Heat a little of the oil over high heat in a deep-sided pan. Fry onion and garlic for 1-2 minutes. Remove and put aside.

2 Heat a little more oil on high. Brown beef in small batches, removing each batch before adding next.

3 Return beef and onion to pan. Add remaining ingredients, stirring to combine.

4 Cover and simmer gently for 1-1½ hours for blade or round, 1½-2 hours for chuck or shin. Stir occasionally. Season to taste. If curry needs thickening, boil with lid off for 10-15 minutes. Serve with rice, yogurt and cucumber, banana and coconut with slices of lime.

Serves 4

ingredients

750g/1½ lb lean beef, diced-round, blade, chuck or gravy beef
1 tablespoon canola oil
1 onion, chopped
2 teaspoons garlic, crushed
1 tablespoon lime pickle
1 tablespoon sambal oelek
(very hot chilli paste)
250mL/8fl oz beef stock

hearty beef
casserole with duchess potatoes

Method:

1 Preheat oven to 180°C/350°F/Gas 4. Trim beef of excess fat, cut into 3cm cubes, toss in sufficient flour to coat. Heat oil in deep saucepan or Dutch oven, brown beef well.

2 Stir in tomatoes, corn and Worcestershire sauce. Transfer to ovenproof casserole dish. Cover and bake 2 hours, stirring occasionally. Remove casserole, increase heat 220°C/440°F/Gas 7.

3 Boil potatoes until soft. Drain and mash with egg, season to taste. Pipe swirls of potato onto greased oven slide. Bake at 15-20 minutes or until golden.

4 Meanwhile, steam or microwave cauliflower and broccoli 8-10 minutes.

5 Serve beef casserole with duchess potatoes, cauliflower and broccoli.

Serves 4-6

ingredients

750g/1½ lb lean chuck steak
2-3 tablespoons flour
1 tablespoon olive oil
420g/14oz can tomatoes, undrained
2x130g/4oz cans corn kernels, undrained
1 tablespoon Worcestershire sauce
4 large potatoes, peeled and diced
1 egg, beaten
300g/10oz cauliflower, broken into florets
300g/10oz broccoli florets

spiced
shredded beef

Method:

1 Place beef, onion, garlic, clove, cumin seeds and water in a saucepan over a medium heat, bring to simmering and simmer, skimming the top occasionally, for 1½ hours or until beef is very tender. Remove pan from heat and cool beef in liquid. Skim fat from surface as it cools. Remove beef from liquid and shred with a fork. Reserve cooking liquid for making sauce.

2 To make sauce, heat oil in a frying pan over a high heat, add onion and chillies and cook, stirring, for 3 minutes or until tender. Stir in tomatoes and 1 cup/250 mL/8 fl oz of the reserved cooking liquid, bring to simmering and simmer for 10 minutes or until mixture reduces and thickens.

3 Add shredded beef to sauce and simmer for 5 minutes or until heated through.

   Note: The cooking time will depend on the cut of meat used. For a complete meal, serve on warm flour tortillas with salad and Green Rice with Herbs.

Serves 6

ingredients

**750g/1½ lb boneless beef chuck, blade or brisket, trimmed of visible fat
1 onion, halved
2 cloves garlic, peeled
1 clove
2 teaspoons cumin seeds
8 cups/2 litres/3½pt water
green chilli and tomato sauce
2 teaspoons vegetable oil
1 onion, chopped
2 hot green chillies, chopped
440g/14oz canned tomatoes, undrained and chopped**

jarkoy
beef and fruit casserole

Method:

1 Trim the fat from the chuck steak. Cut into large cubes. Peel and slice the carrots and onions. Heat a large heavy-based saucepan, add butter or oil and a third of the beef cubes. Toss to brown well on all sides over high heat. Remove and brown the remainder in 2 batches. Add the sliced carrot and onions and sauté a little.

2 Return all meat to saucepan and sprinkle in the flour to cover all the surface. Add the garlic, dill, nutmeg, salt, pepper and beef stock. Bring to the boil over high heat, stirring to lift browned-on juices. Cover, reduce heat to low and simmer slowly for 1 ½ hours.

3 After 1 ½ hours add dried fruits, mint and coriander. Cover and simmer 30 minutes more or until meat is tender. Remove to a heated serving dish. Sprinkle with crushed walnuts and orange juice.

Serves 6

ingredients

1kg/2lb thick-cut chuck steak
3 large carrots
3 medium onions, thinly sliced
2 tablespoons butter or oil
2 tablespoons flour
2 cloves garlic, crushed
1 teaspoon chopped fresh dill
or ½ teaspoon dried dill
½ teaspoon nutmeg, grated or ground
salt and freshly ground black pepper
1 ½ cups rich beef stock
½ cup dried apricots
½ cup dried peaches, cut in quarters
½ cup pitted prunes
1 teaspoon chopped mint
1 tablespoon chopped coriander (cilanto)
½ cup walnuts, crushed
½ cup orange juice

carbonada
griolla

Method:

1 Heat oil in a large saucepan and sauté the garlic and onion. Add veal cubes and quickly stir over high heat to brown lightly.

2 Add tomatoes, stock, thyme, parsley and season with salt and pepper. Bring to the boil, then turn down heat and simmer for 25 minutes.

3 Add the cubed vegetables, corn, rice and dried fruits. Cover and simmer for 25 minutes. Stir occasionally during cooking and add extra stock if necessary. Adjust seasoning before serving.

Serves 6

ingredients

2 tablespoons oil
1 clove garlic, crushed
1 large onion, chopped
1kg/2lb boned shoulder of veal,
cut into 2cm/¾ in cubes
220g/7oz can peeled tomatoes
1½ cups beef stock
1 teaspoon chopped thyme
2 tablespoons chopped parsley
salt and pepper
1 medium potato, cubed
1 sweet potato, cubed
250g/8oz pumpkin, cubed
2 fresh corn cobs, cut into thick slices
½ cup short grain rice
4 dried peaches, cut in half
4 dried pears, cut in half

drumsticks in dill sauce

white meat dishes

The flavor of pork blends well

with a variety of herbs and spices, fruits and vegetables, giving a wide repertoire of tasty dishes. Any piece of chicken can be used in casseroling, providing the bone is still intact . This allows the extra flavors from the bone to be absorbed into the sauce and meat during cooking.

drumsticks
in dill sauce

Photograph on page 745

ingredients

2 tablespoons butter
I kg/2 lb chicken drumsticks
I cup/90g/3oz chopped spring onions
3 tablespoons finely chopped dill
¼ cup/60mL/2fl oz lemon juice
½ teaspoon salt
¼ teaspoon white pepper
I bunch baby carrots, peeled
2 cups water
I chicken stock cube
2 tablespoons cornflour
2 tablespoons water

Method:

1 *Heat butter in a wide-based saucepan. Add drumsticks a few at a time and brown lightly on all sides. Remove to a plate and brown remainder.*

2 *Add spring onions and sauté for one minute. Stir in chopped dill. Add lemon juice, return drumsticks to saucepan, sprinkle with salt and pepper.*

3 *Arrange the carrots over the drumsticks. Add water and stock cube. Bring to a simmer, turn down heat, cover and simmer for 40 minutes until tender.*

4 *Remove drumsticks and carrots with a slotted spoon and arrange on a heated platter.*
Note: *Blend the cornflour with water, stir into the juices remaining in the pan. Stir over heat until sauce boils and thickens. Pour over drumsticks and carrots. Serve immediately with crusty bread.*

Serves 6

chicken
and sweet
peppers

ingredients

2 tablespoons olive oil
12 skinless chicken thighs
I onion, halved and sliced
4 cloves garlic, chopped
2 red and 2 yellow peppers deseeded and thinly sliced
2 tablespoons chopped fresh thyme or 2 TEASPOONS dried thyme
300mL/½pint chicken stock
250mL/9fl oz white wine
salt and black pepper
chopped fresh basil or flat-leaf parsley to garnish

Method:

1 *Heat the oil in a large, heavy-based frying pan, add the thighs and fry for 4-5 minutes on each side, until browned. Remove and set aside. Add the onion and garlic to the pan and fry for 5 minutes or until softened. Add the peppers and fry for a further 4-5 minutes, until slightly softened. Reserve a few pepper slices for the garnish.*

2 *Stir in the thyme, stock and wine, season lightly and bring to the boil. Boil for I-2 minutes, then reduce the heat and add the chicken, mixing well. Cover and simmer for 30-35 minutes, until the thighs are cooked through and tender.*

3 *Remove the chicken, cover and keep warm. Increase the heat and boil the cooking sauce rapidly for 4-5 minutes, until it has reduced and thickened slightly. Season again if necessary. Transfer the mixture to a serving dish, lay the chicken thighs on top and garnish with basil or parsley and the reserved pepper slices.*

Serves 6

braised
rabbit with dried fruit

Method:

1 Wash rabbit and pat dry. Cut into serving pieces. Season with salt and pepper. Heat oil or butter in a large, lidded frying pan or saucepan. Add rabbit pieces and quickly brown all sides on high heat.

2 Remove to a plate. Reduce heat, add onions and cook until golden. Add water and stir to lift pan juices. Return rabbit to the pan, sprinkle in the chopped thyme and add bay leaves. Cover and simmer for 40 minutes.

3 Add the fruit salad and wine, cover and continue to simmer for 30 minutes more, or until rabbit is tender. Add more liquid to saucepan during cooking if necessary. Taste and adjust seasoning. Uncover and stir in the cream. Simmer with lid off for 5 minutes. Serve with rice or mashed potato.

Serves 6

ingredients

1 ½kg/3lb rabbit
salt and pepper
2 tablespoons oil or clarified butter
6 small onions, halved
2 cups water
1 tablespoon chopped, fresh thyme
2 bay leaves
200g/6½oz packet mixed dried fruit
150mL/5fl oz red wine
150mL/5fl oz cream

tarragon
pork with vegetables

Method:

1 Heat butter in large saucepan. Add pork and cook over high heat until browned on all sides. Add onions and leek to pan with meat and cook over low heat for 5 minutes or until onion softens.

2 Add stock, lemon juice, pepper and bay leaves, bring to the boil. Reduce heat and simmer, covered, for 30 minutes turning meat occasionally. Add turnip, potatoes, carrots and celery and simmer, covered, for 15 minutes longer or until vegetables are firm but tender and meat is cooked through.

3 Remove meat and vegetables from pan. Set aside and keep warm. Bring pan juices to the boil and boil, uncovered, for 2 minutes. Stir in redcurrant jelly and tarragon and simmer for 5 minutes. To serve, slice pork, accompany with vegetables and spoon over sauce.

Note: A succulent pot roast of pork with vegetables delicately flavored with fresh tarragon.

Serves 6

ingredients

2 tablespoons butter
1 kg/2 lb boned and rolled
shoulder of pork
2 onions, chopped
1 leek, chopped
750mL/1¼pt chicken stock
3 tablespoons lemon juice
1 teaspoon cracked black pepper
2 dried bay leaves
1 turnip, peeled and chopped
12 baby potatoes, washed and drained
2 carrots, peeled and chopped
2 sticks celery, chopped
3 tablespoons redcurrant jelly
2 tablespoons chopped fresh tarragon

pork
and asparagus casserole

Method:

1 Lightly coat pork in seasoned flour. Empty asparagus and liquid into a shallow microwave casserole with garlic and vermouth. Add pork and any remaining seasoned flour in a single layer in the dish; cover. Cook on power level 5 (Medium) for 15 minutes, turn pork over and cook further 10 minutes on same power.

2 Remove pork to a separate dish, cover and keep warm.

3 Add shallots, grapes and cream and stir into asparagus; season with mustard. Cook on power level 9 (High) for 2 minutes; stir and return pork spooning over the sauce. Cover, reduce power to 5 (Medium) and cook for 2 minutes longer.

4 Stand 5 minutes. Serve with savory cooked noodles and steamed broccoli.

Note: A delicious blend of flavors in a tangy sauce.

Serves 4-6

ingredients

(Microwave)
750g/1½lb pork steaks, leg or shoulder
2 tablespoons seasoned flour
315g/10oz can asparagus pieces
1 clove garlic
2 tablespoons white Vermouth
3 chopped shallots
1 cup sultana grapes
2 tablespoons sour cream
2 teaspoons German mustard

rabbit, olive
and onion casserole

Method:

1 *In a large bowl, combine the rabbit, wine, oregano and bay leaves. Cover, and refrigerate overnight.*
2 *Drain the rabbit and reserve the marinade. Pre-heat oven (to 180°C/350°F/Gas 4..*
3 *Heat the oil in a large frypan and brown the rabbit a few pieces at a time on both sides. Remove the rabbit and place in a casserole dish.*
4 *Brown the onions and garlic in the pan. Once golden, add the paprika. Stir continuously for two minutes, then add the stock and reserved marinade. Bring to the boil.*
5 *Pour onion and stock mixture over rabbit, add olives, and season with salt and pepper.*
6 *Cover and bake for one hour and 15 minutes (or until rabbit is cooked and tender). Garnish with fresh oregano, and serve with plenty of bread (to mop up the juices).*

Serves 4

ingredients

750g/1½lb rabbit portions
375mL/12fl oz dry white wine
3 sprigs fresh oregano
3 bay leaves
80mL/2½fl oz olive oil
220g/7oz baby onions (peeled and halved)
6 cloves garlic (unpeeled)
1 tablespoon paprika
170mL/6fl oz chicken stock
½ cup black olives
salt and freshly ground black pepper
fresh oregano sprigs (to garnish)
crusty bread

Oven temperature 180°C/350°F/Gas 4

fruity
chicken casserole

Method:

1. Lightly coat chicken with flour. Heat oil in large saucepan, add chicken pieces and cook over medium heat for 8 minutes or until golden brown. Remove from pan and drain on absorbent kitchen paper.

2. Add onions and potatoes to pan, cook over low heat for about 5 minutes or until onion softens. Stir in stock, juices and honey. Return chicken to pan, add apricots, apples and prunes. Bring mixture to the boil and simmer, covered, for 20 minutes or until chicken and fruits are tender.

3. Just before serving, stir in olives and thyme. Season to taste.

Note: This Middle Eastern inspired casserole looks great served on a bed of saffron rice and garnished with fresh thyme sprigs.

Serves 6

ingredients

12 chicken wings, rinsed and drained
3 tablespoons oil
3 tablespoons plain flour
2 onions, sliced
12 baby potatoes, scrubbed
250mL/8 fl oz chicken stock
250 mL/8 fl oz apple juice or cider
125mL/4 fl oz lemon juice
125mL/4 fl oz honey
220g/7oz whole dried apricots
220g/7oz dried apples, chopped
90g/3oz prunes, pitted
12 black olives
1 tablespoon chopped fresh lemon thyme

creamy
chicken with sweet potato

Method:

1 Heat oil in large saucepan. Toss chicken pieces in flour. Add to pan and cook over medium heat until browned. Remove from pan and drain on absorbent paper. Set aside and keep warm.

2 Add onions to pan, cook over low heat for 5 minutes or until soft. Stir in curry powder and mustard seeds, cook for 2 minutes stirring continually. Stir in wine, chicken stock and tomatoes, bring to boil then reduce heat.

3 Return chicken to saucepan and add sweet potato. Simmer, covered, for about 30 minutes or until chicken is cooked and potato is tender. Combine garlic, basil, mayonnaise and sour cream in small bowl. Add to saucepan, stirring over low heat until just warmed through. Season to taste.

Note: The combination of chicken and sweet potato with a hint of curry makes a delicious family meal.

Serves 4

ingredients

3 tablespoons oil
8 chicken thighs
3 tablespoons plain flour
2 onions, sliced
I tablespoon mild curry powder
I teaspoon brown mustard seeds
250mL/8fl oz dry white wine
250mL/8fl oz chicken stock
440g/14oz canned tomatoes, chopped
500g/1 lb sweet potato,
peeled and cut into 2¹/₂cm/1in cubes
2 cloves garlic, crushed
3 tablespoons finely chopped
fresh basil
2 tablespoons mayonnaise
2 tablespoons sour cream

pork
hock risotto

Method:

1 Heat butter in large saucepan. Add hocks and cook over high heat until browned all over. Stir in water, bouquet garni and peppercorns. Bring to the boil, reduce heat and simmer, covered, for 1 hour.

2 Sprinkle eggplant (aubergine) liberally with salt, set aside for 20 minutes. Rinse under cold running water and pat dry with absorbent kitchen paper.

3 Remove meat from the hocks and transfer with liquid to a deep casserole dish. Stir in rice, stock, onion and turmeric, cover and cook at 180°C/350°F/Gas 4 for 50 minutes. Remove bouquet garni and discard.

4 Add eggplant (aubergine), peppers and tomato to casserole and cook, uncovered, for 10 minutes or until almost all liquid is absorbed and rice is tender. Stand for 5 minutes and sprinkle with fresh herbs before serving.

Note: Earthy and comforting, this substantial risotto makes an ideal midwinter meal.

Serves 8

ingredients

3 tablespoons butter
4 medium pork hocks
1 L/35fl oz water
1 bouquet garni
1 teaspoon whole black peppercorns
2 eggplants (aubergine),
unpeeled, chopped
salt
375g/12oz long grain rice
375mL/12fl oz chicken stock
1 onion, chopped
1 teaspoon ground turmeric
2 green peppers, sliced
2 tomatoes, peeled, seeded and chopped
chopped fresh herbs, such as parsley,
chives and coriander (cilantro)

Oven temperature 180°C/350°F/Gas 4

chicken
biryani

Method:

1 Heat ghee in a large frypan, cook onions for 2-3 minutes or until golden brown. Remove from pan and set aside.

2 Add chicken to the pan and cook until well browned on all sides. Remove from pan and set aside.

3 Combine ginger, garlic, cumin, cinnamon, cloves, cardamom, nutmeg and flour. Stir into pan and cook for 1-2 minutes. Add stock, yogurt and cream, stirring to lift pan sediment.

4 Return chicken to the pan with half the onions. Cover and simmer for 15-20 minutes. Remove from heat and stand, covered, for 15 minutes.

5 To make rice pilau, heat ghee in a large saucepan. Cook saffron, cardamom, salt and rice for 1-2 minutes. Pour in stock and bring to the boil. Add sultanas, reduce heat and cook gently for 10-15 minutes or until most of the stock is absorbed. Cover and set aside for 10 minutes.

6 Transfer half the rice to a large ovenproof dish, top with chicken pieces, then remaining rice. Drizzle over sauce from chicken, top with remaining onions and cashew nuts. Cover and bake at 180°C/350°F/Gas 4 for 20-30 minutes.

Note: The great Mogul emperors served biryani at lavish feasts on plates so large that two people were required to carry them.

Serves 4

ingredients

3 tablespoons ghee
3 onions, sliced
1¹/₂kg/3 lb chicken pieces
2 teaspoons grated fresh ginger
3 cloves garlic, crushed
¹/₂ teaspoon ground cumin
¹/₂ teaspoon ground cinnamon
¹/₄ teaspoon ground cloves
¹/₄ teaspoon ground cardamom
¹/₄ teaspoon ground nutmeg
¹/₂ teaspoon flour
250mL/8fl oz chicken stock
125g/4oz unflavored yogurt
125mL/4fl oz cream

Rice pilau
2 tablespoons ghee
¹/₂ teaspoon ground saffron
¹/₂ teaspoon ground cardamom
1 teaspoon salt
210g/6¹/₂ oz basmati rice, well washed
1 L/1³/₄ pts chicken stock
2 tablespoons sultanas (yellow raisins)
60g/2oz chopped cashew nuts, roasted

Oven temperature 180°C/350°F/Gas 4

mustard
chilli pork

Method:

1 Trim meat of all visible fat, brush with melted butter and bake at 180°C/350°F/Gas 4 for 25-30 minutes.
2 Heat ghee and oil in a saucepan, cook onions, mustard seeds, garlic and chillies for 2-3 minutes or until onions soften.
3 Stir in cumin, turmeric, brown sugar, water, lime juice and lime leaves. Bring to the boil, then reduce heat and simmer, uncovered, for 10 minutes or until mixture reduces and thickens.
4 Transfer mixture to a food processor or blender. Process until smooth, then return to pan. Slice pork diagonally and add to mustard mixture. Heat through gently and serve.
Note: Perfect pork transformed into an exciting dish for a special occasion. The fiery taste of mustard and chilli is a wonderful complement to the zesty tang of lime.

Serves 4

ingredients

750g/1 ½ lb pork fillets
60g/2oz melted butter
30g/1oz ghee
2 tablespoons peanut oil
3 onions, chopped
1 tablespoon black mustard seeds
2 cloves garlic, crushed
2 red chillies, chopped
½ teaspoon ground cumin
½ teaspoon ground turmeric
1 tablespoon brown sugar
250mL/8fl oz water
1 tablespoon lime juice
8 kasmir lime leaves

Oven temperature 180°C/350°F/Gas 4

chicken
breasts with shiitake mushrooms

Method:

1 *Preheat the oven to 230°C/450°F/Gas 8. Heat 1 tablespoon of the oil in a large, heavy-based saucepan, add the onion and the ginger and fry for 5 minutes or until the onion has softened. Add the shiitake and button mushrooms and the soy sauce and cook for a further 4-5 minutes, until the mushrooms have softened.*

2 *Stir in the stock and wine, bring to the boil, then simmer for 10 minutes. Add the patty pan squash or courgettes and cook for a further 5 minutes or until tender.*

3 *Meanwhile, make 3 slashes in each chicken breast, using a sharp knife. Heat the remaining oil in a large, heavy-based frying pan, add the chicken and fry for 2-3 minutes on each side to brown.*

4 *Transfer the chicken to an ovenproof dish and spoon over the mushroom mixture. Bake for 15-20 minutes, until the chicken is cooked through. Sprinkle with coriander just before serving.*

Note: *Shiitake mushrooms, soy sauce and fresh ginger give this dish an oriental flavor. It's great with plain boiled rice or Chinese noodles and some stir-fried green vegetables.*

Serves 6

ingredients

**2 tablespoons groundnut oil
1 onion, chopped
5cm/2in piece fresh root ginger, finely chopped
200g/7oz shiitake mushrooms, stems removed and caps sliced
150g/5oz baby button mushrooms
2 tablespoons dark soy sauce
300mL/½pint chicken stock
200mL/7fl oz dry white wine
350g/12oz patty pan squash, halved, or courgettes (zucchinis), trimmed and sliced
6 skinless boneless chicken breasts
chopped fresh coriander to garnish**

Oven temperature 230°C/450°F/Gas 8

spanish
style pork casserole

Method:
1 Marinate pork steaks in a shallow dish with garlic, herbs, Worcestershire and vinegar; turning to coat in mixture; stand ½ hour.
2 Prick sausages and place into a shallow dish with sliced onion and capsicum, cover and cook on power level 6 (Bake) for 7 minutes; drain off any excess fat
3 Cover pork steaks and cook for 13 minutes. Add sausage mixture, tomato sauce and beans then cover and cook together another 5 minutes; stand covered 3 minutes before serving. Serve with boiled new potatoes and crisp side salad.

Serves 4

ingredients

(Microwave)
500g/1lb or 4 pork leg steaks
1 teaspoon freshly crushed garlic
1 tablespoons chopped fresh sage
and thyme
2 tablespoons Worcestershire sauce
1 tablespoons red wine vinegar
250g/8oz or 8 pork chipolata sausages
1 medium size onion, sliced
360g/12oz can tomato pasta sauce
1 cup drained canned butter beans

lovely legs
and vegetable casserole

Method:

1 Pour the Tomato and Pesto Sauce into a casserole or baking dish and stir in the water. Place lovely legs in one layer and arrange potato quarters in between. Drizzle over the olive oil and sprinkle with parsley. Cover dish with lid or foil.
2 Place in a preheated oven 180°C/350°F/Gas 4 and cook for 30 minutes. Lift from oven and turn the legs and potatoes. Add the peas and baby corn. Return to oven and cook uncovered for 25 minutes more or until legs and potatoes are tender when tested.
3 Serve hot with crusty bread.

Serves 4-6

ingredients

375g/12½oz jar ready made Tomato and Pesto Sauce
½ cup/120ml/4fl oz water
1kg/2lb chicken drumsticks
4 medium potatoes, peeled and quartered
2 tablespoons olive oil
2 tablespoons finely chopped parsley
250g/8oz packet frozen peas
425g/14oz can baby corn

Oven temperature 180°C/350°F/Gas 4

chicken
rogan josh

Method:

1 Cut each chicken thigh into 4 pieces. Heat the oil in a large heavy-based frying pan and add the peppers, onion, ginger, garlic, spices and a good pinch of salt. Fry over a low heat for 5 minutes or until the peppers and onion have softened.

2 Add the chicken and 2 tablespoons of the yogurt. Increase the heat to medium and cook for 4 minutes or until the yogurt is absorbed. Repeat with the rest of the yogurt.

3 Increase the heat to high, stir in the tomatoes and 200ml/7fl oz of water and bring to the boil. Reduce the heat, cover, and simmer for 30 minutes or until the chicken is tender, stirring occasionally and adding more water if the sauce becomes too dry.

4 Uncover the pan, increase the heat to high and cook, stirring constantly, for 5 minutes or until the sauce thickens. Garnish with coriander (cilantro).

Note: With its combination of Indian spices and creamy yogurt, rogan josh is a real winner. Serve it with rice, a cooling mint raita and some mango chutney.

Serves 4

ingredients

8 skinless boneless chicken thighs
1 tablespoon vegetable oil
1 small red pepper and 1 small green pepper, deseeded and thinly sliced
1 onion, thinly sliced
5cm/2in piece of fresh root ginger, finely chopped
2 cloves garlic, crushed
2 tablespoons garam masala
1 teaspoon each paprika, turmeric and chilli powder
4 cardamom pods, crushed
salt
200g/6oz tub Greek yogurt
410g/13oz can chopped tomatoes
fresh coriander (cilantro) to garnish

Oven temperature 180°C/350°F/Gas 4

braised
pork with apples

Method:

1 *Preheat the oven to 180°C/350°F/Gas 4. Heat the oil in a non-stick frying pan. Add the pork and cook for 5 minutes or until browned, turning once, then transfer to a casserole dish.*

2 *Add the shallots and mushrooms to the frying pan and cook gently for 5 minutes or until softened. Add the flour and cook for 1 minute, stirring. Slowly add the stock and cider, stirring until smooth, then add the mustard and black pepper. Bring to the boil and continue stirring for 2-3 minutes, until thickened.*

3 *Place the apple slices on top of the pork steaks and pour over the sauce. Cover and cook in the oven for 1-1¼ hours, until the pork is tender and cooked through. Garnish with fresh parsley.*

Serves 4

ingredients

**1 tablespoon sunflower oil
4 boneless lean pork loin steaks or loin medallions, about 100g/3½oz each
4 shallots, thinly sliced
175g/6oz mushrooms, sliced
1 tablespoon plain flour
200mL/7fl oz vegetable stock
100mL/4fl oz dry cider
2 teaspoon Dijon or wholegrain mustard
black pepper
2 large eating apples, peeled, cored and sliced
fresh flat-leaf parsley to garnish**

chicken
curry

Method:

1 Cut chicken thighs in half or into 3 pieces. Heat half the oil in a large saucepan, add $1/3$ of the chicken and quickly brown on both sides. Remove to a plate and brown remaining chicken in 2 batches, adding remaining oil when necessary. Remove last batch of chicken.

2 Add onion and cook a little then stir in the Madras curry cooking sauce. Add a liitle water to the can to rinse down remaining sauce (about a $1/4$ can) and then pour into saucepan. Bring to the boil, turn down heat and return the chicken to the saucepan. Cover and simmer for 20 minutes.

Add sultanas, banana and apple and simmer 15-20 minutes more.

Serve immediately with boiled rice.

ingredients

500g/1 lb chicken thigh fillets
2 tablespoons oil
1 large onion, finely chopped
280g/9oz can curry cooking sauce
2 tablespoons sultanas (golden raisins)
2 bananas, sliced
1 green apple, peeled,
cored and cut in large dice

chicken rolls
with an indonesian flavor

Method:

1 Open out the thigh fillets on a large chopping board. Flatten with a meat mallet to an even thinness. Spread each with a teaspoon of rendang curry sauce.

2 Peel bananas and slit in half lengthwise then cut in half to make 4 pieces. Place a piece of banana in centre of each fillet and form into a roll. Fasten with a toothpick.
Heat oil in a wide-based saucepan and brown the rolls on all sides, a few at a time, removing rolls to a plate as they brown. Drain all the oil from the saucepan.

3 To the same saucepan, add rendang curry sauce and the water. Bring to the boil, turn down heat to a simmer and place in the chicken rolls. Cover and simmer 35 minutes, turning rolls once during cooking.

4 Remove rolls to a heated platter and keep hot. If sauce is thin, increase heat and reduce sauce to a thicker consistency. Reduce heat and stir in the coconut milk and simmer 2 minutes. Return rolls to the saucepan to reheat.

5 Saute the pineapple rings in a little butter until lightly coloured and grind over some black pepper. Arrange 1 or 2 slices of pineapple and a chicken roll on each plate, spoon sauce over the roll and sprinkle with a little toasted coconut. Accompany with steamed rice.

Serves 4

ingredients

1kg/2 lb chicken thigh fillets
285g/9¹/₂oz can redang curry sauce
2 bananas
toothpicks
2 tablespoons vegetable oil
¹/₂ cup/120mL/4fl oz water
150ml/5fl oz coconut milk
1 small, fresh pineapple, peeled, and thinly sliced
freshly ground black pepper
2 tablespoons shredded coconut, toasted
steamed rice to serve

spanish
chicken with chorizo

Method:

1 Place the chicken joints in a large non-stick frying pan and fry without oil for 5-8 minutes, turning occasionally, until golden. Remove the chicken and set aside, then pour away any fat from the pan.

2 Add the oil to the pan and fry the onion, garlic and peppers for 3-4 minutes, until softened. Return the chicken to the pan with the paprika, sherry or vermouth, tomatoes, bay leaf and orange rind. Bring to the boil, then simmer, covered, over a low heat for 35-40 minutes, stirring occasionally, until the chicken is cooked through.

3 Add the chorizo and olives and simmer for a further 5 minutes to heat through, then season.

Note: Packed with Mediterranean flavors, this casserole is equally good eaten with rice or crusty bread. You can use stock or orange juice instead of the sherry or vermouth.

Serves 4

ingredients

8 chicken joints, such as thighs
and drumsticks
2 tablespoons olive oil
I onion, sliced
2 cloves garlic, crushed
I red and I yellow pepper,
deseeded and sliced
2 teaspoons paprika
50mL/2fl oz dry sherry
or dry vermouth
410g/13oz can chopped tomatoes
I bay leaf
I strip orange rind, pared with
a vegetable peeler
70g/2¹/₂oz chorizo, sliced
50g/2oz pitted black olives
salt and black pepper

preserves

Pickled vegetable medley

This colourful pickle looks very attractive if vegetables are packed into the jars in layers. The pickle originated in the Middle East but is delicious served with any meat or poultry dish.

¹/₂ cauliflower, cut into florets
I green pepper, cut into strips
I red pepper, into strips
2 green tomatoes, sliced
2 carrots, peeled and sliced
2 stalks celery, sliced
75g/2¹/₂oz salt
I L/I³/₄pts water
250mL/8fl oz white vinegar
I tablespoon sugar
2 red chillies
sprigs fresh dill
2 cloves garlic, peeled

1 *Layer vegetables in a baking dish and sprinkle each layer with a little salt. Set aside to stand for 6 hours. Rinse and drain.*
2 *Place water, vinegar, sugar and remaining salt in a saucepan. Bring to the boil, stirring until sugar and salt are dissolved. Set aside and allow to cool.*
3 *Pack layered vegetables into warm sterilised jars. Place whole chillies, dill sprigs and garlic cloves in jars to give an attractive appearance. Pour over the cold brine. Seal and label. Allow to stand for I week before using.*

Makes 2 litres (3¹/₂pts)

Preserved limes

Nothing is more refreshing than the tart taste of the lime. This recipe will ensure that you have these small precious fruits to enjoy at any time of the year. The limes are ready when the skins are soft and juice has thickened.

25 fresh limes
12 small red chillies
3 large green chillies, sliced
2 cm piece ginger, cut into strips
2 tablespoons black mustard seeds
2 tablespoons fenugreek seeds
4 bay leaves
2 tablespoons sugar
2 tablespoons salt

1 *Cut 8 of the limes into quarters. Squeeze the juice from the remaining limes and reserve.*
2 *Layer limes in a sterilised glass jar. Place red chillies, green chilli slices, ginger, a sprinkling of mustard and fenugreek seeds, a bay leaf and a pinch of sugar and salt between each layer. Cover with lime juice and place muslin cloth over the jar.*
3 *Stand jar in a warm place and add a pinch of sugar and salt every day for four days. Seal and store for 6 weeks before using.*

Makes 2 litres/3¹/₂pts

Using preserved limes

Lemons can also be preserved in this way. Preserved limes and lemons are an essential part of Mediterranean cookery. Usually only the peel and the juice are used in the wonderfully aromatic stews and casseroles of this area. The fruit imparts a unique flavor to these dishes. A white film will often form on the preserved fruit. There is no reason for concern should this occur, just rinse it off before using.

Chutneys and pickles

Sweet mango chutney, pungent pickled radish, preserved limes - they all add that "je ne sais quoi" to the recipes in this book. Yes, you can buy chutneys and pickles, but making them yourself allows you to control the sweetness, the fire or the tartness of the end result.

red hot
gourmet

introduction

introduction

The passionate pursuit of foods that make us gasp for breath and perspire is nothing new. Early attempts at food preservation often involved liberal applications of pepper and other strong-tasting seasonings—the same ingredients used to help mask the taste of decay when victuals had passed there prime. Many of the hottest cuisines originated in very warm climates, where particular foods have long been revered for the ability to induce sweating, thereby triggering a kind of natural air-conditioning when the sweat evaporates. Throughout history pepper, garlic, chiles, and other hot foods have been acclaimed as digestives, antiseptics, antidepressants, and even aphrodisiacs.

Practical benefits aside, certain edibles possess an irresistible quality that keeps human palates begging for more. The fascination with hot stuff—foods capable of producing a mix of pleasure and pain—has developed into a hot love affair, and it's getting hotter every day.

Cuisines the world over rely on certain ingredients with a reputation for feistiness to add heat, not to mention exciting flavor. Just as the name of these foods vary from culture to culture, so do individual tolerances for heat and spiciness: What's exquisitely hot to you may not seem hot at all to someone else. In preparing the recipes in this book, let your own taste and tolerance level be your guide. Adapt the recipes to suit yourself, adding more or less of the following heat sources:

Onions and Garlic: Eaten raw, both onions and garlic release a strong-tasting acid. Cooked at low heat, the acid breaks down and the harshness dissipates. Most varieties of onions and garlic have powerful personalities but are easy to get along with when handled properly. Fresh, firm onions and young, ivory-colored heads of garlic provide the best flavor.

Mustard: The seeds of the mustard plant are virtually flavorless and odorless. But when crushed and steeped 15 minutes in water or other liquid, mustard can be blistering in its effects—literally. The volatile oils in mustard were traditionally considered powerful medicine for a number of ailments, with mustard poultices and foot baths among the most common remedies.

Prepared mustards made from yellow, brown, or black mustard seed run the gamut from mild table varieties to fiery Asian blends. Wasabi, a fire-breathing cousin to mustard, is often served with sushi and other Japanese dishes.

Ginger: Ginger imparts a refreshingly clean, hot taste that adds sparkle to sweet and spicy foods alike. It is available fresh, pickled, candied, and powdered.

Note: For the recipes in this book, powdered ginger is not an acceptable substitute for fresh ginger.

Pepper: A member of the Piper nigrum family, pepper is available in three forms: black peppercorns (the result of drying ripe pepper berries); white (produced by hulling the ripe berries); and green peppercorns (made by pickling the immature berries). Pepper's hot bite and flavor can't be duplicated; like mustard, it releases its heat and flavor only when cracked or ground.

Chile: *Chiles are the hot-blooded relatives of sweet, mild bell peppers, both members of the genus Capsicum. Hot chiles, fresh or dried, are among the most potent of all heat sources. The amount of heat in chiles varies (depending upon the variety, growing conditions, and method of processing). Chiles have 60 percent of the substance that makes them hot— capsaicin— in the ribs and veins, 30 percent in the seeds, and 10 percent in the skin. Because small chiles have a proportionately larger volume of ribs and seeds (the hottest areas) than larger chiles, they usually pack more firepower. One of the hottest is the tiny tabasco, the main ingredient in the famous bottled condiment from Louisiana. Chiles also vary in size (from short to long), shape (from blocky to slim), and colour (from pale green to yellow, orange, or red.)*

There are a multitude of different names for the same chiles, the similarity of varieties can be confusing. For example, the habanero, a H-bomb of a chile native to the Yucatán peninsula, differs slightly in color and flavor from the equally potent Jamaican Scotch Bonnet. Both chiles have their zealous fans, *but the two are generally regarding as different varieties of the same species and can be substituted for one another.*

Note: *A chile by any other name is just as hot; always exercise caution in handling and tasting any chile, especially if it is unfamiliar.*

Any cook can become a red hot gourmet. It's a matter of selecting authentic ingredients, mastering basic techniques, and applying them to well-crafted recipes like the ones developed for this book and the adaptations you'll create yourself. You'll find red hot recipes to tingle your mouth, clear your head, and warm your soul.

fish cakes with relish

soups
&
snacks

A hot bowl of soup or a fiery snack

*with a snappy come-back – either makes a welcome
alternative to luke-warm menu openers. Designed to
fire up your appetite and get a good meal off to a great
start.*

hot and sour
seafood soup

Method:

1 Place shallots, chillies, lime leaves, ginger and stock in a saucepan and bring to the boil over a high heat. Reduce heat and simmer for 3 minutes.

2 Add fish, shrimp, mussels and mushrooms and cook for 3-5 minutes or until fish and seafood are cooked, discard any mussels that do not open after 5 minutes cooking. Stir in lime juice and fish sauce. To serve, ladle soup into bowls, scatter with coriander leaves and accompany with lime wedges.

Note: Straw mushrooms are one of the most popular mushrooms used in Asian cooking and in the West are readily available canned. Oyster mushrooms are also known as abalone mushrooms and range in colour from white to grey to pale pink. Their shape is similar to that of an oyster shell and they have a delicate flavor. Oyster mushrooms should not be eaten raw as some people are allergic to them in the uncooked state.

Serves 6

ingredients

4 red or golden shallots, sliced
2 fresh green chillies, chopped
6 kaffir lime leaves
4 slices fresh ginger
8 cups/2 litres/3¹/₂pt fish, chicken
or vegetable stock
250 g/8 oz boneless firm fish fillets,
cut into chunks
12 medium uncooked shrimp, shelled
and deveined
12 mussels, scrubbed
and beards removed
125g/4oz oyster or straw mushrooms
3 tablespoons lime juice
2 tablespoons Thai fish sauce (nam pla)
fresh coriander leaves
lime wedges

chilli
kumara soup

Method:

1 Place stock, lemon grass, chillies, galangal or ginger and coriander roots in a saucepan and bring to the boil over a medium heat. Add kumara (sweet potato) and simmer, uncovered, for 15 minutes or until kumara (sweet potato) is soft.

2 Remove lemon grass, galangal or ginger and coriander roots and discard. Cool liquid slightly, then purée soup, in batches, in a food processor or blender. Return soup to a clean saucepan and stir in ¹/₂ cup/ 125mL/4fl oz of the coconut cream and the fish sauce. Cook, stirring, over a medium heat for 4 minutes or until heated. Stir in two-thirds of the reserved coriander leaves.

3 To serve, ladle soup into bowls, top with a little of the remaining coconut cream and scatter with remaining coriander leaves.

Serves 4

ingredients

6 cups/1 ¹/₂ litres/2¹/₂ pt chicken stock
3 stalks fresh lemon grass, bruised, or
1 ¹/₂ teaspoons dried lemon grass, soaked
in hot water until soft
3 fresh red chillies, halved
10 slices fresh or bottled galangal or ginger
5-6 fresh coriander plants, roots washed,
leaves removed and reserved
1 large kumara (orange sweet potato),
peeled and cut into 2 cm/³/₄ in pieces
³/₄ cup/185 mL/6 fl oz coconut cream
1 tablespoon Thai fish sauce (nam pla)

fish
cakes with relish

Photograph on page 775

Method:

1 *Place fish, curry paste, coriander, basil and egg white in a food processor and process to make a smooth thick paste. Place mixture in a bowl, add beans and lime leaves (if using) and mix to combine. Cover and refrigerate for 1 hour.*

2 *To make relish, place cucumber, chilli, sugar, vinegar, water and peanuts (if using) in a bowl and mix to combine. Cover and refrigerate until required.*

3 *Using wet or lightly oiled hands, take 2 tablespoons of fish mixture and roll into a ball, then flatten to form a disk. Repeat with remaining fish mixture.*

4 *Heat about 2.5 cm/1 in oil in a frying pan over a high heat and cook fish cakes, a few at a time, for 2 minutes each side or until well browned and cooked through. Drain on absorbent kitchen paper and serve hot fish cakes with relish.*

Note: *Thai recipes such as this one, and some of the others in this chapter and in the Snacks and Starters chapter, are great for barbecuing. For a memorable Thai-inspired barbecue meal, serve your favourite Thai barbecue dishes with a selection of Thai-style salads and dipping sauces. Other recipes suitable for barbecuing include Satay, Fish with Green Mango Sauce, Spiced Grilled Beef and Barbecued Pork Spare Ribs.*

Makes 12-14

ingredients

500 g/1 lb boneless fine fleshed fish fillets
3 tablespoons Thai red curry paste
2 tablespoons chopped fresh coriander leaves
1 tablespoon fresh basil leaves
1 egg white
90 g/3 oz green beans, finely chopped
2 kaffir lime leaves, finely shredded (optional)
vegetable oil for shallow-frying
Cucumber relish
1 cucumber, seeded and chopped
1 fresh red chilli, chopped
1 tablespoon sugar
2 tablespoons rice vinegar
1 tablespoon water
1 tablespoon chopped roasted peanuts (optional)

marinated lime fish

seafood
dishes

seafood is one of the healthiest

meal that you can eat. The recipes included in the following pages from a light but tasty fish with marinated onions to terrific spiced mussels in vinegar.

roasted
garlic fish

Method:

1 *Pat fish dry with absorbent kitchen paper. Place fish in a baking dish and fill cavity with lemon slices, chillies and marjoram sprigs.*

2 *Place garlic in a hot frying pan or comal and cook until skins are charred and garlic is soft. Squeeze garlic from skins into a bowl, add butter and mix to combine. Spread garlic butter over both sides of fish, cover with foil and bake for 40 minutes or until flesh flakes when tested with a fork. Remove foil, place under a hot grill and cook for 3-4 minutes each side or until skin is crisp.*

To serve, drizzle with coconut milk.

Note: *Serve fish with Mexican Red Rice or tortillas and a salad.*

Serves 4

ingredients

1 ¹/₂kg/3 lb whole fish such as bream,
snapper, whiting, sea perch,
cod or haddock, cleaned
1 lemon, sliced
2 fresh red chillies, halved
3 sprigs fresh marjoram
7 cloves garlic, unpeeled
30g/1oz butter
¹/₃ cup/90mL/3fl oz coconut milk

Oven temperature 150°C, 300°F, Gas

seafood tacos

Method:

1. To make filling, heat oil in a frying pan over a high heat, add onion and cook for 4 minutes or until golden. Add tomatoes and cook for 5 minutes. Add fish, shrimp, scallops, chillies, oregano and lemon rind and cook, tossing, for 3-4 minutes or until seafood is cooked.

2. To serve, spoon filling down the centre of each tortilla and scatter with feta cheese. Fold tortilla to enclose filling and serve immediately.

Note: These indulgent tacos are wonderful served with Garlic and Chilli Salsa.

Serves 4

ingredients

8 flour tortillas, warmed
155g/5oz feta cheese crumbled

Seafood Filling
2 teaspoons vegetable oil
1 onion, chopped
2 tomatoes, chopped
375g/12oz white fish, cubed
250 g/8 oz shelled and deveined medium uncooked shrimp
12 scallops
3 medium fresh green chillies, chopped
2 tablespoons chopped fresh oregano
1 teaspoon finely grated lemon rind

grilled scallops
with salsa

Method:

1 *To make salsa, place pineapple, red pepper, chillies, coriander, mint and lime juice in a bowl, toss to combine, then stand for 20 minutes.*

2 *Brush scallops with oil and cook on a preheated hot char-grill or barbecue plate (griddle) for 30 seconds each side or until they just change colour. Serve immediately with salsa and tortilla chips.*

To make crisp tortilla chips, cut day-old tortillas into wedges and shallow fry for 1-2 minutes or until crisp.

Note: *Known in Mexico as Veracruzana sauce and originating from the region of Veracruz, the sauce in this recipe is traditionally served with and used as a cooking sauce for fish fillets and whole fish. It is also delicious served with grilled lamb or veal chops.*

ingredients

30 scallops
chilli or lime oil
crisp tortilla chips
Pineapple salsa
125g/4oz chopped pineapple
¼ red pepper, finely chopped
2 medium green chillies, chopped
1 tablespoon fresh coriander leaves
1 tablespoon fresh mint leaves
1 tablespoon lime juice

Serves 4

spiced
mussels in vinegar

Method:

1 Heat oil in a saucepan over a medium heat, add onions and cook, stirring, for 3 minutes or until soft. Add chillies, oregano, cumin, peppercorns, bay leaves and cinnamon and cook, stirring, for 2 minutes.

2 Stir vinegar and stock into pan and bring to the boil. Add mussels, bring to simmering, cover and simmer for 5 minutes or until mussels open. Discard any mussels that do not open after 5 minutes cooking.
Serve mussels with pan juices.

Note: Try this recipe using clams, cleaned baby octopus or squid.

Serves 4

ingredients

2 teaspoons vegetable oil
2 onions, chopped
3 medium fresh green chillies, chopped
1 tablespoon chopped fresh oregano
1 teaspoon ground cumin
1/2 teaspoon crushed black peppercorns
3 bay leaves
1 cinnamon stick
1/4 cup/60mL/2fl oz apple cider vinegar
1 1/2 cups/375mL/12fl oz fish stock
1 kg/2 lb mussels in shells, scrubbed
and beards removed

fish
with marinated onions

Photograph on page 783

Method:

1 To make marinated onions, place onions, coriander leaves, sugar and lime juice in a bowl, cover and marinate at room temperature for at least 1 hour.

2 Place fish fillets on absorbent kitchen paper and pat dry. Place flour, cumin, chilli powder and ground coriander in a plastic food bag and toss to combine. Add fish and toss to coat with spice mixture, then shake off excess.

3 Heat oil in a frying pan over a medium heat, add fish and cook for 1-2 minutes each side or until flesh flakes when tested with a fork. Serve with marinated onions.

Note: This simple fish dish is delicious served with roasted tomatoes and red and green peppers.

Serves 4

ingredients

4 firm white fish fillets
¹/₂ cup/60g/2oz flour
1 tablespoon ground cumin
1 tablespoon mild chilli powder
2 teaspoons ground coriander
2 tablespoons vegetable oil

Lime marinated onions
3 white onions, thinly sliced
3 tablespoons fresh coriander leaves
1 tablespoon sugar
¹/₂ cup/125mL/4fl oz lime juice

marinated
lime fish

Photograph on page 777 and 783

Method:

1 Place fish in a bowl, pour over lime juice and marinate in the refrigerator, tossing occasionally, for 3 hours or until fish is opaque. Drain off half the lime juice, then add tomatoes, chillies, oregano and oil. Toss and chill for 1 hour longer.

2 Before serving, stand at room temperature for 20 minutes, then scatter with onion, olives and coriander.

Note: Known the world over as ceviche or seviche this classic Mexican fish dish must be made with the freshest fish (never use frozen). Any firm fleshed fish can be used and prawns, scallops, crab or lobster are delicious and elegant alternatives.

Serves 6

ingredients

625g/1¹/₄ lb firm white fish fillets,
cut into strips
1 cup/250mL/8fl oz lime juice
3 ripe tomatoes, chopped
4 pickled jalapeño chillies, sliced
1 tablespoon chopped fresh oregano
¹/₃ cup/90mL/3fl oz olive oil
¹/₂ onion, finely diced
3 tablespoons chopped stuffed olives
2 tablespoons fresh coriander leaves

slow-baked chilli lamb

meat dishes

in this chapter you will find

*delicious new ways to prepare different kind of meats.
What more tempting than a Santa Fe grilled beef or a
roasted chilli duck?*

santa fe
grilled beef

Method:

1 To make spice mix, place onion, garlic, chilli powder, lime rind, cumin, oil and lime juice in a bowl and mix to combine.

2 Spread spice mix over both sides of each piece of steak and place between sheets of plastic food wrap. Pound with a meat mallet or rolling pin until steaks are 5mm/¼ in thick.

3 Cook steaks on a preheated hot barbecue or in a frying pan for 30-60 seconds each side or until tender. Serve immediately with avocado slices, lime wedges and spring onions.

Note: For a complete meal add warm tortillas, Refried Beans and a lettuce salad.

Serves 6

ingredients

6 scotch or eye fillet steaks
I avocado, sliced
lime wedges
2 spring onions, sliced
Spice mix
½ onion, very finely chopped
3 cloves garlic, crushed
I tablespoon mild chilli powder
2 teaspoons grated lime rind
I teaspoon ground cumin
2 tablespoons olive oil
I tablespoon lime juice

chicken
with garlic and pepper

Method:

1 Place garlic, coriander roots and black peppercorns in a food processor and process to make a paste. Coat chicken with garlic paste and marinate for 1 hour.

2 Heat oil in a wok or frying pan over a high heat until a cube of bread dropped in browns in 50 seconds, then deep-fry chicken, a few pieces at a time, for 2 minutes or until golden and tender. Drain on absorbent kitchen paper.

3 Deep-fry basil and mint until crisp, then drain and place on a serving plate. Top with chicken and serve with chilli sauce.

Note: Thai cooks use three types of basil in cooking - Asian sweet, holy and lemon - each has a distinctive flavor and is used for specific types of dishes. For this dish Asian sweet basil, known in Thailand as horapa, would be used.

Serves 4

ingredients

4 cloves garlic
3 fresh coriander roots
1 teaspoon crushed black peppercorns
500 g/1 lb chicken breast fillets,
chopped into 3cm/1 1/4 in cubes
vegetable oil for deep-frying
30g/1oz fresh basil leaves
30g/1oz fresh mint leaves
sweet chilli sauce

Oven temperature 220°C, 425°F, Gas 7

roasted
chilli duck

Method:

1 *Pierce skin of duck all over with a fork, then rub with salt and black pepper and place on a rack set in a baking dish. Place orange and garlic cloves in cavity of bird and bake for 30 minutes. Drain juices from pan.*

2 *Combine chilli powder, paprika, crushed garlic and tequila and rub over duck. Reduce oven temperature to 180°C/350°F/Gas 4 and bake for 40 minutes or until skin is crisp and meat is tender. Just prior to serving, scatter with mint.*

Note: *Serve with a pile of warm flour tortillas and a selection of salsas.*

Serves 4

ingredients

2¹/₂ kg/5 lb duck
sea salt
crushed black peppercorns
1 orange, halved
1 head garlic, cloves separated
2 tablespoons mild chilli powder
2 tablespoons sweet paprika
3 cloves garlic, crushed
2 tablespoons tequila
3 tablespoons chopped fresh mint

slow-baked
chilli lamb

Photograph on page 785 and below

Method:

1. To make chilli paste, place chillies and garlic in a hot dry frying pan or comal over a high heat and cook until skins are blistered and charred. Place chillies in a bowl, pour over hot water to cover and soak for 30 minutes. Drain chillies and discard water.

2. Squeeze garlic from skins. Place chillies, garlic, tomato, oregano, cumin, peppercorns and vinegar in a food processor or blender and process to make a purée.

3. Place lamb in a glass or ceramic dish, spread with chilli paste, cover and marinate in the refrigerator for at least 3 hours or overnight.

4. Transfer lamb to a baking dish and roast for 3 hours or until tender.

   Note: Slice lamb and serve with warm tortillas, vegetables and a selection of salsas.

Serves 6

ingredients

1 ½ kg/3 lb leg lamb, trimmed of visible fat

Chilli herb paste
4 ancho chillies
3 cloves garlic, unpeeled
1 ripe tomato, peeled and chopped
1 tablespoon chopped fresh oregano
½ teaspoon ground cumin
½ teaspoon crushed black peppercorns
2 tablespoons apple cider vinegar

Cooking is not an exact science: one does not require finely calibrated scales, pipettes and scientific equipment to cook, yet the conversion to metric measures in some countries and its interpretations must have intimidated many a good cook.

Weights are given in the recipes only for ingredients such as meats, fish, poultry and some vegetables. Though a few grams/ounces one way or another will not affect the success of your dish.

Though recipes have been tested using the Australian Standard 250mL cup, 20mL tablespoon and 5mL teaspoon, they will work just as well with the US and Canadian 8fl oz cup, or the UK 300mL cup. We have used graduated cup measures in preference to tablespoon measures so that proportions are always the same. Where tablespoon measures have been given, these are not crucial measures, so using the smaller tablespoon of the US or UK will not affect the recipe's success. At least we all agree on the teaspoon size.

For breads, cakes and pastries, the only area which might cause concern is where eggs are used, as proportions will then vary. If working with a 250mL or 300mL cup, use large eggs (60g/2oz), adding a little more liquid to the recipe for 300mL cup measures if it seems necessary. Use the medium-sized eggs (55g/1 1/4oz) with 8fl oz cup measure. A graduated set of measuring cups and spoons is recommended, the cups in particular for measuring dry ingredients. Remember to level such ingredients to ensure their accuracy.

English measures

All measurements are similar to Australian with two exceptions: the English cup measures 300mL/10fl oz, whereas the Australian cup measure 250mL/8fl oz. The English tablespoon (the Australian dessertspoon) measures 14.8mL/1/2fl oz against the Australian tablespoon of 20mL/3/4fl oz.

American measures

The American reputed pint is 16fl oz, a quart is equal to 32fl oz and the American gallon, 128fl oz. The Imperial measurement is 20fl oz to the pint, 40fl oz a quart and 160fl oz one gallon.

The American tablespoon is equal to 14.8mL/1/2fl oz, the teaspoon is 5mL/1/6fl oz. The cup measure is 250mL/8fl oz, the same as Australia.

Dry measures

All the measures are level, so when you have filled a cup or spoon, level it off with the edge of a knife. The scale below is the "cook's equivalent"; it is not an exact conversion of metric to imperial measurement. To calculate the exact metric equivalent yourself, use 2.2046 lb = 1kg or 1 lb = 0.45359kg

Metric		Imperial	
g = grams		oz = ounces	
kg = kilograms		lb = pound	
15g		1/2oz	
20g		2/3oz	
30g		1oz	
60g		2oz	
90g		3oz	
125g		4oz	1/4 lb
155g		5oz	
185g		6oz	
220g		7oz	
250g		8oz	1/2 lb
280g		9oz	
315g		10oz	
345g		11oz	
375g		12oz	3/4 lb
410g		13oz	
440g		14oz	
470g		15oz	
1,000g	1kg	35.2oz	2.2 lb
	1.5kg		3.3 lb

Oven temperatures

The Celsius temperatures given here are not exact; they have been rounded off and are given as a guide only. Follow the manufacturer's temperature guide, relating it to oven description given in the recipe. Remember gas ovens are hottest at the top, electric ovens at the bottom and convection-fan forced ovens are usually even throughout. We included Regulo numbers for gas cookers which may assist. To convert °C to °F multiply °C by 9 and divide by 5 then add 32.

Oven temperatures

	C°	F°	Regulo
Very slow	120	250	1
Slow	150	300	2
Moderately slow	160	325	3
Moderate	180	350	4
Moderately hot	190-200	370-400	5-6
Hot	210-220	410-440	6-7
Very hot	230	450	8
Super hot	250-290	475-500	9-10

Cake dish sizes

Metric	Imperial
15cm	6in
18cm	7in
20cm	8in
23cm	9in

Loaf dish sizes

Metric	Imperial
23x12cm	9x5in
25x8cm	10x3in
28x18cm	11x7in

Liquid measures

Metric	Imperial	Cup & Spoon
mL	fl oz	
millilitres	fluid ounce	
5mL	$^{1}/_{6}$fl oz	1 teaspoon
20mL	$^{2}/_{3}$fl oz	1 tablespoon
30mL	1fl oz	1 tablespoon plus 2 teaspoons
60mL	2fl oz	$^{1}/_{4}$ cup
85mL	2$^{1}/_{2}$fl oz	$^{1}/_{3}$ cup
100mL	3fl oz	$^{3}/_{8}$ cup
125mL	4fl oz	$^{1}/_{2}$ cup
150mL	5fl oz	$^{1}/_{4}$ pint, 1 gill
250mL	8fl oz	1 cup
300mL	10fl oz	$^{1}/_{2}$ pint)
360mL	12fl oz	1$^{1}/_{2}$ cups
420mL	14fl oz	1$^{3}/_{4}$ cups
500mL	16fl oz	2 cups
600mL	20fl oz 1 pint,	2$^{1}/_{2}$ cups
1 litre	35fl oz 1 $^{3}/_{4}$ pints,	4 cups

Cup measurements

One cup is equal to the following weights.

	Metric	Imperial
Almonds, flaked	90g	3oz
Almonds, slivered, ground	125g	4oz
Almonds, kernel	155g	5oz
Apples, dried, chopped	125g	4oz
Apricots, dried, chopped	190g	6oz
Breadcrumbs, packet	125g	4oz
Breadcrumbs, soft	60g	2oz
Cheese, grated	125g	4oz
Choc bits	155g	5oz
Coconut, desiccated	90g	3oz
Cornflakes	30g	1oz
Currants	155g	5oz
Flour	125g	4oz
Fruit, dried (mixed, sultanas etc)	185g	6oz
Ginger, crystallised, glace	250g	8oz
Honey, treacle, golden syrup	315g	10oz
Mixed peel	220g	7oz
Nuts, chopped	125g	4oz
Prunes, chopped	220g	7oz
Rice, cooked	155g	5oz
Rice, uncooked	220g	7oz
Rolled oats	90g	3oz
Sesame seeds	125g	4oz
Shortening (butter, margarine)	250g	8oz
Sugar, brown	155g	5oz
Sugar, granulated or caster	250g	8oz
Sugar, sifted icing	155g	5oz
Wheatgerm	60g	2oz

Length

Some of us still have trouble converting imperial length to metric. In this scale, measures have been rounded off to the easiest-to-use and most acceptable figures.

To obtain the exact metric equivalent in converting inches to centimetres, multiply inches by 2.54 whereby 1 inch equals 25.4 millimetres and 1 millimetre equals 0.03937 inches.

Metric	Imperial
mm=millimetres	in = inches
cm=centimetres	ft = feet
5mm, 0.5cm	$^{1}/_{4}$in
10mm, 1.0cm	$^{1}/_{2}$in
20mm, 2.0cm	$^{3}/_{4}$in
2.5cm	1in
5cm	2in
8cm	3in
10cm	4in
12cm	5in
15cm	6in
18cm	7in
20cm	8in
23cm	9in
25cm	10in
28cm	11in
30cm	1 ft, 12in

acidulated water: water with added acid, such as lemon juice or vinegar, which prevents discoloration of ingredients, particularly fruit or vegetables. The proportion of acid to water is 1 teaspoon per 300ml.

al dente: Italian cooking term for ingredients that are cooked until tender but still firm to the bite; usually applied to pasta.

americaine: method of serving seafood - usually lobster and monkfish - in a sauce flavored with olive oil, aromatic herbs, tomatoes, white wine, fish stock, brandy and tarragon.

anglaise: cooking style for simple cooked dishes such as boiled vegetables. Assiette anglaise is a plate of cold cooked meats.

antipasto: Italian for "before the meal", it denotes an assortment of cold meats, vegetables and cheeses, often marinated, served as an hors d'oeuvre. A typical antipasto might include salami, prosciutto, marinated artichoke hearts, anchovy fillets, olives, tuna fish and Provolone cheese.

au gratin: food sprinkled with breadcrumbs, often covered with cheese sauce and browned until a crisp coating forms.

balsamic vinegar: a mild, extremely fragrant, wine-based vinegar made in northern Italy. Traditionally, the vinegar is aged for at least seven years in a series of casks made of various woods.

baste: to moisten food while it is cooking by spooning or brushing on liquid or fat.

baine marie: a saucepan standing in a large pan which is filled with boiling water to keep liquids at simmering point. A double boiler will do the same job.

beat: to stir thoroughly and vigorously.

beurre manie: equal quantities of butter and flour kneaded together and added a little at a time to thicken a stew or casserole.

blanc: a cooking liquid made by adding flour and lemon juice to water in order to keep certain vegetables from discolouring as they cook.

blanch: to plunge into boiling water and then, in some cases, into cold water. Fruits and nuts are blanched to remove skin easily.

blanquette: a white stew of lamb, veal or chicken, bound with egg yolks and cream and accompanied by onion and mushrooms.

blend: to mix thoroughly.

bonne femme: dishes cooked in the traditional French "housewife" style. Chicken and pork bonne femme are garnished with bacon, potatoes and baby onion; fish bonne femme with mushrooms in a white wine sauce.

bouguet garni: a bunch of herbs, usually consisting of sprigs of parsley, thyme, marjoram, rosemary, a bay leaf, peppercorns and cloves, tied in muslin and used to flavor stews and casseroles.

braise: to cook whole or large pieces of poultry, game, fish, meat or vegetables in a small amount of wine, stock or other liquid in a closed pot. Often the main ingredient is first browned in fat and then cooked in a low oven or very slowly on top of the stove. Braising suits tough meats and older birds and produces a mellow, rich sauce.

broil: The American term for grilling food.

brown: cook in a small amount of fat until brown.

burghul (also bulgur): a type of cracked wheat, where the kernels are steamed and dried before being crushed.

buttered: to spread with softened or melted butter.

butterfly: to slit a piece of food in half horizontally, cutting it almost through so that when opened it resembles butterfly wings. Chops, large prawns and thick fish fillets are often butterflied so that they cook more quickly.

buttermilk: a tangy, low-fat cultured milk product whose slight acidity makes it an ideal marinade base for poultry.

calzone: a semicircular pocket of pizza dough, stuffed with meat or vegetables, sealed and baked.

caramelise: to melt sugar until it is a golden brown syrup.

champignons: small mushrooms, usually canned.

chasseur: (hunter) a French cooking style in which meat and chicken dishes are cooked with mushrooms, shallots, white wine, and often tomato. See also cacciatora.

clarify: to melt butter and drain the oil off the sediment.

coat: to cover with a thin layer of flour, sugar, nuts, crumbs, poppy or sesame seeds, cinnamon sugar or a few of the ground spices.

concasser: to chop coarsely, usually tomatoes.

confit: from the French verb confire, meaning to preserve. Food that is made into a preserve by cooking very slowly and thoroughly until tender. In the case of meat, such as duck or goose, it is cooked in its own fat, and covered with it so that it does not come into contact with the air. Vegetables such as onions are good in confit.

consomme: a clear soup usually made from beef.

coulis: a thin puree, usually of fresh or cooked fruit or vegetables, which is soft enough to pour (couler means 'to run'). A coulis may be rough-textured or very smooth.

court bouillon: the liquid in which fish, poultry or meat is cooked. It usually consists of water with bay leaf, onion, carrots and salt and freshly ground black pepper to taste. Other additives can include wine, vinegar, stock, garlic or spring onions (scallions).

couscous: cereal processed from semolina into pellets, traditionally steamed and served with meat and vegetables in the classic North African stew of the same name.

cruciferous vegetables: certain members of the mustard, cabbage and turnip families with cross-shaped flowers and strong aromas and flavors.

cream: to make soft, smooth and creamy by rubbing with back of spoon or by beating with mixer. Usually applied to fat and sugar.

croutons: small toasted or fried cubes of bread.

crudites: raw vegetables, whether cut in slices or sticks to nibble plain or with a dipping sauce, or shredded and tossed as salad with a simple dressing.

cube: to cut into small pieces with six equal sides.

curdle: to cause milk or sauce to separate into solid and liquid. Example, overcooked egg mixtures.

daikon radish: (also called mooli): a long white Japanese radish. dark sesame oil (also called Oriental sesame oil): dark polyunsaturated oil with a low burning point, used for seasoning. Do not replace with lighter sesame oil.

deglaze: to dissolve congealed cooking juices or glaze on the bottom of a pan by adding a liquid, then scraping and stirring vigorously whilst bringing the liquid to the boil. Juices may be used to make gravy or to add to sauce.

degrease: to skim grease from the surface of liquid. If possible the liquid should be chilled so the fat solidifies. If not, skim off most of the fat with a large metal spoon, then trail strips of paper towel on the surface of the liquid to remove any remaining globules.

devilled: a dish or sauce that is highly seasoned with a hot ingredient such as mustard, Worcestershire sauce or cayenne pepper.

dice: to cut into small cubes.

dissolve: mix a dry ingredient with liquid until absorbed.

dredge: to coat with a dry ingredient, as flour or sugar.

drizzle: to pour in a fine thread-like stream over a surface.

dust: to sprinkle or coat lightly with flour or icing sugar.

emulsion: a mixture of two liquids that are not mutually soluble- for example, oil and water.

entree: in Europe, the "entry" or hors d'oeuvre; in North America entree means the main course.

fillet: special cut of beef, lamb, pork or veal; breast of poultry and game; fish cut of the bone lengthways.

flake: to break into small pieces with a fork.

flame: to ignite warmed alcohol over food.

fold in: a gentle, careful combining of a light or delicate mixture with a heavier mixture using a metal spoon.

fricassee: a dish in which poultry, fish or vegetables are bound together with a white or veloute sauce. In Britain and the United States, the name applies to an old-fashioned dish of chicken in a creamy sauce.

galette: sweet or savoury mixture shaped as a flat round.

garnish: to decorate food, usually with something edible.

gastrique: caramelized sugar deglazed with vinegar and used in fruit-flavored savoury sauces, in such dishes as duck with orange.

glaze: a thin coating of beaten egg, syrup or aspic which is brushed over pastry, fruits or cooked meats.

gluten: a protein in flour that is developed when dough

is kneaded, making it elastic.

gratin: a dish cooked in the oven or under the grill so that it develops a brown crust. Breadcrumbs or cheese may be sprinkled on top first. Shallow gratin dishes ensure a maximum area of crust.

grease: to rub or brush lightly with oil or fat.

joint: to cut poultry, game or small animals into serving pieces by dividing at the joint.

julienne: to cut food into match-like strips.

knead: to work dough using heel of hand with a pressing motion, while stretching and folding the dough.

line: to cover the inside of a container with paper, to protect or aid in removing mixture.

infuse: to immerse herbs, spices or other flavorings in hot liquid to flavor it. Infusion takes from two to five minutes depending on the flavoring. The liquid should be very hot but not boiling.

macerate: to soak food in liquid to soften.

marinade: a seasoned liquid, usually an oil and acid mixture, in which meats or other foods are soaked to soften and give more flavor.

marinara: Italian "sailor's style" cooking that does not apply to any particular combination of ingredients. Marinara tomato sauce for pasta is most familiar.

marinate: to let food stand in a marinade to season and tenderize.

mask: to cover cooked food with sauce.

melt: to heat until liquified.

mince: to grind into very small pieces.

mix: to combine ingredients by stirring.

monounsaturated fats: one of three types of fats found in foods. Are believed not to raise the level of cholesterol in the blood.

nicoise: a garnish of tomatoes, garlic and black olives; a salad with anchovy, tuna and French beans is typical.

non-reactive pan: a cooking pan whose surface does not chemically react with food. Materials used include stainless steel, enamel, glass and some alloys.

noisette: small "nut" of lamb cut from boned loin or rack that is rolled, tied and cut in neat slices. Noisette also means flavored with hazelnuts, or butter cooked to a nut brown colour.

olive oil: various grades of oil extract from olives. Extra virgin olive oil has a full, fruity flavor and the lowest acidity. Virgin olive oil is slightly higher in acidity and lighter in flavor. Pure olive oil is a processed blend of olive oils and has the highest acidity and lightest taste.

papillote: to cook food in oiled or buttered greasepoof paper or aluminium foil. Also a decorative frill to cover bone ends of chops and poultry drumsticks.

parboil: to boil or simmer until part cooked (i.e. cooked further than when blanching).

pare: to cut away outside covering.

pate: a paste of meat or seafood used as a spread for toast or crackers.

paupiette: a thin slice of meat, poultry or fish spread with a savoury stuffing and rolled. In the United States this is also called "bird" and in Britain an "olive".

peel: to strip away outside covering.

plump: to soak in liquid or moisten thoroughly until full and round.

poach: to simmer gently in enough hot liquid to cover, using care to retain shape of food.

polyunsaturated fat: one of the three types of fats found in food. These exist in large quantities in such vegetable oils as safflower, sunflower, corn and soya bean. These fats lower the level of cholesterol in the blood.

puree: a smooth paste, usually of vegetables or fruits, made by putting foods through a sieve, food mill or liquefying in a blender or food processor.

ragout: traditionally a well-seasoned, rich stew containing meat, vegetables and wine. Nowadays, a term applied to any stewed mixture.

ramekins: small oval or round individual baking dishes.

reconstitute: to put moisture back into dehydrated foods by soaking in liquid.

reduce: to cook over a very high heat, uncovered, until the liquid is reduced by evaporation.

refresh: to cool hot food quickly, either under running water or by plunging it into iced water, to stop it cooking. Particularly for vegetables and occasionally for shellfish.

rice vinegar: mild, fragrant vinegar that is less sweet than cider vinegar and not as harsh as distilled malt vinegar. Japanese rice vinegar is milder than the Chinese variety.

roulade: a piece of meat, usually pork or veal, that is spread with stuffing, rolled and often braised or poached. A roulade may also be a sweet or savoury mixture that is baked in a Swiss roll tin or paper case, filled with a contrasting filling, and rolled.

rubbing-in: a method of incorporating fat into flour, by use of fingertips only. Also incorporates air into mixture.

safflower oil: the vegetable oil that contains the highest proportion of polyunsaturated fats.

salsa: a juice derived from the main ingredient being cooked or a sauce added to a dish to enhance its flavor. In Italy the term is often used for pasta sauces; in Mexico the name usually applies to uncooked sauces served as an accompaniment, especially to corn chips.

saturated fats: one of the three types of fats found in foods. These exist in large quantities in animal products, coconut and palm oils; they raise the level of cholesterol in the blood. As high cholesterol levels may cause heart disease, saturated fat consumption is recommended to be less than 15% of kilojoules provided by the daily diet.

sauté: to cook or brown in small amount of hot fat.

score: to mark food with cuts, notches of lines to prevent curling or to make food more attractive.

scald: to bring just to boiling point, usually for milk. Also to rinse with boiling water.

sear: to brown surface quickly over high heat in hot dish.

seasoned flour: flour with salt and pepper added.

sift: to shake a dry, powdered substance through a sieve or sifter to remove any lumps and give lightness.

simmer: to cook food gently in liquid that bubbles steadily just below boiling point so that the food cooks in even heat without breaking up.

singe: to quickly flame poultry to remove all traces of feathers after plucking.

skim: to remove a surface layer (often of impurities and scum) from a liquid with a metal spoon or small ladle.

slivered: sliced in long, thin pieces, usually refers to nuts, especially almonds.

soften: ie: gelatine - sprinkle over cold water and allow to gel (soften) then dissolve and liquefy.

souse: to cover food, particularly fish, in wine vinegar and spices and cook slowly; the food is cooled in the same liquid. Sousing gives food a pickled flavor.

steep: to soak in warm or cold liquid in order to soften food and draw out strong flavors or impurities.

stir-fry: to cook thin slices of meat and vegetable over a high heat in a small amount of oil, stirring constantly to even cooking in a short time. Traditionally cooked in a wok, however a heavy based frying pan may be used.

stock: a liquid containing flavors, extracts and nutrients of bones, meat, fish or vegetables.

sweat: to cook vegetables over heat until only juices run.

sugo: an Italian sauce made from the liquid or juice extracted from fruit or meat during cooking.

sweat: to cook sliced or chopped food, usually vegetables, in a little fat and no liquid over very low heat. Foil is pressed on top so that the food steams in its own juices, usually before being added to other dishes.

thicken: to make a thin, smooth paste by mixing together arrowroot, cornflour or flour with an equal amount of cold water; stir into hot liquid, cook, stirring until thickened.

toss: to gently mix ingredients with two forks or fork and spoon.

total fat: the individual daily intake of all three fats previously described in this glossary. Nutritionists recommend that fats provide no more than 35% of the energy in the diet.

whip: to beat rapidly, incorporate air and produce expansion.

zest: thin outer layer of citrus fruits containing the aromatic citrus oil. It is usually thinly pared with a vegetable peeler, or grated with a zester or grater to separate it from the bitter white pith underneath.

notes